HUMAN SENSES AND PERCEPTION

HUMAN SENSES AND PERCEPTION

G. M. WYBURN
Regius Professor of Anatomy in the University of Glasgow

R. W. PICKFORD
Professor of Psychology in the University of Glasgow

R. J. HIRST
Professor of Logic in the University of Glasgow

Edited by
G. M. WYBURN

UNIVERSITY OF TORONTO PRESS

Published in Great Britain by
Oliver & Boyd Ltd., Edinburgh & London

Published in Canada by
University of Toronto Press

First published 1964

Printed in Great Britain
by Robert Cunningham and Sons Ltd, Alva, Scotland.

HUMAN SENSES AND PERCEPTION

And men should know that from nothing else but from the brain come joys, delights, laughter and jests, and sorrows, griefs, despondency and lamentations. And by this, in an especial manner, we acquire wisdom and knowledge, and see and hear and know what are foul and what are fair, what sweet and what unsavoury. . . . And by the same organ we become mad and delirious and fears and terrors assail us, some by night and some by day, and dreams and untimely wanderings, and cares that are not suitable and ignorance of present circumstances, desuetude and unskillfulness. All these things we endure from the brain, when it is not healthy, but is more hot, more cold, more moist, or more dry than natural, or when it suffers any other preternatural and unusual affliction.

HIPPOCRATES, *On the Sacred Disease*.

Preface

This book offers an assessment of the contribution of the senses to human experience and activity from the viewpoints of biology, psychology, and perception.

Its purpose is to make readily available within one cover the kind of information that a biologist, psychologist, or philosopher might wish to have concerning those aspects of the subject outside his special interest. Thus the student of psychology or philosophy will find here described the structure of the sense organs, their response to certain specific forms of the physical energy of the universe, and the data they transmit to the brain; while the medical man "specialising" in the senses and the nervous system will find in the discussion of perception as a conscious activity the equally important psychological facts and associated philosophical concepts not normally given in the standard medical text books.

It is hoped that the book will in addition have a wider appeal to educational institutes outside the universities, and to the many others who are curious about their sense organs, the origin and nature of sensory experience, and the scope and reliability of the senses as their source of knowledge about the world.

No attempt has been made at integration of the three disciplines which, rightly or wrongly, was considered to be an unprofitable exercise at the present state of our knowledge. The book therefore consists of three parts, each part retaining the characteristic approach of its discipline to the subject.

The book is not meant to be an authoritative treatise incorporating all recent work on the senses and perception, but an effort has been made to present established knowledge and widely accepted interpretations of the facts in as simple and comprehensible a manner as the subject allows; and in the last part a critique of the standard philosophical views is supplemented by a more positive, if unorthodox, theory of perception and of the relation of body and mind it presupposes.

A list of further reading is given at the end of each chapter.

Contents

PART II

PART I

1

General Introduction

Living substance is not something which originated and exists distinct and separate from the non-living substance of the world. It has evolved through cosmic time out of the physical matter of the universe and for its continued growth and evolution requires not only a supply of the world's available energy but the ability to respond to a range of change in the environment, mechanical, chemical, thermal, or electromagnetic. This adaptation to external conditions or irritability is a property common to all forms of life, animal or vegetable. Plants and the vast hordes of simple

FIG. 1:1. The brain as seen from below. The outer covering, or cortex, is the grey matter of the brain with the nerve cells. The surface of the brain is convoluted and fissured and in this way increases the total area of grey matter.

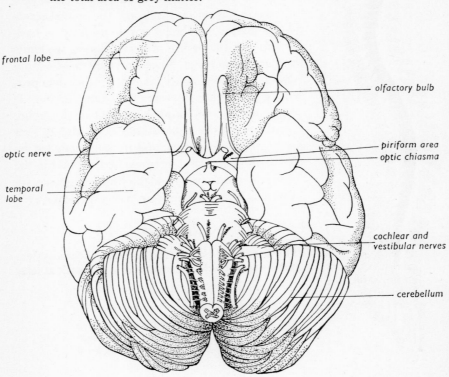

unicellular organisms have a large expanse of surface area. Consequently, most of their substance is in contact with and can respond to changes in the immediate environment as, for example, the spread of foliage which absorbs energy from the sun. The complex multicellular animal forms, on the other hand, with their increased bulk, diminished ratio of surface area, and thus limited external contact, have had to evolve sense organs, structures specially modified to present information about a selection of external changes, together with a centre, the brain and spinal cord (the central nervous system), to receive and organise the incoming information so that appropriate instructions for the necessary responses can be issued to the tissues and organs (Figs. 1:1 and 1:2). While the sense organs provide the information that initiates adaptive behaviour they are not windows giving a view of the external world; they record data in the form of a biological code, and moreover the nature of the data is controlled and modified by the overall intrinsic activity of the organism itself after the manner of automation as we understand it today. Awareness, arising from the stimulation of the sense organs that constitutes perception, *i.e.* seeing, hearing, etc., and the subjective experience of a behavioural response that is part of consciousness, emerges only from a high level of

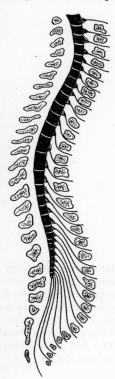

organisation within the nervous system. The skin of a worm has sensory cells and the animal reacts to stimulation, but the worm is unlikely to have anything in the nature of perception as we know it. Perception is not, however, at any level simply a matter of decoding an input of sensory data providing space/time measurement of stimulation. It is an entirely new product created in the brain, in part out of the raw material of the signals sent in by the sense organs, and in part modelled by the total ingoing and outgoing activity within the central nervous system at the time, together with what has been learned from past experience.

The Neuron

The structural unit of the central nervous system is the neuron, which consists of a cell with at least

FIG. 1:2. The spinal cord and its nerves lying within the backbone. It is segmented, with a pair of nerves coming off each segment.

two different kinds of process. There are many types of neuron with a range of size, shape of cell, number, length, and branching of the processes. The largest human nerve cells are about a twentieth of a millimetre in diameter, and the smallest a thousandth of a millimetre or less (Fig. 1:3). Each neuron has one process—the axon—conducting messages away from the cell, while other, more branched processes—the dendrites, of which there may be several—bring messages to the cell. Every nerve fibre within or without the central nervous system is the process of a neuron and therefore the extension of the substance of a nerve cell. Axons may be very long, extending from the brain down the

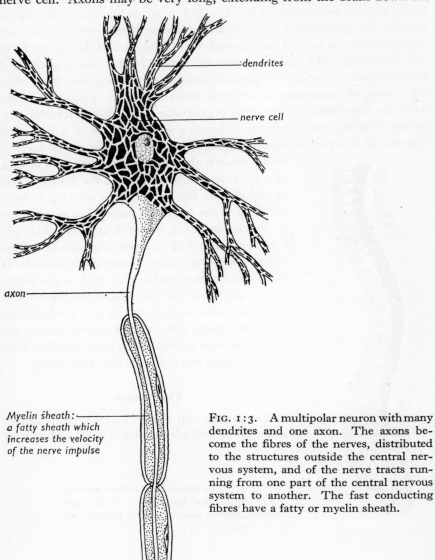

dendrites

nerve cell

axon

Myelin sheath:
a fatty sheath which
increases the velocity
of the nerve impulse

FIG. 1:3. A multipolar neuron with many dendrites and one axon. The axons become the fibres of the nerves, distributed to the structures outside the central nervous system, and of the nerve tracts running from one part of the central nervous system to another. The fast conducting fibres have a fatty or myelin sheath.

spinal cord and vice versa, or to and from the spinal cord in the nerves of the limbs. There are thousands of millions of neurons populating the nervous system, arranged in the columns, groups, or layers forming the

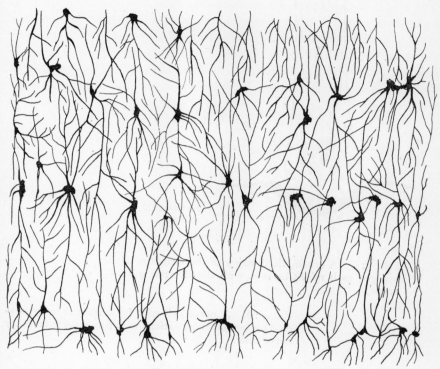

FIG. 1:4. A network of nerve cells and their processes such as is found in the grey matter of the cortex of the brain.

grey matter of the spinal cord and brain, and in small collections outside the central nervous system known as ganglia (Fig. 1:4).

The Synapse

The neurons communicate with one another at junctions termed synapses where a narrow gap separates the respective neurons (Fig. 1:5). In the human nervous system synapses are one-way conducting pathways, so that there is a presynaptic and a postsynaptic neuron. Most neurons have hundreds or even thousands of synaptic junctions with other neurons so that the system is in effect a complicated communications network (Fig. 1:6). The messages from the sense organs are conveyed to the highest "centres" of the brain—the grey matter of the cerebral cortex—by a

HSP B

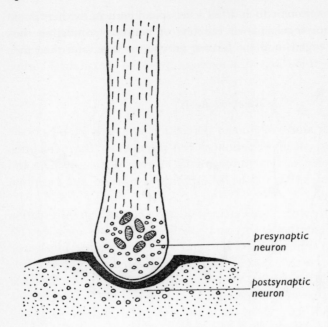

FIG. 1:5. A schematic drawing of the structure of a
synapse as it might be seen with the electron microscope.

FIG. 1:6. A nerve cell with its surface densely covered by synaptic connections with processes from other
nerve cells.

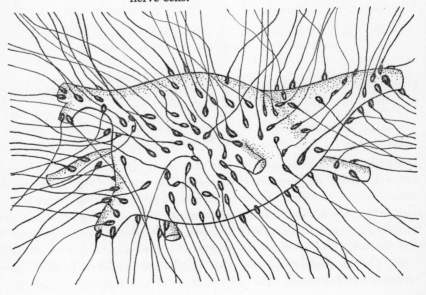

series of relays of neurons which at all levels communicate with adjacent neurons. These neuron relays form the sensory nerves providing the link between the sense organs and the central nervous system, and the nerve tracts running up within the central nervous system to the cerebral cortex.

Electrogenesis

Although the direct study of human perception is largely based on the introspective report, an appreciation of the problem of the perceptual process requires some understanding of the nature of the physical and chemical activity responsible for the collection, transmission, and reception of sensory information.

The ability of the nervous elements to receive all kinds of information about internal and external events and to convert this into messages for transmission to the appropriate brain centres is due to their bioelectric properties, and their activity, or at least the manifestation of it available for recording and measurement, is essentially of the nature of electrical events. There is an electrochemical gradient between the inside and the outside of the neuron, with the inside of the nerve fibre and the nerve cell electrically negative in respect of the outside. This "resting" potential measures from -50 to -100 millivolts and the covering or bounding membrane of the neuron is said to be polarised. The storage of electrical energy in this way is made possible by the special property of the bounding membrane of the neuron with regard to its ion (chemical particles with an electric charge) permeability. When at rest, there is a relatively free diffusion across the membrane of such ions as potassium (cation) and chlorine (anion), which therefore tend to be in equilibrium with respect to both sides of the membrane; but the larger sodium cations with their positive electric charge accumulate on the outside of the membrane, and indeed are responsible for the resting potential. The energy required to sustain this electrochemical gradient is made available from the chemical processes within the substance of the neuron itself. It has been said that the biologist is dealing with information systems in which the signals are transmitted by ions through conduction lines composed chiefly of salts and water.

At least two kinds of electrical activity, or electrogenesis, occur in the nervous system: (1) the non-decremental electrogenesis or nerve impulses characteristic of the conducting elements such as nerve fibres which are electrically excitable, and (2) the decremental electrogenesis developed at the input end of the neurons, which includes sense receptors, postsynaptic membranes, and dendrites of the central nervous system; these are not excitable electrically.

The Nerve Impulse (Fig. 1:7)

When a nerve fibre is stimulated either naturally or electrically under experimental conditions, there is an alteration in the ion permeability of its cell membrane which results in the abolition of the electrochemical gradient, *i.e.* the depolarisation of the membrane, and, as the process continues, an actual reversal of the gradient so that the inside of the nerve at the stimulated point becomes electrically positive relative to the

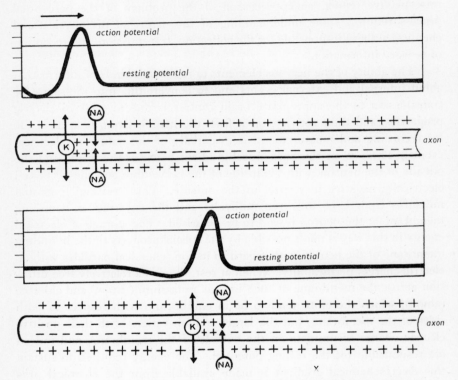

FIG. 1:7. To show spread of the nerve impulse with the depolarisation of the axon membrane (after Katz).

outside. There will now be a flow of electric current along the nerve from this positive site to an adjacent negative site where the electric current acts as a stimulus, and this procedure is then repeated with a further spread of current flow to the next segment downstream, and so on. This electrical change, or "action potential," progressing along the nerve fibre is the basis of the nerve impulse. It can be recorded and measured with the oscillograph and constitutes the unit of the signal code by which messages are conveyed via the nerves and the nerve tracts to their destination in the brain. The nerve impulse, as an item of information, has the following properties:

(1) A certain minimum or threshold stimulation is required to elicit an action potential, which is measured in millivolts.

(2) For any one nerve fibre the action potential remains constant in amplitude and duration irrespective of the strength of stimulation; it is an all-or-none event, like an explosion.

(3) The nerve impulse does not spread along the nerve as an electric current flows along a wire, otherwise it would decay within a relatively short distance. It is a chain reaction and each link of the chain generates an "action potential" like ignition travelling along a fuse.

(4) The large, *i.e.* thick, nerve fibres, like a telephone cable incorporate a special boosting mechanism at regular intervals along their length and so the signal is "pulsed" along and can attain a maximum velocity of 100 metres per second compared to half a metre per second in the small nerve fibres without the boosting mechanism.

(5) The larger the fibres the greater the amplitude of the impulse.

(6) The nerve impulse is the only kind of sensory message received by the brain whether it is from the eye, the ear, the skin or elsewhere.

Decremental Electrogenesis

The postsynaptic membrane at the input end of the neuron is not excitable electrically and therefore is not affected directly by the action potential across a synapse. At the presynaptic or output end the nerve impulses release a chemical substance (chemical transmitter) which affects the ion permeability and so initiates an electrogenesis of the postsynaptic membrane—the postsynaptic potential (P.S.P.). This differs from the action potential in the following ways:

(1) It is not an all-or-none event but can be built up and sustained over a period of time.

(2) It is not conducted but spreads electrotonically, decaying with distance, *i.e.* it is decremental.

(3) It is usually a depolarisation which, when it attains a certain strength, acts as a stimulus and triggers off action potentials at the electrically excitable conducting part of the nerve fibres.

(4) The P.S.P., due to the release of a different kind of chemical transmitter substance, may be a hyperpolarisation which will inhibit or block the passage of the nerve impulse.

It is probable that any one neuron will have both inhibitory and excitatory synapses.

A single impulse arriving at the presynaptic membrane is unlikely to release sufficient chemical transmitter substance to produce an effective

P.S.P., but it will cause some degree of electrogenesis which will be increased by succeeding impulses until it attains sufficient strength to trigger off impulse volleys in the postsynaptic neuron. This is temporal summation. Most neurons have many synapses, and while the activity at any one of these may not be sufficient to generate impulses the combined activity at a number of synapses on the cell surface at any one time may initiate an impulse discharge. This is spatial summation.

Decremental electrogenesis confers on the synapse the special properties of facilitation (in the form of temporal and spatial summation) and inhibition (hyperpolarisation), implying that it does something more than function as a passive conducting unit and can to some extent sort out the messages to be sent on. In terms of the computer mechanism, the neuron is capable of processing diverse input and determining, within limits, the output. Much of the activity of the ramifying dendrites within the grey matter of the central nervous system is a form of decremental electrogenesis.

Sensory Apparatus

The sensory apparatus consists of (1) the sense organs or receptors situated outside the central nervous system, many of them, such as those for pain or touch, placed just under the skin; (2) the conducting elements made up of chains of sensory neurons terminating in (3) a localised area of the grey matter on the brain surface which is the final receiving centre. It should be understood, however, that each neuron in the chain leading up to the brain establishes through its synaptic connexions a vast and complex network of interconnexions with other neurons, so that any volley of incoming impulses will have widespread effects on large assemblies of neurons. Indeed, at present it would seem to be unlikely that we will ever be able to obtain a full record of the total effect of a short burst of sensory input throughout the central nervous system.

General Characteristics of Receptors

Our awareness of the external world is obtained wholly through our sense organs, and is therefore limited to those events which possess the kind and range of energy capable of stimulating them. The human sense organs are mechanoreceptors, thermoreceptors, chemoreceptors, or photoreceptors, sensitive to mechanical, thermal, chemical, and electromagnetic forms of energy respectively. Receptors may consist of specialised nerve endings or the association of these endings with receptor cells. They may be single units like the sense organs of the skin or, as in the special senses such as the eye and the ear, aggregations of receptors.

Specific Stimuli: A receptor is relatively unresponsive to all but one particular kind of energy except perhaps the pain receptors, which appear to respond to any form of stimulus intense enough to be harmful. In addition to this general specificity the individual receptors of a complex sense organ may respond only to a particular range of the exciting energy. For example, receptors in the eye vary in their sensitivity to the different regions of the light spectrum which we subjectively recognise as colour, and separate groups of sound receptors respond to the different frequencies perceived as pitch. Similarly, there are thermal receptors sensitive to a particular range of temperature.

Receptor Potential: The special function of all receptors is to convert the energy of the stimulus into the electrical energy used to discharge the nerve impulses along the conducting elements. The receptors, therefore, act as biological transducers. Our knowledge of the electrical changes that occur within a receptor comes from the study of mammalian mechano-receptors such as the Pacinian corpuscles (Fig. 2:3) which can be seen with the naked eye (they are up to a millimetre in length) and are large enough to be explored with the microelectrode, leading off any electric currents to be amplified and measured with the oscillograph. The transducer action of the receptors initiates an electrogenesis known as the receptor potential which, like that of the postsynaptic membrane, is decremental, capable of being sustained locally and of spreading to the electrically excitable conducting nerve membrane where it acts like a constant electrical stimulus and triggers off volleys of nerve impulses. In what way the various forms of stimulus energy bring about the ionic shifts responsible for the development of the receptor potential is not known, but the details probably vary in the different receptors. In mammalian mechanoreceptors the potential develops within a thousandth of a second after stimulation and its amplitude increases up to a certain maximum with the strength of the stimulus. This maximum varies for each sense organ but may be as much as ten times stronger than a threshold receptor potential, *i.e.* one able to trigger off nerve impulses. The frequency rate of discharge, *i.e.* the number of nerve impulses sent along the nerve in unit of time, is related to the amplitude of the receptor potential and so indirectly to the strength of the stimulus. The relationship between the strength of the stimulus and the impulse frequency is further complicated by the fact that the build-up of the receptor potential is influenced by the velocity of the stimulus, *i.e.* whether the application of the stimulus is sudden or slow. It has been shown, for instance, that in some receptors, *e.g.* the Pacinian receptors, the amplitude of the receptor potential rises with the velocity of the stimulus up to a maximum compression velocity of about 1 mm. per second, which lies within the range of natural stimulation. It is probable that in all receptors the nerve impulses are triggered off from the receptor potentials generated in their nerve terminals at some point in the conducting nerve fibres nearer the central nervous system. There is as yet no conclusive evidence of the existence of chemical transmitter substances in the receptors.

Sensory Units and Receptive Fields: A single nerve fibre links up with groups of receptors by terminal branches, and each receptor group forms a sensory unit which in some way would appear to function as an independent information line with its own receiving cells in the cortex of the brain. The territory from which a sensory unit records stimulation is its receptive field, and this of course varies in size in the different senses, *e.g.* the tactile receptive field in the skin is of the order of square millimetres. It is a general principle that there is a wide overlap of receptive fields and so a single stimulus can be recorded by several sensory units, but the impulse frequency generated in the sensory units concerned will vary according to their position relative to the site of stimulation.

Adaptation: The rate of discharge from a receptor may diminish with prolonged stimulation, and indeed for a time cease altogether. This is particularly characteristic of the "phasic" mechanoreceptors such as touch corpuscles and is the physical basis of "adaptation," the term used to describe the everyday experience that we cease to be aware of some forms of continuous stimulation, *e.g.* the contact of our clothes. "Tonic" receptors adapt more slowly and their frequency of discharge declines to a steady rate depending on the strength of the stimulus, *e.g.* thermoreceptors and proprioceptors. While adaptation is the response of the receptor to one particular aspect of the energy concerned, what information is conveyed in respect of time by the act of adaptation is not at all clear. Phasic receptors may only respond to a change from one state to another, some when the stimulus strength is increased, others when it is decreased. Such "off" and "on" responses may be due to the mechanics of the sensory apparatus as, for example, the mechanoreceptors of the ear, rather than an innate property of the receptors themselves.

Weber Fraction: Every sense organ not only has a threshold stimulus, *i.e.* the minimum amount of energy required to produce a sensation, but it also has a minimum change in stimulus energy that can produce a just noticeable difference in sensation, *e.g.* the smallest difference which makes it possible to distinguish between two weights or the minimum difference in light intensity which can be appreciated in respect of brightness. This minimum stimulus increment or decrement is not a constant value for any one sense organ, but is a ratio of the energy difference between the two stimuli and the energy value of the first stimulus. This is expressed as $\Delta I/I$, the so-called Weber fraction, where $I =$ the energy value of the first stimulus, and ΔI = the additional stimulus energy required to be added to I to produce a just noticeable difference in sensation. This is not, however, as was at one time believed, a universally applicable formula for all sense organs, although there is some relationship between this ratio and the frequency of impulse discharge under certain specific conditions.

Impulse Pattern: The meaningful content of sensory stimulation is coded in the timing and spacing of the nerve impulses, *i.e.* the impulse pattern, and this is determined by (1) threshold value and the rate of adaptation of the receptors, (2) the velocity and amplitude of the impulses, dependent on the size range of the conducting nerve fibres, (3) the differential discharge rate of the various sensory units involved according to the situation of their receptive fields relative to the centre of stimulation, (4) a necessary condition is, of course, that the messages are conveyed to the correct destination—their particular receiving area on the cerebral cortex—along the established communication channels.

BIBLIOGRAPHY

The Neuron

BRAZIER, M. A. B. 1959. Historical development of neurophysiology. *Handbook of Physiology*, **1,** Sec. 1. Amer. Physiol. Soc., Washington, D.C.

CLARK, W. E. LE GROS. 1958. *The Tissues of the Body*, 4th Edn. Clarendon Press, Oxford.

MILLER, W. H. *et al.* 1961. How cells receive stimuli. *Scientific American*, **205,** No. 3.

PALAY, S. L. and PALADE, E. G. 1955. The fine structure of neurons. *J. Biophys. Biochem. Cytol.*, **1,** 69.

WYBURN, G. M. 1960. *Outline of the Central Nervous System*. Academic Press, London and New York.

The Synapse

BREEMEN, V. L. VAN *et al.* 1958. An attempt to determine the origin of synaptic vessels. *Exp. Cell Res.*, Suppl. **5,** 153.

COUTEAUX, R. 1958. Morphological and cytochemical observations on the post-synaptic membrane at motor end-plates and ganglionic synapses. *Exp. Cell Res.*, Suppl. **5,** 294.

DE ROBERTIS, E. 1958. Submicroscopic morphology and function of the synapse. *Exp. Cell Res.*, Suppl. **5,** 347.

PALAY, S. L. 1957. *Progress in Neurobiology*. Vol. II *Ultrastructure and Cellular Chemistry of Neural Tissue*. Ed. by Korey, S. R. and Nurnberger, J. I. Hoeber, New York.

——1958. The morphology of synapses in the central nervous system. *Exp. Cell Res.*, Suppl. **5,** 275.

SJÖSTRAND, F. S. 1961. Electron microscopy of the retina. In *The Structure of the Eye*. Ed. by G. K. Smelser. Academic Press, London and New York.

WYBURN, G. M. 1958. The Joints of the Brain. *New Scientist*, May 8th.

Nerve Fibre

ENGSTRÖM, A. and FINEAN, J. B. 1958. *Biological Ultrastructure*. Academic Press, London and New York.

GEREN, B. B. 1956. *Myelin in Cellular Mechanisms in Differentiation and Growth*. Princeton University Press.

GOLDBY, F. 1961. The Schwann cell, myelin and other tissues associated with nerve cells. In *Recent Advances in Anatomy*. Ed. by F. Goldby and R. J. Harrison. J. and A. Churchill Ltd., London.

Proceedings of the Anatomical Society of Great Britain and Ireland. 1961. Cytology of Nervous Tissue, November. Taylor and Francis Ltd., London.

WEISS, P. 1955. Nervous system (neurogenesis). In *Analysis of Development*. Ed. by B. H. Willier, P. A. Weiss and V. Hamburger. Saunders, Philadelphia and London.

The Nerve Impulse

CRESCITELLI, F. 1955. Conduction and transmission in the central nervous system. *Ann. Rev. Physiol.*, **17**, 243.

GRUNDFEST, H. 1952. Mechanism and properties of bioelectric-potentials. *Modern Trends in Physiology and Biochemistry*. Academic Press, London and New York.

KATZ, B. 1961. How Cells Communicate. *Scientific American*, **205**, No. 3.

NACHMANSOHN, D. 1959. *Chemical and Molecular Basis of Nerve Activity*. Academic Press, London and New York.

TASAKI, I. 1959. Conduction of the nerve impulse. *Handbook of Physiology*, **1**, Sec. 1. Amer. Physiol. Soc., Washington, D.C.

Synaptic Transmission

ECCLES, J. C. 1947. *The Physiology of Nerve Cells*. John Hopkins Press, Baltimore.

GRUNDFEST, H. 1959. Synaptic and ephatic transmission. *Handbook of Physiology*, **1**, Sec. 1. Amer. Physiol. Soc., Washington, D.C.

HEBB, C. O. 1959. Chemical agents of the nervous system. *Int. Rev. Neurobiol.*, **1**, 165.

KUFFLER, S. W. 1952. Transmission processes at nerve-muscle junctions. *Modern Trends in Physiology and Biochemistry*. Academic Press, London and New York.

——1958. Synaptic inhibitory mechanisms. *Exp. Cell Res.*, Suppl. **5**, 493.

2

The Cutaneous Sense Organs

The receptor organs of the skin are terminals of the sensory nerves, some of them enclosed within supporting tissues to form various kinds of microscopic encapsulated bodies (Fig. 2:1). The cutaneous sense modalities are temperature, touch, pain, and pressure. In a broad way it can be said that each cutaneous sense modality has its own kind of receptor, and if there is some experimental evidence to the contrary and a lack of sufficient knowledge to classify all the different kinds of nerve endings found in the skin, it is nevertheless quite definite that there are specific receptors picking up particular kinds of stimuli. Moreover, it is recognised that each sense modality is associated with a size range of nerve fibre and tends to have its own conducting system within and without the central nervous system, while there is a general acceptance of the idea that a

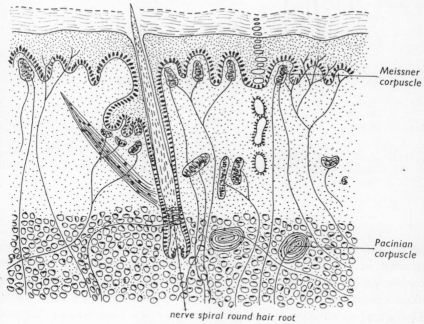

Meissner corpuscle

Pacinian corpuscle

nerve spiral round hair root

FIG. 2:1. A drawing of the skin to show a nerve spiral round the hair roots and other sense receptors.

sensory unit is normally responsible for one kind of sensation only. We do, however, have subjective experiences which cannot be placed in any one of the recognised categories, *e.g.* wetness, hardness, itching, and tickling.

Touch

Among the earliest of the sense organs evolved were the mechanoreceptors informing the organism about movement of parts, vibration, and skin contacts. The primary object of the tactile sense is to feel one's way about in the world, and many animals explore their immediate surroundings by special probing antennae and hairs so that touch is with them a more highly developed and important sense than it is with Man.

The mechanoreceptors we know to be quite definitely concerned with the tactile sense are (1) the roots of the hairs with their spiral of sensory

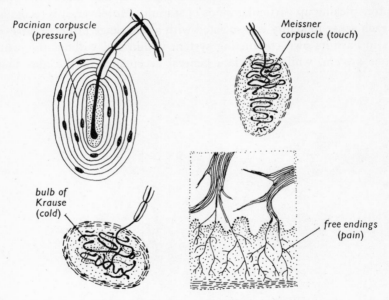

FIG. 2:2.   The sense receptors of the skin.

nerves and (2) the corpuscles of Meissner (Fig. 2:2), encapsulated bodies situated in relation to the peg-like roots of the epidermis. Pacinian corpuscles, found in the deeper tissues around joints and capsules, are more concerned with pressure and kinesthesis (see later) than touch. The actual stimulation of a mechanoreceptor is a compression due to a deformation of the skin and the tissues or, in the case of the hair roots, displacement of the hairs, and a characteristic property of mechanoreceptors is their delicate sensitivity to mechanical stimuli. The effect of experimental stimulation of a Pacinian corpuscle is known in some detail and it has been shown that the corpuscle responds to a minimal movement of the order of ·5μ in a tenth of a second. The receptor element in the Pacinian corpuscle is the nerve terminal enclosed in a sheath made up of

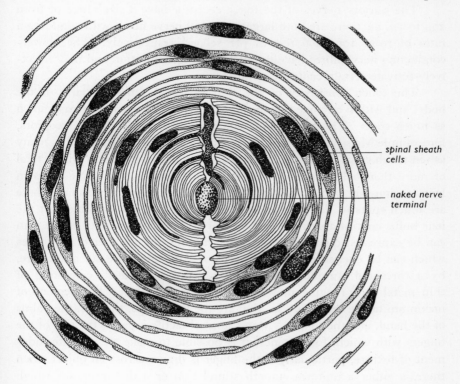

spinal sheath cells

naked nerve terminal

FIG. 2:3. The structure of a Pacinian corpuscle as seen with the electron microscope (after Quilliam). The nerve terminal is enclosed within a sheath made up of concentric cell layers with some intervening fluid. This acts as a compression gauge and picks up the specific stimulus energy.

concentric layers like those of an onion, with some intervening fluid (Fig. 2:3). Pressure will compress the corpuscle with initial displacement of all its layers, including the nerve terminal. Displacement of the enclosed receptor is, however, confined to the onset of compression and does not persist with sustained stimulation. Thus, the activation of the receptor will be limited to the initial stimulation, and the characteristic rapid adaptation of the Pacinian corpuscles is largely a mechanical attribute of the structure. Some Pacinian corpuscles, however, particularly those in the deeper tissues round the joints, are slow-adapting, but whether adaptation is slow or fast may depend on the configuration of the terminal receptor. The receptor potential of the Pacinian corpuscle is set up in less than ·2 milliseconds from the time of stimulation and thereafter spreads from the nerve terminal to the "conducting" nerve fibre inside the corpuscle where it triggers off a volley of nerve impulses.

The sensory nerves of the touch receptor have a size range of from 20μ to 1μ, *i.e.* there are both large and small nerve fibres with conduction rates of from 100 to 6 metres per second respectively. The slower-conducting nerve fibres have impulses of longer duration and may selectively activate certain central neuron systems.

The touch sensitivity of the skin varies in different parts of the body, and within any one region there are specially sensitive areas known as touch spots. The touch spots consist of a group of touch receptors, for example Meissner's corpuscles, in clusters of two or three, and as many as ten touch spots can be found in 1 sq. mm. of sensitive skin with a total of more than half a million over the whole surface. Sensitive spots in hairy regions are said to be localised round the hair bulbs, although there are touch spots in the skin between the hairs, but it is possible that the hair bulbs control a surrounding territory. Tactile sensitivity of the skin can be expressed quantitatively by determining the number of responses which can be elicited over a given area of skin, say half a sq. millimetre, by a threshold stimulus produced by "aesthesiometers" consisting of thin metal rods ranging in weight from ·05 to ·5 gm. The regions of maximum tactile sensitivity in Man are the finger tips, the lips, the palms of the hand, and the tongue. Man's normal tactile organ is the tips of the fingers with which, for instance, it is possible to make an accurate judgment of texture, particularly if the finger is drawn across an object when there is either a uniform smooth stimulation or a discontinuous rough stimulation. In Braille, where the letters of the alphabet are denoted by a combination of raised dots, the blind read with their fingers.

Touch receptors are fast adapters and to maintain a sensation the stimulus must not only have a certain minimum strength but also a minimum rate of change. We are, for instance, much more sensitive to a moving than a static stimulus, and while normally the threshold stimulus will vary according to our preoccupation or otherwise with other sensory events, contact is a good "alerting" stimulus. There are a number of sensations which include an element of touch. Wetness, for example, is touch plus cold, and moisture itself is not necessary as a sensation of wetness is still experienced if the finger immersed in fluid has a waterproof covering. Judgment of hardness or softness brings in an element of pressure. That there are receptors specifically sensitive to touch does not exclude the possibility that touch sensation can be elicited in the absence of such receptors, or that stimuli other than touch may unusually excite the specific touch receptors.

It is possible without visual aid to locate approximately the point on the skin touched, and the degree of accuracy of this tactile localisation depends on the sensitivity of the region. Similarly, if an individual is touched simultaneously by two points, say by the points of dividers, a certain minimal distance between the stimulated points is necessary before a double sensation is appreciated. This is tactile discrimination which, like tactile localisation, varies according to the sensitivity of the region.

Vibration

Vibration is a form of discontinuous pressure which is transmitted through the skin and so affects a wide area of receptors. Curiously, however, there may be a loss of the sense of vibration while both touch and pressure are preserved. It has recently been pointed out that just as we have to learn to interpret particular combinations of speech sounds as words, so it should be possible, with training and appropriate coding of tactile stimuli, to evolve some kind of skin language, particularly as cutaneous sensation is a good break-through attention demanding sense. For instance, we can look and not see, hear and yet be unaware of noise, but we are almost invariably attentive to stimulation of the skin. It has indeed been suggested that of all the cutaneous sense modalities vibration probably has the greatest number of dimensions suitable for use as items of a code delivering messages to the skin and capable of some kind of interpretation. The obvious dimensions are with regard to intensity, duration, frequency of vibrations, and locus. Within a certain range it is possible to appreciate small increases in intensity of vibration. The duration of a burst of vibratory stimulation can, of course, be judged fairly accurately and the comparative lengths of different periods of stimulation assessed with some precision. However, if the total duration of the stimulus is less than a tenth of a second it tends to be felt as a single touch stimulus rather than a discontinuous vibration, and periods of longer than two seconds would be too cumbersome to use as code signals. Between these limits, *i.e.* ·1 and 2 seconds, the average person can distinguish about twenty-five time periods, the steps being of the order of ·005 seconds at the low end and ·15 seconds at the high end of the range.

There are a number of difficulties about coding in terms of appreciation of vibration frequency, and while judgment of frequency rates is reasonably good below 70 cycles per second, above this the ability to discriminate between the different frequency rates, *i.e.* appreciation of skin vibratory "pitch," is conditioned to some extent by its amplitude.

The other dimension, locus, depends on the two attributes of cutaneous sensation—tactile localisation and tactile discrimination—and it should be possible to vary the total pattern of signals received by simultaneous stimulation of different surface areas. It has been found, for example, that if the vibrators are spaced on the chest, under certain circumstances the situation of each stimulator can be identified. One difficulty, however, is that a number of vibrators with exactly the same stimulus pattern and acting at the same time tend to become merged into a single vibration sensation. If, however, there is even a split-second difference in the timing of the stimulus at different sites this will restore perception of multiple point stimulation and will at the same time provide the essential conditions for the perception of movement, what the psychologists call the phenomenon-phi (see p. 176). This phenomenon of cutaneous-phi is an extraordinarily powerful one and highly attention-demanding. For instance, with a ring of vibrators round the body, three across the front and three across the back, energised successively with a ·1 sec. temporal separation, the subject feels a vivid swirling movement which is quite a novel type of sensation because the observer seems to be in the centre of it. Based on such variations of intensity, duration, and locus of vibratory signals, an alphabetical code has been devised and applied to a subject who, after a period of training in this vibratised language could interpret sentences transmitted at the rate of 35 lettered words per minute with a 90 per cent accuracy. With the same spacing as international morse, *i.e.* ·1 second between words and ·005 second between the letters of words, this system requires only ·9 seconds to transmit the average five-lettered English word. The development of skin communication is not just an interesting exercise in psychophysics. From time to time there will be human beings born both blind and deaf or who through accident or disease are deprived of sight and hearing. These unfortunate individuals, apart from their chemical senses, are left with only the skin as a means of communicating with the world and their fellow men. A properly developed tactile communication system could do much to help them. Moreover, during the next century Man is going to venture further and further into space where sound signals such as speech will not be available as the basis of a communications system. In space, Man may have to learn to communicate by contact and to make use of his relatively enormous skin receiving area for this purpose.

Pain

The basic function of the sensory apparatus for pain is to provide the information to initiate the behavioural responses by which the animal deals with harmful influences. As a sensation, pain has a greater range of affective manifestations and a more powerful psychic component than any other form of consciousness. Some of the descriptive epithets applied to pain are smarting, stabbing, quivering, pricking, pinching, thrusting, burning, etc., most of them expressing either a spatial or a temporal dimension. It has been said that there are two elements in pain, the initial sensation and the reaction to the sensation. The stimulus and the state of mind at the time of stimulation share responsibility for the total psychic disturbance caused by pain and it may be difficult to separate out from a condition of misery and suffering the relative contributions of physical pain and of a mental attitude brought about by non-physical factors which, as far as we know, adds nothing to the impulse input. Most religions and many tribal traditions attribute an inherent virtue to fortitude in the toleration of pain, but a combination of innate stoicism and sacrificial ecstasy could be factors in the successful performance of such endurance tests as fire-walking, skin-piercing, and ritualistic self-mutilation. Apart from indifference to pain which is seen during hypnosis, hysteria, and other psychotic conditions, there are records of otherwise normal individuals who are insensitive to pain and who, for example, are indifferent to stabbing or burning injuries. This so-called congenital universal indifference to pain is likely to be due to some defect in the cerebral cortex rather than any interference with pain receptors and conducting pathways.

It has been contended that pain is not a sensation in its own right, but merely the consequence of any excessive stimulation like intense pressure, intense heat, intense cold, etc. Excessive stimulation of any receptor, however, results in a high rate of impulse discharge and it is known that this is not an inevitable characteristic of the conduction of pain impulses. Moreover, there is unequivocal evidence that pain, like touch, has its own receptors, nerve fibres, pathways within the central nervous system, and final receiving centres in the cortex. The pain produced by dazzling light is not the result of excessive stimulation of the photoreceptors of the eye, but is said to be due to spasm of the muscle controlling the size of the pupil. Similarly, painful noise is due to a spasm of the small muscles acting on the eardrum. Above 50 °C. heat becomes a burning sensation and thereafter its receptors and conducting pathways have been shown to be dissociated from the thermal system.

Unlike other modalities, the quality of pain varies not only according to the nature of the stimulus—thermal, mechanical, or chemical—but also according to the organ or tissue stimulated. Brief painful stimulation of the skin is usually described as pricking. It is sharply localised, and if prolonged becomes burning. Pain from the deep tissues—bones, joints,

HSP C

and muscles—is dull, aching, diffuse, and immobilising and if intense can have generalised effects leading to nausea, vomiting and a condition of shock. Many organs—intestines, kidneys, and the brain itself—are insensitive to cutting and burning, but stretching of hollow organs, either by pulling them or from internal distension, produces pain, e.g. distension of the kidneys or of the gall bladder. Both blockage and dilatation of arteries is associated with the sudden onset of severe pain, the headache of migraine is said to be due to arterial dilatation, while ischemia, i.e. an insufficient blood supply, is a cause of pain, for example, in coronary thrombosis or intermittent claudication (spasm of the muscles of the leg). The pain of inflammation is in part due to the tension of the tissues caused by swelling but it also lowers the pain threshold so that normally painless stimuli become painful. Pressure on an inflamed appendix, for example, is painful.

Pain Receptors (Fig. 2:2)

The nerves of the skin form plexiform networks and the great majority of them end in fine branches without any specialised capsule formations. These free terminals are regarded as the pain receptors and are the only kind of nerve ending found in the cornea, the eardrum, or the dental pulp where most forms of stimulation are painful, although it is possible that in the cornea mild stimulation can be interpreted as touch. Similar free nerve endings are found in the serous membranes round the viscera, in the walls of the gut and blood vessels, in the deeper tissues round the joints, and in the covering membrane of bones—the periostium.

The conducting elements in the pain apparatus are the fast, larger fibres where the impulses have a velocity of 15 to 40 metres per second and the slow, smaller fibres with a velocity of less than 2 metres per second. Corresponding to the fast and slow conduction rates, trained observers describe a double pain response following stimulation by pin-prick—an immediate sensation and after an interval a second sensation which is not only of slower onset but more severe, more penetrating, and with a longer after-effect. This is, of course, a subjective observation and appreciation of double pain has not been confirmed by all observers.

Stimulus and Sensation

Painful stimulation of the skin has been classified as pricking, crushing, or burning, each sensation with its separate pathway and therefore characteristic conduction velocity and impulse amplitude. The stimulus energy for pricking is pressure exerted upon a small area, the effect being in inverse ratio to the area excited and reaching its maximum with point stimulation. The significant factor in crushing forms of pain is the duration of the stimulus; the longer it lasts the more intense the pain becomes. Possibly in this type of pain stimulus there is liberation of some chemical substance activating the pain receptors and responsible not only for the intensity of the sensation but also for the persistence of the pain after the stimulus is withdrawn. The stimulus energy in burning sensations is probably of a chemical nature as likewise the pain following injections of hypertonic or hypotonic solutions into mucous membranes, due possibly to variations in osmotic pressure affecting pain receptors. An increase (alkalinity) or a decrease (acidity) of the hydrogen ion concentration can cause pain and certain chemical elements excite pain more readily than others, *e.g.* the potassium ion. Indeed, there appears to be some relationship between pain potential and position in the periodic table.

Skin irritated in different ways such as by continuous scratching, heat, or ultraviolet light (sunlight) becomes hyperalgesic, *i.e.* hypersensitive to painful stimulation so that a light pin-prick, for instance, will cause much more intense pain than in normal skin. It has been suggested that this hyperalgesia is promoted by the liberation of chemical substances by the irritated skin and both acetylcholine (Ach) and 5–hydroxytryptamine (serotonin) have been mentioned in this respect. A pain-producing substance (P.P.S.) has been found in both blister fluid and inflammatory fluid.

Itching, which has its own persistent and demanding quality, is a variety of cutaneous pain. The chemical substance histamine causes itching, and a number of skin conditions where there is intense itching are associated with irritation from histamine-like substances. The relief of itching by rubbing or scratching is possibly a central mechanism, *i.e.* within the brain, whereby an additional or alternative stimulus inhibits the existing one.

Pain from harmful stimulation of deep structures or from disease affecting the internal organs is often felt at some area on the body surface. This is referred pain. Classical examples are (1) pain down the inner side of the arm in a heart attack, (2) shoulder pain due to gallstone colic, and (3) earache from a gastric ulcer. The usual, although not wholly satisfactory, explanation of referred pain is that it is due to a convergence of pain neurons from the organs and the skin either in the spinal cord or higher up in the brain, and as the sensory impulses from the viscera do not normally cause conscious sensation, pain impulses are referred by the central nervous system to the skin receptors sharing the receiving neurons. The receptive field to which the pain is referred may in addition show tenderness, and this has been attributed to a central excitatory state of the neurons in the spinal cord brought about by the impact of pain impulses.

Thermal Sensation

Thermoreceptors

Man maintains a body temperature which varies within narrow limits round 37 °C. (98·4 °F.) and is regulated by a number of internal mechanisms including heat loss or gain through the body surface. We have sensations of cold or warmth with regard to the skin, and appreciation of temperature conditions at the body surface, or "thermal sensitivity," is a cutaneous sense modality like touch and pain, with its own sensory apparatus made up of sense organs or thermoreceptors and their nerve pathways. As thermal sensations result from negative or positive forms of the same kind of stimulus energy it is perhaps surprising to find that there are two quite distinct kinds of thermoreceptors, one for cold and one for warmth, with a functional overlap rather like maximum and minimum thermometers. Such an arrangement gives greater flexibility to our thermal recording system within a smaller temperature range.

The cold receptors are believed to be the minute corpuscle-like structures—the end bulbs of Krause—and the warm receptors the less numerous Ruffini end organs (Fig. 2:2). The cold receptors are placed at a depth of ·18 mm. and the warm receptors at ·3 mm. from the surface. Hence, the time taken to appreciate a warm stimulus is longer than the corresponding time for a cold stimulus. Both warm and cold receptors are in fact terminals of fine nerve fibres enclosed within a capsule. There are a great many other varieties of sensory nerve endings of unknown function just under the skin and possibly some of them act as thermoreceptors. Thermoreceptors, like all sense receptors, perform two separate tasks. They respond to a specific stimulus, in this case thermal, and they are biological transducers.

Thermal sensitivity, like tactile sensitivity, varies in the different regions of the body and is discrete, with cold and warm spots, the proportion of each varying in the different parts of the body with, as a rule, more cold spots than warm spots. Cold spots can quite readily be mapped out with the end of a narrow metal rod but the warm spots are more indefinite. The highest density of thermal sensitive spots is found in the face, and the forehead is particularly sensitive to cold. Presumably such cold and warm spots correspond to areas overlying groups of the respective thermoreceptors.

The Stimulus

The thermal stimulus is the temperature at the level of the receptors and not the actual temperature on the surface of the skin. To be more precise, it is a rate of change in the temperature, except when the constant temperature is outside a certain normal range.

Thermal movement through the skin is determined by what is known as the thermal diffusion coefficient, a combination of a number of factors, and for human skin the thermal diffusion coefficient in depths up to 2 mm. varies from ·0004 to ·0018 cm² per second. Local changes in the blood flow of the skin can also influence temperature conditions round the receptors.

It is possible to record temperature movements at a depth of up to ·6 mm. below the skin and to show that with constant skin temperatures below 20 °C. and above 40 °C. sensations of cold or warmth persist even after the rate of thermal change at the level of the receptors is zero. Within the range 20 °C. to 40 °C. a thermal sensation requires a certain rate of thermal change and will tend to disappear, i.e. adapt, when or shortly after the temperature movement ceases. The greater the difference between the stimulus temperature and that of the skin the longer the sensation lasts, and the nearer the temperature of the skin at the time of stimulation is to 20 °C. on the one hand, or 40 °C. on the other, the smaller the rate of thermal change required to elicit a sensation. For example, +·001 °C. and −·001 °C. are still effective above 38 °C. and below 25 °C. respectively. To put it another way, the temperature level of the skin when stimulated influences the threshold value, i.e. the minimum amount of stimulus energy for both warm and cold sensation. In addition, there is also a time factor. Given a steady rate of change of +·0017 °C. the higher the temperature at the start of stimulation the more quickly does the sensation of warmth appear. Similarly, the lower the starting temperature the more quickly does a rate of change of −·0017 °C. produce a cold sensation.

The total area of skin stimulated also influences its threshold value. If the whole body is exposed the range of thermal indifference (i.e. when there is no thermal sensation with a constant temperature) is narrowed to between 32 °C. and 35 °C., and at 35 °C. even a slow rise of temperature at the rate of +·001 °C. per second, producing a somewhat slower rate in the rise of skin temperature, elicits a sensation of warmth.

There are thus three factors of significance in thermal stimulation. First, the absolute temperature underneath the skin; second, the rate of change of this temperature; and third, the total area of the surface stimulated, i.e. the control system is three-dimensional—thermal, temporal, and spatial.

Stimulation of cold spots by heat above 45 °C. results in a sensation of cold which has been named paradoxical cold, and indeed there is some evidence that a hot sensation arising from stimulation by temperatures of over 45 °C., although introspectively a single subjective experience, is in fact a mixture of warmth and paradoxical cold.

Electrophysiology

In mammals there are specific nerve fibres for warm and cold sensation connected with their respective thermal receptors, and by the use of electrophysiological methods it has been possible to record experimentally the rate of discharge of the nerve impulses of "cold" and "warm" nerve fibres in, for instance, the nerve of the tongue during controlled thermal stimulation of the surface of the tongue.

With constant temperatures within the range 10 °C. to 40 °C. there is a steady discharge of the cold fibres and the temperature eliciting the maximum discharge rate within that range varies for different cold fibres, but the total frequency of impulses in a nerve, *i.e.* the sum of impulses from all its cold fibres, reaches the maximum between 15 °C. and 20 °C. Above 40°C. and below 10 °C. there is no impulse discharge of the cold fibres. The warm fibres have a steady discharge rate at temperatures within the range 20 °C. to 47 °C. with a maximum rate somewhere between 37 °C. to 40 °C. Above 47 °C. and below 20 °C. there is no impulse discharge of warm fibres and there is a low sensitivity of warm receptors, *i.e.* a high threshold value at temperatures between 20 °C. and 30 °C.

Sudden cooling produces an increased discharge rate of cold fibres which then settles down to a new "steady" rate characteristic for the new temperature—the more rapid the temperature change the greater the initial increase in the discharge rate—although this is also influenced by the range of temperature within which the thermal change takes place. Rapid warming of cold receptors leads to an immediate cessation of their steady discharge, but this will be resumed if the final constant temperature is within the range of the normal steady discharge of cold fibres. Slow warming, on the other hand, may only diminish the discharge rate. The warm fibres behave in the same way as the cold fibres, but in reverse order. They respond to rapid warming and then adapt to a new steady rhythm unless the final temperature is outside the limits 20 °C. to 47 °C.

When the temperature of the tongue is raised above 45 °C. a steady discharge of cold fibres is produced. This is the basis of the paradoxical cold and the discharge begins at 45 °C. and attains a maximum about 50 °C. The threshold for paradoxical sensation therefore lies about 5 °C. above the upper limit of the usual range of temperature in which the receptors have a steady discharge rate.

The electrophysiological records of the behaviour of warm and cold fibres are in accord with the observed subjective experience of thermal change. Thus, the existence of the sensation can be related to some change in the total pattern of impulses received by the brain from the thermoreceptors. For example, the persistent cold sensation with temperatures below 10 °C. is associated with complete absence of a steady discharge from all thermoreceptors.

Again, when the forehead is stimulated by cold metal the cold sensation persists after the stimulus is withdrawn, even although the temperature of the skin surface will then be rising. This persistent cold sensation is due to the continuing steady discharge of cold fibres and the low sensitivity of warm receptors within the temperature range 20 °C. to 30 °C.

The fact that there is a discharge of impulses from the thermoreceptors when the temperature is constant, *i.e.* when there is thermal equilibrium as between the outside and the inside of the receptors, indicates that the stimulus is not an exchange of thermal energy. In what way the thermal stimulus excites the receptors to generate their potential we do not know, but most probably it is in the nature of a chemical action governed by temperature.

Many cold-blooded animals have thermal receptors which, within certain temperature limits, have a steady discharge rate and respond to cooling and warming by an increase or decrease in discharge rate respectively. The rattlesnake is said to possess the most effective organ in the animal kingdom for the detection of the radiant heat energy of infra-red rays, enabling it to discriminate warm objects some distance from the body surface.

This elaborate combination and permutation of discharge rates of the different thermal receptors within the temperatures normally encountered by the body give a more than sufficient variety of impulse patterns to provide a thermal calibration which can be read off by the receiving cells of the cortex of the brain and translated into the corresponding sensations. There is evidence that the central threshold for cold "sensation" is higher than the actual threshold value required to produce an increased discharge of the cold thermoreceptors. This implies that there is an input for our thermal "automation" and control mechanism below the level of consciousness.

Central Connexions of the Cutaneous Sense Modalities

Sensory Pathways

Two relay systems (the medial lemniscal and spinothalamic systems), each made up of chains of three neurons, convey the code of impulses from the touch, pressure, pain, and temperature receptors to the primary somatic sensory centre of the cerebral cortex (areas 3, 2, and 1) very largely of the opposite half of the brain. This is the final depot for all sensory information other than that from the special senses. The medial lemniscal system handles two sense modalities—touch and kinesthesis—the spino-

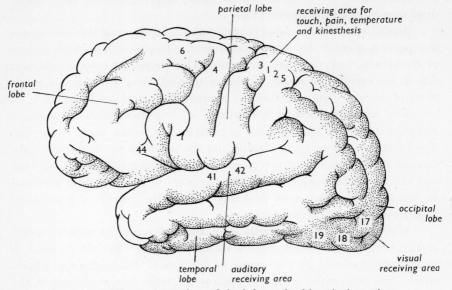

FIG. 2:4.   The outer surface of the left cerebral hemisphere showing the sensory receiving areas.

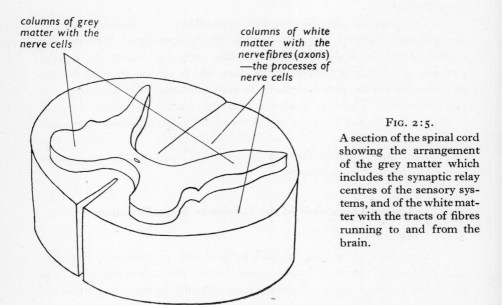

FIG. 2:5.
A section of the spinal cord
showing the arrangement
of the grey matter which
includes the synaptic relay
centres of the sensory systems, and of the white matter with the tracts of fibres
running to and from the
brain.

thalamic handles three—pain, temperature, and other aspects of touch—
and each sense modality has its own neuron relays, *i.e.* the messages are
routed according to the nature of the stimulus energy.

The sensory projection areas as defined today occupy a very much larger portion of the total cortex than was once thought to be the case, and in addition to the primary somatic sensory centre there is now known to be at least one other, the second somatic sensory area (Fig. 2:4). The better known, and probably the more important of the two sensory systems, is the medial lemniscal and its general properties are more or less

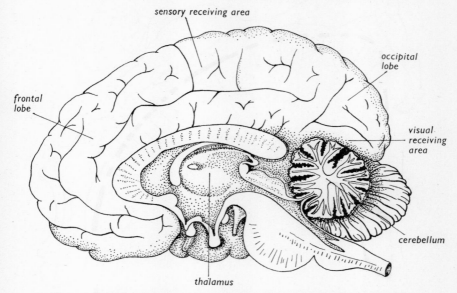

FIG. 2:6. The inner surface of the right cerebral hemisphere showing the thalamus, which is a synaptic relay centre between the second and third neurons of the sensory pathways.

applicable to any sensory pathways. The axons of the three neurons form the nerve fibres of the ascending tracts in the spinal cord and the lower brain, while the relay centres with the synapses between the different orders of neurons are nerve cell aggregates in the grey matter (Fig. 2:5). There is a relay centre for all sensory systems, except the olfactory, in the thalamus, one of the masses of subcortical grey matter in the centre of the brain (Fig. 2:6). While the individual neuron chains have innumerable connexions with other neuron systems and stimulation of the sense receptors affects activity in many parts of the central nervous system, it has been confirmed by physiological methods that the main stream of impulses is contained within their respective pathways.

Sensory Representation

All the primary receiving (sensory) areas of the brain have an orderly representation of peripheral receptive fields, *i.e.* they show a precise topography in respect of receptor surface. Thus, the somatic sensory pathways project something resembling a map of the body surface onto the cortex of areas 3, 2, and 1, and in such a way that the lower limbs are at the top of the brain and the face below (Fig. 2:7). This, however, is a distorted image of the body form as the more sensitive regions with the

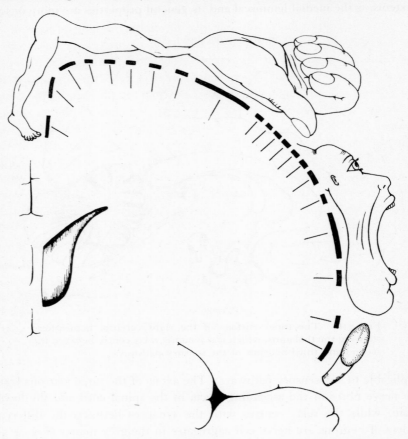

Fig. 2:7.   To show the cortical receiving areas for cutaneous sensation from the different regions of the body (after Penfield).

greater number of receptors and nerve density will require more receiving cells and so a larger extent of cortical surface. The representation of the different parts of the body on the sensory cortex varies in mammals according to the development of particular regions as tactile organs, and in Man the hands have a proportionately large cortical representation.

The receptive field of a sensory unit varies from a maximum of 2 to 3 sq. cm. of skin in the trunk to a few square millimetres at the distal ends of the limbs, and in general the large fast-conducting sensory fibres tend to have a much smaller receptive field than the slow-conducting small fibres. Very little information is, however, available with regard to the comparative sizes of receptive fields activating the second, third (thalamic) or fourth (cortical) order of neurons. In the monkey, experiments have shown that each cortical (fourth) neuron can be activated by a peripheral receptive field which does not change in size, but all parts of this cutaneous receptive field are not equally effective in eliciting responses in terms of the number of impulses per stimulus. There are gradations from a maximum at the centre of the receptive field to a minimum at the edge, but as there is an overlap of peripheral receptive fields the stimulus at the edge of one receptive field may at the same time be approaching the centre of another and so producing an increased response from a different cortical neuron. A touch stimulus on the surface of the body, for example, will activate a small population of cortical cells and the central cells of this activated group with, presumably, the greatest number of relevant synaptic connexions, will have the highest impulse frequency rate. If the stimulus moves across the receptive field the centre of maximum cell activity will also shift, and this arrangement is common to all cell levels throughout the relay system.

Although, therefore, one cortical neuron responds to stimulation of the same peripheral receptive field, stimulation of one point of the skin does not give rise to a point of activity in the cortex, but rather a zone of maximum response surrounded by an area of less intense activity. It follows, therefore, that any one part of the surface of the brain can be activated to some extent by a considerable area of cutaneous surface, the size of which will vary according to its peripheral nerve density. The relationship would thus seem to be a stimulus point on the skin to an area of cortex, and an area of the skin to a cortical neuron. Such an arrangement will obviously aid the capacity of the lemniscal system to appreciate form and recognise contour.

Stimulus Intensity

With an increase in the intensity of the stimulus there is not only an increase in the impulse frequency of the cortical neurons, but in addition a greater number of cortical neurons become involved and so the response of the cortex in terms of total impulse discharge in unit of time increases along with the increase in the strength of the stimulus. A point of some importance is that activation of cortical cells would appear to induce facilitation whereby they become more responsive to a succeeding stimulus, and in this way are better able to deal with natural stimulation which is seldom as brief as experimental stimuli. One significant experimental finding is that the peripheral receptive field for any cortical neuron is surrounded by skin, stimulation of which will inhibit this same cortical neuron. This means that any stimulus produces a group of activated cells and a surrounding zone of inhibited cells, a mechanism that will obviously help in tactile discrimination.

Organisation of Sensory Cortex

As shown in Fig. 2:4, the cortical neurons are arranged in vertical columns, the detailed structure, *i.e.* the cytoarchitecture, varying in different parts of the cortex; in fact the numbers 3, 2, 1, denote cyto-architectural variation within the primary somatic sensory area. Moreover, there is evidence that the neurons of these separate areas are linked to a specific sense modality. Those of area 2, it is said, deal with kinesthesis while those of area 3 are activated by cutaneous stimulation, particularly touch. Thus, the neurons for the sense modalities of any one region lie along the same horizontal strip of cortex.

There are a number of facts which support the idea that the function-ing units of the sensory cortex are not single neurons, but vertical columns of neurons extending down through the layers of the cortex. The organisa-tion of the cortex is therefore in respect of its three dimensions, viz. (1) the sensory map of the body is represented from above downwards, (2) the sense modalities are arranged in areas 3, 2, 1, from before backwards, while the thickness of the cortex, *i.e.* from without inwards, contains the functioning units—the vertical columns of cells. An arrangement of this kind is obviously suited for the precise location of a stimulus with reference to the excited cortical receptors, but we do not even begin to comprehend why the same kind of messages (impulse patterns) have such a diversity of subjective meaning depending on the area of cortex and neuron groups within that area to which they are delivered. We see, we hear, we taste, not only because the messages come from specific receptors but also because they are sent to a particular region of the cortex. Thus we are aware of a touch, a pain, a difference of temperature, or are conscious of a movement following the activation of different neuron groups within the same milli-metre of brain territory.

Cortical Cues

The relay sensory systems retain the specific properties of their receptors throughout the different levels, and the construction and con-nexion of the sensory pathways provide the receiving cortex with anatomical cues in regard to both the quality and location of the peripheral stimulus. The steady response of the slow-adapting mechanoreceptors to constant stimulation will, within certain limits, produce a corresponding steady discharge of a group of cortical neurons and the velocity and amplitude of the delivered impulses reflects the size range of the conducting units of the stimulated receptors. It would, however, be quite wrong to think that the messages sent out from the periphery are delivered unchanged to the cortex in all their dimensions. Above a certain rate of stimulus some neurons of the medial lemniscal system equilibrate to a lower discharge frequency, while other neurons cease to discharge altogether with maximum stimulation, the so-called "cut off" type of response. Moreover, it has been shown that in the lemniscal system the normal response of the postsynaptic cell to single impulses is repetitive discharge. There are other considerations. The impulses are fed into a sensory cortex which maintains an intrinsic electrical activity of its own and the nature of this activity is connected with the state of consciousness. Further, in addition to the medial lemniscal and spinothalamic systems sensory impulses reach the cortex by a slower route via what is known as the reticular activating system because of its effect on the electrical activity of the cortex and thus on the state of consciousness. It should be clearly understood that all the evidence supports the view that the relay systems sort out and convey the raw materials in the form of impulses to the cortex, and it is there and there only that the end product in the form of perceptions is finally elaborated.

Servomechanisms

Modern work has shown that the central nervous system can influence its own sensory input at every level from peripheral receptors to receiving cortical neurons. It has been demonstrated that there are relays of centrifugal fibres running down from the higher cortical centres to connect up with each level of any sensory pathway, and that stimulation of these fibres diminishes or abolishes responses in the sensory pathways. On the other hand, when an animal is lightly anaesthetised there is an increase in the amplitude of the responses in the sensory pathways implying that, in the waking state, such pathways are scanned by some form of inhibitory influence and do not inevitably and indiscriminately accept all incoming messages. The psychological counterpart of this centrifugal sensory control mechanism is the subjective phenomena of habituation and conditioning. The most striking examples of habituation are auditory. If a sound signal is repeated often and regularly the amplitude of the electrical response of the cochlear neurons decreases, and corresponding to this physiological adaptation is the gradual psychological "unawareness" of the sound. Attention can be redirected to the sound by associating it with another stimulus such as an electric shock. This, however, is only temporary. The animal soon becomes conditioned to the other stimulus and the attention again shifts. Indeed, it is commonplace that "attention" can be diverted from a visual or auditory stimulus by some more demanding concurrent event. Thus sensory activity, auditory, visual, or cutaneous, can be affected by systematic intervention in accordance with previous experience, habituation, shifts of attention, etc., and so each sensory system through its servomechanism undoubtedly makes a purposeful contribution to the perceptual content. As experiences are repeated there develops in the brain some economy in terms of the extent of involvement so that it is possible that recognisable signals are eventually reduced to small parcels of impulses representing what might be reckoned the essential items.

Perception

Perception includes, generally, recognition of a particular object or event, and such recognition implies an objective contribution of some sort from the cortex, the nature of which will remain unknown until we have solved the problem of how the sensory input is evaluated, is modified by previous responses, and stored as memory. Obviously, although sensory messages are delivered to specific receiving cortical areas this is but the beginning of an intricate mingling and confluence of activity from all over the brain towards the fabrication of a perception.

That perceptions are not simple unitary events can be convincingly demonstrated with regard to pain. The psychic component of pain can be modified and largely eliminated by the surgical procedure of frontal lobotomy performed occasionally for the relief of intractible pain. This operation involves cutting off communication between the frontal lobes of the brain and the thalamus. The pain is not abolished by the operation but thereafter the patient, although admitting the pain is still there, does not complain or appear to be unduly distressed by it. It is suggested that in the case of pain the frontal lobes, on the basis of information received from the thalamus, normally contribute an affective component responsible for the general mental disturbance.

Inevitably there is the question of how far perceptions are in fact true recordings of the stimuli which initiate them, and this introduces the principle of uncertainty into the interpretation of psychological from physiological processes.

Consciousness

It has already been noted that in addition to the direct route such as the medial lemniscal system there are secondary ascending sensory systems within the reticular formation which deliver their responses to widespread regions of the cortex and not to the recognised receiving cortical areas. If the reticular formation of anaesthetised monkeys is destroyed, leaving only the direct sensory pathways intact, the animals remain in coma, *i.e.* a state of unconsciousness. These secondary sensory pathways are therefore regarded as activating mechanisms alerting the cortex to a state of awareness.

With the present state of our knowledge there is, however, little to be gained by speculating on the quantity and quality of physiological activity associated with consciousness. To do so is to assume, first, that we are in a position to define what is meant by consciousness as distinct from the response to stimulation, an assumption which could certainly be contended; and secondly, even if we could offer a definition, that it necessarily had a basis of the kind of physiological activity within our comprehension. Nevertheless, there is now a record of observations on the effect of loss of consciousness (natural or experimentally induced sleep following injury) on the one hand, and of the effect of electrical stimulation of the reticular formations on the intrinsic electrogenesis of the cortex on the other, which encourages speculation about and theories of consciousness.

BIBLIOGRAPHY

BISHOP, G. H. 1946. Neural mechanisms of cutaneous sense. *Physiol. Rev.*, **26**, 77.

BUDDENBROCK, W. VON. 1958. *The Senses.* University of Michigan Press.

GELDARD, F. A. 1953. *The Human Senses.* Wiley, New York.

CLARK, W. E. LE GROS. 1958. Sensory experience and brain structure. *J. Ment. Sci.*, **104**, 1. No. 434.

HUTCHISON, J., TOUGH, J. and WYBURN, G. M. 1948. Comparison of the cutaneous sensory pattern of different regions of the body. *Brit. J. Plast. Surg.*, **1**, 131, No. 2.

LEWIS, T. 1942. *Pain.* Macmillan, New York.

MONTAGNA, W. 1960. *Advances in Biology of Skin.* Vol. 1. *Cutaneous Innervation.* Pergamon Press, London.

MOUNTCASTLE, V. B. and POWELL, D. P. S. 1959. Central Nervous mechanisms subserving position sense in kinesthesis. *Bull. of John Hopkins Hosp.*, **105**, No. 4.

ROSE, J. E. and MOUNTCASTLE, V. B. 1959. Touch and kinesthesis. *Handbook of Physiol.*, **1**, Sec. 1. Amer. Physiol. Soc., Washington, D.C.

SWEET, W. H. 1959. Pain. *Handbook of Physiol.*, **1**, Sec. 1. Amer. Physiol. Soc., Washington, D.C.

WALSH, F. M. R. 1942. The anatomy and physiology of cutaneous sensibility. A critical review. *Brain*, **65**, 48.

WYBURN, G. M. 1961. Biological thermometers. *New Scientist*, **9**, 328.

ZOTTERMAN, Y. 1959. Thermal sensations. *Handbook of Physiol.*, **1**, Sec. 1.

3

Proprioceptors

The lowliest of organisms have sense receptors excited by movement and change of position in space. They are mechanoreceptors, stimulated by tissue deformations, tensions, stretching, compressions, changes in length etc., and are present in the wings of insects, in the cuticle over the joints of spiders, and in the skin of worms. The information obtained from the mechanoreceptors in the form of generated impulses controls the reflex responses to gravity forces and aids the regulation and direction of movement. At this level of organisation the nervous system is not concerned with the kind of awareness implied in the voluntary act when similar stimuli in similar circumstances do not necessarily produce the same response.

Normally we see any movement or change of position of the whole or any part of the body, but even without vision we are still aware of movement and the new position taken up by the body or part of the body as a result of the movement. The information necessary for this awareness is provided by mechanoreceptors grouped as the special and general proprioceptors. The special proprioceptors are the sense organs for the vestibular mechanism and are situated within the skull. The general proprioceptors are the receptor organs for "kinesthesis" or the sense of joint movement and position.

Kinesthesis

The general proprioceptors are distributed widely throughout the ligamentous structures of joints and the deep tissue planes. Around the joints both small encapsulated and free nerve endings are disposed in such a way that different groups are stimulated during the various phases of a movement. The immediate exciting stimulus is a compression of the receptors caused by tissue deformity which will initiate the ionic changes responsible for the generation of the receptor potential. When a joint moves the rate of discharge of a group of proprioceptors increases according to the speed and degree of movement, and thereafter decreases to a steady state determined by the final position. During movement of a joint, different populations of receptors will be stimulated in turn according to

36

their position relative to the axis of movement, and the response from any one group continues over about 15° of rotation, the range varying for different joints. Some receptors have their maximum response at full flexion, others at full extension, or in some intermediary position.

The Pacinian corpuscles in the deeper tissues, including capsules and ligaments of abdominal and thoracic organs, are excited by displacements, pressures, and tensions affecting individual organs and tissue territories, and in this respect they can be regarded as general proprioceptors.

The general proprioceptors and the touch receptors share the lemniscal system and are arranged within the general topographical pattern which is projected onto the cortex where, however, they have their own cortical units. It has indeed been observed that such units may be arranged in pairs with one active and the other silent when the joint moves in one direction, and vice versa with movements in the reverse direction. This would provide a helpful cue in discrimination of both the rate and extent of joint rotation. It is said that the elbow and wrist are sensitive to angular variations of position of 15' to 20' of arc, and that the thumb and forefinger may be able to detect, on the basis of variations in angular position, a difference in thickness of about 0·15 mm.

Normally the kinesthetic sense makes little demand on our attention and only exceptionally are we aware of an effort to make the proper response. During each step, for instance, we lift the foot from the ground neither too much nor too little; we reach out for some object without sensibly assessing the distance, yet such conscious movements are controlled continuously and throughout their entire duration by the incoming discharge signals from the general proprioceptors which provide step by step the data necessary for the successful completion of the purposeful act. The importance of our muscle joint sense becomes evident when from disease or injury its messages are prevented from reaching the brain. Visual judgment alone is not sufficient, and attempts to perform simple tasks such as eating, drinking, writing, or putting on clothes are uncoordinated, clumsy, and may be unavailing.

While each muscle and tendon has its own sense receptors—the muscle spindle and the Golgi tendon organ—acting as recorders for the elaborate nervous machinery which regulates the locomotor apparatus operated by the muscles, it is now generally agreed that muscle receptors make no contribution to our kinesthetic sense.

Special Proprioceptors

These consist of a system of minute intercommunicating membranous sacs and canals filled with the fluid endolymph and enclosed, along with the

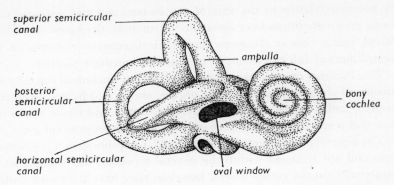

FIG. 3:1.   The bony labyrinth which is carved out of the temporal
bone in the side wall of the skull.

organ of hearing, in the bony capsule sculptured out of the temporal bones
on each side of the skull—the labyrinth (Fig. 3:1). They record movements of the body as a whole relative to the environment, *e.g.* rotation or
linear acceleration either actual or passive (as in a train or other moving
object), and movement of the head relative to the rest of the body. There
are three semicircular canals, horizontal, superior, and posterior, each
about $1\frac{1}{2}$ cm. in circumference and 1 mm. in breadth, and situated with
reference to the three planes of the body, horizontal, vertical, and anteroposterior (Fig. 3:2). Because of the relative positions of the two bony
labyrinths, the plane of the posterior canal of one side is parallel to that
of the superior canal of the other. Each canal has an expanded end, the
ampulla, and opens into a common chamber, the utricle, communicating

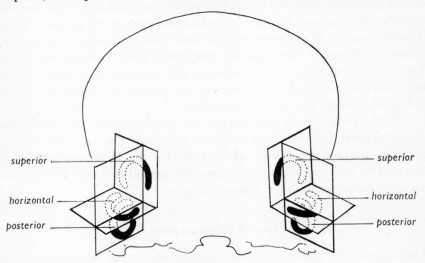

FIG. 3:2.   A drawing to show the plane of the semicircular canals.

indirectly with the smaller saccule which in turn is connected by a short duct to the organ of hearing, the cochlea (Fig. 3:3). The horizontal canal is tilted slightly downwards so that it forms an angle of about 30° with the horizontal plane when the head is erect, while the superior and posterior canals form angles with the saggital plane. The immediate receptor structures are the sensory cells placed on the crista, or shelf, projecting into the ampulla of each canal. A sensory cell has a synaptic junction with one or more terminal nerve fibres and about 50 sensory hairs projecting from its free end into narrow channels within a gelatinous structure, the cupula, hinged onto the crista and extending almost to the roof of the ampulla. The cupula resembles a hood covering the sensory epithelium and its mechanical properties are those of a spring-loaded pendulum (Fig. 3:4). The utricle and the saccule have each a receptor organ, the macula, with similar sensory cells whose hair processes are in contact with a mass of gelatinous substance containing concretions of calcium carbonate known as the otoliths, with a specific gravity heavier than the surrounding endolymph (Fig. 3:5). When the head is in a normal position the maculae of the utricles lie approximately in the horizontal plane with the otoliths in contact with the hair cells, while the saccular maculae form an angle of about 30° with the vertical plane.

Semicircular Canals

The adequate stimulus for the semicircular canals, which work in pairs one on each side, is angular acceleration from rotation of the head in the transverse, vertical, or anteroposterior axis, *i.e.* tilting the head backwards, forwards, turning the head round, or tilting it from side to side. At the beginning of rotation or of a change in the speed of rotation, *i.e.* acceleration, the fluid endolymph, because of its inertia, lags behind the movement of the canal as a whole and so exerts a backward pressure on

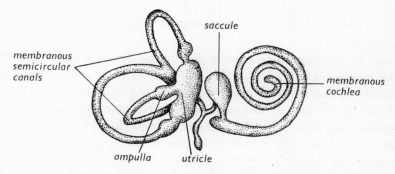

FIG. 3:3.   The membranous labyrinth which is placed inside the bony labyrinth.

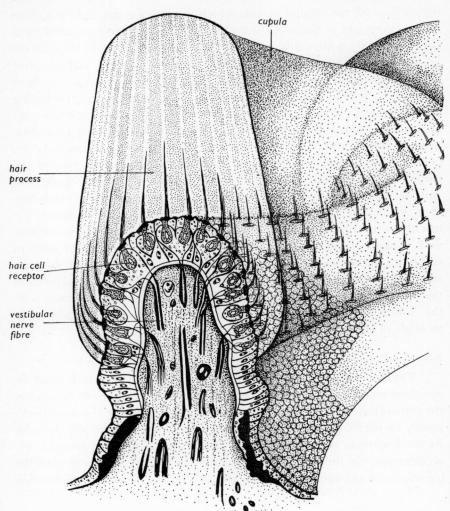

cupula

hair process

hair cell receptor

vestibular nerve fibre

FIG. 3:4.   The membranous ampulla of a semicircular canal.

the cupula, bending it like a swing door in the direction opposite to that of the movement (Fig. 3:6). This will in turn cause some tension and deformity in the enclosed hair processes of the sensory cells, which is the stimulus for the development of their receptor potential. Cupular movement can be initiated by pressure changes equal to ·00,004 gm. of water. Thirty seconds is said to be the natural period of the cupula functioning as an elastic pendulum. When rotation stops the cupula will swing in the opposite direction owing to backlog of the endolymph and it may be anything up to half a minute before it returns to a resting position,

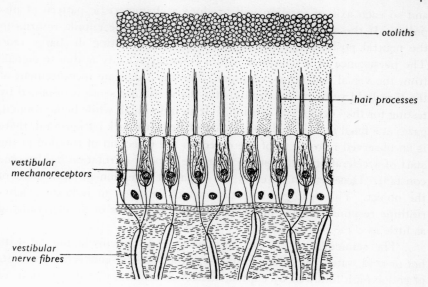

FIG. 3:5. The macula.

during which time there is the sensation of rotating in the opposite direction, the reason for the feeling of giddiness.

While the most effective stimulus for any pair of ampullae is rotation of the head in the plane of their canals, angular acceleration in intermediate planes may well stimulate a combination of the ampullae of the different canals. There is a resting discharge rate for the receptor cells with the cupula in a neutral position and an increase or decrease in the discharge rate according to the direction of deflection of the cupula, so that a single receptor can in this way signal rotation in either direction. As the canals work in pairs, the cupular movement on the two sides during any one rotation will be in opposite directions relative to their respective canals,

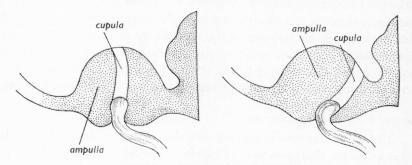

FIG. 3:6. To show the effect of acceleration on the cupula of a semicircular canal (after Dohlman).

and so each axis of rotation will produce a characteristic pattern of impulses. If the speed of rotation remains constant the cupula returns to the neutral position and the receptors resume a resting discharge rate. The persistence of a sensation with a constant velocity is due to signals from the visual and other receptors. The most delicate measurement of the threshold value of the stimulus for the vestibular sense is obtained by testing for the "oculogyral illusion." If an individual, while being rotated, gazes at a fixed illuminated object viewed against a dark background, there is an observed movement of the object in the direction of rotation at the start of acceleration which stops when the velocity of rotation has become constant. Deceleration reverses the apparent direction of movement of the object. The oculogyral illusion, which is taken to indicate a labyrinthine response, begins to appear with accelerations or decelerations of as little as $0 \cdot 12^2$ per sq. second.

The semicular canals can be stimulated by syringing the ear with hot or cold water, the caloric response, which sets up convection currents of endolymph followed by cupular deflection and associated sensations of dizziness.

Utricle and Saccule

When the head is at rest and there is no movement of endolymph we are still aware of its position. In this case the necessary information comes from the maculae of the utricle and the saccule. The stimulus mechanism in the maculae is tension deformity of the hair processes of the sensory cells from the weight of the otoliths which obey the laws of gravity. For example, a neutral position of the head denoting equilibrium with regard to the saggital (midline vertical) plane is indicated by equal stimulation of the right and left maculae and so a balance of similar signals arriving at both sides of the brain, while if the head is tilted to one or other side the responses from the two sides will be different. Similarly, forward or backward tilting alters the gravity pressure of the otoliths in relation to the macular surface as would also, for example, standing on the head. In addition the maculae respond to the movements of endolymph in linear acceleration, centrifugal, and coriolis forces. Two types of macular receptor have been described, one responding to tilting of the head by increased discharge, and the other when the head returns to "equilibrium."

Central Vestibular Mechanisms

The nerve filaments synapsing with the receptor cells of the ampulae and maculae are short processes of bipolar nerve cells. The long processes form the vestibular nerves which enter the hind brain, where they form intricate relay systems linking up with those parts of the central nervous system concerned with posture, balance, and movement. It is now established that there is a final receiving centre in the cerebral cortex where certain neurons respond to stimulation by particular groups of the special proprioceptors.

Unlike many animals, *e.g.* the foal, Man at birth is unable to cope with the forces of gravity and requires a long period of training and learning. Thereafter, however, it becomes automatic, much of it at subconscious level. We remain erect and retain our balance as the centre of gravity shifts when moving or being moved by tensing muscle groups to steady the necessary joints. This is a response to signals relayed to the central nervous system by the proprioceptors, including the vestibular apparatus, which can initiate reflex responses of various kinds. An example of a "labyrinthine" reflex is the movement of the eyes known as nystagmus. As the body is rotated the eyes move slowly in the opposite direction, fixing the gaze as long as possible, and then swing quickly back in the direction of rotation to fix a new object and begin again moving slowly in the direction opposite to rotation. When rotation stops nystagmus will continue but the quick component will be in the reverse direction, corresponding to the deviation of the cupula and add to the subjective experience of rotating in the opposite way, producing a sense of giddiness. Nystagmus may occur in any plane but is most commonly horizontal.

In Man, the special proprioceptors do not dominate our sense of equilibrium to the same extent as in many lower animals such as reptiles and birds, in whom the postural reflexes are more intimately and rigidly controlled by the labyrinthine apparatus—in the pigeon, for example, the head remains in normal position irrespective of the position of the body. Congenital deaf mutes without functional canals or vestibular sacs can cope satisfactorily with a normal range of locomotor procedures with the aid of vision. Deprived of sight, however, there are obvious postural and balancing difficulties.

It has been questioned if vestibular discharges reaching the cortex can be equated with "sensation." Movement and gravity forces affect many receptors other than the special proprioceptors. Acceleration, deceleration and abnormal posture will alter the position of abdominal organs, cause tension of their ligaments, and vascular changes from shifts in blood volume. Moreover, subjective experiences of rotation are very similar when the surroundings and not the individual are being accelerated as, for example, when a neighbouring train starts to move out of the station, and this is obviously not due to direct stimulation of the vestibular mechanism. We all, however, have difficulty in being able to describe the phenomenal except in terms of a physical event, and the different kinds of feeling that can be aroused by bodily rotation are not easy to separate out introspectively from the various responses required, such as adjusted balance, co-ordinated vision, etc. Quoted in favour of a vestibular sense is the experience of sinking slowly while under water and the awareness of the direction of gravity while under water when there is no kinesthesis involved. It would be very difficult to believe that vestibular information is excluded from the attention-demanding subjective experience of, for example, post-rotational giddiness, even taking into consideration the other sources of stimulation. Certainly we normally accept proprioceptive information without question and there is no recognition, memory, or interpretation involved in a "vestibular" situation such as there might be, for instance, in connexion with some visual or auditory experience. To that extent, therefore, it will not involve the affective aspects of cerebral activity but there is little reason to doubt that the highest levels of the central nervous system are constantly dealing with adjustments to the force of gravity, including the contribution from the special proprioceptors.

In recent times high-speed flying has provided an ideal experimental background for the study of the labyrinth in response to angular, radial, or linear acceleration. Normally a pilot relies mainly on vision for data with regard to the position of himself and his plane. Without vision, the information from the labyrinth alone may, in certain circumstances, lead to a false interpretation of the actual situation. There are, for instance, sensations of tilting forwards and/or backwards with rapid linear acceleration and deceleration. Thus at night, a pilot suddenly decreasing speed has the impression of tilting forward, *i.e.* diving, although his instruments assure him otherwise. The need for flashing rather than steady light signals when flying is connected with the oculogyral illusion—the apparent movement of a point source of light when banking, for example, or if stared at continuously over a period of time.

The most common physiological disorder of the labyrinths is motion sickness in the form of car sickness, sea sickness, or air sickness, and is associated with a regularly repeated motion at a fairly low frequency of the order of, say, ten times a minute. Rapidly repeated motion does not cause sickness. The feeling of nausea or sickness must have its origin in the cerebral cortex as a result of incoming sensory impulses, and, as we know, it can be aroused by a great many different forms of sensory stimulation—visual, chemical, physical, or visceral.

BIBLIOGRAPHY

CAMMIS, M. 1930. *The Physiology of the Vestibular Apparatus.* Clarendon Press, Oxford.

GARDNER, E. 1950. Physiology of moveable joints. *Physiol. Rev.*, **30,** 127.

GERNANDT, E. E. 1959. Vestibular mechanisms. *Handbook of Physiol.*, **1,** Sec. 1. Amer. Physiol. Soc., Washington, D.C.

LOWENSTEIN, O. 1950. Labyrinth and equilibrium. Physiological mechanisms and animal behaviour. *Symp. Soc. Exp. Biol.*, **4,** 60.

SHERRINGTON, C. S. 1906. *The Integrative Action of the Nervous System.* Yale University Press.

WENDT, G. R. 1951. Vestibular functions. *Handbook of Experimental Psychology.* Wiley, New York.

4

Hearing

Properties of Sound

Sound energy can be generated by any sort of motion, usually of a vibrating body, and is transmitted in the form of waves, like the ripples radiating from a stone thrown into a pond. Air is the usual conducting medium but sound is also conducted through solids and fluids, but not in a vacuum; space is soundless. The velocity of sound in air is about 1100 feet per second (740 miles per hour) at normal temperature, about four times this speed in water, and a still greater velocity in solids. The nature of the sound energy is a to-and-fro movement of the particles of the medium, *e.g.* the molecules of air, in such a way that there are alternating areas of

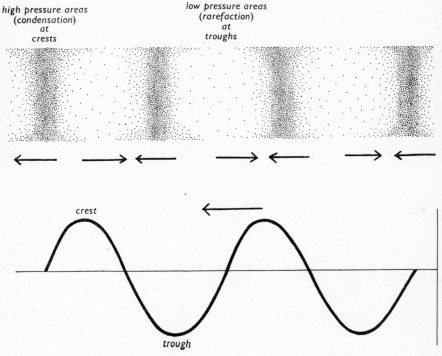

FIG. 4:1. Sound waves (after Pierce and David).

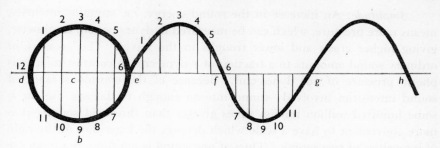

FIG. 4:2.   Simple harmonic motion, as in the vibrations of a tuning
fork, shown as a projection of circular movement.

condensation and rarefaction, and this disturbance moves progressively
through the air until it is lost in heat (Fig. 4:1). Just, however, as the
waves of the sea do not carry the same body of water with them, the air
does not move bodily from place to place, but rather the sound waves
resemble a field of wind-blown corn where the stocks remain fixed in
the ground. The simplest form of sound wave, such as those sent out by
a vibrating tuning fork, is the harmonic or sinusoidal wave, representing
the projection of uniform circular movement on a time axis where the
crests are areas of maximum pressure (condensation) and the troughs are
areas of minimum pressure (rarefaction) (Fig. 4:2).

Physical Properties of Sound Waves

Frequency: The time taken to complete the cycle of pressure changes
is the period of the wave, and the distance travelled by the wave front in
one such period will be the wavelength. Given a constant velocity, the
number of waves passing any given point in unit of time, or the frequency,
will be proportional to the wavelength, the shorter the waves the higher
the frequency and vice versa. This physical attribute of sound waves—
their frequency—we subjectively interpret as pitch or tone. For example,
middle C of the musical scale, with a wavelenth of 4·31 ft., has a frequency
of 256∼ (cycles per second) while the C an octave above that, with a
wavelength of 2·61 ft., has a frequency of 512∼.

The human ear appreciates frequencies between 20∼ and 20,000∼.
Below 20∼ we are conscious of vibration rather than sound. Many
animals, cats, dogs, rats, for example, can hear tones much higher in
frequency than 20,000∼, the so-called ultrasonic waves, and bats are
credited with hearing ultrasonics of 90,000∼. The musical scale has a
frequency range of from about 16∼ (the largest of the organ pipes) to
about 5,000∼, and the discrete steps or tones which have a simple arith-
metical ratio to one another have been selected on a subjective rather than
an objective basis.

Amplitude: An increase in the sound energy, *i.e.* stimulus intensity, means more pressure, which can be measured in dynes per sq. centimetre, giving higher crests and lower troughs to the waves. The pressure of ordinary sound amounts to a fraction of 1 dyne/cm² in contrast to atmospheric pressure of 10^6 dynes/cm². Because of the enormous range of sound intensities involved—sound intense enough to damage the ear is some hundred million million times greater than threshold sound—it is more convenient to have a scale which denotes the logarithm of the ratio of intensities of two sounds. Thus, if one sound is ten times more intense than the other they are said to differ by 1 bel. The intensity level of sound, subjectively appreciated as degrees of loudness, is measured in decibels ($\frac{1}{10}$ bel) with a scale varying from zero which is around threshold sound, to over 140 db. when sound becomes painful. In such a scale, 0 db. simply expresses a ratio of 1 to 1 and is meaningless without a reference level—the standard reference is a 0 db. pressure level of ·0002 dyne/cm². Zero in the decibel scale represents the least noise that can be heard in quiet surroundings, *i.e.* near sound threshold. A hundred times louder is 20 decibels, about the sound level of a whisper, a million times stronger is 60 decibels, the sound level of normal conversation, while the noise from a nearby jet plane measures about 160 decibels. The formula relating intensity level in dynes to loudness level in decibels is applied to the calibration of the instrument used to test hearing, the audiometer.

Harmonics or Overtones: Normally few of the sounds we hear are pure tones represented by a simple sinusoidal wave. A stretched string or wire when plucked vibrates not only as a whole, its fundamental frequency or 1st harmonic responsible for the tone, but also in fractions of the whole—halves, thirds, quarters, fifths, etc.—the higher harmonics or overtones which are incorporated with the fundamental frequency into a complex wave form (Fig. 4:3). The frequency of the 2nd harmonics (halves) will be twice, and of the 3rd harmonics (thirds) will be three times that of the fundamental frequency, and thus the harmonics are all in simple mathematical ratio to one another. The overtones give the quality to a musical note, for example the distinctive "timbre" of different musical instruments—middle C in the piano as compared to middle C on the violin—and confer the individual characteristics on the human voice.

Resonance: Solid bodies and vibrators (tuning forks, wires, strings, etc.) have a natural periodicity determined by a number of factors—tension, length, mass—and they can be forced into sympathetic vibration by sound waves whose frequencies correspond to their natural periodicity. In this case the sound is enhanced and the body is said to "resonate." When a periodic force is applied to a body it gives a "transient" response at its natural frequency and this "transient" dies out or is damped down

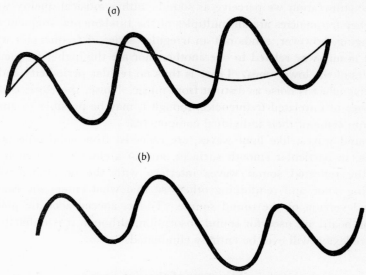

FIG. 4:3. (a) Pure, or simple, tones of frequency F and 3F.
(b) Compound tone with a fundamental frequency plus
its second harmonic.

by a number of factors that together constitute the mechanical impedance
of the body. Although the ear responds to forced vibrations we are not
troubled by any of its transients and can therefore conclude that it possesses effective mechanical impedance.

Tubes or pipes filled with air, *e.g.* organ pipes, have resonant frequencies and when excited produce complex sound waves with a fundamental frequency giving the tone and the higher frequencies of the 2nd,
3rd, harmonics etc., constituting the overtones. They also act as resonators and if the ear is close to the open end of a pipe there is reinforcement
of any extraneous sounds around its resonant frequencies. For example,
when we put a seashell to our ear the resonances of the shell emphasise
these frequencies in the surrounding noise that resemble the sound of the
sea. Acoustic resonators are responsible for the characteristic sound
qualities of reed instruments.

The human vocal tract functions as a resonator and in fact by changing
its dimensions, both length and breadth, it can act as a whole series of
resonators, each with its distinctive resonant frequencies. The frequency
range of the speaking voice extends over a few hundred cycles but can be
increased to the order of thousands in the trained singing voice.

Noise: So far we have been discussing sounds that are periodic, *i.e.*
they repeat regularly in terms of time and can be broken up into component sinusoidal frequencies. The physical regularity of this kind of

acoustic stimulation we perceive as sounds with a musical quality where the higher frequencies are all multiples of the fundamental frequency. A bell ringing, however, sends out an irregular series of frequencies which are not in any way related to one another, nor are the higher frequencies multiples of the lower ones. There is thus no regular periodicity and the subjective effect is noise as distinct from music. Noise, therefore, consists of a series of unrelated frequencies, though it may be possible to analyse them into some of their individual components.

Sound waves, like light waves, are reflected from solid objects and surfaces, in particular smooth surfaces, and in a closed space such as a room the reflected sound waves interfere with the oncoming waves, cancelling some and reinforcing others so that what enters the ear is a distorted version of the sound source. Today, special acoustic plasters and fibreboard are used for sound absorption, although it is unlikely that sound reflexion will ever be entirely eliminated.

Structure of the Ear

The sense receptors for hearing are mechanoreceptors, and they transduce the stimulus energy of the sound waves into receptor potentials which

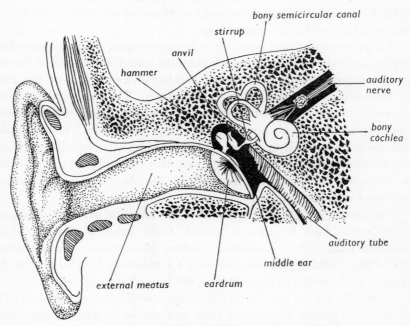

FIG. 4:4.   The three parts of the hearing apparatus.

trigger off the nerve impulses providing the input of information with regard to their amplitude and their frequency, subjectively interpreted in terms of loudness and pitch, together with the duration of the sound and its location in respect of direction and distance.

The organ of hearing has three parts—the outer, middle, and inner ear, the sensory organ proper (Fig. 4:4). The outer ear—the auricle and the canal leading to the tympanic membrane of the eardrum—acts as an ear trumpet, catching the sound waves, although unlike the large sensitive ears of many animals, human auricles are mainly ornamental and we move our heads rather than our auricles. The cone-shaped tympanic membrane seals off the outer from the middle ear, a small air-filled cavity in the temporal bone on each side of the skull about half an inch high and a quarter of an inch broad. Straddling this cavity there is a system of tiny mechanical levers in the form of a chain of the three smallest bones in the body named, because of their shape, the hammer, the anvil, and the stirrup. The handle of the hammer is attached to the eardrum, the head is joined to the anvil which is joined to the stirrup, and the footplate of the stirrup fits into an opening in the inner ear—the oval window (Fig. 4:4). The middle ear communicates with the back of the nose by a narrow tube and in this way maintains atmospheric pressure on each side of the eardrum.

The inner ear, the front part of the labyrinth of the temporal bone (Fig. 4:5) is a bony tunnel spiralling $2\frac{3}{4}$ times round a central pillar $\frac{1}{4}$ in. in height and hence appropriately known as the cochlea. The cochlea is divided by a partition, partly bone and partly membrane—the basilar membrane—into upper and lower spiral passages (Fig. 4:5). Occupying the upper partition, its floor the basilar membrane, is a soft tube—the

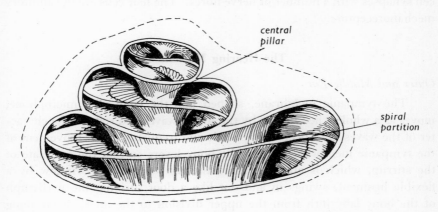

FIG. 4:5. The spiral bony cochlea in section showing upper and lower divisions.

membranous cochlea (Fig. 3:3)—and the two divisions filled with fluid—
the perilymph—communicate at the apex. The upper division is continuous at the base of the cochlea with the vestibule of the labyrinth and
has the oval window closed by the footplate of the stirrup. The lower
division terminates at the base of the cochlea and has the round window
closed by a membrane. The length of the membranous cochlea from base
to apex is about 35 mm. and it contains a fluid—the endolymph—plus
the organ of Corti. The spiral shape of the cochlea, it is said, prevents
movement of the fluid contents during angular and linear acceleration of
the head. The basilar membrane, 35 mm. long, ·5 mm. broad at the apex,
and ·04 mm. at the base, *i.e.* near the stirrup, is made up of about 24,000
fibres welded together in a soft ground substance. It is not, however,
under tension but as a result of its graded variation in width and stiffness
the physical characteristics, such as the mass and elasticity of the basilar
membrane, vary by a factor of at least a hundred from base to apex. The
organ of Corti stands on the basilar membrane and consists of 5,000 pairs
of tiny girders—the rods—forming a continuous spiral archway from
base to apex of the cochlea (Fig. 4:6). Flanking this archway there are
three rows of outer hair cells and one row of inner hair cells totalling
altogether about 17,000 in each ear. The hair cells are fixed at two points;
the neck is firmly held within a reticular lamina hinged on the outer rods,
and about fifty sensory hairs, each from ·2µ to ·5µ thick and 4µ long,
project from the apex of a sensory cell into the gelatinous substance of
the flange-like tectorial membrane which is free at one end and hinged
at the other (Fig. 4:7). The base of the hair cells and the termination of
the cochlear nerve fibres form synaptic junctions. There are about
28,000 nerve fibres each related to a number of hair cells, while each hair
cell synapses with a number of nerve fibres. The hair cells are the auditory
mechanoreceptors.

The Hearing Mechanism

Outer and Middle Ear

The tympanic membrane, shaped like the cone of a microphone,
moves as a whole when driven by the sound waves and reflects the character of the waves in respect of amplitude and frequency. The movement of
the tympanic membrane acts on the bony levers so that the footplate of
the stirrup, which is attached along the rim of the oval window by a
flexible ligament, swings in and out like a door, driving the perilymph
of the bony labyrinth from the upper division to the apex, down along
the lower division to the round window where the closing membrane
moves in and out in the opposite phase to the footplate of the stirrup.

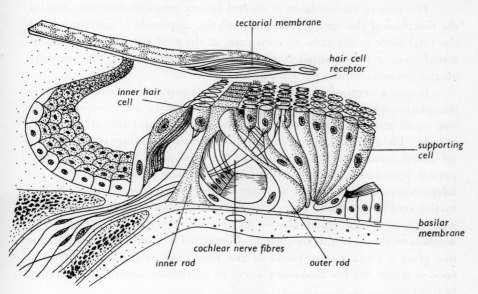

FIG. 4:6. The organ of Corti situated on the basilar membrane.

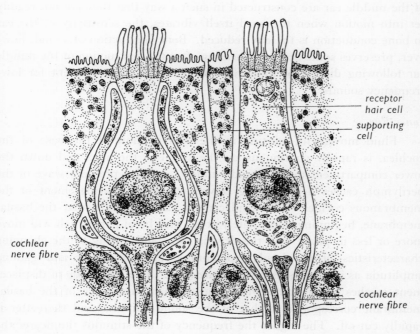

FIG. 4:7. The auditory mechanoreceptors, i.e. the hair cells of the
organ of Corti.

The area of the eardrum is around twenty times greater than that of the footplate of the stirrup, and although the amplitude of movement and the total force is the same in each case, at the oval window it is concentrated over a much smaller area and so will exert a correspondingly greater pressure on the perilymph.

Just as a decrease in the size of the pupil protects the eye from overstimulation by strong light, so overstimulation of the ear is prevented by two small muscles, one attached to the eardrum and the other to the stirrup. The tympanic membrane and the ossicles faithfully reproduce the air sound waves by pressure waves of the perilymph, and provide a near perfect impedance match between the air and the intracochlear fluid for frequencies about 500∿, in this way making a considerable contribution to the sensitivity of the ear. The resonance frequency of the external auditory meatus is about 4000∿ to give an increased sensitivity of 10 decibels to sound of this frequency. Combined with middle ear resonance this gives a frequency response of the whole ear over the range 800 to 6000∿ which fits the frequency curve of maximum sensitivity of human hearing.

Sound waves are conducted through the bones of the skull and bypassing the middle ear affect the cochlea directly, but as the bony levers of the middle ear are constructed in such a way that they are not readily set into motion when the head itself vibrates, the sensitivity of the ear to bone conduction is thereby reduced. Bone conduction of sound, however, preserves some degree of hearing after the destruction of the middle ear following disease or injury and is relatively more efficient for low-frequency sounds.

Inner Ear

Fluid movement, starting at the oval window at the base of the cochlea, is rapidly continuous up the spiral to the apex and down the lower compartment to the round window, and this pressure wave of the perilymph causes a succeeding travelling wave of displacement of the membranous cochlea. The displacement affects in particular the basilar membrane, beginning immediately at the stiff basal part which will move more or less in phase with the driving force and, owing to the changing characteristics of the basilar membrane, losing velocity and gaining amplitude as it progresses towards the apex. The amplitude of displacement reaches a maximum where the resonant frequency of the basilar membrane corresponds to that of the sound stimulus and thereafter is rapidly cut off. The higher the frequency of the stimulus the nearer the point of maximum amplitude is to the base of the cochlea where the basilar membrane is narrowest, and it shifts towards the apex as the

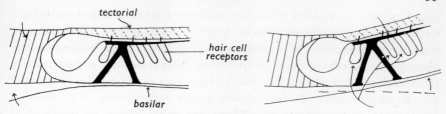

FIG. 4:8. To show how movement of the organ of Corti causes
bending of the hair processes of the auditory receptors (after von
Bèkèsy).

stimulus frequency decreases. Thus, the basal end of the cochlea will
move in response to all frequencies within the audible range; at 2000 ∿
the displacement wave probably does not travel much beyond the mid-
point of the membranous cochlea, while at 100 ∿ it reaches almost to the
apex, and below this the basilar membrane moves more and more as a
unit until at 50 ∿ the entire cochlear partition is moving in phase with
maximum amplitude near the apex. Although the displacement wave
pattern is determined primarily by the basilar membrane, all the walls of
the membranous cochlea move in phase with one another and it bends not
only in its long axis, *i.e.* from base to apex, but also transversely. This
results in a shearing action between the reticular lamina and the tectorial
membrane, causing a vibratory bending of the hair processes of the
mechanoreceptors which is the immediate stimulus generating the graded
receptor potential, or cochlear microphonics, of the hair cells (Fig. 4:8).
The maximum stimulation of the receptors with, up to a certain limit,
correspondingly stronger cochlear microphonics, occurs at the position of
greatest displacement of the membranous cochlea which in this way

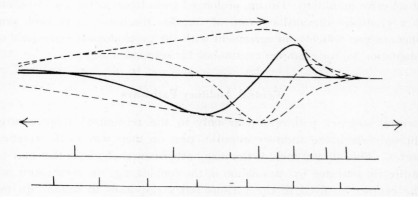

FIG. 4:9. The travelling wave of displacement of the mebranous
cochlea. (After Pierce & David).

functions as a mechanical frequency analyser, the pattern of the displacement wave varying throughout its length according to the frequency of the driving force, *i.e.* the sound waves (Fig. 4:9). This constitutes the place principle contribution to frequency discrimination, *i.e.* our ability to appreciate pitch. It follows that the basal part of the cochlea is essential for the appreciation of high-pitched sound and injuries of this region result in high-tone deafness. There are other effects of mechanical stimulation of the cochlear structures associated with the development of the receptor potential; for instance, external and internal hair cells are not equally sensitive to the radial and longitudinal bending of their hairs, and electrical events other than cochlear microphonics arise from cochlear activity, including a positive electrical potential of some 80 millivolts.

Auditory Nerve

The auditory nerve responds to sound stimulation such as a single click with a volley of impulses followed by a second burst due to repetitive firing of some of its fibres. A continual steady tone below 4000~ elicits very small impulse volleys reproducing the frequency of the stimulus, although of course no single nerve fibre responds to every sound wave. Below 1500~ the stiff basilar membrane at the base of the cochlea moves more or less in phase with the stimulus so that each sound wave acts as an individual stimulus.

This relationship between sound stimulus and impulse frequency obviously can provide the brain with additional information for pitch discrimination. These two receptor mechanisms, the place principle and the volley frequency, cannot wholly account for the remarkably fine pitch discrimination of the human ear which is only made possible by some further elaboration within the brain itself involving, perhaps, some kind of selective inhibition. During prolonged stimulation of the cochlea there is a gradually diminishing rate of impulse discharge, a physiological phenomenon which is in agreement with the psychological experience of adaptation to, for example, continuous background noise.

Central Auditory Pathways

Central auditory pathways refer only to the recognised relay centres through which the auditory impulses pass on their way to the cerebral cortex. They do not include the many other neural elements that may be indirectly activated by stimulation of the cochlea, *e.g.* the cerebellum and the centres involved in the various reflex responses to sound. In the auditory cortex the impulse patterns are translated into sound sensations in respect of frequency (pitch) and intensity (loudness). They also initiate such voluntary motor acts as turning the head towards the sound source, and their more widespread diffusion throughout neighbouring brain territories will be correlated with affective experiences such as recognition, recollection, pleasure, or distress. Whereas in other somatic sensory systems there is, as we have seen, a well-defined number of neuron relays, usually up to four, the characteristic of the auditory pathways is the complexity and multiplicity of their connexions with up to six or more relaying neurons. Neuron I are bipolar cells of the spiral ganglia within the central pillar of the bony cochlea with short processes, the post-synaptic terminals of the mechanoreceptors, and long processes, the fibres of the cochlear nerve, which terminate in the brain stem by synapsing with the cells of neuron II. Other relay centres in the brain stem are the superior olivary nucleus and the inferior colliculi, one of the largest and most highly organised of the subcortical sensory centres. The last link in the pathway is from the medial geniculate body to the auditory region of the cortex (Fig. 2:4). The auditory pathways have crossed and uncrossed fibres so that the brain centres receive information from both ears. Auditory impulses also reach the brain by the reticular activating system and as a result sound stimuli can produce arousal reactions.

Central Mechanisms

Although each cochlear nerve fibre synapses with a number of cells of neuron II and each cell has synapses with a number of nerve fibres, there is an orderly grouping of the neurons according to their receptive fields so that they will respond preferentially to a specific range of frequencies. For example, if the receptive field is at the base of the cochlea the cell groups will respond to high frequencies, and to low frequencies when the receptive field is at the apex. This, however, only holds for threshold stimuli, and as the intensity of the stimulus increases, the range of frequency response of the cells widens towards the lower end of the scale, but not towards the upper end. It would therefore be more correct to say that at above threshold intensity neuron II, like the cochlear nerve fibres, responds to all the stimulus frequencies up to a "high" limit. A similar arrangement and response is found in the other relay centres, although in the inferior colliculus the frequency-band response above threshold intensity widens for high as well as low frequencies. There is some spatial order in the auditory cortex in that low-frequency units are at the posterior end and high-frequency units at the anterior end, but only a small proportion of all the cortical neurons which respond to auditory stimulation are tone sensitive, and these respond to a wider frequency band at threshold intensity than subcortical neurons. There is, however, less increase of the frequency band with stronger stimulation, and any increase is equal for

high and low intensities. Thus, cochlear nerve fibres which respond at
threshold intensity to 2000∼ only may respond to all tones lower than
2000∼ but none higher, when the intensity of the stimulus is increased,
while the tone-sensitive cortical units respond at threshold intensity to a
frequency band centering round 2000∼ which, however, widens very
little either way with increased intensity of stimulation. Stimuli dimensions are changed in other ways throughout the auditory pathways. The
response to a click is both amplified and extended in time in the higher
centres at the level, for example, of the inferior colliculus. The amplification may be due to the involvement of larger numbers of units and the
dispersal in time to a diversity of synaptic relays, or to some feedback
mechanism within the nucleus itself.

In general, it can be stated that there is a broad correlation between
the arrangement of the receptive units along the cochlea and the disposition of the cortical neurons and thus between the frequency of the
stimulus and the tone sensitivity of the responding cortical neurons. It
may be significant that from lower to higher auditory centres there is a
progressive dispersal of tone-sensitive units with a diminishing ratio of
frequency specific to non-frequency specific units which reaches its
lowest in the auditory cortex. Somewhere in the auditory relay system,
most probably in neuron II, there must be a switchover from a system of
units which are both tone- and noise-sensitive to one which is noise-
sensitive only, probably sorted out by synaptic points between the first
and second neurons.

The trained ear can distinguish differences of half a tone or less, and
it is difficult to account for this precision of pitch discrimination on the
facts so far recorded. The auditory pathways contain elements with a
spontaneous discharge rate, increased by stimuli of certain frequencies,
and others whose spontaneous discharge rate is correspondingly inhibited.
Moreover, the auditory impulses are fed into a continuously changing
background of intrinsic cortical electrical activity and, as already noted,
the auditory system like other sensory systems includes centrifugal control
mechanisms. Fibres descend from the cortex to the receptors and the
lower neurons whereby their sensory responses can be regulated, and it is
fair to assume that the activity throughout any level of the auditory
apparatus can be modified in relation to existing events in both lower and
higher centres, and reduced or even obliterated by preceding auditory or
other sensory stimulation. From all this it is obvious that analysis of the
manner of projection of fibre pathways onto the cortex and the response of
cortical neurons to stimulation of these fibres is one of the more simple
and straightforward aspects of a plan whose complexity we are just
beginning vaguely to comprehend.

Sound Perception

A combination of physiological tests and psychological observations has given us quantitative and qualitative data concerning the capabilities and limitations of our auditory apparatus and some idea of the way in which the brain, through the organ of hearing, can extrapolate physical events in our environment, in this case the disturbances caused by bodies in motion.

Pitch

Frequency and intensity are the physical attributes which together or separately arouse the sensations associated with sound. While pitch, denoting the position in the musical scale, is most directly related to frequency it is also influenced by intensity in the same way as luminosity can affect colour. Greater intensity decreases the tone of low-frequency sounds and raises the tone of high-frequency sounds. This shifting of the pitch as a result of increased sound intensity can probably be explained in terms of the mechanics of either the middle ear or the cochlear receptors but it would be interesting to compare, if it were possible, the total impulse pattern reaching the cortex when the same tone is heard with two sounds at different frequencies and intensities. Fortunately, musical instruments with their complex sound waves, fundamental frequencies plus overtones, preserve a stable pitch whether played loudly or softly. The reason is said to be related to the prominent harmonics of tones in the region of maximum sensitivity (2000-4000∿) which are in some way anchored by them so that the frequency pattern of impulses is preserved. Movement of the sound source relative to the listener can also affect the pitch, *e.g.* the whistle of an approaching train lowers in pitch as it rushes by—the so-called Doppler effect. Similarly, as already noted, there is no one-to-one relationship between the loudness and sound intensity, *i.e.* the stimulus energy. The sensitivity of the ear varies according to the pitch, and thus of two sounds of the same intensity but different pitch one may be louder than the other.

Loudness

Loudness is the subjective attribute of sound which is related to stimulus intensity. The physiological correlates of stimulus strength are most commonly said to be the number of impulses reaching the cortex in unit of time. With sound, however, it is not at all clear that there is any such simple relationship between loudness and impulse quantity. Both the total number of nerve fibres involved and the impulse rate of any single fibre are also part of the frequency analysis. Quite possibly loudness involves some selective inhibition at various points along the auditory pathways, but there is as yet no straightforward explanation. As a subjective assessment loudness level has a psychological scale and can be expressed in either phones or sones. If a tone of 1000~ at an intensity of 40 db. is taken as a loudness level of 40 phones, other frequencies can be adjusted in intensity to obtain equal loudness contours. Such contours show that the loudness level of low-frequency tones grows with increasing intensity much faster than that of high-frequency tones. An abnormally rapid increase in loudness is often present in cases of unilateral deafness, and even though the threshold of the deaf ear is much higher than that of the normal ear, the loudness increases so rapidly in the deaf ear that sounds of high intensities are equally loud to both ears. This is called recruitment of loudness.

Intensity Threshold

This can be expressed in terms of the amount of pressure on the eardrum required to arouse an audible sensation, *i.e.* the minimum audible pressure. On this standard the ear is a remarkably sensitive stimulus recorder with maximum sensitivity within the frequency range of 2000 to 4000~ when the threshold stimulus has an intensity level of 6 to 8 db. below zero, corresponding to an audible minimum pressure of ·0001 dynes/cm². which, it is calculated, causes a movement of the tympanic membrane of the order of 10^{-9}cm. It has been stated that such a movement of the eardrum would imply movement of the basilar membrane as small as the diameter of a hydrogen molecule.

Hearing tests are carried out with the audiometer, calibrated in decibels with a different zero (threshold) for each frequency, and the amount in decibels by which a sound must be increased above zero to render it audible gives a measure of the hearing loss over a particular range of frequency. Defects over frequency ranges are known as tonal gaps or tonal islands. High-frequency tonal gaps are common in old age in the male. The frequencies which are of special significance in the hearing of ordinary speech sounds are 500, 1000 and 2000~ and any hearing loss for these frequencies means a hearing defect for speech.

Intensity Discrimination

One difficulty in investigating the Weber fraction $\Delta I/I$, *i.e.* by how much the stimulus has to be increased in intensity to produce a just noticeable difference is that compared to the eye two sound stimuli cannot be presented for discrimination at the same time. $\Delta I/I$ has been found to vary with both the frequency and the intensity level. Differential sensitivity is greatest in the region of 2000~ which is within the frequency range of maximum absolute sensitivity, and $\Delta I/I$ has been given as ·05 at 2500~ and intensity of 100 db. At 35~ and intensity of 5 db. it is as high as 7·5.

Frequency Discrimination

Frequency discrimination, or ΔF, is the ability to detect a just noticeable difference in pitch when the frequency is varied, and it is a function of both the absolute frequency at which the measurement is made and of the intensity. $\Delta F/F$ is roughly constant within the higher frequencies for a given intensity. Below 4500~ ΔF by itself is constant. There are probably very wide individual variations in the ΔF, which may indeed explain the marked difference of opinion about the average number of possible discriminable frequencies for which the figures given vary from 1500 to 11,000.

A theoretical consideration of the ΔI and ΔF would suggest that the human ear has the potential to discriminate a total of around 400,000 sounds. This in practice is quite unrealistic and a recognition of differences in pitch and loudness of sounds separated by definite intervals of time would reveal a very much broader classification. For example, there are something like fifty different speech sounds or phonemes in a modern language.

In addition to pitch and loudness, sound conveys a subjective sense of volume and density. Low notes from an organ appear to have volume in that they are more pervading and could be described as large, whereas high-pitched tones or squeaks take up little room and could be described as small, e.g. the shrill tones of the piccolo. Experimentally it can be shown that volume can be manipulated by variables of frequency and intensity. Density applies to those qualities of a note which make it appear hard or compact such as high-pitched tones, in contrast to the loose or dispersed quality of low tones.

Aural Harmonics

Like all sound transmission systems the ear distorts the sound waves reaching it by forming its own harmonics, so that even if a pure tone without overtones is presented to the ear, what we hear is this tone plus the aural harmonics. With moderate stimulation these harmonics appear in ascending order of magnitude, the first being more prominent than the second, the second than the third, etc.; but at high intensities certain harmonics become proportionately greater at the expense of the remainder, so that in terms of the sound engineer the distortion of the ear is both non-linear and asymmetrical when the system is forced into vibration by waves of moderate amplitude.

Combination Tones

If an ear is stimulated simultaneously by two pure tones of different frequencies, combination tones may be heard in addition to the fundamentals, and if the frequency differences between the two sounds is small, "beats" occur. Combination tones are described as difference tones (with a pitch equal to the frequency difference between the two stimulating tones) and summation tones (with a pitch equal to the sum of the frequencies of the two tones). There are also first, second, and third orders of difference and summation tones.

A beat consists of a regular loudening and softening of the tone and the number of beats per second indicates the frequency difference between the two tones. Thus, a difference of only one cycle will produce a slow beat once per second. Beats are useful aids in tuning instruments such as the piano, as with two perfectly tuned "generators" there will be no beats. In the middle pitch range a frequency difference producing four to five beats per second may give a pleasant sensation which, however, can become unpleasant with further separation of the frequencies of the two tones. This occurrence of beats indicates the limitations of the ear as an acoustic analyser of frequency differences.

If two or more tones produce a pleasant effect when sounded together they are said to be consonant, and if they have an unpleasant effect they are dissonant. Certain intervals in the musical scale are recognised as being consonant and others dissonant, but this may to some extent be a matter of culture and training. The most consonant interval is the octave, because here the even-numbered harmonics of both notes coincide and reinforce each other. With dissonant tones, on the other hand, there is a roughness resulting from the "beating" of harmonics separated by small frequency differences.

Masking

When two tones of different frequencies, one much louder than the other, are simultaneously "led" into the same ear, the weaker sound is not heard at all. It is said to be "masked" by the stronger one and can only be heard when the intensity is increased by an amount above its threshold value, which is a measure of the masking strength of the stronger tone. The masking effect is greatest between tones of adjacent frequencies, particularly in the high-frequency ranges, and is primarily a function of the cochlear mechanism, as when the two sounds are delivered into different ears its effect is not nearly so marked. Masking can be used to jam and "interfere" with radio broadcasting.

Auditory Fatigue

There is some evidence that the cochlea can become fatigued. Following a continuous stimulation of one ear a less intense tone will thereafter appear equally loud to the other ear, which could mean that the first ear is "adapting", or less probably that the second ear has become sensitised by the continuous tone submitted to the first ear. In this connexion it should be noted that the speech sounds received in one ear may be made to appear louder by the introduction of a continuous noise in the other ear, or conversely the removal of the steady noise may weaken the speech sounds heard in the other ear.

Sound Localisation

Listening with both ears we can locate approximately the direction of a sound source. The necessary cues are differences in the arrival time and the intensity of the sound stimulus reaching the two ears although, of course, the two sound "images" fuse into one sound perception, just as there is image fusion in binocular vision. With frequencies below 1500∼ a time difference of a few milliseconds in the arrival of sound at the two ears means that the "phase" (crest or trough) at any one time will not correspond in the two ears. In the case of high frequencies where the half wavelength of sound is less than the distance separating the ears, there is an averaging process which is said to extract the fluctuating envelopes of the sound wave, i.e. the line joining the wave amplitudes. Intensity differences are more marked with short-wave high-frequency sounds when the head casts a shadow so that the sound is louder in the ear turned towards it.

With suitable techniques and the use of headphones both the arrival time and the intensity of sound stimulus can be experimentally controlled for each ear. If, for instance, a sound is equally intense for both ears, but there is a delay of a few milliseconds in reaching, say, the right ear, it will appear to come from the left ear, but if the intensity of the sound to the right ear is sufficiently increased it will then appear to be centred in the head. Correspondingly, when the same sound reaches our ears from two points, one distant and one nearer, we tend to hear it as coming from the nearer point as the time of the arrival of the two sounds differs by some milliseconds, and this illusion persists unless the sound from the distant point is increased in intensity.

In any normal group of people a barrage of voices reaches the listener, and binaural hearing is important not only for detecting the direction of sound but also for separating sounds on the basis of differences in arrival time at the two ears. Thus, head rotation by producing such time differences facilitates speech discrimination. It has been pointed out that an individual can listen to and repeat a spoken message more or less concurrently, and moreover if different messages are fed simultaneously through headphones to each ear the individual can shadow one message at will but while doing so is totally unaware of what is reaching the other ear.

Experiments have demonstrated that a sound image cannot be sub-jectively placed in a distinct position relative to another one unless the two sounds have already been separated as Gestalten, *i.e.* sound perception. Thus two known voices can be separated but two simultaneous unknown noises cannot. A person of normal hearing derives much of the impression of subjective space from such image separation and it might be said that subjective space means to us the disposition of various visual or sound images within it.

As has already been noted, a characteristic of the auditory system is its bilaterality with an increasing overlap of the pathways from the two ears from lower to higher centres. Destruction of one ear, in fact, may have little effect on the total hearing acuity. Nevertheless, it has been found that whereas a sound source in the mid plane produces equal activity in the right and left cortex, if to one side of the midline it produces a greater response in the opposite cortex, and the farther away the stimulus is from the midline the greater is the difference in the cortical response on the two sides.

Quality and Fidelity

The aim of good sound recording and transmission is the faithful reproduction of voice or music, *i.e.* quality and fidelity, or what is known today as hi-fi. This means, amongst other things, the preservation of the relative intensities of the harmonics or overtones. The weak point in most sound systems is the electromechanical unit, the pick-up or micro-phone and the loudspeaker. Even with the best of loudspeakers, for example, the intensity can fluctuate by as much as 10 db. over the fre-quency range, while with the bad speaker this may amount to 40 db.

Electromechanical components are also limited in the dynamic range (intensity) they can handle without producing non-linear distortion (gramophone records have a dynamic range of about 50 db.), the best example of which can be heard by turning up the radio to full volume. The effect of such distortion is to increase greatly the loudness of the high-pitched relative to that of the low-pitched sounds. Paradoxically, sound systems with a narrow frequency band are less prone to distortion than those with a wide frequency band.

Listening to "live" music we have the advantage of binaural hearing as the sound reaching the two ears differs in arrival time and intensity. To reproduce the sound perspective and so give the impression of "live" music any sound system requires to incorporate binaural or stereophonic devices. Stereophonic reproduction is attained by a system of microphones placed in different positions, each connected up to its corresponding loud speaker. Two such pairs can differentiate the left and the right, and two others can represent the vertical dimensions. Stereo sound is now used with the new large-screen motion pictures. No matter, however, the improvisations of the sound engineer, there will always be a difference between listening in the concert hall and listening to the reproduction in the home.

Deafness

There are two main types of deafness, conductive and perceptive. Conductive deafness is caused by interference with the passage of the sound waves through the external and middle ear. There is never complete loss of hearing in conductive deafness as bone conduction of sound remains. In most types of conductive deafness, the amplification provided by hearing aids is generally of great assistance. Perceptive deafness is caused by damage to the cochlear mechanism or the auditory pathways, and can vary from minor degrees of hearing loss confined to an upward shift of the threshold to complete loss of hearing. Hearing for the upper frequencies is more commonly affected than for the lower, and indeed a gradual perceptive loss for high frequencies occurs with old age. A modern cause of loss of hearing is the use of the antibiotics of the streptomycin group which have been shown to produce degeneration of the hair cells and destruction of the organ of Corti. Deafness tends to produce differences in the voice and speech patterns. In perceptive deafness there is a tendency to speak too loudly, while in conductive deafness the tendency is to speak too softly. The acoustic effects of the loss of high-frequency sound which is often found in perceptive deafness can be appreciated by considering what happens in a telephone where there are no, or very weak, frequencies above 3000 ~ and in consequence it is often necessary to ask for a repetition of certain words. This "interference" with telephonic communication and some aspects of perceptive deafness may be associated with distortions of the consonant sounds which have distinguishing characteristics in the high-frequency areas. Thus, a perceptive deaf person with high-frequency loss may fail to hear children speaking or telephone or door bells ringing. The surprise at hearing one's own voice recorded for the first time is due to the loss of the effect of bone conduction on its volume, pitch, quality, and articulation.

Hearing and Speech

The infant learning to speak depends greatly on hearing its own voice and in this way correcting its own vocal efforts, a form of feedback control. Just how much this is an essential part of speech learning becomes apparent in the very difficult task of speech-training congenitally deaf children. Although for the most part unaware of this feedback mechanism, we all require to hear ourselves speak and if, for example, the feedback is experimentally delayed even by a fraction of a second there is a tendency to stammering and incoherent articulation.

Although our hearing organ is no more efficient than that of any other vertebrates, indeed in respect of acuity and frequency range it is less so, our central cerebral mechanism for dealing with the information is vastly superior to that of any other living forms. Thus the extent and variety of the finished products—sound perceptions—and the use we have been able to make of these to communicate by and comprehend the spoken word exceeds anything even remotely possible in other species.

Perhaps because we cannot close our ears as we can close our eyes, sound has a greater power for psychological disturbance than vision, although Man's world is predominantly a visual one. Sound perception seems to include a dynamic element. It is the screech of the hurricane and the roll of the thunder that brings terror to the storm, and the overall emotional reaction to the anguished cry or the Wagner fortissimo is for most of us a mental experience surpassing anything achieved by visual excitation.

BIBLIOGRAPHY

Békésy, G. von and Rosenblith, W. A. 1951. The mechanical properties of the ear. *Handbook of Experimental Psychology*. Wiley, New York.

Bergeijk, W. A. van, Pierce, S. R. and David, E. E. 1960. *Waves and the Ear*. Heinmann, London.

Davis, H. 1951. Psychology of hearing and deafness. *Handbook of Experimental Psychology*. Wiley, New York.

——1957. Biophysics and physiology of the inner ear. *Physiol. Rev.*, **37**.

——1959. Excitation of auditory reception. *Handbook of Physiology*, **1**, Sect. 1. Amer. Physiol. Soc., Washington, D.C.

Galambos, R. 1954. Neural mechanisms of audition. *Physiol. Rev.*, **34,** 497.

Licklider, J. C. R. 1951. Basic correlates of the auditory stimulus. *Handbook of Experimental Psychology*. Wiley, New York.

Meyer, M. M. 1950. *How we Hear, how Tones make Music*. Branford, Boston.

Pierce, J. R. and David, E. E. 1958. *Man's World of Sound*. Doubleday, New York.

Wever, E. G. 1949. *Theory of Hearing*. Wiley, New York.

——and Lawrence, M. 1954. *Physiological Acoustics*. Princeton University Press.

Wyburn, G. M. 1957. How and what we hear. *New Scientist*, March 21.

5

Vision

Light

All living substance is sensitive to light, seeks it, avoids it or, like the green plants, absorbs it as energy for its chemical processes. The eye has developed to a high degree the photosensitivity present as a rudimentary activity throughout organised substance, and can thus be regarded as a specialisation to gain additional information from the light stimulus. The specific stimulus generators for the visual receptors are the units or quanta of radiant energy. Of the known range of radiant energy in our world, extending from the short cosmic rays at one end to the long radio waves at the other, only a small part—about a seventieth—supplies the stimulus energy for light, and is accordingly known as the visible spectrum. This visible radiant energy is made up of groups of light quanta of different energies, and according to the wave concept such groups have different wavelengths (λ) determined by their energy, ranging from 350 to 740 mμ (μ is one thousandth of a millimetre, and mμ is one thousandth of μ). The different regions of the visible spectrum can also be designated by wave number indicating the number of wavelengths to a centimetre (the shorter the wavelength the greater the wave number) and the energy of a quantum of light is thus inversely proportional to its wavelength.

Light Stimulus

There are two physical attributes of light significant as a visual stimulus:

1. Its wavelength, which is defined by the energy of the corresponding light quantum and varies over the different parts of the visible spectrum. This is the basis of colour discrimination and subjectively we perceive the different light wavelengths as the colours of the spectrum.

2. Its amount of radiant energy, defined by the energy flux through unit area in unit time. The luminance of a surface, perceived by us as brightness, is proportional to the amount of radiant energy coming from the unit area of that surface.

The essential event in the production of a visual sensation is absorption of light quanta by pigment substances in the photoreceptors which

67

initiates a photochemical reaction starting off the chain of events terminating in "seeing." Obviously, if the photoreceptors are to function during continuous illumination the photochemical change must be reversible, with a simultaneous process of alteration and regeneration of the pigments.

When the stimulus energy is confined to light of a specific wavelength (monochromatic light) we perceive a particular colour, presumably due to its selective absorption by the visual pigments in the photoreceptors, but stimulation of the eye by all the light of the spectrum or a combination of certain parts of it, is perceived as white light. Unlike the trained ear, which can pick out separate tones in a complex sound, the eye cannot see the constituent colours in white light.

The physical unit denoting the amount of radiant energy may be measured in "ergs." Subjectively we assess the strength of the light stimulus or the amount of the radiant energy as degrees of brightness. The direct effect of more radiant energy, *i.e.* increased stimulus intensity, is absorption of more light quanta with a more extensive photochemical change producing stronger excitation of neural elements and hence sensation of brighter light. Brightness, like loudness, is thus our index of the strength of the generating stimulus and the instruments for measuring light intensity—photometers—are designed on the principle of comparing an unknown with a known standard of brightness. The amount of light from a point source is measured in candlepower, and the illumination at a given point is inversely proportional to the square of its distance from the source. The metre candle is defined as the intensity of illumination at a distance of one metre from a point source of one candlepower (measured, say, in ergs per sq. cm. per second). The luminance reflected from a perfectly diffusing surface with illumination of 10,000 metre candles is a Lambert and one thousandth of this is known as a millilambert. The intensity of light illuminating the retina is expressed in "Trolands," defined as the illumination of the retina through a millimetre pupil by light from a surface with a luminance of 10^{-4} Lamberts. There is a confusing number of alternative units used to measure luminosity.

Invisible Radiation

All invisible short-wave radiation, *i.e.* less than λ 300 mμ, has a chemical action on living tissues, ranging from the sunburn of ultraviolet rays to the more damaging effects of ionising radiation, including X-rays. Most short-wave radiation is absorbed by the tissues of the eye although, of course, X-rays penetrate the eye and reach the retina, and there is some evidence that given a sufficient intensity λ 300 mμ can be seen as light. It is possible to take photographs using ultraviolet radiation, and this kind of photography is particularly useful in dealing with fossil remains as any organic material is made to fluoresce and so stands out more clearly. Many arthropod eyes are photosensitive to ultraviolet rays and bees, for example, have their maximum light sensitivity in this part of the spectrum.

At the other end of the visible spectrum the long infra-red rays (λ 700 mμ) although transmitted are felt as heat and not seen as light. Given, however, a sufficiently strong source it is said that wavelengths of up to 10,000 mμ can cause a sensation of light. Infra-red rays are less scattered by atmospheric particles, and infra-red photography using specially sensitised plates is therefore particularly useful in aerial survey work, giving clearer detail than photography with ordinary light. Landscapes, however, with green trees and meadows look as if they are covered with snow. Infra-red photography has other practical application and it may, for instance, render legible otherwise totally undecipherable documents.

Light Source

Ordinary daylight is the visible range of radiant energy corresponding roughly to the solar radiation utilised by the green plants. Normally, however, much of the light entering the eye is not emitted directly from its source, but indirectly from surrounding objects. Light is either transmitted, absorbed, or reflected and scattered from solid, fluid, or gaseous particles and so in this way provides information about the environment.

Artificial sources of light are classified as hot or cold light. Examples of a hot source are an incandescent light where electricity makes a tungsten wire glow either in a vacuum or in a bulb filled with a chemically inert gas such as nitrogen, argon, or crypton. Under such conditions, however, only about 10 per cent of the radiation is in the visible spectrum and more than 90 per cent is in the form of heat. Cold light in the form of a fluorescent light is much more efficient. One form of fluorescent lamp contains mercury vapour which undergoes an ionising change (affecting its electrons) with a direct discharge emitting a strong ultraviolet radiation which causes a substance coating the inside of the tube, to glow, *i.e.* to fluoresce. Fluorescence is due to the transfer of radiant energy to the particles of the fluorescing substance, as a result of which these particles emit radiation of longer wavelength than the absorbed radiant energy. In this way the invisible ultraviolet radiation causes the substance to emit visible radiation. Phosphorescence of non-living matter, where the material has a natural emission of visible radiation, is due to radioactivity; but what is commonly referred to as phosphorescence in living organisms or, to be more precise, bioluminescence, is the result of chemical processes within the organisms.

HSP F

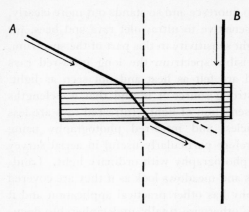

FIGURE 5:1.
Refraction. A = Oblique and B = Perpendicular ray entering and leaving a sheet of glass.

Refraction

Rays of light, in passing obliquely from one transparent medium to another of different optical density, *e.g.* from air to glass, are bent or refracted, and the amount of bending or refraction is expressed as the refractive index of the medium, for example, the refractive index of water is 1·3. In the case of a sheet of glass with plain surfaces, oblique rays are reflected to an equal degree on entering and emerging, though in opposite directions, *i.e.* towards and away from the perpendicular respectively, so that the incident and emergent rays are parallel (Fig. 5:1). In a prism with converging sides the rays will be bent both on entering and emerging towards the base of the prism, and so in convex lenses, which can be regarded as built up of a number of prisms with the base towards the centre of the lens, parallel rays will be brought to a meeting point or focus (Fig. 5:2). Light rays passing through the centre of the curvature of a lens, *i.e.* through its principal axis, are not, however, refracted. The converging power of a convex lens is related to the curvature of its surfaces, the greater the degree of curvature the greater the refractive power,

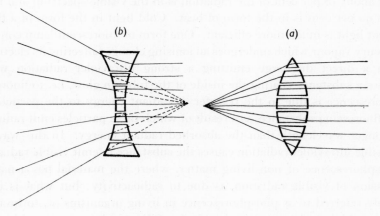

(b)   (a)

FIG. 5:2.   Refraction by (*a*) a convex lens, (*b*) a concave lens.

expressed as 1 diopter in a lens with a focal length of 1 metre. With a focal length of 2 metres the converging power is half a diopter, and with a focal length of half a metre it is 2 diopters.

Structure of the Eye

The vertebrate eye has evolved from a great variety of invertebrate photosensitive apparatus, ranging from a simple increase in the sensitivity of surface cells, unicellular eye spots consisting of one specialised receptor cell with associated pigmented mass, to the more complex multicellular eye. There are two basic types of invertebrate multicellular eye: (1) The camera-type eye consisting of a pigment-surrounded cup lined with receptor cells forming a retina, in some species placed far enough away from a dioptric (refracting) system to receive some kind of image. (2) Groups of units known as ommatidia. Each ommatidium has an investing sheath of pigment cells, a ring of receptor cells at the proximal end of a dioptric system, and operates as a separate photometric unit. This is the typical arthropod eye found, for example, in crabs, centipedes, and insects, and is particularly effective as a detector of movement.

Although the ommatidium eye does not appear to be equipped to form any definite image there is, nevertheless, evidence of pattern and form perception as, for example, the identification of flowers or recognition of various courtship gestures. This implies a synthesis within the central nervous system of the summated information from individual ommatidia and a level of awareness.

The same transducer mechanism operates in all photoreceptors, namely a photochemical reaction of the pigment molecules which are arranged in the ommatidium within densely packed tubules.

Structure of the Human Eye

The human eyeballs are slung within the orbital cavities of the skull and are approximately spherical with a diameter of about one inch, but the posterior five-sixths is a segment of a larger sphere than the anterior sixth which bulges in front. The centre of the anterior curvature of the eyeball is the anterior pole, and of the posterior curvature the posterior pole, while the straight line joining the two poles is known as the optic axis, and the circumference of the eyeball midway between the two poles is termed the equator. The optic nerves are attached to the eyeballs a little to the inner side of the posterior pole, and the optic axes of the two eyes are nearly parallel, converging slightly behind.

The eye consists of a light-receiving part—the retina—comparable to the plate or film in a camera with the photoreceptors and neural elements, and the light-transmitting part—the dioptric system—concerned with focusing the image on the retina (Fig. 5:3).

The inside of the eyeball contains (1) a transparent jelly-like material, the vitreous body, which fills the posterior five-sixths, (2) a watery fluid, the aqueous humour, occupying the front part, and (3) a crystalline lens situated on the front of the vitreous body. The wall of the eyeball has three layers. The outer layer, the sclera, is a tough fibrous membrane replaced in front by the transparent almost circular cornea about half a

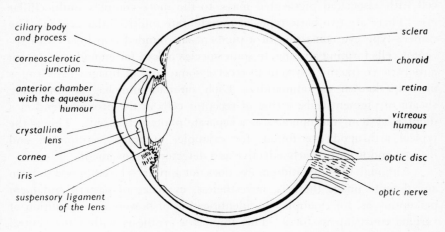

FIG. 5:3.   A section of the eye.

millimetre in thickness. The optical transparency of the cornea is maintained by the activity of its cells and it becomes opaque almost immediately after death. Contact lenses may, to begin with, interfere with the cell activity including the normal exchange of substances, in particular oxygen, necessary for the nutrition of the corneal tissue, causing swelling and temporary opacity of the cornea.

The middle vascular layer consists, from the back to the front of the eye, of the choroid, the ciliary bodies, and the iris. The choroid, dark brown in colour, has blood vessels and scattered pigment cells. The ciliary bodies, placed just behind the corneosclerotic junction, consist of about 70 folds forming a radial fringe round the eyeball. These are covered with a pigmented epithelium and include the muscle of accommodation, the ciliary muscle. The iris is a muscular diaphragm surrounding the central aperture of the pupil through which light reaches the lens. It has blood vessels, pigmented epithelium, and the scattered pigment cells responsible for the colour of the eyes. In white races nearly all newborn babes have blue eyes as the pigment of the iris does not appear until some weeks after birth, but pigment is present at birth in the brown-eyed babies of dark races. The size of the pupil is controlled by the reflex opening and closing of the muscular diaphragm, regulated by the amount of light falling on the retina.

The Retina

The lining of the eyeball, the light-receiving retina, is constructed of the following cell layers; a pigmented epithelium immediately adjacent

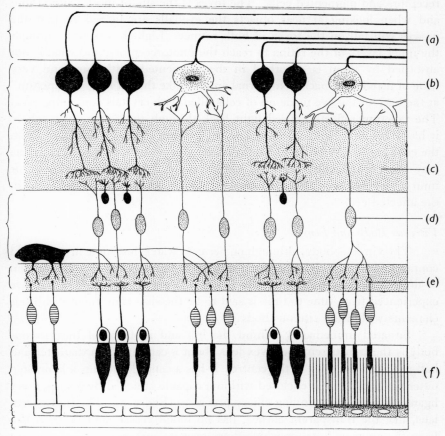

Fig. 5:4. The layers of the retina.
(b) = Layer of ganglion cells
(d) = Layer of bipolar neurons
(f) = Layer of rods and cones.

to the choroid, a layer of photoreceptors—the rods and cones—several layers of nerve elements including the bipolar neurons with their processes and, situated next to the vitreous body, a layer of ganglion cells whose axons are fibres of the optic nerve (Fig. 5:4). In the living subject the retina, examined through the pupil with an "opthalmoscope" appears red due to the underlying vascular choroid except for a pale circular area, the optic disc, to the nasal side of the midline, the point of convergence of the axons of the ganglion cells to form the optic nerve. The optic disc is 1·5 mm. in diameter, has no photoreceptors, is therefore insensitive to light, and consequently known as the "blind" spot of the retina. At the centre of the retina, *i.e.* the point on the visual axis, there is a depression, the fovea, about ·4 mm. in diameter and here there is only a layer of cone receptors and pigmented cells. The fovea is the site of most acute vision, and when looking at near objects the eyeballs are turned so that the images will fall on the fovea of both retinae. Light has to pass through the inner layers of the retina to reach the photoreceptors, and what is not absorbed by them is absorbed in the pigmented epithelium and very little of it reflected back. Nocturnal animals like the cat have a "tapetum" at the back of the eye made up of cells filled with crystals containing zinc. The tapetum reflects unused light back through the retina again where it has a second chance to stimulate the photoreceptors. The glow from the cat's eye in the dark is the light reflected from its tapetum. The retina may become detached from the wall of the eyeball following disease or injury, and unless replaced surgically there is permanent loss of sight in the affected eye.

Vitreous Body and Lens

The vitreous body, although 99 per cent water, has some firmness and contains fibres by which it is attached to parts of the retina. The impression of dots or threads floating slowly before the eye which most of us have experienced from time to time is said to be the slow movement of fibrous elements within the vitreous body.

Situated immediately behind the iris and in front of the vitreous body is the transparent biconvex lens about a centimetre in diameter and half a centimetre thick at the centre. It has a central nucleus, a laminated outer covering, and is enclosed within a capsule attached by a suspensory ligament to the surrounding ciliary processes (Fig. 5:3). The transparent lens, like the transparent cornea, has no blood vessels and is nourished from the aqueous humour which flows over its surface carrying, amongst other substances, a supply of sugar (glucose) for the lens tissues. Conditions involving some abnormality in the chemical cycle of the sugars, *e.g.* diabetes, by indirectly affecting the vitality of the lens may cause lens opacities, commonly known as cataracts. Babies born with defects in their sugar cycle develop cataracts and become blind, but more usually the condition occurs in later life.

To function as an efficient optical apparatus the eyeball, which collapses immediately after death, must keep its shape. During life there is an internal pressure or intraocular tension maintained by the capillary blood pressure and the circulation of aqueous humour which is diffused from the capillaries of the ciliary body and absorbed by a vein at the corneosclerotic junction. Blockage of this vein prevents the circulation of aqueous fluid and causes a dangerously high intraocular tension, a condition termed glaucoma which may if untreated lead to loss of vision.

Visual Pathways

Unlike other sense organs the first, second (bipolar cells) and third (ganglion cells) visual neurons are within the peripheral sense organs (Fig. 5:5). The visual fibres, which are the axons of the third neurons (ganglion cells) and form the innermost layer of the retina nearest the centre of the eyeball, converge on the optic disc to form the optic nerves. Each optic nerve is stated to have about a million nerve fibres grouped according to the situation of their parent ganglion cells on the retina (the electron microscope has now enabled us to see many small nerve fibres previously invisible and it seems likely that light microscopic counts of optic nerve fibres are a gross underestimation). The two optic nerves join on the under surface of the brain at the optic chiasma and separate again to form the optic tracts. At the chiasma the nerve fibres from the nasal half of each retina cross over so that each optic tract contains fibres from the outer or temporal half of the retina of its own side and from the inner or nasal half of the retina of the opposite side (Fig. 5:6). As we have seen, the fibre pathways of other sense organs cross more or less completely to the opposite side of the

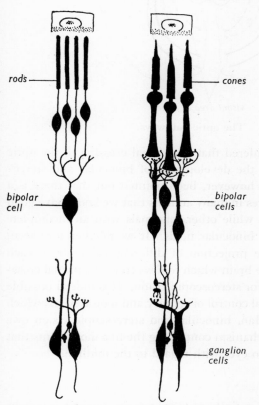

rods

cones

bipolar cell

bipolar cells

ganglion cells

FIG. 5:5.   The three neurons of the retina.

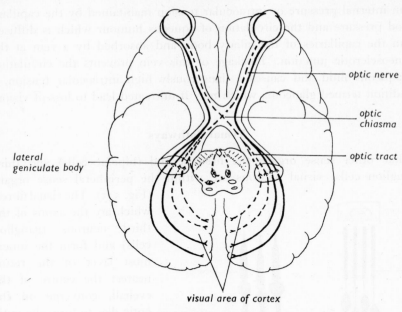

optic nerve

*optic
chiasma*

optic tract

*lateral
geniculate body*

visual area of cortex

FIG. 5:6.   The optic pathways.

brain, and it is generally considered that the partial crossing of the optic
nerve fibres has evolved with the development of binocular and stereoscopic vision in Man. It has, however, been pointed out that there is a
complete crossing of visual fibres in many animals that we know have good
stereoscopic vision, *e.g.* birds, while other mammals with an incomplete
crossing have only very small binocular fields. It would therefore seem
unjustified to assume that the projection of different halves from each
retina onto the same side of the brain which follows from the partial crossing is an essential mechanism for stereoscopic vision. It is indeed possible
that with the increasing cerebral control of sensory and motor events which
has reached a maximum in Man, binocular and stereoscopic vision owe
something to the precision mechanism controlling the fine movements that
regulate the position of the two eyes with regard to the midline.

Lateral Geniculate Body

Most of the fibres of the optic tract terminate in synaptic junctions
with the cells of the lateral geniculate body, the lower visual centre on the
under surface of the brain. Others, known as pretectal fibres, form
connexions with the neurons whose axons convey messages to the muscle
regulating the size of the pupil and thereby the amount of light falling
on the retina. The cells of the lateral geniculate body are arranged in six
layers of grey matter, and it is said that the crossed and uncrossed fibres

of the optic tract end around the cells of alternate layers, *e.g.* layers 1, 4, and 6 for the crossed fibres and 2, 3, and 5 for the uncrossed fibres. During binocular vision corresponding activated retinal points, *i.e.* one point from the outer half of the retina of one eye and one from the inner half of the retina of the other eye, will produce a stimulated linear strip through the six layers of the lateral geniculate body, and possibly this linear strip projects as a unit onto the visual cortex. In lower vertebrates the lateral geniculate body, although the final receiving centre for visual information, has a relatively simple structure and its complicated organisation in Man would indicate that it does something more than merely serve as a relay station; but its specific contribution to visual function has yet to be ascertained. One significant fact is the very large area of the lateral geniculate body receiving fibres from the fovea, an indication of the importance of this retinal receptor area.

Visual Cortex (Fig. 2:6).

The final visual pathway is the grouping of the axons of the cells of the lateral geniculate body to form a tract terminating in synaptic connexions with about 145 million receiving cells of the visual cortex, the grey matter of the occipital lobe at the back of the brain. The visual cortex on each side will therefore obtain information from the temporal half of one retina and the nasal half of the other retina, *i.e.* with regard to objects in the opposite field of vision, by which is meant the opposite side of the vertical midline so that, for instance, the left visual cortex is concerned with the right field of vision and vice versa (Fig. 5:7).

The arrangement of the neurons of the visual cortex is in general that of the cerebral cortex elsewhere, *i.e.* six layers, each with its characteristic cells. There is a point-to-point topographical representation of the retina on the cortex, that is to say, stimulation of one part of the retina activates a specific area of visual cortex and in a general way the periphery of the retina projects onto the front of the visual cortex and the fovea to the back, but in such a way that the small fovea occupies almost as much of the visual cortex as the rest of the retina. The figures given are 1 mm. of visual cortex to 2 minutes of visual angle at the fovea, the same area of cortex for 18 minutes of visual angle just outside the fovea, while in the more peripheral retina the ratio is much higher. This would mean that one foveal cone receptor would give information to the order of a hundred or more cortical cells, which quantitatively at least indicates the possibility of a more detailed analysis of the light stimulus.

There is some experimental and clinical evidence that the foveal retina is represented bilaterally, *i.e.* on the visual cortex of both sides, but this is not confirmed anatomically and the incomplete loss of foveal

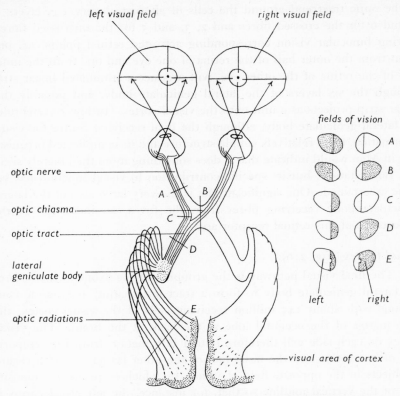

left visual field   right visual field

fields of vision

optic nerve

optic chiasma

optic tract

lateral
geniculate body

optic radiations

A
B
C
D
E

left   right

visual area of cortex

FIG. 5:7. To show the extent of blindness of the visual fields resulting from damage to the part of the visual pathways indicated
by *A, B, C, D, E*. (After Fulton.)

vision with destruction of one entire visual cortex could have some other
explanation.

Formation of the Image on the Retina

Making up the dioptric system of the eye are cornea, aqueous humour,
lens, and vitreous body. As the cornea and the aqueous humour have
approximately the same refractive index the eye can be said to have three
refractive surfaces—the anterior surface of the cornea, and the anterior
and posterior surfaces of the lens. The compound optic system of the eye
can be simplified to the so-called reduced schematic eye with a single
refractive surface situated 1·3 mm. behind the cornea, to give a total
refracting power of over 58 diopters and bring the image to a focus on
the retina 24·14 mm. behind the anterior surface of the cornea. Given
the refractive indices of the media of the dioptric system and the distances

between their respective curvatures, it is possible to construct the pathway of the light rays passing from an object into the eye where it forms both a smaller and an inverted image on the retina (Fig. 5:8). This has been confirmed experimentally by observing the back of an excised eye from which the scleral and choroid coats have been removed, and inversion of the retinal image can also be demonstrated in the living subject in the following way. An individual with very little pigment in the choroid, *i.e.* of a fair colour, is asked to look at a lighted candle (in a darkened room) placed well to the outer side of the eye. An inverted image of the flame can be seen showing through the inner wall of the eyeball. It should be clear that the expression "retinal image" indicates a pattern of light

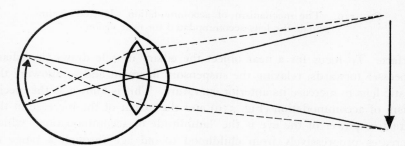

FIG. 5:8.   To show the formation of the image on the
retina.

falling on the retina, and that the actual seeing of an object requires the co-operation of the brain. If "inverting" spectacles producing an "erect" image are worn, objects will at first be seen upside down, but after a week or two the visual world gradually rights itself. The brain is now rationalising visual cues in the light of information received from the other sense organs, touch, gravity, etc.

The greatest distance from the eye at which an object can be seen clearly is its "far point," and in the normal eye this is more than 20 feet away when parallel rays of light are brought to focus on the retina. The corresponding shortest distance or "near point" varies from 7 to 40 cm. depending upon age.

Accommodation

In a camera the image is focused on the photographic plate by moving the lens nearer or farther away, but the eye focuses for near objects by increasing the convexity of the lens (the lens in the eyes of some fishes, however, moves). At rest, for instance, when looking at a distant object the anterior surface of the lens, because of traction exerted on the lens capsule by the suspensory ligament, is less convex than the posterior

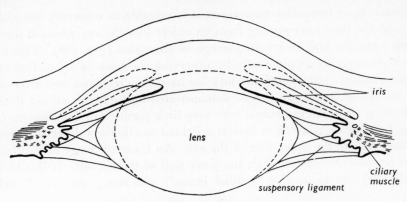

FIG. 5:9.   The mechanism of accommodation. Dotted outline
equals the lens accommodated for near vision.

surface.   To focus for a near object the ciliary muscle draws the ciliary
processes forwards, relaxing the suspensory ligament and so allowing the
elastic lens to increase its anterior curvature. This is known as the mechanism of accommodation (Fig. 5:9) and the extent of the increase in the
refractive power of the eye is the "amplitude of accommodation" which
decreases progressively from childhood to old age through a range of
from 16 to 1 diopters. In other words, with advancing years the near
point gradually becomes more distant and may be as much as a metre
away compared to 7 centimetres in early life (Fig. 5:10).

Accommodation for near objects is accompanied by the convergence

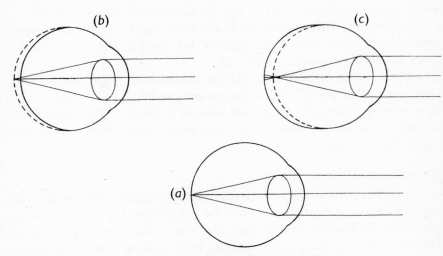

FIG. 5:10.   Normal and abnormal vision.
(a) Normal eye; (b) Long sight where the eyeball is too short; (c) Short
sight where the eyeball is too long.

of the eyes, *i.e.* the turning of the eyeballs towards the midline and con-
striction of the pupil. This ensures that the image falls on the fovea of
both retinae. The light rays passing through the peripheral parts of a
complex lens are refracted more strongly than those passing through the
centre, so that the outer rays cross at a point nearer the lens than the
inner rays. This is known as spherical aberration and tends to produce
a blurred image (Fig. 5:11). In the eye, spherical aberration is largely

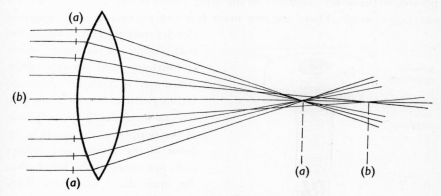

FIG. 5:11.   Spherical aberration.
(*a*) = focal point of outer rays; (*b*) = focal point of inner rays.

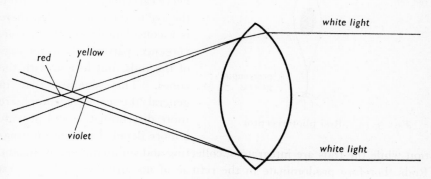

FIG. 5:12.   Chromatic aberration.

corrected by the fact that the central nucleus of the lens has a higher
refractive index than the cortex and in addition the iris tends to shut off
light rays from the periphery of the lens. All lenses refract rays of different
wavelengths differently, short violet rays more strongly than the long red
rays; this is chromatic aberration (Fig. 5:12). Fortunately chromatic
aberration is not significant at the red end of the spectrum and because
of the Purkinje shift (see later) will be at a minimum in photopic vision.

In addition, the yellow lens acts as a colour filter, cutting off the far edge of the violet spectrum.

The Photoreceptors

The retina is formed as a direct outgrowth from the embryonic brain and as, in addition to the receptor structures, it includes the second and third neurons, the bipolar and ganglion cells, it is in this respect comparable to the lower "centres" of the other senses placed within the central nervous system. There are two main types of photoreceptor; elongated slender rods used for seeing in the dark—night or scotopic vision (colourless)—and shorter thick cones used in daylight—photopic vision (with colour). There are only cones at the fovea, only rods at the periphery, *i.e.* towards the front of the retina, and neither rods nor cones at the blind spot, the optic disc. Elsewhere there are both rods and cones, and 120 million rods and 6 million cones serve the million fibres of the optic nerve carrying the messages from the eye to the brain so that there is a considerable degree of convergence, particularly in the case of the rods, but less so with the cones. This signifies that in general the cone receptors are more discriminative and provide a more detailed kind of informa-

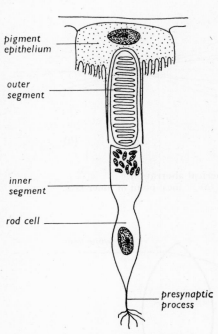

pigment epithelium

outer segment

inner segment

rod cell

presynaptic process

FIG. 5:13.   Rod photoreceptor.

tion while the rods are integrators, collecting and summating light quanta. Rods therefore predominate in the retinae of nocturnal animals, *e.g.* rat or toad, and cones in the retinae of certain snakes and birds with daylight vision only. The apparent random distribution of rods and cones over much of the retina implies a peripheral mechanism for dealing with light stimuli quite different from the "place principle" frequency analysis of the cochlea. The photoreceptors are basically similar in design with (*a*) rod or cone-shaped transducer parts, *i.e.* where the stimulus generates the receptor potential, and (*b*) rod and cone fibres, regarded as the first neuron, with a nucleus and a process, which is the presynaptic element of the synapse with the second or bipolar neurons (Fig. 5:13).

Rod Receptors

The rod-shaped part consists of an inner and an outer segment connected by a narrow strip of cytoplasm in which there is an arrangement of filaments. The outer segment of human rods is about 24μ long and 3μ wide ($\mu=$ one thousandth of a millimetre) and a variable extent of the outer segment is in contact with projections of the pigmented epithelial cells of the retina. It is filled with regularly stacked discs, seen in electron microscopic sections as double lines representing the kind of lamellar arrangement of molecules found in many other intracellular bodies and indicating a catalytic system to deal with specific chemical processes. Molecules of the visual pigment, rhodopsin, are laid out along the discs and make up 40 per cent of the weight of the outer rod segments. The inner segment has no discs, but contains aggregations of intracellular bodies known as mitochondria, which is taken to mean that this is a chemically active part of the photoreceptor, possibly directly concerned with the generation of the receptor potential. In fishes and birds the inner rod segment is contractile, lengthening in the light and contracting in the dark. The rod fibre, terminating in the synaptic body, is invaginated by the postsynaptic elements of the bipolar neurons. Each rod receptor has synaptic connexions with a number of bipolar neurons, and each bipolar is in contact with groups of rod receptors (Fig. 5:5).

Cone Receptors

The cones, bulkier than the rods, also have inner and outer segments. The outer segments can be as short as 6μ outside the fovea and as long as 30μ at the fovea. They have the same content of stacked discs as the rods, which is presumably related to the disposition of the cone visual pigments, and their inner segments also contain mitochondria. In many animals, e.g. pigeons, there are coloured oil globules in the inner cone segments. The cone fibre has a nucleus and a process synapsing with the bipolar neuron (Fig. 5:5) and at the fovea there may be a one-to-one relationship between the cones, the bipolars, and the ganglion cells.

Visual Pigments

The ability of the receptors to capture and use light energy to produce electrogenic change is due to the absorption of light quanta by the pigments in their outer segments, which initiates a photochemical reaction. There are four known visual pigments, two of them—rhodopsin and iodopsin—found in the human photoreceptors. All four are of the chemical group, the carotenoid-proteins. The carotenoid part, known as a retinene, is responsible for the colour and the photosensitivity and is chemically related to vitamin A. The proteins are opsins—scotopsins in rhodopsin and photopsin in iodopsin—and although not in themselves photo-sensitive they obviously influence the particular properties of the respective visual pigments.

The details of the breakdown and regeneration of the visual pigments, the chemical cycle involved in the activation of the receptors, is known in some detail for rhodopsin, which is therefore generally regarded as a working model for the photochemical system. Rhodopsin, the pigment found only in the rods, is pink in colour as it absorbs the blue/green part of the spectrum and transmits red, is bleached by light and broken down to a mixture of the retinene and opsin, and the retinene is thereafter reduced to vitamin A. It is regenerated from the bleached products in one of two ways; (1) a spontaneous interaction of the retinene and the opsin which also produces the energy to (2) oxidise vitamin A into a retinene which then reacts with the opsin to form rhodopsin. This is a slower process requiring the presence of the pigmented cell layer of the retina which is thought to provide the necessary supply of vitamin A. The pigmented epithelium, the outer layer of the retina, i.e. placed next to the choroid, is a single row of cells with finger-like processes extending round the outer segments of the rods and, to a lesser extent, of the cones. These processes have granules of melanin-like pigment which are said to migrate into them during exposure to light and to be concerned with the regeneration of the visual pigment. All the retinenes require vitamin A for their synthesis and it is now well established that deficiency of vitamin A is connected with night blindness and structural changes in the retina. While light initiates the breakdown of the rhodopsin, once started the cycle can be completed in the dark.

The only visual pigment so far extracted from the cones is the violet iodopsin, differing from the rod pigment in the nature of its protein—photopsin instead of scotopsin—but as appreciation of colour requires some analysis of the light stimulus by the photoreceptors in respect of its quantum energy (as indicated by the wavelength) it is assumed that there must be a corresponding variety of cone visual pigments.

The bleaching of visual pigment with the liberation of the retinene is a relatively slow process and so cannot be responsible for the practically instantaneous transducer action which causes the nervous excitation following within a fraction of a second of stimulation. The development of a receptor potential implies some change in ion concentration to produce depolarisation, but as with all receptors we know very little about the chemical or physical details of the immediate transducer mech-anism. The formation of a stable pigment requires a close fit between the molecules of the retinene and the opsin, and it has been shown that what light does is to isomerise the retinene molecule, i.e. change its configuration so that it loosens off from the opsin, and this in some way almost instantaneously produces conditions favouring depolarisation. What matters in rod stimulation is the number of quanta acting on the rods and not their energy content. One quantum acts on one molecule of rhodopsin and there are 10^8 molecules of rhodopsin in a rod. There is, however, no chain reaction leading to the bleaching of a number of molecules but there is probably some amplification mechanism. Over the range of night vision the total number of pigment molecules bleached is very small; the figure given is ·015 per cent per hour.

Scotopic and Photopic Vision

The retina is often described as a sense organ with a double function —rod or scotopic vision without colour, and cone or photopic vision with colour—but the rods and cones act together over intermediate ranges of light intensity and we cannot make any categorical statement that the rods do not function at high intensity or the cones at low intensities of light. Visual sensitivity, which simply means the ability to see and distinguish objects clearly, is related to the concentration of the visual pigment so that with constant illumination as the visual pigments bleach to a steady level (maintained by the regenerative process) there is an accompanying fall of visual sensitivity to a corresponding steady state. It is a common experience to be temporarily blinded when changing from light to darkness or from darkness to light and a certain time is needed, for instance, before we begin to see in the dark, the so-called dark adaptation time, which in fact corresponds to the interval necessary for the reformation of the bleached rhodopsin. After long exposure to strong light full rod dark adaptation time is as much as half an hour, compared to the cone adaptation time of six minutes required to regenerate cone pigment. Much of the adaptation process in the rods takes place during the bleaching of the first small fraction of rhodopsin and the regeneration of the last small particle. The bleaching of as little as 0·006 per cent of rhodopsin lowers the visual sensitivity by a factor of eight; and after, for instance, only 7 per cent of rhodopsin has been bleached the rods cease to function while the cones continue to function after half their pigment has been bleached. There is the interesting question, therefore, why do cones function with half their pigment and rods cease to function, at least in scotopic vision, long before that?

The visual pigments do not absorb equal amounts of lights of different wavelengths (the spectral colours) and this can be represented graphically by their absorption curves which relate the amount of light absorbed to its wavelength. As the amount of light absorbed determines the smallest quantity of light energy needed to give a visual sensation, *i.e.* the threshold

HSP G

stimulus level, the absorption curve should more or less correspond to a "visibility" curve showing the relative light sensitivities. Although, for example, scotopic vision is colourless, the rods are not equally sensitive to the different spectral colours and the scotopic visibility curve reveals a minimum threshold value for light of λ 507 mμ (greenish blue light) which means that in the dark the eye is most sensitive to light of this

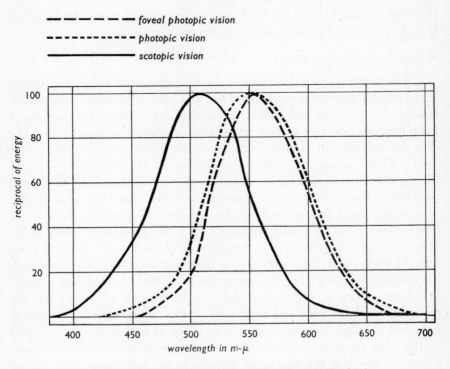

FIG. 5:14. Visibility curves. (After Best & Taylor.)

wavelength, indeed a thousand times more sensitive than to the red light of longer wavelength (Fig. 5:14). This fits the absorption curve of rhodopsin with its maximum absorption of light of λ 507 mμ. The photopic visibility curve, on the other hand, shows a minimum threshold value for light of λ 550 mμ (the yellowish green part of the spectrum) and this change from the wavelength sensitivity of the dark to that of the light-adapted eye is known as the Purkinje shift. Because of the Purkinje shift, bluish objects are brightest in twilight to give way to red as the morning light strengthens, and thus in a garden at dawn red flowers appear black and blue flowers are grey or white (Fig. 5:14).

Electrical Activity of the Retina

Complex electrical changes occur in the retina when it is illuminated and their record is known as an electroretinogram (E.R.G.). This can be obtained in the living subject with "leads" between the cornea and other points in the body, or capillary microelectrodes can be inserted into the retina of the excised eyes of cold-blooded animals. The E.R.G. is something quite distinct from the impulse discharge carried by the optic nerve to the brain, and indeed one of the unsolved problems is how the E.R.G. is related to the train of impulses sent along the optic nerve. The E.R.G. is present in all vertebrate eyes, and although in some respects it differs in rod as compared to cone eyes, it is not yet settled where the electric changes are developed, whether in the receptors, the bipolars, or both, but it is known that the ganglion cells are not involved.

In the human and frog retinae, where there are both rods and cones, the E.R.G. recorded during photopic vision is different from that recorded during scotopic vision. This does not necessarily mean that the one is due to cones and the other to rods, as it may depend to some extent on the adaptation changes within the receptors or the nerve cells of the retina itself. One of the tasks for the future is to obtain more information about these differences in the E.R.G. denoting not only rod and cone components, but also the different responses connected with colour vision. Current colour vision theories assume that there are photochemical substances with different absorption curves, and there are some features of the E.R.G. in the light-adapted eye which could indicate specific spectral sensitivity. Electrophysiologically the significance of colour vision at the retinal level is (1) the specific sensitivity of individual receptors, and (2) how this is coded in the impulse discharge generated in the ganglion cells.

Bipolar and Ganglion Cells

Undoubtedly the intermediate neurons—the bipolars—not only conduct information from the receptors to the ganglion cells, but can alter the nature of this information. Except at the fovea, large numbers of the retinal neural elements converge onto each ganglion cell, and the area of the retina occupied by the elements converging onto a single ganglion cell is its receptive field, in the frog a circular area with a diameter of about 1 mm. The size of a receptive field may vary according to the state of adaptation and the intensity of the stimulus as an inhibitory zone surrounds most of the receptive fields, but this inhibition decreases in the dark-adapted eye. Again, there are overlapping receptive fields and the discharge from one may be inhibited by stimulation of adjacent receptive fields.

There are ganglion cells (whose axons are the optic nerve fibres) that only discharge with the onset of the stimulus—"on" cells—those that only discharge when the stimulus stops—"off" cells—and the great many whose discharge is confined to the onset and the cessation—"off/on" cells. Again, a ganglion cell may transmit information from both rods and cones, and its sensitivity therefore varies according to the light intensity. There is thus a great complexity of electrical events within the retina itself and no simple correlation exists between the response of the receptors and that of the ganglion cells, *i.e.* the optic nerve fibres. Indeed, it is possible that no two optic nerve fibres will carry the same impulse pattern at any one time.

The eye differs from all other sense organs in that its first integrating centre—the retina—can move with the eye which, in fact, is never still even with a "fixed" gaze, and so it is in a more favourable position to deal with the "off/on" effects of the changing boundaries of light, shade, and colour which make up the world as we see it. Such "off/on" differentials seem to be required to give a proper image definition.

Stimulus and Impulse Frequency

In the invertebrate (ommatidium) eye the impulse frequency of a nerve fibre is found to vary more or less directly with the intensity of the stimulus and the state of adaptation. With short flashes of light the impulse frequency is influenced both by the duration of the flash and its intensity, *i.e.* the total photochemical change. This temporal summation only holds for periods of up to ·2 second. In the dark-adapted eye the same intensity produces a greater impulse frequency because, presumably, of the increased sensitivity. The impulse frequency is also affected by the light wavelength so that it is impossible for animals like *Limulus* (King crab) to "discriminate" colour on the basis of the impulse frequency rate of its optic nerve fibres.

In the vertebrate eye there is no direct relationship between stimulus intensity and impulse frequency of the optic nerve fibre as the discharge rate can be influenced by both visual and spectral sensitivity. In the dark-adapted eye, for example, it can be shown to be related to the absorption curve of rhodopsin, while in the light-adapted eye the same optic nerve fibre may have a different discharge rate corresponding to the change in visual sensitivity, thereby showing that it can serve both cone and rod receptors.

In the retina of both the frog and the cat it has been demonstrated experimentally that there are ganglion cells giving a maximum response in terms of impulse frequency to stimulation with light at λ 560 mμ, the so-called "photopic dominators"; others vary in their response pattern with the Purkinje shift of scotopic vision and there may be as many as four different impulse frequency rates which could be the result of integration within the neural layers of the retina of messages received from different kinds of photoreceptors.

It has been shown that there is a direct correlation of impulse frequency of the retinal elements and the critical fusion frequency (C.F.F.) (see later) and moreover it is known that the C.F.F. can be used as a measure of brightness.

Performance of the Eye

The efficiency of the eye as an optical device for recording visual events from light stimulation can be measured in terms of visual thresholds, visual acuity, and intensity discrimination.

Visual Threshold

The visual threshold is the least amount of light energy required to give rise to a visual sensation. Much of the light entering the eye is absorbed by its tissues or reflected back out again, and what matters in a visual sensation is the number of quanta of light absorbed by the photosensitive pigments. The lowest absolute threshold value is for light of λ 507 mμ in the dark-adapted eye, *i.e.* with scotopic vision, and thereafter the visual threshold level at any one time depends on (1) the state of adaptation of the eye, *i.e.* scotopic or photopic vision, (2) the wavelength of the stimulating light, (3) the part of the retina stimulated, and (4) the size and duration of the stimulus. Ideally, the absolute threshold should be expressed in numbers of absorbed light quanta, and it has been said that the total quanta absorbed by rhodopsin in order to see a flash of light is probably not more than fourteen. In terms of illumination the absolute threshold has been given as ·000,001 millilamberts, but this of course varies according to the extent of the retina stimulated and the duration of the stimulus, and one function of the retinal neural elements will obviously be to summate the effects of quanta absorption in space and time. It has been calculated, for example, that an image covering 1·5 cm.² of peripheral retina will fall on 20 million rods, and at absolute threshold such a field of rods will absorb only a total of 3500 quanta per second. Assuming that each light quantum acts on a single molecule of pigment and that the primary photochemical reaction lasts ·1 second, then if on a very dark night a rod absorbs one quantum of light every ten minutes it will be excited for only ·1 second every ten minutes. In full moonlight, 20,000 times brighter than absolute threshold, the rods absorb on average

4 quanta per second but the total amount of rhodopsin bleached is still surprisingly small—the figure given is ·015 per cent per hour. The extraordinary sensitivity of the eye can perhaps be more readily understood by the statement that given a perfectly transparent atmosphere, the light emitted by a standard candle would be visible at a distance of nearly a mile.

The threshold level rises very steeply from the green towards either end of the spectrum. In photopic cone vision the lowest threshold is obtained by stimulation of the fovea with light of around λ 550 mμ, *i.e.* the yellow-green part of the spectrum where, however, the eye may be as much as 100,000 times less sensitive than when fully dark-adapted. For monochromatic light the threshold level varies not only with the wavelength but, within limits, according to the size and duration of the stimulus. With small fields all the light falling within a given area and during a given time is summated up to a certain size of field which depends on the wavelength and the part of the retina on which the image falls.

Visual Acuity

Visual acuity is probably most commonly thought of as the ability to see very small objects representing the "minimum visible." Related to this, but of more practical importance, is the ability to see as separate objects two closely approximated points or parallel lines at a given distance from the eye, *e.g.* the letters of words in small print. This is the "minimum separable" or resolution (comparable to tactile discrimination) which

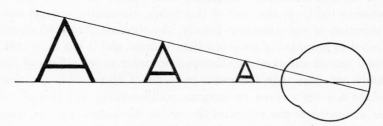

FIG. 5:15.   Visual acuity. (After Best & Taylor.)

enables us to see and distinguish the minute detail in our surroundings. It can be measured and is then expressed as the reciprocal of the angle subtended at the nodal point of the eye, viz. the visual angle, by the space between two points situated at the minimum distance apart at which they can just be distinguished as separate entities (Fig. 5:15). Stated in this way, resolution for the normal eye is about 1, which means that the average person can distinguish two separate points when the visual angle is 1 minute. When an object is moved away from the eye and its visual angle becomes progressively smaller, details of form and structure which could be discerned when they subtended an angle of a minute or more at the near point become gradually imperceptible. It is an everyday experience that in order to see an object at a distance as clearly as when it is near the eye it would need to be increased proportionately in size. A well-known eye test which is really a test of visual acuity is "Snellen's test type," in which the individual reads decreasing sizes of printed letters from a distance of six metres. Another target for testing visual acuity is a black "Landolt" ring with a gap equal to the thickness of the ring and about a fifth of its diameter.

"Scotopic Acuity": If a Landolt ring is situated in the middle of the visual field so that the gap subtends an angle of 1° at the eye, then at an illumination corresponding to ten times the absolute threshold specially trained subjects can detect the position of the gap in about 50 per cent of trials, although the light absorption per rod at this illumination is still only about ·002 quanta per second, *i.e.* one quantum every ten minutes, which is slightly lower than the absorption of light from a dark sky. In full moonlight the gap in the ring can be seen when it subtends an angle of only 3' at the eye. Acuity of rod vision depends on the degree of illumination. With, for instance, a flash of light there will be a random distribution of quanta absorbed and the brighter the flash the denser the distribution. With low illumination an object of diameter smaller than the mean distance between the absorbed quanta will naturally not be detected, and what determines the accuracy of vision is therefore the pattern of the quantum excitation of the retina, although one acting quantum is not sufficient to detect a light stimulus (as already noted a visual sensation requires the absorption of several quanta within a limited area of the retina and within a period of less than ·1 second). What is probably significant in the physiological summation of the effects of light quanta in the dark-adapted retina is not the single rod but rather the visual units or the receptive fields, each converging on one optic nerve fibre. It has been pointed out that one of the difficulties with absolute threshold experiments is the fact that the eye seldom "sees" absolute darkness and the visual field is filled with *"Eigenlicht,"* the eye's own light in the form of luminous clouds or "phosphenes," due possibly to spontaneous activity in the nerve fibres.

"Photopic Acuity": The maximum resolution of the eye in foveal vision and bright light is seven times greater than in full moonlight, corresponding to a gap subtending an angle of about 0·4', roughly the angular separation of the cones. Tactile discrimination is related to the spacing of the receptors, but in the retina there is no space between the receptors which are placed in contact with one another. With a visual

angle of 1′ the images of two points on the retina are about 4·5μ apart and would therefore be separated by at least one unstimulated cone receptor. This, however, for a number of reasons would seem to be an over-simplification of the problem. Even when staring fixedly at some object there are small imperceptible "saccadic" movements of the eye so that retinal images are moving to and fro over groups of from three to four receptors. It is possible to arrange experimental conditions whereby the retinal image remains fixed at one point on the retina, and with this unnatural immobility the image tends to fade and reappear alternately in whole or in part.

The maximum visual acuity or resolution is at the fovea which has the smallest receptive fields, i.e. ratio of receptors to optic nerve fibres, but there is no functional isolation of these receptive fields, and any single stimulus will initiate complex patterns of excitation and inhibition. The visual acuity at the extrafoveal retina is said to be much worse than would be expected from the quality of the projected retinal image having regard to the fineness of the pattern of the receptors, but with over a hundred million rods and cones converging onto one million optic fibres there are here relatively large receptive fields with, in consequence, some loss of detailed information. There is thus no ready and simple explanation of resolution at the level of receptor stimulation, and we cannot discount an essential contribution from more central visual neurons.

Resolution not only varies in different parts of the retina but also with intensity and wavelength of the light stimulus. Given, as is generally accepted, a more or less random distribution in the retina of photoreceptors of different threshold values, obviously at low intensity levels the stimulated receptors will tend to be farther apart, and thus the receptive surface will, under these conditions, act as a coarse-grained photographic plate capable of reproducing only limited detail. As the intensity increases more and more receptors become involved and the retina will now act as a fine-grained photographic plate and reproduce a more detailed picture. With vastly increased stimulus intensity giving an extremely high illumination, all the receptors will be stimulated to the maximum. There will no longer be any differential and the result is "glare" with an inability to distinguish objects clearly as, for example, with the dazzle of bright sunlight reflected from snow.

The resolving power of the eye is greater with monochromatic than with mixed light, probably due to the absence of chromatic aberration. The best resolution is obtained in photopic vision with yellow light (λ 575 mμ) and the worst with blue light, very likely because of the much larger receptive field of the blue mechanism and its low sensitivity at the fovea.

Intensity Discrimination (ΔI)

The eye, like other sense organs, not only gives information about the intensity of stimulation which in general we appreciate as degrees of brightness, but can also discern differences in stimulus intensity and recognise the brighter of two objects. Because it has both scotopic and photopic vision and so adapts to wide variations of illumination, the eye can detect stimulus differences through a remarkable range of light intensities. The dark-adapted eye (scotopic vision) deals with a level of illumination below ·01 millilamberts, while the light-adapted eye (photopic vision) can detect differences with light stimuli several million times stronger. The Weber fraction $\Delta I/I$ representing the incremental ratio for just noticeable differences is only approximately applicable to vision. At the lowest intensities the Weber fraction is around 1, while at the highest intensities it is as little as $\frac{1}{167}$, and this would suggest that although the rods have a very much lower threshold, the cones are more sensitive to actual differences in illumination.

There is no direct relation of stimulus intensity to brightness, and equal intensities of light of different wavelengths are not equally bright. Our assessment of the brightness of some object is affected by the content of the visual field, both the background and other objects. A black background makes a white object brighter, and grey is darker against a white than against a black background. The state of adaptation of the eye, *i.e.* its immediate past experiences, can also influence the quality of brightness. With coloured lights brightness contrast is often accompanied by colour contrasts; a grey on a coloured background becomes tinged with the hue complementary to the background colour so that against a green background it looks quite different from grey against a red background.

Binocular Vision

What is seen of the external world with one eye (monocular vision) constitutes its visual field. The visual field is not flat, but is a section of a hollow sphere corresponding to the bowl-shaped surface of the retina and its dimensions are referred to in terms of the angle it subtends, viz. 160° in the horizontal and 145° in the vertical meridian. Owing to the shadow of the nose the visual field has a smaller nasal and a larger temporal "half." Light from the temporal half of the visual field falls on the nasal half of the retina and vice versa (Fig. 5:7). In most individuals the two eyes are not equal in every respect and near objects, for instance, are lined up with reference to one eye—"sighting dominance." This can be demonstrated by closing each eye in turn when the object shifts when the dominant eye is closed. There is also acuity dominance, and in a high

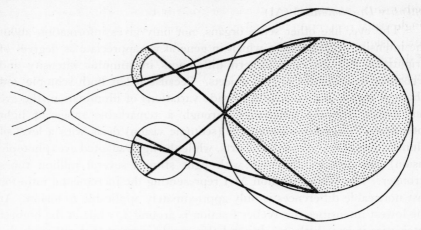

FIG. 5:16. Showing monocular and binocular fields of vision.

proportion of individuals the left eye is both sighting and acuity dominant.
Every student learns that the field in a monocular microscope is brighter
for one eye.

In most animals there is some overlap between the two visual fields,
attaining a maximum in Man and monkeys where the eyes are situated in
front and not at the sides of the head so that only a small part of the outer
quadrant of each field of vision is monocular (Fig. 5:16). The light from
points of the large binocular "overlap" will fall on opposite halves of the
two retinae, *e.g.* the temporal half of one and the nasal half of the other
(Fig. 5:17), so that each point
on the temporal half of one
retina (or fovea) will correspond to a point on the nasal
half of the other retina. With
the crossing of the optic nerve
fibres at the chiasma the impulses from corresponding
retinal points will convey a
combined pattern of impulses
and activate adjacent areas of
the same visual cortex, to-

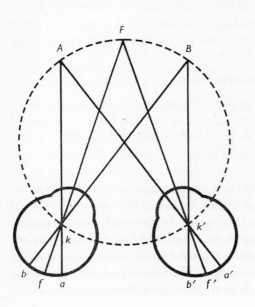

FIGURE 5:17
To show corresponding retinal
points. (After Best & Taylor.)

gether with the respective monocular contributions. The "fusion" into a single visual perception takes place in the brain, as it also does with monocular vision when each side of the brain is activated by the respective halves of the retina. If, for some reason or other, for instance paralysis of an ocular muscle, the two eyes are "lined up," differently as in squinting, and the

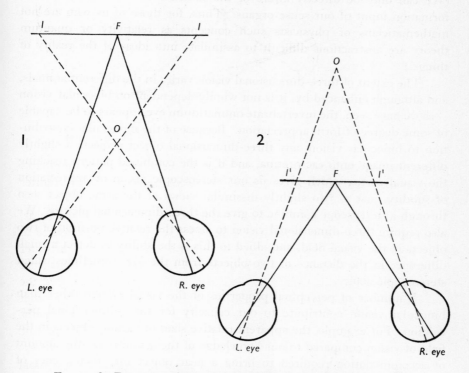

FIG. 5:18. Demonstrating physiological diplopia from the projection of retinal images falling on non corresponding points of the retina, i.e. on different sides of the fovea.
1 : With eyes fixated at distant point F, nearer object O can be seen double at I—crossed diplopia.
2 : With eyes fixated at near point F, more distant object O can be seen double at I'—uncrossed diplopia.

images do not fall on the corresponding retinal points, this will cause some conflict of information reaching the brain, subjectively interpreted as two images, i.e. double vision or diplopia (Fig. 5:18). Binocular rivalry occurs when different visual fields, e.g. different in colour, are presented separately but simultaneously to each eye and instead of a single fused image there is an alternation of the image or the persistence of one to the exclusion of the other, e.g. looking down a monocular microscope with both eyes open.

Three-Dimensional Vision

To frame visual concepts of space, solidity, depth perception, to judge distance, size, velocity, etc., and so obtain the maximum information about our world and its events, we need to be able to "see" in three dimensions. (We can only be directly aware of the dimensions scanned by the information input of our sense organs. Thus, for those of us who are not mathematicians or physicists such concepts as relativity or quantum theory are abstractions difficult to assimilate into ideas of the reality of things.)

The extent of three-dimensional vision varies in the different animals, and although enhanced by, it is not wholly dependent on binocular vision —as we have seen, the invertebrate ommatidium eye appears to be capable of some degree of form appreciation. Because of the monocular contribution to binocular vision, any three-dimensional object projects a slightly different image onto each retina, and it is the combined pattern reaching the visual cortex which gives us our stereoscopic vision or appreciation of solidity, just as two slightly dissimilar views of the same object seen through a stereoscope combine to give the three-dimensional picture. We also require three-dimensional vision to assess the relative position of two objects in the visual field, and allied to this is the ability to detect a small difference in the distance of two objects from the eye, sometimes called stereoscopic acuity.

A number of perceptual properties of the visual system other than binocular vision contribute to our capacity for three-dimensional perception. For example, the apparent relative sizes of various objects in the field of vision compared to our knowledge of the actual sizes; the amount of accommodation required to bring a near object into focus; cues of colour and shadow in relation to relief and distance; linear perspective, by which is meant the fact that parallel lines receding into the distance appear to converge, e.g. looking down a long stretch of railway track (the artist gives depth to his picture by drawing objects in this way); and parallax, the known experience that if an observer moves, near objects appear to move in the opposite direction while those in the background move in the same direction.

Unlike the young of many species the human infant is not born ready for independent existence and few, if any, of the sense organs perform their "adult" task at birth. This immaturity also applies in some measure to vision, in particular three-dimensional vision, and the perception of form and depth improves with practice and experience. The "Gestalt" theory of psychology assumes that Man is born with an innate ability to recognise form, e.g. circles, triangles, or cubes, and that it is in fact part of his visual heritage, but there is the contrary opinion that the infant has to learn about form, building up the more complicated from the simple in the same way as words are built up from speech sounds. Recent work suggests that the right answer incorporates something of both points of view: that Man in fact has a certain innate ability to use his three-dimensional vision, and that the human infant can, to some extent, use not only physiological but such psychological cues as linear perspective and parallax well enough for the recognition at an early stage of those forms significant for survival, for example, the form of the human face, just as chickens immediately after hatching peck at food particles. There is no doubt, however, that time and experience are required for the development of the full potential of three-dimensional vision and that we have to learn, for example, the significance of the distribution of light and shadow in the recognition of relief, intaglio (depressions), and curves.

Perception of Movement

We have all had the experience of gazing at an object and at the same time being aware of something moving "out of the corner of the eye." The extrafoveal or peripheral retina is particularly sensitive to movement, and as long as any vision remains we have movement perception. The readiest explanation of our sense of movement is the successive stimulation of receptors leaving a trail of "on/off" discharges which give some indication of direction and total displacement. This would certainly account for the apparent movement of external objects when the observer is stationary in a travelling train, but it does not explain all the aspects of movement perception. We are not only conscious of movement when the eyes are stationary and the image moves across the retina, but also when the eye follows the moving object so that its image remains fixed on the fovea. Here, perception of movement is obviously influenced by the rotation of the head. On the other hand, when the gaze is changed from one object to another the image of intervening objects sweeps across the retina, but there is no sense of movement. Obviously, the interpretation of movement is not wholly based on the simple mechanics of events at the periphery, but involves activation of the brain by a certain spatio/temporal pattern of impulses such as can be produced experimentally, for instance, by stimulating the retina alternately with one of two targets separated by a certain distance and at certain time intervals. The avian eye has a pleated projection from the retina—the pecten—which it is believed increases the sensitivity to small moving shadows. If this be so, it would certainly be a useful contribution to the panoramic avian vision which dominates the sensory input in the bird.

There are many examples of optical illusions of movement, *i.e.* apparent or paradoxical movement. For example, after looking at a continuously moving object—a waterfall or out of a train window—and then transferring the gaze to a stationary object, this will appear to move in the opposite direction with the same speed, although nothing actually changes in position, or again, when the eye is following a moving object the stationary background appears to move in the opposite direction. The normal small saccadic jerks of the eye which occur at the rate of about four per second do not cause any sensation of movement. Indeed, individuals who, because of muscular paralysis, have lost their saccadic jerks are conscious of the movement of static objects in their visual field. A number of alternative and in part psychological theories have recently been advanced to explain this relation of eye movements to the stability of objects in the visual field.

Flicker

The ability to distinguish between an intermittent and a steady stimulus is found in many animals including the arthropods and crustaceans. If the retina is stimulated intermittently by flashes of light at a certain rate of stimulation there is a sensation of flicker, but if the number of flashes per second is increased beyond a certain frequency the discontinuous sensation becomes continuous. This is known as the Critical Fusion Frequency (C.F.F.). The rather unpleasant flicker effect is said to be due to each flash falling upon the retina along with the positive after-image (see p. 182) of the preceding stimulus. This causes an abrupt cessation of the first sensation and, by contrast, a more brilliant succeeding sensation. A common method of producing intermittent stimulation which provides a useful test for some aspects of visual function is the interruption of a steady light by a rotating sectored disc with equal open and closed parts where the number of flashes per second can be controlled by increasing or decreasing the speed of rotation. The C.F.F. varies with the light intensity, the stimulus size and, to a lesser extent, with the light wavelength, and also tends to vary under standard conditions in the same individual from time to time. It ranges from a figure of 15 per sec. with low intensity stimulation up to 60 per sec. with high intensity stimulation. As the C.F.F. is, within certain limits, directly proportional to the logarithm of the light intensity, it can be used experimentally as an accurate method of comparing the brightness of differently coloured lights. At the C.F.F. the level of perceived brightness is less than that from continuous stimulation by light of the same intensity. Known as the Talbot effect, this indicates that the brain is averaging the amount of total illumination received during the light and dark intervals; with a white sector the resultant sensation at the C.F.F. might be some shade of grey, or with alternate sectors of red and white the sensation at the C.F.F. would be pink.

Colour

Colour is a sensation,[1] *i.e.* it is a product of the activity of the nervous system and is not an inherent property of the radiant energy of the visible spectrum. Animals without the necessary sensory and neural apparatus have no colour vision, and those with a coneless retina, for example, look out on a world of uniform grey. Colour vision occurs widely throughout the animal kingdom, *e.g.* bees, butterflies, some fishes, amphibia, some reptiles, and birds, but very few mammals outside the primates. The colour mechanism is not necessarily the same in all animals. Pigeons and chickens have coloured oil droplets in their cone segments, and there is evidence that these colour droplets alter the spectral sensitivity of the cone pigment sufficiently to provide a basis for colour vision.

Colour Mixtures

If the light reflected from a coloured surface is analysed with a spectrometer it may be found to be a mixture of colours of different wavelengths, and in this case what we see as a single colour is the result of a stimulus input with ingredients from many spectral regions. It is known that any spectral colour (one estimate is that there are around 300 of them) and also white, can be matched by combining different amounts of light from the long, *e.g.* 650 mμ (red), middle, *e.g.* 530 mμ (green), and short, *e.g.* 460 mμ (blue) wavelength regions of the spectrum. Red, green, and blue are therefore termed the primary colours. A number, but not all of the spectral colours can be matched by a combination of two colours. For example, a red (λ 671 mμ) plus a green (λ 560 mμ) will yield a spectral yellow of λ 589 mμ. If the two lights are from widely separated parts of the spectrum their combination produces white light, *e.g.* yellow of λ 580 mμ plus blue of λ 479 mμ, and they are termed complementary colours. In any set of three primary colours, however, no single one of them can be formed by a mixture of the other two.

Mixtures of spectral colours can be experimentally produced by the use of filters or rotating discs. To obtain a match in brightness as well as in hue, it is necessary to have the correct amounts of radiant energy of each of the primary colours, and this can be expressed as $aC = xB + yG + zR$,

[1] This statement raises certain philosophical questions which are discussed on pp. 301-2.

where x, y, and z are the amount of the primary colours and add up to a, the amount of brightness of the perceived colour. With different sets of primaries (from the same general regions of the spectrum) there are correspondingly different values for x, y, and z. All spectral colours can now be specified as amounts of the three primary colours and charts have been constructed, for instance the C.I.E. chart, from which any colour can be "read off" as so much red, green, and blue light. Colour mixtures with spectral lights are therefore additive and provided that the stimulation of the receptors adds up to the same answer in terms of the total impulse response, the same colour is seen. For instance, equal amounts of red, green, and blue give the same receptor response as the whole spectrum, and thus a white sensation.

Pigment mixtures, on the other hand, are subtractive, and yellow, which is not a primary spectral colour, is a primary pigment colour. A yellow pigment appears yellow because it absorbs much of the blue light of the spectrum, reflecting the yellow, green and red—the green and red combining in the eye to become yellow. A blue pigment, on the other hand, absorbs all the red and yellow light of the spectrum. Thus, when yellow and blue pigments are mixed, the only light left unabsorbed to be reflected is green. A mixture of spectral yellow and spectral blue, however, adds up to white.

Colour Qualities

We are aware of three qualities of colour—brightness, hue, and saturation.

Brighter light, we normally assume, means more light and more intense stimulation. Given equal amounts of energy of lights of different wavelength, however, they are not necessarily equally bright. Blue (λ 477 mμ), for example, has a low luminosity or brightness compared to green (λ 530 mμ), and luminosity plotted against the wavelength is not a straight line but a "photopic luminosity curve." The more light quanta absorbed, the greater the photochemical reaction and the brighter the sensation. Basically what matters, therefore, is the number of quanta of different light wavelengths absorbed by the respective photosensitive pigments.

Hue is how we describe the sensation experienced from stimulation by light of various light wavelengths, e.g. red for long, blue for short, and green for the middle wavelength etc. Except for one or two fixed points on the spectrum, hue is to a limited extent influenced by stimulus intensity and most colours on being brightened shift slightly towards either the yellow or the blue. For example, it is necessary to increase the wavelength of brightened red and decrease the wavelength of brightened green in order to retain the original hue, one aspect of the so-called Bezold-Brücke effect. Hue discrimination (λΔ) as distinct from intensity discrimination (ΔI) is a measure of the capacity of the eye to detect changes in wavelength in terms of changes in colour. Passing through the spectrum there are said to be around 150 just noticeable differences but these are not equally spaced throughout the spectrum. For example, yellow changes to orange with a difference of λ 10 mμ, but there is very little change of hue between λ 460 mμ and λ 470 mμ, *i.e.* the hue discrimination is low with the short wavelength and increases with the longer wavelength light.

Saturation of a colour implies its purity in the sense that it is not diluted with white light, and in this respect might be compared with pure tones. Red, for example, is more saturated than pink and in general the colours at either end of the spectrum are the most saturated.

Colour Vision Theories

Trichromatic

Although today colour mixing is an applied science of some importance, the physiological processes involved in colour vision at the different levels of the visual apparatus still present a problem. As all the colours we see can be produced by mixtures of not more than three spectral colours it is logical to assume that a three-colour (trichromatic) mechanism can provide the visual apparatus with the necessary items of information for colour discrimination. The simplest model of such a trichromatic system would have three visual pigments, each with a different absorption maximum (λ max) (Fig. 5:19), *i.e.* specific spectral response, in three types of receptor each sending out messages along three separate channels to the brain. We can all, however, name not just three but a dozen or more main colours and numerous shades of colour so that assuming, as the trichromatic theory does, that light stimuli are in the first instance converted by the visual receptors into electrical activity denoting a ratio of the three variables, there must be a further treatment by the neural apparatus of this preliminary sorting out of the stimulus input to give the information required for our range of colour discrimination. Thus, whereas the cochlea sorts out the frequency items of the sound stimuli and so codes an extensive range of "variables" the photoreceptors pass on to the visual neurons information with regard to only three main variables.

Although it has been said that "even today no one can say with complete certainty that he has ever had a cone pigment in a test tube" there is indirect evidence, from experimental procedures involving the spectral analysis of the light reflected from the retina of living individuals, of the existence of visual pigments with different absorption maxima. For example, there would seem to be, at any rate in the cones of the fovea, a red-sensitive pigment (erythrolabe) and a green-sensitive pigment (chlorolabe), presumably giving the photochemical responses for two of the primary colours, the red and green mechanisms. There are, indeed, indications that only two types of receptor normally function at the fovea and that here colour matches are dichromatic, *i.e.* based on mixtures of

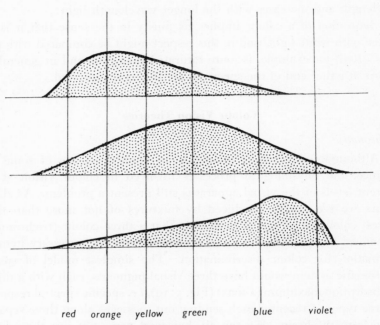

red   orange   yellow   green   blue   violet

FIG. 5:19.   Diagram to illustrate the sensitivity of the three primary colour receptors (after Helmholtz).

two colours. So far there is no experimental evidence for the existence of a blue mechanism at the fovea, but blue is known to have a very large receptive field, probably due to the convergence of numbers of blue receptors onto one optic nerve fibre, and any light experimentally confined to the fovea is necessarily limited to a very small area.

Man has evolved from nocturnal ancestors, and over the greater part of the human retina there are still many more rods than cones. Despite the fact, therefore, that scotopic vision is colourless it is not surprising that the rods, as the retina's most abundant receptor, have been considered possible contributors to colour vision, particularly with regard to the blue mechanism, and this is encouraged by a number of observations:

1. Unlike the red and green mechanism blue operates far forwards

on the retina and because of its widespread distribution it is thus often the first colour to be affected in disease of the retina.

2. Twilight vision has a quality of blueness about it.

3. There are two kinds of rods in the frog's retina, purple rods and green rods.

The unanswerable argument against the implication of rods in colour vision is its incompatibility with the spectral sensitivity of rhodopsin.

Opponens-Pairs

A modification of a straightforward trichromatic theory of colour vision is what is known as the opponens-pairs theory (Hering theory) (Fig. 5:20). This still assumes the existence of three kinds of photo-sensitive material but the final messages sent out by the retina are based on three paired processes—red/green, yellow/blue, and white/black. These processes are regarded as opposite and antagonistic so that the response must be either red or green, blue or yellow, black or white, and there is no sensation which could be properly described as greenish red or bluish yellow; rather the binary combinations would be a fusion of members of different pairs, greens and blues, or yellows and greens. Black and white are thus mutually antagonistic and in the absence of any external stimulus it is assumed that the visual system is in a condition of equilibrium associated with a neutral grey sensation.

Many psychophysical phenomena show a clear linkage between colour pairs and find a ready explanation in terms of this opponens-pairs theory, for example, the predominance of red and green with low luminosity while yellow and blue increase with increase in luminance (Bezold-Brücke phenomenon); the so-called foveal tritanopia, viz. as stimulus size diminishes discrimination between yellow and blue becomes progressively worse than that between red and green. Again, colour vision can gradually be put out of action experimentally by using excessively high stimulus intensities. The course of events is, first, the green drops out completely and is replaced by white, then the red becomes a brilliant yellow, and lastly the whole spectrum appears white, except a blue tinge at the short and a yellow tinge at the long wavelength ends. Thus, the blue/yellow system appears to remain long after the red/green has disappeared. On the basis of such experiments it is assumed that there is a stable primordial blue/yellow system and a secondary, less stable, red/green system.

The concept of an opponens-pairs mechanism certainly fits in with the current knowledge of the electrophysiology of the visual neurons. Any optic nerve fibre or ganglion cell, for example, may have both "off" and "on" phases of discharge with electrical changes of opposite sign which will thus be mutually inhibitory.

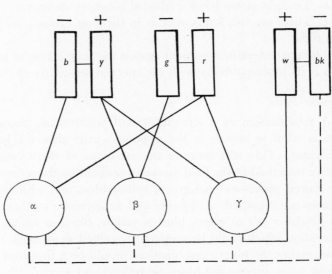

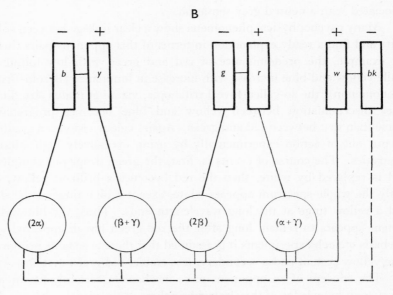

FIG. 5:20. Illustrating possible working schemes for an opponens-pairs theory with three photosensitive materials (α, β, γ) in separate retinal units as in A, or with two or more combined in a single receptor unit as in B.

Dominator Modulator

A more objective approach to the problem of colour vision is the investigation of the impulse responses of the ganglion cells or optic nerve fibres to stimulation of the retina with light of different wavelengths. It has been shown, for example, that a number of retinal elements respond to a broad range of spectral colours. The function of such elements, named photopic dominators, is to make a large range of wavelengths available for vision. Other retinal elements respond only to specific wavelengths. These are named modulators, and their activity is interpreted to mean that they act as wavelength discriminators. In the dark-adapted eye there is only one type of response, that of the scotopic dominator whose activity corresponds to the scotopic visibility curve.

Psychological

In everyday situations the visual field is a complex one and has to be interpreted in terms of colour interactions. It has been pointed out that such interactions contribute differences which are of significance in perception and that a particular colour quality is probably determined by a particular state of the nervous system rather than by the activity of one neural element. There is indeed psychological justification for maintaining that the quality of a particular colour sensation represents a state of sensory equilibrium varying from time to time with the actual stimulus input, just as our appreciation of what constitutes silence depends on the general level of background noise at any particular time.

Evidence has recently been put forward which seemed to provide strong support for a dichromatic interpretation of colour vision (Land's theory) but this has not found general acceptance, and a satisfactory explanation of the subjective phenomenon on which this theory is based can be given within the established facts of three primary colour mixtures.

From this brief survey of what is known about how the visual apparatus produces colour vision from light stimuli, it will be apparent that the problem is far from solved, and there is still no single theory that supplies the answer to all the facts of colour perception.

Colour Blindness

There is, of course, individual variation in detailed colour discrimination and appreciation, so that in any group of people there are likely to be small differences in the matching of two colours, and of course we all have our personal preferences in colour. As distinct from these individual characteristics, there are defects which amount to blindness in respect of one or more colours. Colour blindness can result from injury or disease, but is more commonly a hereditary disease and, like haemophilia, is a sex-linked inheritance. This means that, with the odd exception, it is the males who are colour blind (about 8 per cent of males compared to less than $\frac{1}{2}$ per cent of females have some colour abnormality) and they have inherited this defect from the mother who, as a general rule, has herself no colour abnormality but is "carrying" a genetic defect received from a colour-blind father. The fact that we give the same name to the sensation caused by light of specific wavelengths does not necessarily mean that we all have the same "experience," and an inherited colour defect may only be exposed after positive tests for colour matching. Colour blindness can be broadly grouped under the following headings: (1) Monochromasia with total colour blindness, (2) Dichromasia with defects at some part of the spectrum leaving colour discrimination dependent on two primary mechanisms, (3) Anomalous trichromasia with some weakness in respect of a particular region of the spectrum.

1. *Monochromasia*: This is a rare form of colour blindness and only a few cases have been studied in any detail. Monochromats have no colour vision and see everything in terms of grey. Although they can see in daylight their visibility curve is more scotopic than photopic, and in most cases there is greatly reduced visual acuity.

2. *Dichromasia*: There are two main groups—red/green blindness and blue/yellow blindness. By far the most common type of colour blindness is a red/green defect, with inability to distinguish between red and green. There are two types of dichromatic red/green blindness; (*a*) protanopia where the red end of the spectrum is shortened and consequently seen mainly as black, and the maximum spectral sensitivity has shifted towards the blue, and (*b*) deuteranopia where there is also confusion of red and green because both are seen as yellow. Both protanopes and deuteranopes are colour-blind at the fovea and see the whole spectrum in shades of blue and yellow.

Tritanopia, or yellow/blue blindness, is a relatively rare condition and occasionally occurs following injury or disease of the visual apparatus. Tritanopes have a characteristic confusion of blue and yellow. Their colour spectrum is largely red and green or greenish red, and thus corresponds to foveal colour vision. As already mentioned, some degree of physiological tritanopia is normal and there tends to be loss of discrimination between yellow and blue at the fovea as the size of the stimulus decreases.

3. *Anomalous Trichromats*: There is a variety of minor forms of colour blindness, many of them with poor discrimination between reds and greens but with no absolute loss of red or green sensitivity. Such minor defects are fairly common throughout the population and quite

widespread differences exist in matching, for example, spectral yellow by a mixture of red and green—the so-called Rayleigh match.

While many of the observed facts of colour blindness can be in part explained on the basis of a trichromatic mechanism, the colour linkage which is prominent in the dichromats—red/green or yellow/blue— certainly suggests some functional association of these colour pairs within the visual apparatus.

After Images

The visual sensation invariably lags behind any brief light stimulus, sometimes imperceptibly, but under certain conditions for a matter of minutes when it is known as the "after image." After images are classified as (a) positive, and (b) negative.

(a) When the eyes are closed following a brief intense stimulation, e.g. a glance at strong sunlight, a positive after image resembling the first stimulus in colour and shape may persist, or sometimes there is a succession of colour contrasts. Provided the total amount of the light stimulus, i.e. intensity/duration, is equal the after images are exactly the same whether the stimulus is delivered within a fraction of a second or distributed over two seconds, and this would suggest that such after images are due to the persistence of photochemical activity.

(b) If, instead of closing the eyes, they are directed to a brightly illuminated surface, there appears against this white background a dark image. If the first stimulus is a coloured light, then the image is its complementary colour, e.g. green or red, blue or yellow. This is a negative after image. By projecting a negative after image onto its complementary colour, extremely vivid saturated colours can be obtained. These negative after images not only move with the eyes but alter in size with a change in fixation from near to far vision. There is no entirely satisfactory explanation of negative after images, but they provide a further demonstration of a linkage factor in colour vision.

Central Mechanism of Vision

All but a fifth of the fibres of the optic nerve terminate in the lateral geniculate body. The remainder, as already noted, end in the midbrain region and are concerned with the reflex control of the size of the pupil and the movements of the eyeballs.

Lateral Geniculate Bodies

Each optic nerve fibre synapses with a group of cells although, due to the complexity of the arrangements within the lateral geniculate body, any one cell is probably affected by impulses from a number of fibres so that a given territory can be influenced by adjacent retinal points in addition to those projecting directly onto it. It has been said that the number of fibres entering the lateral geniculate body is greater than the number leaving it, but the margin of error involved in counting nerve fibres and the possible variation from individual to individual invalidates any assumption of convergence of visual function at this level. The stratification of the geniculate body in Man and monkey into six layers of cells is associated with their large binocular fields and the projection of corresponding retinal points through the crossed and uncrossed fibres onto alternate layers.

Although it is known that monkeys, for example, can still respond to light stimulation after removal of the visual cortex, this does not tell us very much about the function of the lateral geniculate body in normal monkeys or normal Man. As elsewhere in the visual pathways there are elements responding to the onset of stimulation ("on" cells), to the cessation of stimulation ("off" cells) and to both onset and cessation ("off/on" cells) and these tend to occur in groups within the cell layers. Of more significance, there are cells or groups of cells with peak responses to particular light wavelengths and cells that give "on" responses to one primary colour, e.g. blue, and "off" responses to its complementary colour, yellow. It is obvious, therefore, from its complex structure and organisation that the lateral geniculate body does something more than passively relay the information received via the optic tract, and that in some way or another what is passed on to the brain differs from what is received from the retina, in particular concerning the messages sent out by the photo-receptors to indicate light of specific wavelength.

The Visual Cortex

Visual experience, i.e. conscious seeing, arises from the activity within the visual cortex where the optic pathways terminate. Visual sensations can also be elicited by experimental electrical stimulation of quite wide areas of the cortex, the so-called visual association areas, presumably implicated in the imagery which dominates so much of our mental processes. The central mechanisms of vision, as distinct from the eye as a peripheral photoreceptor, are concerned with the correlation of items of perceptual experience with the different dimensions of the light stimulus, intensive, spatial, temporal, and spectral, i.e. degrees of bright-ness, location or shape of objects, movement and discontinuous stimulation, and colour vision.

Destruction of the entire cortex of one side results in blindness of the opposite field of vision—homonymous hemianopia. An individual may, however, be unaware of quite large visual defects which can be compensated for by movements of the eyes, or subjectively by unconsciously filling in to complete a visual perception; indeed, we normally do this with familiar objects which we can recognise from a fleeting glimpse of a small part.

As in the lateral geniculate body, particular areas of the cortex respond maximally to light stimulation of specific areas of the retina and, as the fibres of the optic pathway conveying messages from corresponding points in the two retinae terminate in adjacent areas of the cortex, localised injuries to the visual cortex cause defects in the right or left visual fields respectively.

Electroencephalogram (E.E.G.)

As would be expected from the complex arrangements (cytoarchitecture), number, and varieties of the cells involved, the electrical response of the visual cortex to light stimulation is both more complicated and prolonged than elsewhere in the optic pathways. The impulse patterns conveyed from the retina along the optic pathways are fed into a visual cortex, which has its own spontaneous activity in the form of the rhythmic changes in electrical potential which are widespread throughout the cerebral cortex and can be recorded as the electroencephalogram (E.E.G.). Something is known about the nature of this spontaneous activity and how it is affected by light stimulation or by experimental stimulation of the optic pathways, and here and there it has been possible to link particular visual phenomena with particular patterns of cortical activity. In the "resting" visual cortex when the eyes are shut its electrical activity, known as the alpha rhythm, consists of oscillation of potential of about 50 millivolts occurring every ten seconds. In contrast to the all or none impulses generated by the axon of a neuron there is, as we have seen, a graded response of the dendrites which can sustain activity and act like a steady current stimulus, lowering the threshold and favouring repetitive discharge of the neuron. It is therefore probable that the duration and extent of the waves of potential in the cortex are influenced by the extensive ramification of the dendrites of its cells. When the eyes are opened and the cortex is presumably excited, the alpha rhythm becomes broken up.

Colour

While we have an accurate knowledge of the anatomy of the visual cortex, including precise details of the projection of the retina, we have still a great deal to learn about the kind of information brought to the visual cortex with respect to colour vision, brightness, binocular vision, etc. Although many vertebrate eyes are in structure like the human eyes and capable therefore of a differentiated response to spectral light, it does not follow, indeed it is unlikely, that they have the colour experience of Man which requires a visual cortex capable of analysing the different messages sent through from the retina. The response of the cells in the visual cortex of the monkey to electrical stimulation of the optic nerve or following light stimulation of the retina have been reported and indicate that (1) the single cortical cell can respond to stimulation of the optic nerve both at threshold and at high intensity, which would seem to indicate that one cortical cell can be activated more or less directly from one ganglion cell and that there is no convergence on the cortical cells, but rather divergence from retina to cortex. This need not imply that under "natural" conditions messages are necessarily transmitted unchanged from retina to cortex or that meaningful signals would not evoke characteristic responses; (2) cells in the visual cortex respond to stimulation of the retina by monochromatic light, for example, there are red "modulator" cells, and moreover such cells can respond to monochromatic stimulation of either retina. There is, however, no evidence of a spatial organisation of colour, i.e. groups of neurons with the same spectral sensitivity like the columns of cortical cells for the separate cutaneous modalities, or the tonal bands of the auditory cortex, but rather adjacent cells can respond to different colours. This may in part explain one outstanding difference between hearing and seeing. The trained ear can analyse vibration and perceive the different tones in a complex sound, whereas stimulated by a mixture of the appropriate red and green lights the eye sees only one colour, viz. yellow. There is a fairly wide range in the arrival time at the cortex of impulses travelling over long distances at relatively low velocities, and it has been suggested that conduction velocity could be an additional factor in colour discrimination at cortical level.

It is known that in the dark-adapted eye, i.e. scotopic vision, there is a time frequency distribution of discharge pattern according to the wavelength of the stimulating light. For instance, with λ 600 mμ the peak frequency is attained at ·03 seconds, with λ 520 mμ at ·17 seconds, and with λ 460 mμ at ·24 seconds after stimulation, and that this time frequency factor is incorporated in the information passed on to the cortical cells where it might provide one item in the coding for colour discrimination in photopic vision. An interesting finding in such experiments was that at ·03 seconds (with a peak frequency for red) there was a secondary peak for violet light, interesting because we see the short-wave violet as a mixture of red and blue.

Brightness

Brightness is the quality we ascribe to the appearance of the stimulating "target" and is thus different from energy "flux," which implies the total illumination entering the eye which will, within certain limits, depend on the size of the stimulating target and the duration of the stimulus. Thus, a small area may at any one time appear brighter than a larger area, although the total flux is less. Monkeys whose visual pathways have been experimentally destroyed and prevented from projecting onto the cortex are capable of appreciating total flux differences at the level of the lateral geniculate body, but not differences in brightness, which would therefore appear to be a cortical function. In general, the more intense the stimulus the greater the number of impulses generated in any one conducting unit. As we have seen, however, impulse frequency coding is also involved in intermittent and monochromatic stimulation. Thus, as with loudness (although perhaps to a lesser extent) there is no unique correlation between the number of impulses reaching the visual cortex in unit of time and our appreciation of degrees of brightness. It has, however, been possible to correlate, for example, points on the scotopic visibility curve as determined by the impulse frequency of retinal units with psychophysical measurements of brightness. This means that the cortex can average out from the messages sifted through the complex retinal and geniculate neurons something indicating the extent of the photochemical reaction to the stimulus.

Critical Fusion Frequency (C.F.F.)

The determination of the C.F.F. is at cortical level. During "flicker" the activity in the optic nerve waxes and wanes with sufficient amplitude and at such rates that the cortical activity must also be affected, but because of the more sustained nature of its non-decremental activity it is doubtful if the cortex can respond at the same rate as the peripheral mechanism. What evidence there is indicates that while the alpha rhythm of the cortex can be driven to some extent by intermittent stimulation, the main effect is on the amplitude of the waves of cortical activity which tends to decrease as the frequency of stimulation is increased. Thus, the amplitude at a stimulation rate of 20 per second is half that when the rate is 10 per second, and twice that when the rate is 40 per second. Obviously, at the C.F.F. the nature of cortical activity resembles its response to a continuous stimulation.

Brightness Enhancement

Intermittent stimulation below the C.F.F. may be more effective than steady stimulation of similar intensity in producing brightness (this should not be confused with the Talbot effect at or over the C.F.F.). This is known as brightness enhancement and in Man has its maximum effect at the stimulation rate of 10 per second. This perceptual phenomenon has been correlated with studies of the effect of intermittent stimulation of the optic nerve on the activity of the visual cortex. It is known that following stimulation of the optic nerve at a rate corresponding to the alpha rhythm there is increased amplitude of the electrical responses in the cortex, whereas with a more continuous stimulation there is a shift of the cortical rhythm with, as we have seen, a tendency to decreased amplitude.

Despite the steadily increasing reports and records of the electrical activity of the visual cortex under different experimental conditions it seems very doubtful if we can ever hope to achieve anything like a complete link-up between its physiological and psychological functions, and even if we do it may only emphasise, as has been suggested, that it is at present meaningless to ask ourselves how these material processes are translated into conscious psychological units.

BIBLIOGRAPHY

BARTLEY, H. S. 1959. Central mechanisms of vision. *Handbook of Physiology*, **1**, Sec. 1. Amer. Soc. Physiol., Washington, D.C.

BEST, C. H. and TAYLOR, N. B. 1961. *The Physiological Basis of Medical Practice.* 7th Edn. Baillière, Tindall and Cox, London.

BRINDLEY, C. S. 1960. *Physiology of the Retina and Visual Pathways*. Edward Arnold, London.

CLARK, W. E. LE GROS. 1949. The laminar pattern of the lateral geniculate nucleus considered in relation to colour vision. *Docum. opthal.*, **3**, 57.

DUKE-ELDER, Sir S. 1961. *Anatomy of the Visual Pathways. System of Ophthalmology*, Vol. II. Henry Kimpton, London.

FRY, G. A. 1959. Image-forming mechanism of the eye. *Handbook of Physiology*, **1**, Sec. 1. Amer. Physiol. Soc., Washington, D.C.

GALIFRET, Y. (Ed.). 1960. *Mechanisms of Colour Discrimination*. Pergamon Press, London.

GRANIT, R. 1955. *Receptors and Sensory Perception*. Oxford University Press, London.

MANN, I. and PIRIE, A. 1946. *Science and Hearing*. Pelican Books, London.

PIRENNE, M. H. 1961. Light quanta and vision. *Endeavour*, **20**, 80.

PIRIE, A. 1958. The biochemistry of the eye related to its optical properties. *Endeavour*, **17**, 68.

SMELSER, G. K. (Ed.). 1961. *The Structure of the Eye*. Academic Press, New York and London.

STYLES, W. S. 1952. Colour vision, a retrospect. *Endeavour*, **11**, 33.

WALD, G. 1953. *Eye and Camera. Scientific American Reader*. Simon and Schuster, New York.

——1958. Photo-chemical aspects of visual excitation. *Exp. Cell. Res.*, Suppl. **5,** 389.

——1959. The Photoreceptor process in vision. *Handbook of Physiology*, **1,** Sec. 1. Amer. Physiol. Soc., Washington, D.C.

6

Chemoreceptors

Our world is so predominantly visual that we tend to belittle the importance of the chemical senses, perhaps the oldest and most widely distributed of the senses existing in both invertebrate and vertebrate animals. The chemoreceptors in the forward antennae of certain flies are used to sample food supply, and other insects and many mammals, *e.g.* rodents, depend almost entirely on chemical information not only for the selection of food, but also for the recognition of predators and choice of mate. Taste and smell contribute something more to the wellbeing of Man than the simple pleasures of eating and drinking, and those unfortunate enough to have lost both taste and smell would testify that the chemical senses are indeed essential for the satisfactory assimilation of foodstuffs.

Taste

Receptors

The taste receptors forming the "taste buds" are found primarily in the tongue and scattered sparsely throughout the structures at the back of the mouth. The surface of the tongue is not smooth, but has projections or papillae, especially prominent at the back. The taste buds are situated in the cellular walls of the papillae, at the sides, the tip, and particularly in relation to the so-called circumvallate papillae behind (Fig. 6:1). Seen with the microscope each taste bud, about ·1 mm. in length and half as broad, consists of a cluster of up to twelve leaf-like cells cemented together at the apex which lies below the surface in the taste pit (Fig. 6:2). A slender process of material secreted by the cells usually projects from the taste pit, and fine nerve twigs terminate as expansions on the surface of the taste cells. Up to two hundred taste buds may be associated with a single papilla and their total number in Man is of the order of 10,000. They tend to atrophy and decrease in number with age, hence the jaded palate of the elderly epicure seeking new and exotic dishes to stimulate his dwindling taste sensation. The nerve fibres for the taste buds are linked by three neurons to that part of the cortex of the brain which has the sensory receiving cells for the tongue (area 1).

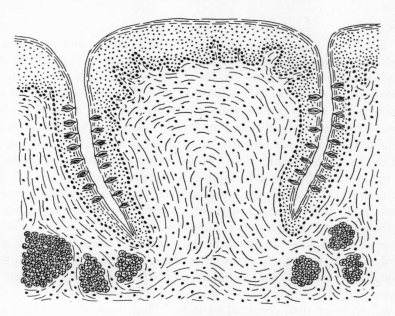

FIG. 6:1. A circumvallate papilla with taste buds.

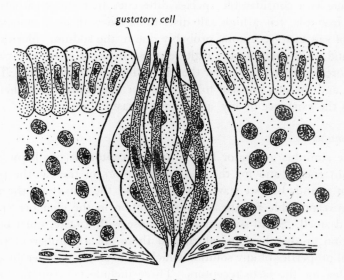

gustatory cell

FIG. 6:2. A taste bud.

Basic Tastes

There are four basic tastes—sour, salty, bitter, and sweet—and blended in various combinations these four tastes are responsible for the many flavours of the food we eat, just as the colours we see are mixtures of three primary colours. Most flavours, however, owe something to the sense of smell, and it is a common experience that food has little savour when a "cold in the head" puts smell out of action. The surface of the tongue is not uniformly sensitive to all kinds of tastes. We taste sweet with the tip of the tongue, sour with the sides, and bitter with the back, and so the small flake of tobacco is only recognised when it reaches the back of the mouth. It might, in consequence, be expected that the groups of taste buds in these areas would only respond to a specific taste, but in fact the position is rather more complicated. It is experimentally possible to record the impulse discharge in the nerve of a taste bud when it is stimulated with substances of different tastes, and it has been shown that although taste buds have a maximum sensitivity to one particular taste as indicated by the discharge of a greater number of impulses, they can respond to more than one kind of taste. Thus, each of the four basic tastes will stimulate groups of taste buds which also respond to one or more of the other three tastes, but the frequency ratio of the group discharge will be different for each taste. Moreover, it has been possible to demonstrate that each cell of a taste bud responds to more than one basic taste and thus behaves as the bud as a whole.

There is a considerable species difference in taste sensitivity. The rat, for example, has a high salt discrimination with a spontaneous discharge of salt taste receptors, probably due to the sodium chloride in the saliva, and while there is very little response to sugar in the cat it appears to be more sensitive than either the rat or the rabbit to quinine. The cat, the pig, and the dog are said to have "water taste fibres" but there is no proof of the existence of any specific water taste fibres in Man.

The Stimulus

The stimulus generator for the photoreceptors is, we know, quanta of radiant energy and for the mechanoreceptors of the ear the pressure waves of sound, but we have yet to disclose the nature of the specific stimulus responsible for the transducer action in the chemoreceptors of taste and smell. Sapid substances, *i.e.* those with a taste, must be either in solution or dissolved in saliva, and there are a number of physico-chemical properties of any solution which could singly or severally provide a stimulus for the taste receptors. These include (1) osmotic pressure, which depends on the total concentration and molecular weight of all dissolved substances, (2) molecular size, (3) osmolality, *i.e.* the "effective" molecular weight of electrolytes, which is the molecular weight of the substance divided by the number of ions per molecule. For non-electrolytes the molecular weight is also the effective molecular weight. Electrolytes are substances which, when in solution, can conduct electricity and contain ions as dissociated particles with an electric charge. Those with a positive charge are cations and those with a negative charge are anions. (4) In this respect the ratio of the weight of anions to the weight of cations in physiological salts, indicated as G, appears to be of some significance. G for free acids will, of course, be numerically equal to the anion weight. (5) Other significant properties are related to the pH ($pH = \log (H^+)$), *i.e.* the concentration of hydrogen ions and electrical conductivity, and to this list may be added a physiological factor, viz. (6) the rate of diffusion of ions and solutes into and out of cells. Such a group of physicochemical properties belongs to no one level of chemical structure but involves atoms, ions, molecules, and specific chemical groupings.

The Sour Taste: The chemical characteristics of an acid are exerted in respect of the content of free, *i.e.* dissociated, ions of hydrogen which are cations. The degree of sourness is broadly related to the degree of dissociation of the acid, *i.e.* the concentration of hydrogen ions, although solutions of the inorganic acids—hydrochloric, nitric, sulphuric—of the same pH are not necessarily equally sour. Moreover, for a threshold stimulus as tested by the response of the taste fibre, the hydrogen ion concentration of weak organic acids such as acetic is less than that of inorganic acids such as hydrochloric, and above threshold level most organic acids are more sour than inorganic acids of the same pH. Clearly, the pH by itself is not the exclusive factor concerned in the sour taste, and some basic physiological mechanism complicates the relation between sourness and acidity. It has been suggested that the electrical conductivity of a solution, itself indirectly related to the pH, influences the sour taste which has also been attributed to the rate at which the acid penetrates the cell or becomes adsorbed onto the cell surface. Some of the amino acids taste sweet and picric acid is intensely bitter.

The Salt Taste: Common salt (NaCl) where sodium is the cation and chloride the anion, gives the only "pure" salty taste. All substances, however, with a salty taste are soluble salts dissociating in solution into discrete cations and anions, both of which contribute to the taste stimulus. Thus, in a series of sodium salts (chloride, bromide, acetate, etc.) the taste elicited will vary with the anion, and similarly in a chloride series (sodium, calcium, potassium, etc.) taste differences are conditioned by the cations. Because of species differences in taste sensitivity it is not possible to relate the stimulating efficiency of electrolytes to single properties of either the anions or the cations. For instance, in a cation series (with the anion chloride) tested for degrees of saltiness, NH_4 is top of the series for the carnivores but is preceded by lithium and sodium for rodents. Again, sodium is a more effective stimulus in rodents than in carnivores, and this has been related to the relatively low sodium/potassium ratio in the red blood cells of rodents, indicative of a species difference in the ionic properties of receptor membranes.

There is some recent evidence that the significant physicochemical properties linked to a salt taste are (1) the effective molecular weight, *i.e.* the molecular weight of the salt divided by the number of ions per molecule. With common salt the molecular weight is 58 and there are two ions, sodium and chloride, to give an effective molecular weight of 29; (2) the ratio of the weight of the anions to cations; this is referred to as *G*. *G* for common salt has a value of 1·45. Where the value of *G* is as high as 2·5 the salt taste tends to change to bitter.

As far as the sour and salty tastes are concerned, therefore, the chemo-receptors provide information with regard to the ion population and ratio of distribution within a solution with a speed and precision which far exceeds anything likely to be equalled in the foreseeable future by labora-tory procedures. It is possible that with the sour and salty tastes the stimulus mechanism consists of a loose binding of ions to a taste receptor surface by a non-enzymatic process like that which links them to proteins, and species variations could then be attributed to differences in the molecular configurations at the sites on the receptor surface.

Salts of heavy metals, such as mercury, with a high molecular weight have a metallic rather than a salty taste and some lead salts, particularly lead acetate, actually taste sweet. The metallic taste of such highly dis-sociated salts as copper sulphate could be due to interference with the function of the taste buds from the adsorption of heavy metal cations by their contained protein.

The Sweet Taste: The sweet taste is associated mainly with organic compounds such as the alcohols, glycols, sugars, ketones, some amino acids, and synthetic sweeteners of the saccharine group, and thus there is no one chemical "group" common to all "sweet" substances. In a homo-logous series of substances, *e.g.* alcohols and glycols, there may be a quite sudden change from sweet to bitter with an increase in molecular weight, and even where the higher members of such a series become less soluble in water, they may have a more powerful sweet taste. Again, quite small changes in the spatial arrangement of the atoms or groupings within the molecule may produce wide differences in taste. Saccharine, which is five hundred times sweeter than sugar, can become converted into a tasteless compound by a small substitution change in a molecule. There are examples of optical isomeres where the dextrorotatory isomer is sweet and the levorotatory isomer is tasteless.

Of the various physicochemical properties already mentioned as potential taste stimulus generators, only osmotic pressure is a possible cause of sweet taste of sugars, and in consequence it has been supposed that there are taste buds with receptors which respond specifically to osmotic pressure. Very dilute solutions of common salt taste sweet, not salty. The effective molecular weight of sodium chloride is a tenth of that of a sugar such as sucrose, and consequently a 1 per cent solution of sucrose and a ·1 per cent solution of sodium chloride will have the same osmotic pressure (2 to 3 atmospheres). As there is no longer a sufficient concentration of the "salty" factor in a ·1 per cent solution of sodium chloride, there remains only the osmotic pressure difference, and so dilutions of this order have the same sweet taste as a 1 per cent sugar solution. Synthetic sweeteners such as saccharine are very different from sugars and so far there is no explanation of their effect on taste buds.

The Bitter Taste: The bitter taste, like the sweet taste, is elicited by substances of widely different chemical composition, including complex nitrogen compounds such as quinine, caffeine, strychnine, and nicotine. It is often found in combination with the sweet taste and many sweet substances such as saccharine have an "after bitter" taste which becomes apparent as the stimulus moves from the front to the back of the tongue. As inorganic salts increase in molecular weight they tend to taste bitter, and it is suggested that the high value for G in neutral salts introduces bitterness. Again, with an increase in the length of the carbon chain of organic molecules there may be a change from sweet to bitter.

Taste Theories

There is at present no satisfactory theory to explain the stimulus mechanism for all four basic tastes, but a number of facts have now accumulated which indicate some working principles. Certain drugs like gymnemic acid reduce the sensitivity to sweet and bitter but leave the salt and sour tastes unaffected, and as individual taste receptor units can respond to salt and sugar the conclusion is that the gustatory cells have specific receptor sites sensitive to sugar on the one hand and salt on the other. Again, it may be that all the taste buds respond to osmotic pressure representing the total concentration of all the dissolved substances and also to the hydrogen ion concentration of the solution or differences between the pH of the solution and that of the cell. The bitter taste of Epsom salts may imply the response of bitter receptor sites to a high value of G added to stimulation of the salt taste buds. There are too many chemical objections to the suggestion that tastes can be generated through interference with one or more enzymes in the gustatory cells for a catalytic theory to be seriously considered.

Threshold and Intensity Discrimination

The determination of a threshold taste stimulus is a difficult task and in general it is advisable to employ a small panel of experts. The taste sensitivity is most appropriately expressed in terms of the molar concentration of the solution used, as this figure indicates the actual number of molecules in a known volume of the tested solution. The threshold sensitivity is influenced by a number of factors and at best is an arbitrary figure. The two most important variables are temperature and the part of the tongue stimulated. It is well known that the taste of food is influenced by its temperature, and good cooks salt foods at the right time when neither too hot nor too cold, while confectioners know the optimum conditions for sweetening their candy. The relation between temperature and taste sensitivity is not, however, a simple one. The threshold for salt tastes, for example, rises, *i.e.* the sensitivity decreases, with the rise in temperature from 17 °C. to 40 °C., whereas the threshold for sweet tastes is at its lowest, *i.e.* sensitivity is maximum, around 35 °C.

Not all parts of the tongue's surfaces are, of course, equally responsive to all kinds of taste stimulus and, as already noted, bitter solutions are most readily appreciated at the back, sweet at the tip of the tongue, acids along the edges, and the salty taste evenly distributed over the tongue except at the top surface which is insensitive to taste. The figures given for absolute threshold values range from $2 \times 10^{-2}M$ for a sugar solution to $4 \times 10^{-7}M$ ($M =$ molar concentration) of quinine sulphate.

While the absolute threshold for taste is very much larger than that for smell, the size of the increment necessary to produce a just noticeable difference, *i.e.* ΔI, is about the same. This means that the Weber fraction $\Delta I/I$ for taste is the same as for smell and ranges from about half to a tenth. The Weber fraction is, however, influenced by the quality of the taste, and the differential sensitivity for sweet taste, for instance, is higher than for bitter taste. It is also affected by both the intensity and the temperature.

It has been found possible to compare the stimulus intensities of solutions of different tastes, and for this purpose a psychological "scale" of taste has been devised. The unit is the "gust," defined as the psychological strength of a 1 per cent sucrose solution. In this way the strengths of all four basic tastes have been specified in terms of a common denominator and, for example, it is possible to detect a salt solution that tastes half as strong as the standard sugar solution.

Taste Mixtures

Most natural tastes are mixtures of two or more of the primary tastes, but like the colours they are unitary and do not break up spontaneously into their components. Thus, sodium bicarbonate can be described as a mixture of salt and sour, or potassium bromide as salt and bitter. Metallic taste can be regarded as having sweet, bitter, and salt components. If the four primary taste qualities merely blended in an additive way, then it would be possible to predict the taste of a known mixture, but if there are mutual interactions between the four systems this will not be possible. The evidence to date implies that there are interactions and in many cases it is impossible to predict the taste from a mixture of basic tastes—sweet, sour, and salt, for instance, all interact with one another in the direction of mutual enhancement while the bitter taste is generally uninfluenced by the others.

The results of combining solutions of different tastes are at present rather contradictory. Acids seem to increase the saltiness of a salt, yet salt reduces the sourness of acids. Again, the presence of salt increases the sweetness of sugar, but whereas all sugars seem to reduce the sourness of acids all acids do not necessarily suppress the sweet taste, and neither hydrochloric nor acetic acid have any effect on the sweetness of sucrose. One interesting experimental result is an increased discharge rate of a taste fibre responding to the mixture of sugar and acid compared to its response to either stimulus alone, indicating that taste "interactions" have a "central" effect. A similar electrophysiological response in terms of the discharge frequency of the taste fibres occurs when glucose and sucrose solutions are mixed, and the sweetness of the mixture is greater than would be predicted by the simple addition of the equivalent sweetness value for each component. There are obviously so far little-understood complications and complexities in taste reactions.

Attempts have been made to analyse food products in terms of some qualitative standards for sweet, bitter, sour, or salty, and one surprising result of such analyses is that most food flavours obtain a very low ranking in terms of these various taste scales, implying that flavour is more a matter of odour than taste.

Adaptation

Continuous stimulation reduces the sensitivity of taste receptors, *i.e.* they show adaptation, and the stronger the stimulus the longer the adaptation time, *e.g.* the low concentrations of salt cease to taste salty in about 20 seconds whereas with stronger concentrations the taste lasts for up to 2 minutes. It is significant that increasing the temperature of a solution prolongs its adaptation time so that it continues to taste after the same solution at a lower temperature would have ceased to taste.

Electric Taste

The passage of a direct electric current through the tongue is followed by an acid taste at the cathode and an alkaline taste at the anode. There are two possible explanations for electric taste; (1) that the taste buds are stimulated by the concentration of the corresponding ions at the cathode and the anode resulting from electrolysis, (2) the electric current causes actual depolarisation of the receptor by ionic transfer across the cell membrane. Both explanations involve an electrochemical reaction.

It is interesting that there have been in recent years a number of reports from patients that certain substances can be tasted a few seconds after being injected into their blood stream.

Taste Individuality

There is, of course, a wide range of taste preferences among individuals often based on social, cultural, or racial habits although there is an almost universal aversion to bitter tastes. Acceptance or rejection of food because of taste can be modified by general constitutional conditions and thus excess of salt in the diet may lead to its rejection, whereas in salt starvation there will be a distinct preference for it. Another example cited is the case of the small boy who compensated for a renal insufficiency with an excessive intake of table salt, and there is often a strong preference for sugar with a low blood-sugar level. Such temporary likes and dislikes cannot be explained by any difference in the sensitivity of taste receptors, and the strange cravings of pregnant women are not due to a change in taste sensitivity but have a psychosomatic basis.

Taste Blindness

It has been known for some years that certain substances, of which phenolthiourea (P.T.C.) is an example, taste strongly bitter to some individuals but are tasteless to others, and following standard tests with P.T.C. it has been found that about two-thirds of British males are tasters and one-third non-tasters, with a somewhat similar distribution in other European populations. Taste blindness is an inherited condition but is different from colour blindness in that the error is confined to a particular group of substances and there is no concomitant loss of the bitter taste.

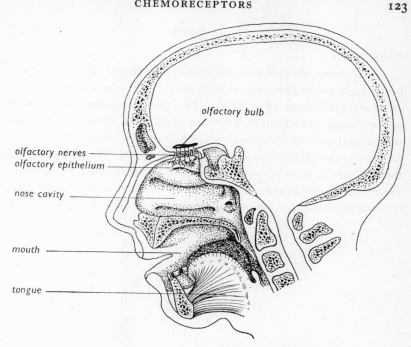

FIGURE 6:3
The nasal cavity with olfactory
epithelium.

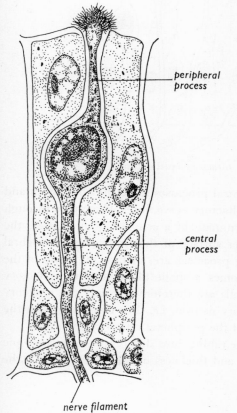

FIGURE 6:4
An olfactory receptor.

Smell

Receptors

The organ of smell is the square centimetre or so of the lining membrane high up on the walls of each side of the nose cavity, known as the olfactory epithelium (Fig. 6:3). The chemoreceptors are bipolar cells approximately 0·01 mm. in length and half again as broad placed amongst the normal cells of the olfactory epithelium (Fig. 6:4). They have short processes, the olfactory rods, running up to the free surface of the epithelium where they terminate in cup-like expansions fringed with up to 1,000 hair-like filaments from 1μ to 2μ in length. It may be that these fringing filaments are the actual sensitive parts functioning like the sense

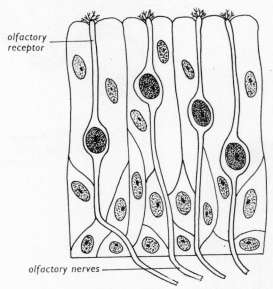

FIG. 6:5.   The olfactory epithelium.

receptors in skin. The longer central processes leave the epithelium and collect into bundles forming the olfactory nerve fibres which pass through the bony roof of the nose to terminate in a strip of brain matter, the olfactory bulb, lying on the under surface of the front of each cerebral hemisphere (Fig. 1:1). The long processes are, in fact, the axons of the bipolar cells and each axon becomes a single filament of the olfactory nerve (Fig. 6:5). The bipolar cells are therefore not only the olfactory receptors but also the first olfactory neuron, *i.e.* they constitute both the transducer and conducting part of the peripheral olfactory apparatus.

The olfactory receptors of the rabbit show differences in microscopic structure which affect the length and thickness of the olfactory rods, the size of the terminal expansion, and the number of its filaments. The olfactory rods are arranged round the periphery of the supporting epithelial cells in such a way that they are separated by an interval of at least 1μ and there are up to 10 around each cell, giving a density of rods of approximately 120,000 per sq. millimetre. This would mean for the rabbit something of the order of 50 million receptors for each nose cavity.

Olfactory Pathways

The olfactory bulbs develop from the cerebral hemisphere which in fact evolved as the "smell brain" in relation to the olfactory sense. The olfactory neural apparatus is therefore unique in that its receptors as the

mitral cells (2nd neuron)

glomeruli   olfactory nerves
(1st neuron)

FIG. 6:6.   The structure of the olfactory bulb.

first peripheral neuron are directly connected with the cerebrum, unlike all the other senses with relay centres in lower parts of the central nervous system. The central processes of the first neuron, the bipolar cells, synapse with the processes of about 60,000 second neurons, the mitral cells, within the olfactory bulb (Fig. 6:6). The arrangement in the rabbit is said to be that about 26,000 receptors pass their information through

24 mitral cells and so there is a high degree of convergence and thus of spatial summation. The axons of the mitral cells form a tract which terminates in what is the smell area of the cerebral cortex, and thus is equivalent to the cortical receiving centres of the other senses. Presumably it is here that smell sensations are elaborated and the different kinds of smell recognised, *i.e.* olfactory discrimination. The smell area of the cortex has connexions with many other parts of the brain and in this way makes its contribution to the sensory component of conscious activity. As in the eye and ear, messages are sent back from the brain to the olfactory receptors (centrifugal) which can, to some extent, regulate their response to stimulation. It could be said, therefore, that not only is smell an indirect recording of physical or chemical molecular energy, it also incorporates a personal interpretation reflecting past experience, existing, and proleptic activity.

Central Mechanism

Sensory discrimination relies primarily on the existence of receptors capable of selective response to the variables of the stimulus generator of the sense organ, and there is some evidence that different smells excite a maximum response in particular groups of olfactory receptors, and that there is in fact a mosaic of receptor sensitivities in the olfactory epithelium. It has already been noted that there are structural differences in the receptors. Electrical changes caused by the potentials generated in the receptors can be recorded from the surface of the olfactory epithelium (an olfactogram) when it is stimulated by odorous substances. The amplitude of the electrical response varies in different regions of the olfactory epithelium according to the density of the receptors, and the records confirm that localised groups of receptors are particularly sensitive to certain odours. The shape, the duration, and the latency period (the time interval from the application of the stimulus to the beginning of the response) of a graphically recorded response is related to the strength of the stimulus. The olfactogram also shows that during continuous stimulation the response of the olfactory epithelium declines from a peak to a lower level, and that its sensitivity to different substances can be reduced by repeated or prolonged stimulation. This is the physiological measure of the psychological experience that we get accustomed to, or cease to be aware of a smell after a certain time—subjectively we adapt. By similar experimental procedures it has been possible to show that groups of mitral cells (2nd neurons) are also selectively sensitive to categories of receptors and so to particular kinds of smell. Units have been recorded from the olfactory bulb which, for example, show specific sensitivity to substances such as acetone, ethyl acetate, etc., and impulses from one region of the smell organ always reach the same area of the olfactory bulb. In the rabbit, a spontaneous electrical activity of the olfactory bulb with a wave frequency of from 70 to 100 per second persists after destruction of the olfactory epithelium. This intrinsic activity may be altered or suppressed during olfactory stimulation, but it is never completely abolished for long and its return may indicate physiological adaptation. Physical and chemical properties of the stimulating substance such as volatility and water solubility can affect the nature of the response of the olfactory bulb as seen in the record, and some of these responses have a shortened latency and a more abrupt rise than others. It is plain, therefore, that the olfactory sense, like the other special senses, has an adequate neural apparatus to make use of the variables of the impulse code and sort out the information which it delivers to the cerebral cortex in terms of both the strength and diversity of smell properties of stimulating substances.

Stimulus

We know even less about the nature of the smell stimulus than we do about the taste stimulus, and can only speculate on the particular chemical or physical properties of a substance required for smell. It follows that, unlike sound and colour which can be accurately linked to certain frequencies or wavelengths, we have no clear ideas about the physical basis of the different smells we encounter. There are, however, certain essential conditions for smell. When one breathes through the nose the air stream does not pass over the olfactory epithelium, which is high up in the cavity, but reaches it indirectly by radiation and convection currents. When one makes a deliberate attempt to smell, sniffing diverts the air stream up to the olfactory receptors. To smell, a substance must therefore be volatile but it does not follow that the most volatile substances have the strongest smell, as the stimulus factor is intrinsic to the molecules. Musk, a powerful odorant used to make perfumes, has a low volatility and water, with its relatively high vapour pressure which is a measure of the facility with which the molecules escape into the surrounding atmosphere and therefore related to volatility, has no smell. If substances require to be in a gaseous state before they can smell, the physicochemical properties of solutions listed as possible sources of the taste stimulus are not eligible for consideration as the stimulus generators for smell; and as it would seem that whatever its precise mechanism smell is a molecular property, it follows that the more molecules of an odorous substance that reach the receptors the more powerful the stimulus and the stronger the smell. The molecular properties currently regarded as possible stimulus generators for smell are:

1. *Infra-red Absorption*: The molecules of all odorous substances

absorb infra-red radiation of wavelength (λ) 2μ to 20μ as energy used in molecular vibration. The absorption is selective and the wavelength of the absorbed radiation corresponds principally to the fundamental vibrational frequencies of the molecule. For example, the frequency of vibration of the C—O↔H group (as present in all alcohols) is always approximately 10^{14} per sec. corresponding to a wavelength of 3μ. As a first approximation only molecules having a hydroxyl group will absorb radiation at this wavelength; in so doing the absorbed energy appears first as an increase in the amplitude of vibration of the atoms in the group, and then as heat as a result of intermolecular collisions. The body surface, including the olfactory epithelium, emits infra-red radiation and one rather improbable suggestion is that their absorption by nearby molecules produces a thermal change which acts as a stimulus generator. The possible olfactory significance of infra-red absorption is also commonly discussed in terms of the "Raman shift," which might be described as quantised abstraction of energy from incident radiation as observed in the change in frequency of the non-Rayleigh scattering. The energy abstraction is exactly equivalent to the energy absorption processes involved in the infra-red region of the spectrum. Another variant to this theory could involve the behaviour of the olfactory epithelium rather in the fashion of a crude spectrometer with ability to detect and measure the intensity of the infra-red radiation with respect to wavelength.

There are objections to the infra-red theory, as indeed there are to all smell theories, and it is pointed out that optical isomers with identical infra-red absorption spectra can have distinctive smells. Such an objection is not, however, entirely insuperable as there is always the question of (a) impurities, (b) whether or not the infra-red radiation is polarised, and (c) if the isomers are adsorbed onto the receptor surface the contacts are not symmetrical and so their interaction could be different.

2. *Polarity of Molecules*: The properties of the elements vary according to their place in the periodic table. Fluorine, for example, is a highly electronegative magnetic element with a powerful attraction for the electrons of other atoms. The electronegativity of the halogen atoms falls in the order F≫Cl>Br>I. Another factor might be the density of the electrical charge over the surface of the atom; thus the fluorine atom, with its great power to attract electrons from the nearby atoms in the rest of the molecule, will have a high negative electrical charge distributed over the very small surface of this atom. On the other hand, the iodine atom has a comparatively small charge distributed over the very large surface of this bulky atom. The size of the halogens falls in the order I>Br>Cl>F. The overall polarity (dipole movement) of the molecule could have some physiological effect, particularly on the ions of a receptor membrane. None

of the elements which occur free in nature normally smell; thus free hydrogen and sulphur have no smell, but when combined as H_2S the arresting characteristic is smell. Of the elements which are naturally in a combined state the halogens—chlorine, bromine, iodine, and fluorine—all have an odour.

3. *Molecular Configuration*: This means the shape of the molecule in respect of the arrangement of its atoms and groupings which could affect its behaviour with regard to either adsorption onto the receptor surface or absorption into the receptor material. Geometrical isomers, for example, the "cis" and the "trans" forms of a substance which differ only in the position of the substitution groups, can have distinctive smells, and as previously noted optical isomers can also smell differently. Apparently a minor change in the composition of a molecule, for example the substitution of OH for H, may abolish smell, while the introduction of an amino group can greatly increase the smell.

4. *Catalytic Action*: The structure of the terminal part of the olfactory rods with its fringe of filaments suggests a mechanism for capturing molecules. A further interpretation of the adsorption theory linked with molecular polarity and configuration suggests that odorous molecules might inhibit or otherwise interfere with catalytic reactions so that the change in the concentration of reaction products excites a receptor. There are many valid objections to such a catalytic theory, including the fact that some substances are effective olfactory stimulators in concentrations as low as $10^{-13}M$.

5. *Water and Fat (Lipid) Solubility*: The surface of the olfactory epithelium is likely to have a protective film of fluid (probably mucus) while the receptor membrane includes many lipid molecules. Water-soluble and fat-soluble molecules will therefore interact more readily, but in different ways, with the receptors. In the homologous series of organic compounds such as the family of alcohols with the series of lower to higher alcohols ascending according to the number of carbon atoms in the molecule, *i.e.* the length of the carbon chain, $CH_3(CH_2)_nOH$ when $n = 0$, 1, 2, 3, etc., odour as well as taste intensity tends to increase as the carbon chain lengthens, *i.e.* up the series; but there is an actual decay in the olfactory stimulating effectiveness of the long-chain alcohols as observed by testing them in increasing concentrations, compared to the rise in effectiveness of higher concentrations of the short-chain alcohols. This could well be associated with diminished water solubility of the larger long-chain carbon molecules, while the absolute increase in odour intensity of many of the higher members of homologous series could be due to their increased lipid solubility. There would seem to be, however, a number of factors involved, particularly in the medium and long-chain alcohols,

and the range of stimulating effectiveness of any homologous series may
well be due to a convergence of a number of physicochemical properties
of the molecule to a peak at different points in the series. There is, for
example, some indication that their smell stimulating power is related to
their thermodynamic activity.[1]

6. *Chemical Composition*: Some compounds of quite different composition smell alike and again, certain smell resemblances are due to
chemical similarity; compounds of phosphorus, bismuth, and arsenic are
said to smell like garlic; sulphurs are universally disagreeable, while the
esters are responsible for the fragrant odours of flowers. Other compounds,
for example the amines, change their odour with dilution; and ambergris,
while repulsive in concentrated form, is pleasant in dilution, and indeed
is used in this form as a constituent of perfumes. Many metal surfaces not
only pick up odours but modify or distort them, and this is not in any way
related to the purity of the metal, at any rate in the case of either copper
or aluminium.

While, therefore, there are some facts, a certain number of rules, and
many interesting observations concerning smell, what particular molecular
property or, as seems more probable, constellation of properties, stimulate
the smell receptors and what particular changes they produce to give, for
instance, the flower its fragrance, each individual a personal odour, and
mortifying flesh its stench, is still largely a matter for speculation. A
complete understanding of all that happens physically and chemically
between the stimulating substance and the olfactory chemoreceptors must
await full analysis of the membrane structure of the receptors at molecular
level.

Odour and Odour Mixtures

The different kinds of smell we are able to recognise greatly out-
number the vocabulary available to describe them, at present limited to
such broad "subjective" terms as fragrant, putrid, fruity, spicy, burnt, etc.
From time to time schemes of basic smell modalities have been suggested,
but none of them is satisfactory and today there are no established basic
smells corresponding to the four basic tastes or the three primary colours.
A chemical grouping of odorous substances—paraffin, hydrocarbons,
esters, etc.—according to the analysis of their electrical responses in the
olfactory bulb, does not supply a comparable subjective classification.
In the absence, therefore, of recognised basic smells, the whole question
of odour mixtures is necessarily unsettled. Most of the smells we ex-

[1] Thermodynamic activity is defined as partial free molar energy referred to as a
standard state and is numerically equal to the relative saturation of the vapour of the
compound.

perience in any one day are likely to be mixtures in the sense that more than one kind of molecule is involved in the receptor stimulation.

The modern method of gas chromatography has shown that the odours emanating from natural substances, vegetable or animal, are extremely complex and quite obviously involve a large number of ingredients. Analysed in this way the smell of flowers and fruits has been shown to consist of at least a hundred volatile substances, some known and others unknown, and roast coffee, it is said, owes its attractive fragrance to around sixty different volatile components. Thus, many well-known "unitary" odours associated with particular natural products in fact arise from a complexity of chemical stimulation with simultaneous excitation of groups of receptors, and the single sensation we experience is the brain's interpretation of the ratio of response from the different groups of receptors involved.

Odour mixtures can be produced experimentally in two ways, (1) by mixing two odorous liquids or vapours in a container and sniffing the combined product, (2) by presenting a different odour to separate sides of the nose—"dichorhinic" mixing. This is of course an unnatural procedure as normally the same mixture is sniffed through each nostril, but it has a number of experimental advantages over the first method where chemical interaction may produce an entirely new product with its own characteristic smell.

In contrast to the confident prediction that can be made of the result of colour mixtures, odour mixtures may produce (a) a unified or "gestalt" sensation, particularly if the odours of the ingredients of the mixture resemble one another qualitatively, (b) a loose "blend" in which first one odour and then the other is perceived, (c) neutralisation so that there is no smell, or (d) a complete masking of one odour by the other.

Practical interest in odour mixtures is of course concerned with neutralisation and masking. On the one hand it is argued that complete neutralisation only occurs from chemical interaction and is not true physiological mixing. On the other hand it is known, as a matter of practical experience, that certain odours tend to cancel one another: for example, Peruvian balsam can be used to neutralise the odour of iodoform, and the expert florist can arrange not only the coloured but also the olfactory components of the bouquet to make it equally attractive to eye and nose. The removal of unpleasant odours by the use of so-called deodorants is of course recognised commercial procedure, but we have very little information with regard to how this result is achieved physiologically, whether peripherally by the successful competition of the deodorant molecules for receptor sites, or more centrally from the interpretation of the combined effect of receptor stimulation. It is obvious that the whole problem of odour mixtures and its wide commercial implications is still very much at the experimental stage.

Threshold and Intensity Discrimination

The term olfactometry is used to describe methods of finding the absolute threshold of olfactory stimulation, and the various forms of apparatus devised for this purpose are known in general as olfactometers. They are designed for the most part to ensure that a constant amount of the substance to be tested is delivered to the olfactory mucous membrane at each trial, and one method involves the use of a box enclosing the subject's head to provide an effective seal between the subject and the external atmosphere. The term "olfactie" is sometimes used to denote a threshold unit and indicates the number of molecules per c.c. of the stimulus at threshold. Some idea of the very high olfactory sensitivity compared to that of taste is given by the absolute threshold for vanillin, which is of the order of two-millionth of a milligramme per cubic milli-metre of air; and as an example of the very small quantities required for smell stimulation it has been pointed out that "one gram of muscone can throw off molecules at the rate of a million a second and lose only one per cent of its weight in a million years." The significance of this statement is that one gram of muscone has a very strong smell. It is said that a man can easily detect the smell of perspiration on a sheet of paper over which a person wearing shoes has walked at normal speed.

While it is notoriously difficult to make comparative statements of relative olfactory sensitivity in different species, recent work indicates that the difference in absolute sensitivity between, for instance, the dog and Man, is not as great as might be expected, and in fact that the absolute sensitivity of the dog's olfactory receptors is no greater than those of Man. However, the very much larger area of olfactory receptive surface in the dog, said to be as closely packed with receptors as the retina over an extent of surface greater than that occupied by the photoreceptors and auditory mechanoreceptors combined, gives a greater potential diversity of receptor sensitivity which would account for the superiority of the dog's olfactory mechanism in discriminating between different odours. The Weber fraction for smell varies in Man according to the stimulus intensity. When this is low it may have a value close to 1 and diminishes to ·2 with high intensities. It is therefore no more constant for smell than for the other special senses. While gas chromatography will give quantitative data with regard to smell, our nose still provides a vastly superior mech-anism for detecting one smell in the presence of another.

Adaptation

Not only is there a very marked adaptation to smell, that is to say we become used to a smell and cease to be aware of it fairly quickly, but certain odours change their quality with continuous stimulation. For example, nitrobenzene has at first a bitter almond odour and if the stimulus is continued this changes to the smell of tar. Again, continuous stimulation by one particular smell may dull sensitivity to another. An example of this is the camphor smell which affects the threshold of other substances like oil of cloves, eau de Cologne, and ether, and the effect is reciprocal. The physiological correlates of adaptation in terms of electrical responses have already been noted.

Civilised man tends to place, perhaps, too little value on his sense of smell apart from food and drink, but there is the odd individual particularly sensitive to smells and moreover the olfactory mechanism can, when necessary, replace our visual sense in large measure in the interpretation of the remote environment. In this connexion there is the oft-quoted account of Helen Keller's very accurate description of a passing countryside gained entirely from her acutely developed sense of smell. Perhaps because for most of us events in the daily round are registered by what we see and what we hear, smell is less dominant in our introspective life than either vision or hearing. Nevertheless, a smell can trigger off a memory just as vividly as a snatch of tune or a glimpse of a once familiar scene.

BIBLIOGRAPHY

ADEY, W. R. 1959. Sense of smell. *Handbook of Physiology*, **1**, Sec. 1. Amer. Physiol. Soc., Washington, D.C.

ADRIAN, A. D. 1954. The physiological basis of perception. In *Brain Mechanisms and Consciousness*. A Symposium. Blackwell, Oxford.

BEDICHEK, R. 1960. *The Sense of Smell*. Michael Joseph, London.

CLARK, W. E. LE GROS. 1956. Observations on the structural organisation of olfactory receptors in the rabbit. *Yale J. of Biol. Med.*, **29**, No. 2.

GELDARD, F. A. 1950. Somesthesis and the chemical senses. *Ann. Rev. Psychol.*, **1**, 71.

HAGENSCHMIT, A. J. 1953. *Smell and Taste. Scientific American Reader*. Simon and Schuster, New York.

KALMUS, H. and HUBBARD, S. J. 1960. *The Chemical Senses in Health and Disease*. Thomas, Springfield, U.S.A.

MONCRIEFF, R. W. 1944. *The Chemical Senses*. Wiley, New York.

NICOL, H. 1959. Towards a theory of taste. *The Brewers' Guild J*. London, E.C.1.

PFAFFMANN, C. 1959. The sense of taste. *Handbook of Physiology*, **1**, Sec. 1. Amer. Physiol. Soc., Washington, D.C.

PART II

7

Perception of Space, Size, and Distance

Consciousness, Behaviour, and Perception

From the point of view of psychology, perception must be regarded as a conscious activity. It will be seen later that there is some evidence for "unconscious" or "subthreshold" forms of perception, but it is a question whether consciousness even of a minute degree can be excluded from such phenomena, and also whether these expressions are psychologically meaningful at all. In the field of sensation it is acceptable to speak of many sensory phenomena as not entering consciousness, but even then it is not easy to think of consciousness arising fully fledged at a particular point. It must arise gradually in the course of the development of the integrative processes which give rise to perception and, if anything, the concept of a sensation, rather than that of perception, is artificial, and is a product of scientific theorising. Perception is known from direct experience.

It follows that a study of perception on a behaviourist basis would have to exclude consciousness. A behaviourist could study behaviour, but not conscious perception. To admit the study of conscious perception to psychology might be said to abandon behaviourism but most psychologists, who are orientated behaviouristically, take up a position in which studies like that of conscious perception are admitted.

All studies of perception in animals are therefore inferential. We infer from behaviour that animals must have certain perceptual processes, implying that they are in some measure conscious, although there is the difficulty that animals have brains and sense organs somewhat different from our own. In dealing with human beings there is the advantage of being able to hear verbal reports of their experiences including perceptions, but these verbal reports do not in themselves allow us direct entry into other persons' experiences. We infer from their words that their experiences must have been of such and such a kind, and these experiences will include their perceptions if they mention them.

Psychology therefore differs from all other natural sciences because it includes in its subject-matter, either by direct reference or by implication, phenomena which find no place in them, although its methods and aims are those of a natural science.

The experimental psychology of perception sets up controlled condi-

tions under which the human subject may observe his perceptions introspectively, report upon them verbally, and carry out behavioural responses
in addition to words, from which his perceptual experiences may be
inferred. With animals the direct introspective observations of the
individual subject are excluded and verbal responses are not possible,
although expressive sounds, which only differ from words in not being
organised into a systematic language, may still be included in the forms
of behaviour from which experience may be inferred. Many examples of
the experimental study of perception will be discussed in this and the
next chapters.

The problem of the psychological explanation of perception is important, and most present-day psychologists will think that this explanation must be in terms of physics, chemistry, biochemistry, and physiology.
No place would be found for a "mentalistic" explanation, which could
not be reduced to the terms of these sciences. Consciousness, however,
is an essential aspect of all perceiving and, as far as we know, it must
play a fundamental part in it. The question whether consciousness can
be explained itself in terms of the natural sciences mentioned above, or
whether its presence constitutes a new state of affairs which creates a
presumption of a different kind of explanation, is still an important one.
Since it seems that consciousness must be included as an agency among
psychological functions, psychology is a natural science in terms of
method but a mental science in terms of its subject-matter.

Gestalt Psychology

The development of Gestalt psychology, associated with the names of
Wertheimer, Kohler, and Koffka, has in the last forty years or so completed a revolution which had been taking place for a much longer period
of time. Its essential principles will be illustrated by examples in the next
section. The first is the principle of "figure and ground" by which every
perception is a pattern related to a background of other experiences or their
absence. The second principle is that of "segregation" and "differentiation" by which the patterns of stimuli form certain structures in perception
owing to their special properties. The third principle is that of "closure"
by which incomplete structure patterns tend to be completed in perception.
The fourth is that of the "good Gestalt" by which one perception will
tend to supersede a weaker perception based on the same structure pattern.
The fifth is the principle of "isomorphism" by which it is claimed that
events in the brain correspond in structure to what is perceived. This is
more doubtful than the first four.

It has been perhaps the greatest achievement of Gestalt psychology to make clear that perceptions are not built up out of ultimate sensory elements, a view widely held in the nineteenth century. Any suggestion that the ultimate content of consciousness consists of particles of sensation has been generally abandoned today, and although the concept of elementary sensations is necessary to physiological psychology, it is essentially an abstraction.

On the contrary, in perception we are faced directly with organisations and structures in experience which cannot be split into ultimate components, although they can be analysed scientifically in various ways and for various purposes. We must think of perception and of mental functions in general as developing by the differentiation of a continuum, rather than by the aggregation of ultimate particles. This theory was supported before Gestalt psychology appeared on the scene, but Gestalt psychology has had the advantage of an experimental approach.

Figures, Shapes, and Areas

Early work on Gestalt psychology demonstrated the essential principles of the perception of figures, shapes, and areas. Even the smallest point

FIG. 7:1. This may be seen either as a vase or as two faces. One of the earliest of this type of drawing showed Marie Antoinette looking at Louis XVI, and a great many variations of the fundamental pattern have been produced. It is a good example of alternating "figure" and "ground".

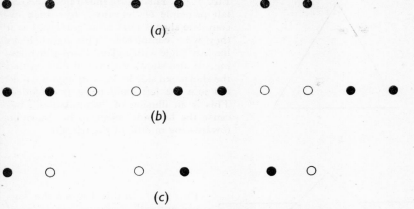

(a)

(b)

(c)

FIG. 7:2. In (a) the dots are perceived in pairs because some are closer together than others. In (b) they are seen in pairs because some are qualitatively alike and others different. In (c) these two factors of perceptual organization are combined, and it is apparent that nearness is more important than similarity in determining the structure perceived. (After Wertheimer, by permission of Springer-Verlag, Berlin, and Michael Wertheimer.)

FIG. 7:3. Here four kinds of stimuli are combined, and the percipient sees a rectangle of columns of dots and circles, which is a general "ground" for an upright cross of large dots and a diagonal cross of small crosses. (After Wertheimer, by permission of Springer-Verlag, Berlin, and Michael Wertheimer.)

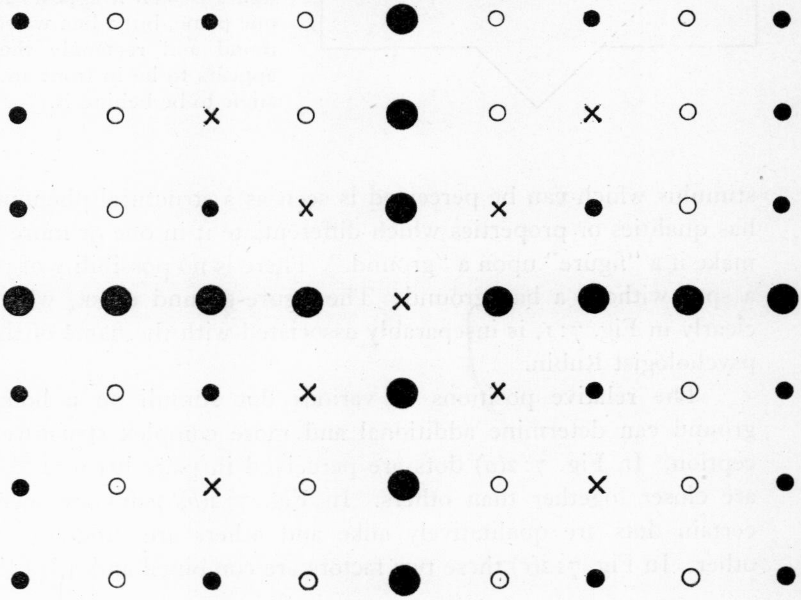

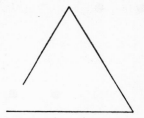

FIG. 7:4. This figure illustrates the Gestalt principle of "closure", by which incomplete shapes tend to be perceived as if they were completed. This figure looks like a triangle with a piece of one side missing. It also shows the optical illusion that the shortened side looks as though it would not join the left hand point if extended. This is an illusion of "assimilation", because the left side seems to be drawn in towards the middle of the triangle.

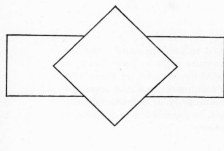

FIG. 7:5. In this diagram the "figure-ground", "closure" and "good Gestalt" principles are combined, and we tend to see a square or diamond superimposed on a rectangle. The diamond tends to seem nearer than the rectangle, which forms a "ground" for it.

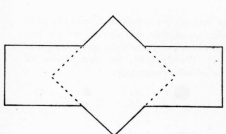

FIG. 7:6. A simple adjustment makes the ten-sided figure in 7.5 quite prominent, although "closure" of the diamond and rectangle still tends to occur. When the ten-sided figure is seen it appears to be all in one plane, but when we see the diamond and rectangle the diamond appears to be in front and the rectangle to be behind it.

stimulus which can be perceived is seen as a structural phenomenon. It has qualities or properties which differentiate it in one or more ways and make it a "figure" upon a "ground." There is no possibili y of perceiving a spot without a background. The figure-ground effect, which is seen clearly in Fig. 7:1, is inseparably associated with the name of the Danish psychologist Rubin.

The relative positions of various dot stimuli on a homogeneous ground can determine additional and more complex structures in perception. In Fig. 7:2(a) dots are perceived in pairs because certain dots are closer together than others. In Fig. 7:2(b) pairs are seen because certain dots are qualitatively alike and others are different from each other. In Fig. 7:2(c) these two factors are combined and it is evident that nearness in space is more important than similarity of quality in determining the structure perceived.

It is easy and fascinating to show that such principles if elaborated and extended in many ways, which may be left to the imagination of the reader, can account for a large range of perceptual phenomena and, where different principles of organisation conflict, ambiguous patterns may be produced. Fig. 7:3 illustrates a simple development. Here four kinds of stimuli are combined, and the percipient sees a rectangle of columns of dots and circles which is the general "ground" and upon which is superimposed an upright cross of larger dots and a diagonal cross of small crosses, namely two distinct "figures."

These phenomena were of such far-reaching significance for psychology that their study has formed a major branch of the subject in the last forty years. The processes of "differentiation" and "segregation," and the "figure-ground" phenomenon illustrated above, are in general little affected by learning, but are provided for in the organic basis of mental life, although they have a history of development in each individual. The two other important principles must be mentioned, however, in this very brief section, namely "closure" and "good Gestalt."

Closure is illustrated by Fig. 7:4. The pattern looks like an equilateral triangle with part missing. The missing part is, so to speak, filled in by the process of perception, and if part of such a figure is covered up, it still looks like a triangle or other figure accordingly. The good Gestalt principle is illustrated in Fig. 7:5. We see a rectangle behind and a square in front and, incidentally, the rectangle is completed by the principle of closure. We do not see a ten-sided outline with two right-angled line patterns inside it. Nevertheless, the ten-sided figure may easily be made prominent as in Fig. 7:6 by an adjustment of the stimulus pattern presented.

The conditions under which good Gestalten tend to form and to combine or conflict with each other, and those under which closures operate more and less effectively, and the other factors determining structural organisation in perception, have been the subject of numerous interesting experimental studies. Sufficient has been said here to show that these phenomena underly and ramify through the whole of perception, not only in the visual field, but in other sensory modalities as well. Many of them can be readily duplicated with sound patterns, and in touch, movement, and other fields of perception. For example, the perception of rhythm in music, dancing, and poetry is very largely based on Gestalt principles. The difference between melody and accompaniment is a figure-ground phenomenon, and in harmony and counterpoint complex configurational factors are at work. In the less structured sensory modalities, however, such as taste and smell, these principles are less obvious.

Figural After-Effects

A phenomenon closely related to the perception of figures, areas, and shapes is that called the figural after-effect, and it has received considerable attention recently in experimental psychology on account of the possible light it might throw on the brain processes underlying perception. This

I

X_1

T_1 X_2 T_2

FIG. 7:7. This illustrates a figural after-effect. If the viewer first fixates the upper cross for 10 to 20 seconds and then transfers his fixation to the lower cross, it will appear on account of the after-effect of the black rectangle I, that the rectangle T_1 is not in line with T_2 but below it. (After Köhler and Wallach.)

phenomenon is illustrated in Fig. 7:7. In this, X_1 and X_2 are fixation points, I is the "inspection" figure and T_1 and T_2 are the "test" objects. Point X_1 is fixated for about one minute, and then the fixation is transferred to X_2. The two objects T_1 and T_2 are exactly in line, but after fixation of X_1 the object T_1 appears lower than T_2, as if it were pushed down by the after-effects of perceiving I. All manner of effects of this kind can be produced, and it is clear that the inspection of any visual object gives rise to them, provided the "inspection" objects concerned are clearly segregated from their grounds, and the "test" objects are rightly placed. Circles, curves, and other objects and patterns may be affected, and vision is not the only sense modality in which such after-effects may occur, because they are found in auditory and kinesthetic perception. Apparently figural after-effects occur in the brain rather than in the sense organs stimulated because they may be transferred from one eye to the other. Presumably many perceptions in everyday life are influenced by them to some extent, but it is unlikely that they are important factors in ordinary perception.

Optical and Sensory Illusions

We should include here optical illusions, which are called by this name in order to distinguish them from the illusions which are due to unconscious influences in perception and which are mentioned in Chapter 10. Optical illusions are of great interest to the psychologist, and occur in a large variety of different forms. In general they are due to special properties of the figures perceived in conjunction with special characteristics of the visual functions as a whole, including brain processes. For the most part the mechanisms underlying them are far from being clearly understood, and may be very complex.

One of the simplest optical illusions is the peculiar effect in perceiving parallel or nearly parallel straight lines close together, which makes them look curved in such a way that the middle parts seem nearer together than the ends, if they are long enough or near enough together. This is not easily seen in an illustration on a small scale but it was well known to the Greeks, and in the Parthenon, for example, the architects carefully made the long, apparently parallel, horizontal lines slightly wider apart in the middle so that the illusion was compensated satisfactorily for the majority of viewers. This was in all probability also the reason why Greek pillars were made to bulge slightly in their middles. If the slight bulge is just right most people will see the column as if it neither bulges nor seems thinner in the middle. Later architects, forgetting the purpose of the imperceptible bulge, incorporated a visible bulge into most perpendicular columns and this became a senseless convention of column construction. Most readers will be able to recall seeing pillars so crudely designed as to look almost barrel-shaped.

A well known illusion of size is the effect of smaller or larger circles surrounding another circle. In Fig. 7:8 the central circle has the same diameter in (a) and (b). It is clear that in (a) it looks larger than in (b). In Fig. 7:4 the incompleted side seems to be at the wrong angle.

Such illusions, of which there are a great number, must be distinguished from purely physical effects, which give deceptive appearances to familiar objects or experiences. The bent appearance of a stick when put

partly into a pool of water is an example of a physical "illusion." In this
case the effect is not strictly an illusion at all, in the psychological sense,
but is due to the refraction or bending of light rays coming from the
submerged part of the stick as they pass from water to air. The change in
pitch of the whistle of a train as it passes is also a purely physical "illusion."

Illusions may have been called optical for convenience, but they may
occur in any sense modality. In the modalities of touch and kinesthesis
there is the size-weight illusion and this usually involves vision too. A

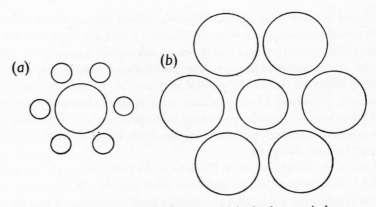

FIG. 7:8 An illusion of contrast in which the larger circles surrounding the central circle in (b) tend to make it look smaller than
the central circle in (a). (Adapted from *Psychology: An Introduction
to the Study of Behaviour*, by H. C. Lindgren and D. Byrne. New
York: Wiley.)

large object if seen, handled, and lifted, seems heavier than a small one
of exactly the same mass. A famous illusion of touch is Aristotle's crossed-
finger illusion. If the right forefinger and middle finger are crossed, and
a pencil is placed between their tips so that it touches the left side of the
forefinger and the right side of the middle finger, it may seem like two
touches with separate pencils.

Alternating illusions and reversible figures are interesting. The best
known of these is the cube drawn after the fashion of an architectural
drawing, without regard to the effects of perspective. This is illustrated
in Fig. 7:9(a). If we look at it we may see a solid cube for a time and then,
unexpectedly, and perhaps owing to a change of fixation point or even of
conscious attitude alone, it may appear as if hollow. In the same group
are the stair case illusion (Fig. 7:9(b)), which may look as if seen from
above or below, and certain well known ambiguous drawings, such as
Boring's wife and mother-in-law picture which is illustrated in Fig. 7:10.

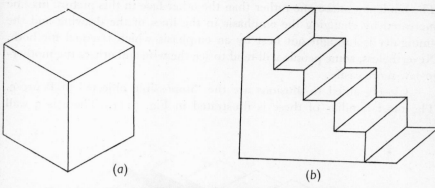

(a)   (b)

FIG. 7:9.   The Necker isometric cube (a) may be seen either as
solid or hollow cube, according to whether the central corner seems
near or far away. Similarly the staircase (b), also drawn isometric-
ally, may seem like an overhanging cornice. (Adapted, by permission of the publishers, from *Elements of Psychology*, by D. Krech
and R. S. Crutchfield, New York: Knopf, 1958.)

FIGURE 7:10
This drawing may be seen
either as the "wife" or the
"mother-in-law". (Adapted
from Boring, after Katz.
Similar to a figure in *Elements of Psychology*, by D.
Krech and R. S. Crutch-
field. New York: Knopf,
1958, by permission of the
publishers.)

The tendency to see one rather than the other face in this picture may be increased by changing the emphasis in the lines of the drawing and the ambiguity is brought out best by an emphasis which is equal for both. Nevertheless, some people will tend to see the wife and others the mother-in-law more easily.

Closely allied to illusions are the "impossible objects" of Penrose. The most familiar of these is illustrated in Fig. 7:11. There is a wall

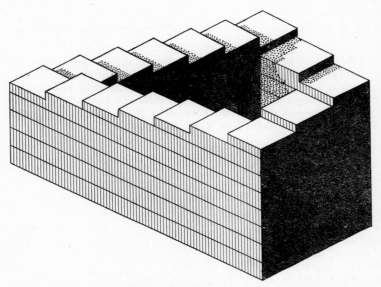

FIG. 7:11.   An "impossible" object, drawn by adjustments of perspective and shadow effects. (After Penrose and Penrose, by permission of the Editor of the *British Journal of Psychology*.)

which apparently ascends in steps but, after turning three right angles, like the wall of a building, it joins with itself at the original height.

Many illusions are possibly to be explained on the Gestalt theory of "isomorphism," according to which patterns of excitation in the brain are supposed to be identical in organisation with the patterns perceived, even when in three dimensions. These excitations may have the property of repelling or attracting each other, and in the sagging together in appearance of long parallel lines there would seem to be attraction, while in the circle illusion there would be repulsion. In ambiguous figures the Gestalt principles favouring one pattern may be just as strong as those favouring another. Then a change of emphasis owing to a verbal instruction, or simply a spontaneous change of "attitude," may favour one pattern at the expense of the other.

Camouflage

The hidden or "embedded" figure, illustrated in Fig. 10:2, is an example of camouflage. This is a phenomenon which depends on the pattern to be hidden fitting into a larger and more complex pattern, or upon the principal outlines of the pattern being cut up by subsidiary outlines into smaller parts which do not look like it. For disguise and deception other principles may be used, as in the fish, which has a large and obviously eye-like pattern near its tail, so that it seems to be facing in the opposite direction. Colour camouflage is common, and it is interesting that the colour blind are often able to see objects which would be camouflaged by colour patterns for the normal. Camouflage obviously exists for the vision of lower animals in much the same way as for Man, because it is an important factor in adaptation to the environment and in protective coloration and appearance. Thus the characteristic patterns of the giraffe and zebra not only split their shapes into "meaningless" sections, but also fit into the light-and-shadow patterns of their environment. Gestalt psychology gives explanations of camouflage in which closure and the principles of the good Gestalt and figure and ground are usually at work. What might seem to be the most glaring design when seen in isolation, may cause a given object to become part of the ground rather than be seen as a figure upon it, and parts of the design may from good Gestalten in combination with the background, while other parts may close in combination with other parts of the background and destroy the unity of outline of the objects, which will then be effectively hidden.

Perception of Space

Monocular Space

The visual perception of space is dependent on a number of factors which act in monocular vision. These should be mentioned before binocular and stereoscopic vision. In the first place there are the impressions of depth and relative distance produced by the apparent convergence of parallel lines which recede away from the eye. These effects can be seen in Fig. 7:12(a) and (b). Non-parallel and curved lines are affected in the same way, of course, but it is easiest to show the effect with parallel lines which are straight. The relative change of position of objects as the eye position changes also gives rise to impressions of relative distance. If an object appears to occlude or cut off part of another object, then it tends to appear as if nearer. This is illustrated in Figs. 7:5 and 7:12(a). The factors of closure and the good Gestalt play important parts, and so do the phenomena of figure and ground because, other things being equal, the figure always seems to occlude the ground and appears as if nearer and more sharply defined than it. This is shown in Fig. 7:13. One may see the dotted areas as the ground and the clear areas as the figure, or vice versa, and these modes of perception may alternate, but

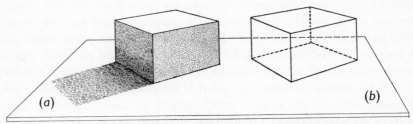

FIG. 7:12. (a) This illustrates the effect of convergence of parallel lines, occlusion of background, and the influence of graduated shadows in creating an impression of depth. (b) This shows how the absence of shadows and the suggestion of background objects through an outline give the impression of transparency.

whichever parts are seen as the figure appear nearer and clearer than the parts seen as the ground. Thus the impression of depth may be given in monocular vision by a flat pattern.

Another factor is that of relative movement, and it is closely connected with the factor of occlusion just mentioned. A fast and a slow-moving object might appear to be at the same distance, but if the slow moving one is occluded by the fast one then there is a clear impression that the fast one is nearer. Similarly, if a moving object is occluded by stationary or more slowly moving objects, it appears to be farther away, and an experiment illustrating this might be carried out in such a way that the objects were at the same distance. For example, if in Fig. 7:14 an object were made to move from A to B and then disappear, and a similar

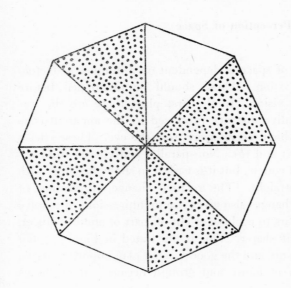

FIGURE 7:13
The "windmill" figure in which it is possible to see either the dotted or the white areas as the "sails" of a "windmill". Whichever parts form the "figure" seem nearer and more definite than those which form the "ground". (After Boring.)

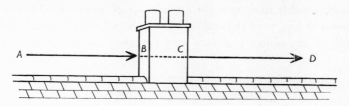

FIG. 7:14. If an object is made to move from A to B, then to disappear momentarily, and thereafter to move from C to D, it will
appear to be farther away than the chimney stack.

object from *C* to *D* after a momentary interval, the viewer would have the
impression that a single object passed behind the chimney stack. This,
however, leads us into the field of the perception of movement, to be dealt
with in a later chapter.

Other important factors in space and distance perception are those of
relative sharpness of outline, relative clearness of detail, and the relative
size of familiar objects. Blue, purple, and violet objects in landscapes tend
to seem more distant than red, yellow, and green ones, because these
colour effects are associated with the impression of distance in natural
scenery. It is generally held that cold (blue and green) and less saturated
colours look farther away than warm and more saturated colours. Exacting
experiments in a room with movable walls which could be made various
colours, however, have not upheld the frequent assumption of artists and
others that colours have large or consistent distance effects, apart from
associated experiences and the influences of boundaries and contours.
Those objects with sharper outlines, showing more detail and larger in
perspective size, will appear nearer, although very large objects with little
or no detail and vague outlines will tend to seem far away, especially if
blue, violet, or purple in colour.

Shadows are very important in creating the impression or experience
of depth and solidity. The eye in perception is intensely sensitive to
shadows, and all artists know that the degree of darkness and the exact
shapes of shadows are extremely important in their work. In Fig. 7:12
the object (*a*) on the left looks definitely solid, while the object (*b*) on the
right might be flat or hollow and, since there is the suggestion that the
background appears through it, the object tends to look transparent. The
gradation of shadows is extremely important, the darkest part of object
(*a*) being that between the shadowed side and the shadowed part of the
table, because the more exposed parts tend to be illumined by adventitious
light. In drawing a face subtle use of shadow gradations is required to
control the appearance of solidity and therefore of the most delicate
nuances of expression.

It is impossible to reverse the appearance of hollowness of objects like those shown in Fig. 7:15 (b) and (c) by a direct effort of thought and, if the shadowing of any object is drawn very precisely and accurately, then the

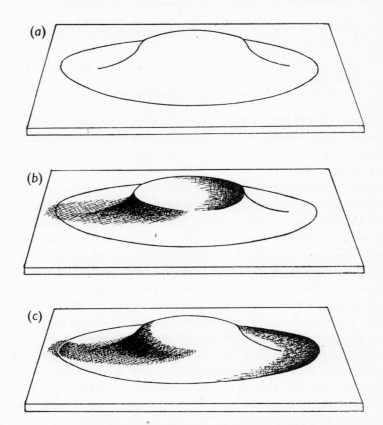

FIG. 7:15. The effect of strong shadows from a single source of illumination gives an impression of solidity and/or hollowness which is very difficult to reverse, and is deceptively real. The same outline which appears in (a) may be made to look hollow like a crater as in (b) or solid like a knob in a circular depression as in (c) simply by adding shadows in different ways.

impressions of solidity or of hollowness are so strong as to be deceptive. Since many of the shadows used by artists are themselves seen in complicated perspective shapes, the precise details of their structure are of almost uncanny importance in painting.

Binocular and Stereoscopic Vision

Stereoscopic vision was an important development in the evolution of perception. All the effects just mentioned may occur in monocular

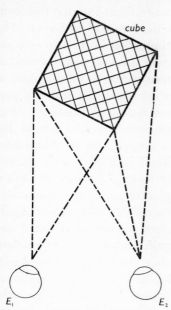

FIGURE 7:16
The different appearances of a cube from the positions of the two eyes are shown in plan on this figure.

vision. Apparently in the more primitive animals which have two eyes placed one at each side of the head and have monocular vision, as in most fish, each eye deals independently with one side of the environment. In other animals, such as the horse and cow, the eyes are so placed that there is some overlapping of the fields of vision. They have panoramic vision, and within the areas of overlap a given object will present slightly different appearances to the two eyes. In Man, with fully developed binocular vision, not only are the fields of vision of the two eyes

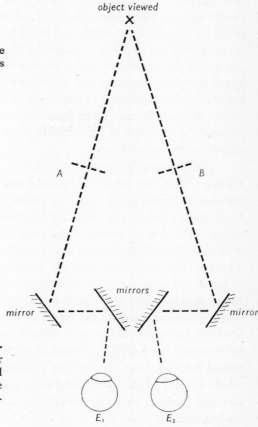

FIG. 7:17
Diagram of the Wheatstone or mirror stereoscope, or range-finder. For the range-finder the object viewed will be at X. For the stereoscope the two disparate pictures to be combined will be at A and B.

largely overlapping, but the eyes are closely co-ordinated so that they converge and bring the images of the object onto the foveae of both eyes. The slight differences, or disparities, in retinal stimulation in the two eyes are illustrated by Fig. 7:16 and, within wide limits, are not seen. Instead of seeing double, the person sees the object as stereoscopic, or solid-looking in space. This transformation of the small retinal disparities into the perception of solidity is a most important and interesting phenomenon. Fig. 7:17 illustrates the possibility of vastly increasing binocular retinal disparation by a system of mirrors as used in a range-finder or Wheatstone stereoscope. The two eyes may receive stimuli as if they were six feet apart, and then the impression of depth or relative distance of objects viewed is enormously increased without any corresponding magnification of the object. In this connexion it should be noted that binoculars magnify the retinal stimulus area and improve accurate perception of detail and outline, but they do not correspondingly magnify the effects of stereoscopic distance cues or retinal disparity in perception. In consequence, objects seen through binoculars tend to appear flat, as if cut out of sheets of cardboard and placed one close behind the other. The stereoscopic cues could be magnified to correspond with the magnification of retinal stimulus areas only if the two object glasses of the binoculars had an appropriately greater distance between them, as if our eyes were placed six or ten feet apart in space, as with the Wheatstone stereoscope. This is done by long-distance range-finders where, however, the problem is the deduction of the distance of an object from the measurement of the angle of convergence of the rays of light incident on the two widely separated object glasses of the range-finder.

The problem of binocular vision is closely related to that of range-finding. The two eyes act unconsciously as a range-finder because the amount of convergence required according to the distance of the object from the observer provides unconscious cues of distance in binocular vision. The interaction of these cues with the further cues of clearness of detail normally indicating near objects is disturbed in using binoculars. The eyes converge little, as for a distant object, but there is much detail, as for a near object, and we have to learn to focus for an object apparently large, detailed, and near, and at the same time to converge as little as would be appropriate to viewing a distant object. The conflict of factors tends to make binoculars less efficient for visual perception than would be expected on purely geometrical grounds. These points are all mentioned here to show that normal perception is a complex function of the whole system of the eyes and brain, and not simply a question of geometrical optics. In using binoculars one has to learn a new system of co-ordinations.

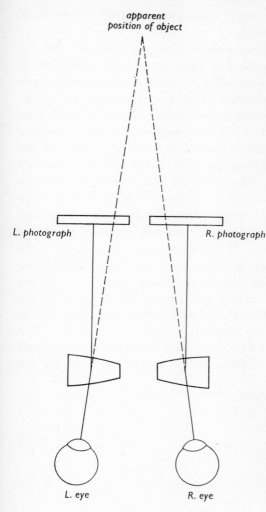

apparent
position of object

L. photograph

R. photograph

L. eye

R. eye

In the prism or Brewster's stereoscope, illustrated in Fig. 7:18, it is possible to present to the eyes two photographs of the same object taken from positions as far apart in space as the eyes themselves, one photograph to each eye, and to combine them so that they are seen in binocular vision as one picture. Then retinal disparity

FIGURE 7:18
Diagram of the Brewster or prism stereoscope.

FIGURE 7:19
The pairs of lines and dots are viewed in a stereoscope so that the two halves of the figure are super-imposed in binocular vision. Lines or dots $B + B^1$ look farther away than $A + A^1$ in binocular combination. (After E. B. Titchener, by permission of John B. Titchener.)

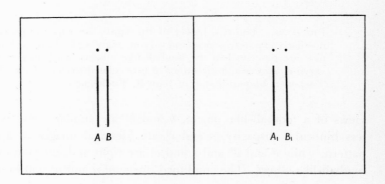

A B   A₁ B₁

is established as in normal stereoscopic vision and is not itself perceived, of course, but the object appears solid.

Many people think that the degree of binocular disparity and the question whether it is to the temporal or nasal side may have little effect. These doubts, however, may be dispelled by studying Titchener's cards with a standard Brewster stereoscope. Fig. 7:19 shows that a single-appearing dot or line may be made to look nearer or farther away than another. Lines (or dots) A and A^1 are in corresponding places, but line (or dot) B^1 is temporally displaced from B for the right eye. In the stereoscope only two lines and dots are seen, but $B + B^1$ looks farther away than $A + A^1$. If, however, the card is cut in half and the halves are turned upside-down, or if they are exchanged without turning them upside-down, then $B + B^1$ looks nearer than $A + A^1$, because the disparity is now to the nasal side. Indeed, it is not necessary to have a stereoscope for such experiments. If one fixates a pencil point near the eyes and holds the diagram at arm's length, the two halves of the diagram may be made to fuse in crossed vision. A little practice and skill are required to converge the eyes on the pencil point but to focus on the diagram. Then the line (or dot) $B + B^1$ will look nearer than $A + A^1$ because crossed vision reverses the disparity.

Another card, illustrated in Fig. 7:20, shows how degree of disparity determines degree of apparent depth. In it a and a^1 are right and left

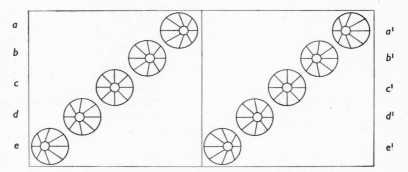

FIG. 7:20. The two halves of the figure are super-imposed binocularly in a stereoscope, and varying degrees of solidity or hollowness are perceived in the fotoball-like objects, according to their varying degrees and directions of binocular disparity. (After E. B. Titchener, by permission of John B. Titchener.)

views of a football-like object, b and b^1 are similar views with slightly less binocular disparity, c and c^1 are identical images of a similar flat pattern, while d and d^1 and e and e^1 are right and left views of a hollow football-like object. The combined image of a and a^1 will be much more bulbous than that of b and b^1, while c and c^1 in binocular combination will look flat. The $d\,d^1$ and $e\,e^1$ combinations will look hollow, $d\,d^1$ being more hollow than $e\,e^1$. If now the card is cut in half and the halves are reversed in the stereoscope, $a\,a^1$ and $b\,b^1$ will look hollow while $d\,d^1$ and $e\,e^1$ will look solid, $b\,b^1$ being less hollow than $a\,a^1$, and $d\,d^1$ being less bulbous than $e\,e^1$.

If the two eyes were placed one above the other in the head, instead of side by side, we should expect perpendicular disparity to give stereoscopic and depth effects rather than lateral disparity. The fact that it does not may be shown by means of a card with two pairs of perpendicular lines upon it as in Fig. 7:19. If it is cut in half and the two halves are placed in the stereoscope sideways, either way up, no sideways position gives any impression of differences in the relative distances of the dots or lines. It is an intriguing speculation what vision might have been like had three eyes been established in evolution, and whether "trinocular" vision would have been of any biological advantage.

A stereoscopic pair of photographs of the moon may be cut in half and reversed in the stereoscope and the moon will tend to look hollow, like the inside of an illuminated translucent hemisphere. What kinds of objects may be made to look hollow in this way is an interesting psychological question. In general the answer is that an object seen with reversed binocular disparity will look hollow if the hollowness does not conflict with other major cues for solid vision such as shadows, and if it is the sort of object which might be met with in a hollow form. It is almost impossible to make a human face look hollow. In a pair of stereoscopic photographs of a complex scene such as a view of the Sphinx and Pyramids, if the retinal disparity is reversed some fragments within the whole may seem hollow while the main parts tend to appear persistently solid.

The present tendency in psychology is to minimise the importance of binocular and stereoscopic vision in space perception, but it would be hard to overestimate its importance for accurate vision. Stereoscopic vision underlies all precision of movement and manual skill, as well as giving us the foundation of the accurate comprehension of the external world on which our conceptual systems of science and philosophy are ultimately based. In Man not only is vision the dominant mode of perception, but stereoscopic vision is the predominant way of seeing all external objects. It is surprising what can be achieved with one eye, but it can never compete effectively with stereoscopic binocular vision.

Where binocular disparation is so great that fusion of images cannot occur, then one of the images is normally suppressed and some training may be necessary to make the subject realise it is there at all. If we hold up the right forefinger near the eyes with the left in line with it farther

away, and then fixate the left forefinger, it is possible to see the right
forefinger nearer but rather vaguely, and any more distant objects also
rather vaguely beyond the left forefinger. If we now try the experiment
of closing first one and then the other eye we shall realise that the more
distant object and the nearer (right) finger are seen in double images
(diplopia), the images appropriate to the less dominant eye being normally
suppressed in binocular vision. Nevertheless, these double images add
their weight to stereoscopic effects.

Size and Shape

The apparent relative sizes and shapes of objects seen in perspective in
monocular or binocular vision, are subject to a further important controlling factor often called size or shape constancy, or "phenomenal
regression" to the "real" object, to use the expression suggested by
Thouless. In this connexion no metaphysical problems are raised or
intended to be raised when the terms "phenomenal," "regression," and
"real" object are used. The "real" size or shape is simply the size or
shape which would be ascertained if the object could be measured directly,
instead of being seen in perspective at a certain distance from the observer.

Many constancy phenomena can be demonstrated by simple experiments which anybody can repeat at home. The apparent shape of a circular
plate, for example, seen in perspective at a certain distance is not as
narrow an ellipse as geometry would predict. It is much more nearly
circular. In fact the plate continues to appear more nearly circular than
would be expected whatever the perspective shape, and there is a compromise between the "real" circularity and the perspective shape predicted. The geometry of the experiment is illustrated in Fig. 7:21.
Thouless believed that the phenomenon of shape constancy accounted for
some non-perspective drawings by famous artists who drew what they
"saw" and not what they ought to have seen according to geometrical
theory. A good example is the famous painting of his yellow chair by
Van Gogh. Indeed, it may be false to teach anybody to draw accurately
according to perspective because nobody sees in that way. As an index of
phenomenal regression Thouless employed the formula $\log P - \log S / \log R - \log S$, where P is a measure of the apparent or phenomenal shape or
size, S of the stimulus, and R of the "real" shape or size. The application
of this formula to the results of the shape experiment can be seen from
Fig. 7:22, in which the diameter of the "real" circle seen is R, its diameter
in perspective is S, and the diameter of the ellipse chosen as equivalent to
it by the viewing subject is P. There are very considerable individual
differences in constancy phenomena, and the adoption of the "stimulus"

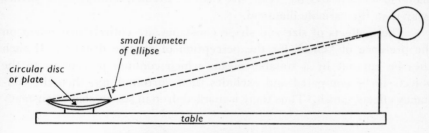

FIG. 7:21.   This illustrates the perspective view of a plate seen on a
table by a person sitting at a distance from it.

attitude as contrasted with the "object" attitude reduces it. Artists, who
probably utilise the "stimulus" attitude, have less constancy than the
average individual.

Size is subject to similar influences. This can be demonstrated using
the apparatus illustrated in Fig. 7:23 in which a diamond may disappear
into a slot. If this diamond is placed at a distance of one metre, and a
standard diamond having twice as large a diagonal at two metres, then
according to the rules of perspective the two diamonds should appear to
be of equal size. In fact they do not, and the "variable" diamond must
be made much larger than predicted according to perspective to make
them look the same. There is a compromise in that the more distant

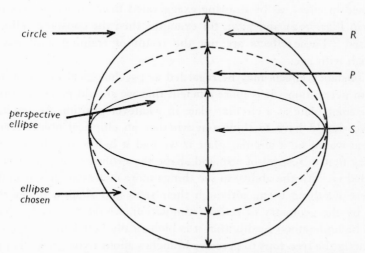

FIG. 7:22.   The "real", "perspective" and "phenomenal" shapes
of a circle seen in perspective like the plate in Figure 7:21. (After
Thouless, by permission of the Editor of the *British Journal of
Psychology*.)

diamond looks nearer its "real" size than we predict, although it is farther away than the variable diamond.

These effects of size and shape constancy are entirely dependent on the presence of "cues" for the perception of relative distance. If such cues be cut out by a suitable means which confines perception to the objects to be compared and excludes their surroundings, then the constancy effects vanish. Thus there is marked drop in size or shape constancy

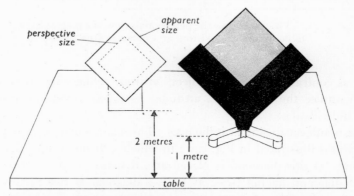

FIG. 7:23. The "perspective" and "phenomenal" sizes of a diamond seen at a distance of 2 metres, and the variable or comparison diamond at a distance of one metre. (Apparatus invented by Thouless.)

in monocular as compared with binocular vision. Also, if the cues can be increased in effect, as by drawing exaggerated lines of perspective on the tables in Figs. 7:21 and 7:23, for example, then the constancy effects are increased. These effects are not the result of training and may even diminish with age.

Constancy effects may be regarded as psychological forms of adjustment in perception. It is more efficient that we should perceive and react to a circular plate as a circular plate in whatever position we see it, than that we should have to think out whether an elliptical object seen at a distance would be a circular plate if we had it before us. In general we may say that in respect of size and shape the evolution of perception has provided us with the ability to see things more or less as they would be if we were handling them, although their sizes and shapes, if determined solely by the geometry of retinal stimulation, would be greatly changed. It can be understood readily that it is biologically better for an ape swinging among the tree-tops to perceive branches about to be grasped approximately the sizes and shapes they would have if actually handled, rather than strictly in stimulus or perspective sizes and shapes, which continually change with varying distances. Thus the discoveries of constancy phenomena have revolutionised our understanding of perception in many ways, and they have shown that the mechanism of perception is an integrating system between stimulus and behaviour. For example, when we aim and shoot at a flying pheasant we do not aim at an object continually diminishing in perspective size as it flies away, but at a normal-appearing pheasant.

As mentioned before, if the subject adopts the "stimulus" attitude, his impressions of size or shape may be surprisingly accurate, and this may be achieved either by making allowance for the effects of distance or by comparing the angles subtended by the objects.

If, however, he adopts the "object" attitude, then the effects of constancy or phenomenal regression are marked. Which attitude is adopted may be decided by individual habits of perception, by the experimenter's instructions to him, or by other conditions prevailing at the time. For example, it is probably easier to adopt the "stimulus" attitude in relation to objects of unknown size, especially if the distances are great, and the "object" attitude for objects of familiar size at short distances, but all such generalisations are likely to have exceptions.

Closely related to constancy phenomena is the fact that lenses do not give apparent magnification as great as would be calculated on optical principles. We tend to see an object more nearly the size it should be if seen without the lens, than the size predicted on the basis of retinal image dimensions alone.

Constancy Phenomena in General

These constancy phenomena occur widely in perception in other sensory modes than vision. Katz has shown that colours are not seen strictly according to the nature of the various lights reflected by objects under given conditions, but more in accordance with what other cues indicate that these colours would be if the objects were seen in uniform and standard lighting. For instance, although incandescent electric lights are very yellow in comparison with daylight, they do not make ordinary objects seem abnormally yellow. Indeed, even the fluorescent lighting we are now becoming familiar with is not as deceptive as the physicist would predict. The "white" fluorescent tube lights grossly exaggerate some parts of the spectrum, and delicate colour matching by them is very difficult or impossible. This is worse than for the usual incandescent filament lamps because, owing to the peculiar mixture of spectral lights given out by fluorescent lamps, the illumination they give actually looks almost white, whereas that of ordinary lamps does not. The eye is less deceived than would be expected by mercury vapour and sodium vapour lights because the first is clearly blue and the second yellow, and in both cases the illumination is by very narrow spectral bands. With these lights we tend to see the colours of objects as if changed, but not as much as would be predicted in terms of the illumination alone. The eye tends to compensate for the distortions of the colour of familiar objects, but the apparent disturbances of colour are smaller than might be expected. However, while even artists seem to be able to tolerate the use of fluorescent tube lighting in picture galleries, probably because the illumination seems to be by white light, it is not likely that sodium or mercury vapour lights would be tolerated since they cut out many hues altogether.

It is easy to set up a simple laboratory experiment in which colour constancy can be measured for any colour, but red is convenient. A colour wheel, with red and grey sectors of the same brightness illuminated by a beam of white light, is compared with a white-and-black-sectored colour wheel which is illuminated by a beam of red light. This experiment is

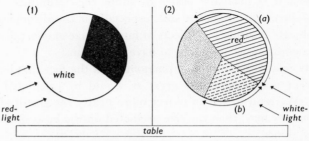

FIG. 7:24. This illustrates the different proportions of grey and red paper on a rotating disk (2), illuminated by white light, which are required to match a given proportion of black and white paper on another disk (1), illuminated by red light. (a) shows the proportion of red required without reduction screen, and (b) shows the additional amount of red required when the reduction screen is used.

illustrated in Fig. 7:24. The red colour wheel looks red because it reflects mainly the red components of white light, but the white and black wheel looks red because it reflects the red light which illuminates it. If the reds are chosen carefully the two wheels may be adjusted to match in apparent colour. Now they are viewed through a "reduction screen" which, in this case, is a large sheet of cardboard with two holes cut in it through each of which a small part of one of the wheels may be seen. Viewing through this screen will show that the red disk has been made much less red than objectively necessary to match the other, and the difference between the direct comparison and the comparison through the reduction screen may be measured by a simple psychophysical procedure. This difference is due to the fact that under normal viewing conditions the white and black disk looks like a grey disk illuminated by red light, while the red and grey disk looks like a red disk illuminated by a white light. Colour constancy tends to make the subject see the white and black disk as much less coloured than it is, unless it is seen through the reduction screen which cuts out the perception of the differences between the beams of red and of white light illuminating the disks, and gives an objective comparison.

Another field in which constancy phenomena play a big part is that of the perception of the upright and of the horizontal. If we are in an aeroplane which tilts while turning or circling we do not perceive fully the changes from the horizontal and vertical, which may be very great. Much depends on the suddenness of the changes, however, but the perceptual system rapidly adjusts itself, taking the floor and upright parts of

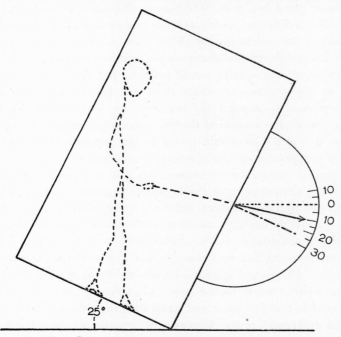

FIG. 7:25. This illustrates the "phenomenal" horizontal chosen by a person in a room tilted at 25°, which is a compromise between the true horizontal and the tilt of the floor. (After Beveridge, by permission of the Editor of the *British Journal of Psychology*.)

the vehicle as the standards for the horizontal and vertical. As an aeroplane tilts to circle and land we may feel the floor to be relatively horizontal while the ground below appears to be at an almost dangerous angle. In the same way, if a person inside a closed box is tilted at various angles, but asked to indicate the horizontal on a scale with a pointer, he will tend to give a compromise between the true horizontal and the "horizontal" represented by the floor of his compartment, as in Fig. 7:25. When we are in an aeroplane or other fast-moving vehicle which tilts with respect to the normal perpendicular, the centrifugal sideways forces due to the angular acceleration to a great extent counteract or combine with the normal action of gravity and give us a new direction for "down" in terms of the influences acting on the otoliths in the saccule and utricle. On the other hand, when we are in a stationary position in a large tilted box, like that illustrated in Fig. 7:25, the gravitational cues are normal, but the visual and kinesthetic cues lead us to tend to perceive the frame of the box as "upright" and the floor as "horizontal."

Perceptual constancy has been shown to affect the velocity of moving objects and also the relative loudness of sounds. Thus, two objects moving at the same speed but seen at different distances, do not appear as if moving at such different speeds as would be predicted on the basis of the movements of the retinal images alone. Sounds of the same intensity but from sources at different distances are not as different in apparent loudness as the law of inverse squares would predict. Perceptual size constancy is possible in any situation in which there are distance cues and does not only or necessarily depend on binocular or stereoscopic vision. For instance, Sonoda has measured the size constancies of objects seen monocularly as if inserted at certain points in flat pictures which had various degrees of perspective effects in their construction.

In general, constancy phenomena are due to a psychological system by which the environment of the organism is perceived in an apparently constant form to a great extent, although it may undergo many objective changes. This apparently constant environment has been called by Koffka the "behavioural" environment, because it is towards this phenomenal environment that we behave, rather than towards the environment of physically determined stimuli. In all likelihood it is when there is a failure to adapt oneself to the new "horizontals" and "verticals" of a moving vehicle that giddiness and nausea set in, although there are large individual differences in the degrees to which one person is liable to these effects and another is not.

The Distorted Room

Ames showed that it is possible to build a room the shape of which, illustrated in Fig. 7:26, is distorted in such a way that every point in it is in line with the projection of another point which could be in a normally rectangular room when we look into it in monocular vision through a small aperture in its front wall. Usually it is made so that the sides are perpendicular and parallel with the forward line of vision (which is a compromise) but the back slopes away to the left, the bottom descends, and the top ascends away from the observer. When this is done, of course, the back part of the room on the left is actually much further away than the monocular visual cues would suggest, and objects placed in the two positions *A* and *B* will look as if at the same distance. Nevertheless, they

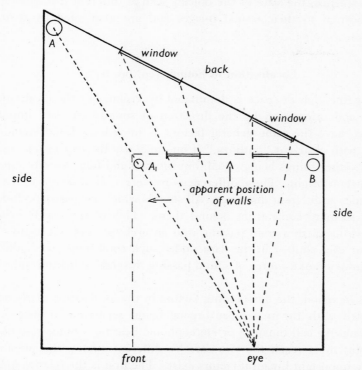

FIG. 7:26. Plan of the distorted room of Ames, to show the real positions of the walls and windows and their apparent position to an observer looking monocularly through the eye-hole. (After Ames; adapted by permission of the publishers from *Elements of Psychology*, by D. Krech and R. S. Crutchfield. New York: Knopf, 1958.)

may be of the same size and then the distant one will look much larger than the near one, because it seems to be at the same distance.

It is said that a distorted room was also constructed for binocular vision. All the distortions in it would, of course, be curves, and its construction was entrusted to a firm of shipbuilders who specialise in building tridimensional curved objects such as ships. When it was completed, it is reported that the workmen said that there must be something wrong with the design because when they looked into it—binocularly of course—the room appeared rectangular and neither curved nor distorted. This, however, is exactly what was wanted, and was predicted by the theory underlying its construction.

The distorted room gives conditions of perception which are the very opposite of those leading to perceptual constancy, because it acts as a tridimensional reduction screen in which distance cues are cut out and, in consequence, the sizes of the objects seen at different distances appear in proportion to their retinal images and are unaffected by their real distances.

Localisation of Sounds (cp. pp. 63-4)

Man's perception of space is dominated by vision, but the localisation of sounds and orientation by the direction of sounds are very important. Here we have the same general factors as in vision. Loud sounds and sounds with clear-cut "outlines," if one may use the expression, seem to be near, other things being equal, but muffled and faint sounds appear to be of distant origin. These differences are very well observed in listening to thunder at different distances. All sounds which are partly occluded by objects seem to come from behind them. This is very easily observed when we listen to a train passing into an archway and out again. Even with our eyes shut or in the dark under such conditions we should have the impression of a source of sound passing through or behind some other object.

As in vision, the outstanding factors in the localisation of sounds are connected with the two sense organs being separated in space. This gives what we call binaural or stereophonic hearing. Since sounds from any point must reach the two ears by different routes, the possibilities of three important binaural factors exist. The first is the relative loudness factor. For short distances a sound reaching the nearer ear will be slightly louder than it is in the other ear because its intensity is inversely proportional to the square of the distance it travels. The second factor in binaural hearing is that of time differences. This applies to sounds of short duration or sounds which have a sudden beginning, like clicks. The nearer ear will receive the sound waves first (Fig. 7:27).

The third factor affecting binaural hearing is that of phase differences. There has been much dispute about whether this factor can possibly have any effect on perception, but now its significance is generally conceded. The sound waves reaching the two ears may strike them in different phases, and one ear may be receiving the air compressions (or "crests") while the other receives the rarefactions of air (or "troughs"). Again, the effect depends on the angle at which the oncoming sound waves strike the head, and the relation of the distance apart of the ears to the wavelengths of the sounds heard. This whole subject is highly complex and cannot be dealt with fully here, but we can say that in general the sound seems

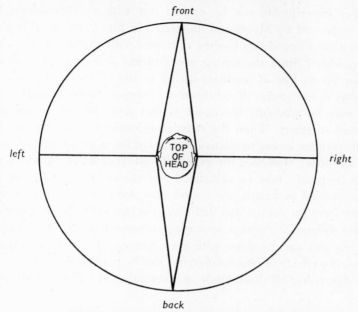

FIG. 7:27. This diagram illustrates the fact that sounds from the front or back of the head have the same distance to travel to the two ears while sounds from the sides have to travel a shorter distance to one ear than to the other.

to come from the side which is leading in phase, just as it seems to come from the side which is louder or leading in time.

It has been shown by experiments that phase differences are most important in the localisation of low-pitched sounds up to about 1000∼ and loudness differences for high-pitched sounds, but in the region of 3000∼ neither phase nor intensity differences are available to any extent, and localisation for sounds of about this frequency is poor.

Experiments on sound localisation can be carried out with the sound perimeter by means of which a click is made in an earphone suspended from a stand above the subject's head and moved into various positions equidistant from the centre between his ears while his eyes are shut. This is illustrated in Fig. 7:28. Sounds from the front (or back) reach the two ears from equal distances, and there are no time or loudness differences. Consequently, front and back are very readily confused. A slight ability to distinguish front and back may be due to differences in the quality of sounds produced by the "sound shadows" from the head and external ears. Sounds from the left or right, however, give the greatest time and loudness differences in the two ears, and left and right are almost never confused.

HSPM

Other experiments can be carried out with the "trombone-tube" apparatus devised by Myers and illustrated in Fig. 7:29. In this a single sound is passed round two lengths of tubing with U-shaped slides to the ears separately. Since the tubing is cylindrical and constant in diameter there can be no loss of loudness owing to the effects of distance. If a continuous sound source of subthreshold intensity from an audiometer is used it may be gradually increased so that time differences are greatly diminished in effect. Then the remaining localisation effects are due to phase differences, unless to relative changes of intensity owing to resonance in the two tubes. However, the expected resonance differences for a sound of given frequency may be calculated and allowed for. If the trombone slides are varied in length, the sound may seem to come first from one side, then from the centre, and then from the other side in accordance with the phase differences, always appearing to come from the side leading in phase. As this can be done with pure sounds of several different frequencies, the effects of phase difference can be made quite clear.

In discussing all three kinds of binaural cues—time, loudness, and

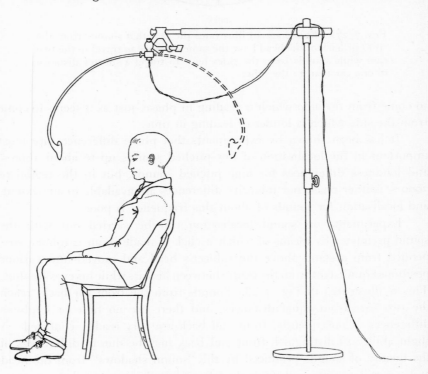

Fig. 7:28. The "Gallows" apparatus, or sound perimeter, a swinging arm carrying a microphone, by means of which clicks may be produced at various positions around the head.

phase differences—it is important to say that the psychological localisation of the sound is perceived without any awareness of the stimulus differences as such. This is parallel to the effects of stereoscopic vision in so far as it is not dependent on conscious perception of the binocular differences. The ability to move the head so that the maximum use is made of the difference between the two ears is also important. Thus it is possible to "point" the face towards a source of sound so that the sound appears neither to the left nor to the right unless slight head movements are made. In many animals, like the donkey, which have large external ears or pinnae, these organs are mobile and can be "aimed" at sound sources, and one ear may move independently of the other.

Localisation of objects by hearing is important for the blind. It is not likely that they have enhanced auditory acuity, but they become expert in using auditory cues not consciously noted by others. It has

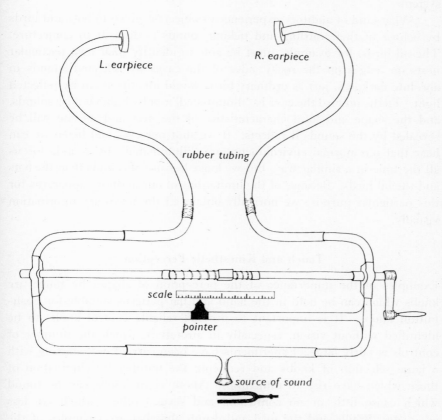

FIG. 7:29. The "Trombone-Tube" apparatus of Myers, by means of which a sound may be made to travel different distances to the two ears without loss of intensity owing to distance.

been shown that the blind normally notice changes in the reflexion of sounds from objects in their neighbourhood and so can avoid them. For instance, a blind man uses the tapping sound of his stick to help him perceive that he has come to the end of a wall.

This use of sounds sent out and reflected back from objects is a kind of localisation system to which the term "sonar" has been applied in parallel with the more familiar "radar" systems now widely used on aircraft and ships, and it is now well established that bats can find their way through complex objects such as the branches of trees by means of the ticking sounds which form the basis of a "sonar" system. Navigational cues are provided by variation in the ticking rate according to the complexity of the objects to be avoided. Similarly, the oil birds of Venezuela and the swiftlets of Borneo, which live in absolutely dark caves, are able to avoid obstacles and to fly accurately in the caves by the aid of a sonar system.

What kind of auditory experience of objects is given to bats and birds by echoes of their rattling and ticking sounds is difficult to conjecture. The oil birds, for example, must be able to identify their own particular nests on ledges on the rocky sides of the caves by reflected sounds in absolute darkness, just as ordinary birds would identify them by reflected light. To the oil bird the cave is "illuminated" not by lights but by sounds, and the shape and local characteristics of the nest and its site will be revealed by the sounds it reflects. If we shut our eyes and listen we can hear that our normal environments are "illuminated" by sounds for us all the time in a similar way, but we make less use of sounds than the bats and the oil birds. Because of the limitations of our auditory apparatus for this particular purpose we normally obtain all the necessary information visually.

Touch and Kinesthetic Perception

Examples of the importance of the perception of shapes by touch are knobs which can be held in the hand and flat patterns suitable for push-button knobs. It is important to provide reliable control knobs to be identified without vision, especially in aircraft in which the number of controls is fairly large. Experiments have been carried out, starting with a large selection of knobs and reducing the number by elimination of those which gave rise to difficulties. About eight knobs can be found which cause little or no confusion, and several others which are less adequate. Braille and the deaf-and-dumb alphabet are examples of the use of tactile perception for reading and for talking. Russian psychologists have made a machine with six points which can emerge as projections on a little plate about half an inch square and which may be felt by the finger tip, and form distinct patterns corresponding to each of the letters of the words on a printed page which is scanned by a "viewing" lens that moves along the lines of print automatically, letter by letter. This enables the blind deaf mute to read a book, if it is printed in suitable type.

Where kinesthesis is added the problem is much more complex and interesting. The expert pianist or violinist does not have to look at his hands or at the instrument. The visual information on the sheet music, or the memory of it, is translated automatically into appropriate arm, hand, and finger movements through kinesthetic and tactile perception to produce the sounds intended. Similarly, the expert horn player can pick out any note on the instrument, which has a range of about three and a half octaves, almost exclusively by the appropriate lip tension and air pressure, in conjunction with pitch. Considering the enormous range of tensions required, and that they are not in a linear series but are based on a series of increments which increase as the pitch ascends, this is quite a remarkable achievement.

Harper has shown that judgments about the quality of "firmness" are important in cheese-making and in the grading of many food products, and that they must enter into many other activities. "Firmness" is a unique perceptual quality involving the integration of tactile and kinesthetic data, and characteristic of the deformation of materials under pressure by the hand or fingers. It may be derived from materials as different as an elastic solid, like vulcanised rubber, of which the amount of deformation is proportional to the pressure applied, and a stiff liquid like Californian bitumen, of which it is the rate of deformation which is proportional to the pressure. "Firmness" therefore relates to materials like putty, clay, dough, soft plastics, plasticine, and very stiff liquids. The sensitivity of judgments of "firmness," the variability of these judgments in an individual or between individuals, the extent of their improvement with practice or training, and methods of estimating and testing them are all of considerable practical and theoretical importance.

BIBLIOGRAPHY

General

ALLPORT, F. H. 1955. *Theories of Perception and the Concept of Structure.* Chapman and Hall, London; Wiley, New York.

BEARDSLEE, D. C. and WERTHEIMER, M. 1958. *Readings in Perception.* Van Nostrand, London and New York.

ELLIOT-SMITH, G. 1927. *Essays on the Evolution of Man.* Oxford University Press, London.

GELDARD, F. A. 1953. *The Human Senses.* Chapman and Hall, London; Wiley, New York.

JOHNSON, D. M. 1961. *Psychology: A Problem Solving Approach.* Harper, New York.

KOHLER, W. 1930. *Gestalt Psychology.* Liveright, New York.

KOFFKA, K. 1935. *Principles of Gestalt Psychology.* Harcourt Brace, New York.

KRECH, D. and CRUTCHFIELD, R. S. 1958. Elements of Psychology. Knopf, New York.

LINDGREN, H. C. and BYRNE, D. 1961. *Psychology: An Introduction to the Study of Human Behaviour.*

PIÉRON, H. 1952. *The Sensations, their Functions, Processes, and Mechanisms.* Muller, London.

POLYAK, S. 1957. *The Vertebrate Visual System.* University of Chicago Press, Chicago.

TITCHENER, E. B. 1901. *Experimental Psychology: A Manual of Laboratory Practice,* Vol. I, Part II. Macmillan, New York.

Visual Perception

AKISHIGE, Y. (Ed.). 1961. *Experimental Researches on the Structure of the Perceptual Space.* Kyushu Psychological Studies, No. II, iv, xx-xxix.

BEVERIDGE, W. M. 1935. Racial differences in phenomenal regression. *Brit. J. Psychol.,* **26,** 59-62.

——1939. Some racial differences in perception. *Brit. J. Psychol.,* **30,** 57-64.

DAY, R. H. and LOGAN, J. A.; STORY, A. W.; TERWILLIGER, R. F.; WILSON, J.; and SUTHERLAND, N. S. 1961. Figural after-effects. (Papers.) *Quart. J. Exptl. Psychol.,* **13,** 193-228.

GIBSON, J. J. 1950. *The Perception of the Visual World.* Houghton-Mifflin, Boston.

ITTELSON, W. H. 1952. *The Ames Demonstrations in Perception.* Princeton University Press, Princeton.

KATZ, D. 1935. *The World of Colour.* Routledge and Kegan Paul, London.

KILPATRICK, F. P. (Ed.). 1952. *Human Behavior from the Transactional Point of View.* Dept. of Navy, Washington, D.C. Institute for Associated Research, Hanover, N.H., U.S.A.

McEWEN, P. 1958. Figural after-effects. *Brit. J. Psychol. Monogr.* Supp. **31.** Cambridge University Press, London.

McKENNEL, A. C. 1960. Visual size and familiar size: individual differences. *Brit. J. Psychol.,* **51,** 27-35.

NEWHALL, S. M., BURNHAM, R. W. and EVANS, R. M. 1958. Color constancy in shadows. *J. Amer. Opt. Soc.,* **48,** 976-984.

PENROSE, L. S. and PENROSE, R. 1958. Impossible objects: a special type of illusion. *Brit. J. Psychol.,* **49,** 31-33.

SONODA, G. 1961. Perceptual Constancies observed in Plane Pictures. In Experimental Researches on the Structure of the Perceptual Space. Ed. by Y. Akishige. *Kyushu Psychological Studies,* No. II, iv, xx-xxix.

THOULESS, R. H. 1931. Phenomenal regression to the real object. *Brit. J. Psychol.,* **21,** 239-359.

——1931. Phenomenal regression to the "real" object. II. *Brit. J. Psychol.*, **22**, 1-30.

——1932. Individual differences in phenomenal regression. *Brit. J. Psychol.*, **22**, 216-241.

VERNON, M. D. 1937. *Visual Perception*. Cambridge University Press, London.

——1937. The perception of distance. *Brit. J. Psychol.*, **28**, 1-11 and 115-149.

——1952. *A Further Study of Visual Perception*. Cambridge University Press, London.

Auditory Perception

BEATTY, R. T. 1932. *Hearing in Man and Animals*. Bell, London.

BROADBENT, D. E. 1958. *Perception and Communication*. Pergamon Press, London and New York.

CRANBROOK, The Earl of. 1960. Feeding habits of noctule bats (*Nyctalus noctula*), and notes on the feeding habits of the long-eared bat. *Suffolk Naturalists' Transactions*. **XI**, Parts II and III.

GRIFFEN, D. R. 1955. "Sonar in Bats" and "Sonar in Birds". *Twentieth-Century Bestiary*, 147-164. Simon and Schuster, New York.

——1958. *Listening in the Dark*. Yale University Press, New Haven.

——1960. *Echoes of Bats and Men*. Heinemann, London.

Tactile Perception

GREEN, B. F. and ANDERSON, L. K. 1955. The tactual identification of shapes for coding switch handles. *J. Appl. Psychol.*, **39**, 219-226.

HARPER, R. 1952. Psychological and psycho-physical studies of craftsmanship in dairying. *Brit. J. Psychol. Monogr.* Supp. **28**. Cambridge University Press, London.

JENKINS, W. O. 1947. The tactual discrimination of shapes for coding aircraft-type controls. In Psychological Research in Equipment Design. Ed. by P. M. Fitts, U.S. Government Printing Office, Washington, pp. 199-205.

8

Perception of Time, Movement, and Causality

Changing and Successive Stimuli

We are not equipped with special sense organs for perception of movement of objects outside our own bodies, or for time and causality, and there are no fundamental "stimuli" for these experiences in the sense in which there are special stimuli for colours, sounds, and other familiar sensations. Time, external movement, and causality, in other words, are no more direct sensory experiences than distance, solidity, or hollowness. They are perceptual experiences due to integration of other sensory data and are not reducible to special sensations.

As stated in the last chapter, perceptions and not sensations are the ultimate components of experience. Sensations are products of scientific theorising (cp. 136). They are inferred by the psychologist as the necessary basis of perceptions, or implied by carefully planned and conducted experiments in which special stimuli are isolated and separated as far as possible from their usual backgrounds or settings in experience. Thus, to find and measure the effect of stimulation with a certain wavelength of light we have to make an elaborate apparatus to isolate it as far as practicable. The person may then report about the experience, but it is always necessary to realise, (1) that there must be a background of other experiences of some kind, (2) that no background will be without its effect on the experience produced by the isolated sensory stimulation, and (3) that absence of other stimulation is in itself a kind of background. The practical problem will be to reduce these effects to the minimum since we can never eliminate them altogether.

In what ways, then, do the experiences of time, external movement, and causality differ from direct sensory experiences? They differ because they are special products in experience of certain kinds of sensory data in combination. Thus, owing to our highly controlled experiments we are confident that the sensation of sky-blueness is produced by a certain wavelength of light impinging on the retina. We believe it would still be produced if we could stimulate the necessary minimum receptor field in isolation, and indeed that it would be much more saturated than any blueness we normally experience, because it would be free from the impurities due to adventitious effects and surrounding excitations of other receptors. On the contrary, we cannot isolate a stimulus for time, external movement, or causality experience, but must rely on the relationships between various stimuli to produce them. It will be seen that experiences of time are produced by stimuli occurring in succession. These could be isolated, but if they were, then they would not give rise to the impression of time passing. Similarly, experiences of movement and causality are produced by stimuli in succession in time and also in certain spatial relationships. These stimuli could also be isolated but then the impressions of movement and causality would disappear. There are, of course special kinesthetic and vestibular receptors to provide information with regard to movements of the body in part or as a whole.

Perception of Time

The conditions under which various combinations of stimuli give rise to temporal experiences are parallel in a very interesting way to those of space perception. Just as a single dot is simply an interruption of a spatial uniformity and has no other structure except the sharp gradation of contrast between itself and its background, so a momentary stimulus is an interruption of a uniformity of duration. If, however, two or more dots or stimuli occur, they are linked in perception spontaneously in a special manner which must be due to the integrative action of our psychophysiological organisation, and is not explained by conscious synthesis, judgment, inference, or deduction.

This may be illustrated again by diagrams on a flat page similar to those used for the illustrations of the perception of dot patterns in Fig. 7:1. Fig. 8:1 makes this clear, and in it (*a*) shows a single isolated stimulus in a uniform duration experience, (*b*) illustrates a pair which are apprehended as linked and enclosing a time interval, while (*c*) shows a more elaborate experience of time patterning. In Fig. 8:1 (*d*) and (*e*) one can see the origin of temporal rhythms and, as everybody knows, in music and poetry the additional sensory differences of stress, here represented by large and small dots, are integrated into the sequence, giving a characteristic and flowing temporal pattern.

Piéron concludes that the minimum perceptible time interval for two visual stimuli in succession is about one-tenth of a second, whereas for hearing, touch, and kinesthesia it is about one-hundredth of a second. Thus, Binet and Courtier found that in playing five notes of a scale on the piano in sequence, time intervals of the order of one-hundredth of a second could be varied with precision. Music obviously depends on such subtle adjustments as these.

Experiments on "filled" and "unfilled" intervals with the Leipzig time-sense apparatus, which enables us to make a precisely measured interval between the two taps, either filled with other taps or unfilled, usually show that unfilled intervals seem shorter. Similar experiments can be carried out with spatial stimuli. On the other hand time intervals filled with interesting activities which do not excite anxiety tend to be underestimated, and intervals filled with the imaginary anticipation of

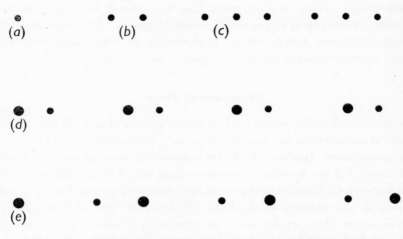

FIG. 8:1. This illustrates the influence of time differences and variations of stress in rhythmic arrangements of sounds. (After Wertheimer. By permission of Springer-Verlag, Berlin, and Michael Wertheimer.)

feared events such as the period of waiting before a serious operation, a trial, or punishment seem long. Nevertheless, a man who spent four days in complete isolation in a soundproof room and who signalled at irregular intervals his estimate of the time of day, gained more than four hours in the first day but subsequently readjusted his guesses so that he was only forty minutes in error at the end. It is suggested that he learned to judge the time by various internal cues, such as the recurrence of hunger, which are normally overlooked.

There is also the phenomenon of assessment of the passing of time under normal conditions. In some experiments sleepers, when wakened at intervals and asked to estimate the time, were correct to within a quarter of an hour. Certain individuals can decide to wake up at a specified time and do so to within a few minutes. For such people a decision to waken at a certain time means, it is believed, that they sleep less soundly than usual and that their sleep is more or less continuously disturbed. It is almost certain that they respond to noises, such as birds singing. This is merely an extension of the ordinary capacity to awake at the same time each morning which becomes a habit for many of us.

Experiments suggest that there is a "chemical clock" in the physiological system which is affected by body temperature almost according to a definite law (Arrhenius's equation). A subject counted intervals of one

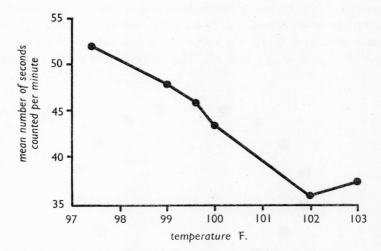

FIG. 8:2. A graphical representation of the dependence upon body temperature of the estimated number of seconds in a timed minute, in an experiment by Hoagland. (See Table I.)

minute in estimated seconds during various stages of a fever and her counting was affected in a surprisingly steady manner by her body temperature, as shown in Table 1 and Fig. 8:2. This reminds us that it is possible to tell the air temperature from the rate of chirping of certain crickets in New England.

TABLE I

The Dependence of Time Estimation upon Body Temperature

Order	Temperature	Mean No. of Seconds counted per Minute
1	103·0 °F.	37·5
2	102·0 °F.	36·0
5	100·0 °F.	43·5
3	99·6 °F.	46·0
4	99·0 °F.	48·0
6	97·4 °F.	52·0

Perception of Movement

The Phi-Phenomenon (cp. p. 20)

The phi-phenomenon is the impression of movement between two or more stationary stimuli given successively in time and near each other in space. It is illustrated by Fig. 8:3. The dots are electric lamps wired so that 1, 4, 7, 10, 13, and 16 are lighted first and then extinguished after a momentary interval, and 2, 5, 8, 11, 14, 17 are lighted next, and then in the same way, 3, 6, 9, 12, 15, and 18, and so on indefinitely, beginning again with 1, 4, 7, 10, 13, and 16. The observer will tend to see an oval

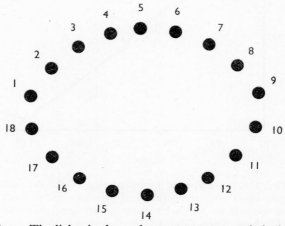

FIG. 8:3. The lights in the oval arrangement are switched on and off in three groups, 1, 4, 7, etc.; 2, 5, 8, etc. and 3, 6, 9, etc., and in consequence of the successive groups of flashes there is an appearance of clockwise movement.

ring of lights moving clockwise if the spacing and time are appropriate. Anti-clockwise "movement" would be produced in a similar way by reversing the order of illumination of successive groups, and all manner of other movement effects can be imitated by appropriate devices. For example, in Glasgow at one time there was a very clever imitation in coloured lights of a bearded Highlander lifting a glass of whisky to his lips and putting it down again; the glass filled and emptied appropriately. Since the basic psychological factor is the stimulation of two retinal points in near succession, it may be seen that the phi-phenomenon is the essential principle underlying seen movement on the cinema screen and in television. A series of "frames" or still photographs is taken on the cinema film and, if they are in close enough succession and the objects photographed do not move too fast, the numerous changes of position fuse into a continuous apparent "movement." A tremendous slowing of the process in which, for instance, we take one photograph every few hours, speeded up for visual presentation, may give the impression of plants growing, and so on. If the frames are too widely spaced in time, or if the objects photographed move too quickly so that the successive points are too widely spaced, then a fluttering effect is produced, and it is well known that in their early days cinemas were popularly called "the flicks."

There are many conditions which contribute to the phi-phenomenon, such as the distance apart, time intervals, and intensity of lights. Similarity plays a part and, in the case of three circular spots the movement might pass as easily from any one to any other, but if two of them are

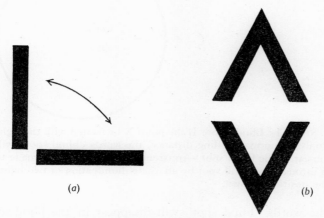

(a) (b)

FIG. 8:4. Two different types of movement, produced by alternate illumination of figures in different positions. The upright line in (a) seems to rotate to its horizontal position and back, but the V-shaped figure in (b) "flops" over from one position to the other. (After Korte; similar to figures in *Elements of Psychology* by D. Krech and R. S. Crutchfield. New York: Knopf, 1958. By permission of the publishers.)

crosses, movement is more likely to occur between them because they are alike, than between a cross and a circle, which are different. In Fig. 8:4, the upright line in (a) may seem to rotate to the position of the horizontal line and back if they alternate. In (b), however, the movement may occur in the third dimension and the figure seems to turn through space towards the observer into its new position and back again. Without doubt the temperament and personality of the observer, his degree of suggestibility, and the instructions themselves are very important factors. A significant point is the difference between an impression that there is movement between the points, which may occur when they are widely separated, and actually "seeing" the first point move across to what seems to be its second position. Thus many people see movement across a road between

Belisha beacons if their timing is not absolutely coincident. The various problems cannot be dealt with fully here, but, as noted in Chapter 5, the phi-phenomenon is not an effect produced by stimulating adjacent retinal receptors successively, because experiments may easily be set up to show that it will pass through the blind spot where there are no receptors. This is illustrated in Fig. 8:5. If the point X be fixated in vision with the right eye only, the left being closed, and the page is held about normal reading

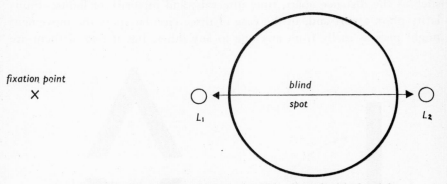

FIG. 8:5. The Blind Spot. If the point X be fixated with the right eye only, at normal reading distance, the words "blind spot" will disappear in the blind spot. Apparent movement may be made to pass through the blind spot by alternate illumination of two lights in the positions shown.

distance, the words "blind spot" will disappear in the blind spot itself and movement might be made to pass through this spot by alternate illumination of two stimulus lights in the positions shown. Evidently the phi-phenomenon must have a central and not a peripheral basis in the nervous system.

Perception of External Movement (cp. p. 97)

Direct visual perception of the actual motion of external objects never occurs. If, for instance, the eyes fixate a given point or object and other objects pass across the field of vision stimulating a succession of retinal elements, each element gives a momentary response and then passes into a refractory phase before it can respond again. This succession of responses is no different from that produced by the successive stimuli of the cinema when the momentary pictures are provided by the photographer, whereas in ordinary vision they are provided by the eye. While moving bodies or changing shapes may stimulate adjoining retinal elements, as already noted it is not an indispensable condition for movement perception.

If, instead of fixating a still object we fixate a moving point and

follow it with the eye, then the objects in the background usually appear
stationary. This is not always true, but depends on which set of objects
in a given scene tend to form the ground or framework, and which the
figure. For example, if we watch a man cycling along a roadway he
usually appears as the figure and the roadway and surrounding countryside
as the ground; the man and not the roadway moves. If, however, we look
at the moon on a night when the clouds are passing rapidly over the sky,
the clouds may seem to be the ground and the moon the figure, racing
along against them. Again, a passenger in a train moving off slowly may
have the impression that a stationary train alongside it has started to
move in the opposite direction, while if the adjacent train moves off instead
he may have the impression that his own train has started. The impression
or illusion that it is the other train which is moving depends partly on
the movement of the passenger's own train being so gentle that the vestibular apparatus is not stimulated enough to give perception of movement
of his body, and on the absence of vibration. Otherwise, it is clear that the
decisive factor in apparent movement may be the distinction between
figure and ground. Which train appears as figure and seems to move, and
which as ground and seems stationary, may depend purely on the passenger's attitude, mental set, or mode or direction of attention at the
critical moment.

After-Effects of Movement

If one stares steadily at, or fixates, the centre of a rotating spiral of
the kind illustrated in Fig. 8:6 and continues fixation after rotation has
stopped, the spiral now appears to expand or to contract according to the
direction of rotation, and this effect will last some seconds and gradually
fade away. This after-effect, which is due to cerebral activity, can be
transferred to other objects. If the spiral is first rotated clockwise it
seems to contract and the after-effect (counter-clockwise rotation) then
makes it seem to expand. If the fixation point is now transferred to a page
of print, or to a cross or other figure, then the print or cross will appear
to contract or expand according to the original direction of rotation of the
spiral.

The after-effects of movement are experienced in everyday situations.
For example, if a person whirls round and stops suddenly he may feel that
he is rotating in the opposite direction for a moment. Another common
experience is the impression, when a lift stops descending or ascending,
that the sides of the shaft are moving in the opposite direction. In such
an experience the lift usually appears as the "ground" and the shaft sides
as the "figure," and thus the after-effect seems to be in the "figure"
rather than in the "ground," as would be expected from what has already

been said. These experiences are after-effects of movement and are different from the experiences of the moving trains mentioned previously.

Fig. 8:6.   If the spiral is fixated for a time while rotating and then stopped, it will appear to expand if the rotation was clockwise, but to contract if it was anti-clockwise. (After Krech, D. and Crutch-field, R. S. from *Elements of Psychology*, 1958, by permission of the publishers, Messrs. Alfred A. Knopf, New York.)

Movement of Celestial Bodies

Although the earth is moving in its orbit round the sun at a relatively high speed, it does not seem to move because its distance from any celestial body with which its position could be compared directly is too great; the phi-phenomenon is not experienced under these conditons. As the sun comes near the horizon, however, one is able to see the relative change of position of the earth and sun as the distance from the edge of the sun to the horizon decreases, as shown in Fig. 8:7, and especially when they "touch," but it is the sun and not the earth which appears to move. This is because the earth forms the "ground" in this perceptual situation and the sun forms the "figure." The apparent movement of celestial bodies, except meteors, is therefore always the result of change of apparently static positions, and is subject to the psychological laws of "figure" and "ground."

Other experiences of movement in external bodies may be similar.

When one object creeps towards another, or when objects smoothly change shape without fulfilling conditions which would correspond to the phi-phenomenon, movement may be perceived. It might then be said that movement is "inferred." Sometimes this is true, as when we notice that there has been a change and think to ourselves that a certain object

FIG. 8:7. As the sun "approaches" the hillside it is "inferred" to move because the space between it and the hillside becomes smaller and smaller, although it is not actually perceived as in motion.

must be moving, but when we just perceive or have the impression that it is moving rather than stationary, as a result of more rapid changes of shape or position, then there is no conscious inference but the impression of movement is experienced through the action of the perceptual system, just as solidity is experienced without our seeing double.

In the end it is true, therefore, that there is no such thing as the direct perception of the actual movement of external objects. Often it can be absolutely imitated by the phi-phenomenon and there is no reason to suppose that the normal perception of fast-moving objects differs from this imitation in any essential way. With very slow moving objects it is either an impression due to change of relative position or shape or both, or it is a deduction from independently observed facts. Perception of movement would be absolutely the same in a universe which disappeared from existence utterly and was recreated in a succession of different but stationary forms sufficiently frequently. A cat running across the floor or a bird flying would look precisely the same if it were annihilated and re-created fifty times a second.

Stroboscopic Effects

Successive stimulation can not only make us perceive movement in stationary objects, as in the phi-phenomenon, but it may also be used to make bodies in motion appear stationary. Instruments known as stroboscopes are used for this purpose. The stroboscope is an electronic or other device which produces very short flashes of light at regular intervals, and the rate of flashing can be accurately controlled from very slow to very fast. If a rotating piece of machinery, such as a rapidly moving crank in an engine, is illuminated by such an instrument, the flash rate of the stroboscope can be adjusted to the speed of rotation of the crank or to a fraction or multiple of it, in such a way that the illuminated crank appears to remain in one position. The expression "appears to remain" is used, because, however short the flash may be, the crank must move to some extent while it lasts, but it will be perceived as if perfectly still and can be inspected visually in its "position" by a mechanic. So definite is the impression of stillness that it is reported that many fingers have been lost by unsuspecting people who tried to touch the moving object to test the theory that it was not stationary. Obviously, the perception of stillness by successive flashes requires a flash rate above the critical fusion frequency (cp. pp. 98-9).

If the flash rate is slightly less than the speed of rotation of the crank, each successive illuminated position will be a trifle in advance of the previous one and the crank will appear to be rotating very slowly in the actual direction of rotation. If the flashing rate is greater than the speed of rotation of the crank, then each flash will illuminate the crank in a position slightly behind that previously seen, and it will appear to rotate in the direction opposite to that of actual rotation. Similar paradoxical rotation effects are often evident in the cinema. For instance, spokes of wheels may appear to be rotating forwards, remaining stationary, or rotating backwards as in Fig. 8:8 according to the relative acceleration of the vehicles and the rate of exposure of the cinema frames. Such illusions are a combination of the phi-phenomenon, flicker fusion, and stroboscopic illumination.

It has been shown that in reading the eye makes several fixation points on a line of print and there is no perception during the eye movement from one fixation point to another, or back to the next line of print. If, however, we arrange a ring of dots on a disc and rotate it at such a speed that the rate of movement of the dots is the same as the rate of movement of the eye from one fixation point to another, it is easy to perceive a single dot moving continuously during an appropriate eye movement. The reason why perception does not normally occur during an eye movement is that the stimuli pass over the retina at a speed greater than the critical fusion frequency, unless we fixate continuously an object moving sufficiently slowly, such as a bird flying.

It is easy to imagine auditory effects similar to the stroboscopic effects just described. The sound track of a cinema film is continuous, although the visual track is divided into successive frames. If, however,

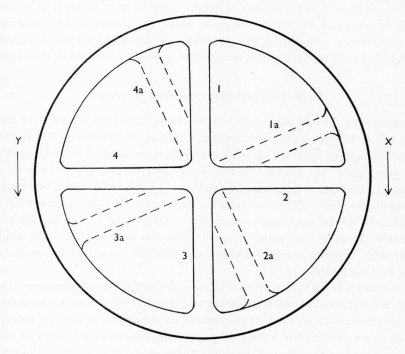

X = direction of real rotation

Y = direction of apparent rotation

FIG. 8:8.   If a wheel rotating clockwise is photographed first when the spokes are in the positions shown by the solid lines, and next when they are in the positions of the dotted lines, and so on, and if these photographs are used as the successive frames of a cinema film, then the film when projected will show the wheel as if rotating anti-clockwise.

the sound track were divided in an appropriate manner and the audience were viewing, for example, a battleship firing its big guns at a submarine some miles away, the timing might be arranged so that the visible and audible explosion of one shot hitting the submarine was immediately followed by the audible and visible explosion of the next shot being fired from the battleship and, after a momentary interval during which neither the visual nor the sound track recorded anything, the same happened again and again. Then one could have the impression that the submarine was firing at the battleship, particularly if the guns of neither were themselves visible in the photographs, but only the smoke and flames. The reader may think of other examples in which vision is not a necessary adjunct.

It would appear, therefore, that real stillness is no more directly perceived than real movement because, under certain conditions moving objects appear stationary, while under other conditions stationary objects seem to move. Moreover, the apparent direction of movement may be indecisive with respect to the actual direction of movement of the object.

Further Experiments on Seen Movement

If an oblique line is made to move sideways across the visual field from top left to bottom right, its apparent direction of movement will depend on the shape of aperture through which it is seen, as shown in Fig. 8:9. In this figure, (a) shows the real movement of the line, (b) shows its apparent movement when seen through a horizontal slot, and (c) through a vertical slot while (d) shows its apparent movement when seen through a circle. If several such lines are seen through several circles placed horizontally, however, the apparent movement is as shown in (e). The reader may draw his own inferences about the effect of the ground or frame on the moving figure.

From this we may turn to relative speeds of apparent movement, and Fig. 8:10 shows how an experiment may be devised to enable the subject to equalise apparent rates of movement in two trains of dots of different sizes upon continuous bands of paper and seen through slots of sizes proportional to the sizes of the dots. If the subjects make the adjustment for equality of rate of movement, the dots twice the size of the small ones, seen through an aperture twice the size of the small aperture, are made to move about twice as fast as the smaller dots.

The apparent movement of the cart wheel may be used as an illustration of the remarkable analytic and synthetic powers of perception in relation to the actual stimulus objects and their settings. The point on the surface of a wheel in contact with the ground is motionless, while the point at the top will be moving forwards at twice the speed of the vehicle, and the points at the horizontal extremes will be moving up or down according to their positions, and also forwards. If a black wheel is made to roll along a blackened table in a dark room with a very small light spot at some point on its circumference so that only the light spot is seen, then this spot will appear to move in a "cycloid" manner as shown in Fig. 8:11(a). If we also have a light spot at the hub, this will seem to move forward at

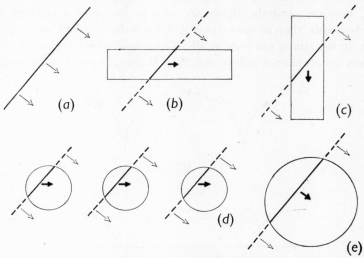

FIG. 8:9. In this figure (a) shows the real direction of movement of a line and (b), (c) (d) and (e) show its apparent movement when seen through different slots. (After Krech, D. and Crutchfield, R. S., *Elements of Psychology*; New York: Knopf, 1958, by permission of the publishers.)

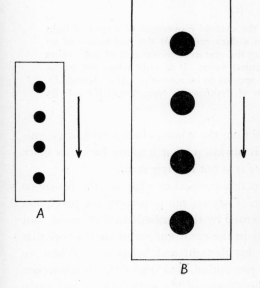

A

B

FIGURE 8:10
The dots in *B*, twice the size of those in *A*, and seen through an aperture twice the size, will be made to move about twice as fast as those in *A*, in order to appear to move at the same speed. (After Brown. From *Elements of Psychology*, by Krech, D. and Crutchfield, R. S., New York: Knopf, 1958, by permission of the publishers.)

a steady speed as shown in Fig. 8:11(*b*). When the whole setting is visible, however, and the lights are seen to be upon a rotating wheel rolling forwards, then as shown in Fig. 8:11(*c*) the "cycloid" movement of a point on the rim is not seen at all. The whole wheel appears to rotate, and many people cannot believe that there is always a point on its periphery

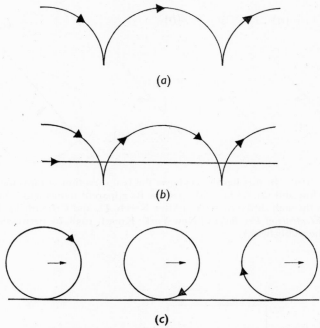

(*a*)

(*b*)

(*c*)

Fig. 8:11. This illustrates (*a*) the cycloid movement of a spot of light near the rim of a wheel seen in a dark room, (*b*) the movement of an additional spot at its hub; and (*c*) the apparent movement of both spots when the wheel is seen in a lighted room. It is only when the whole wheel is seen that the movement appears to be rotatory. (After Krech, D. and Crutchfield, R. S., *Elements of Psychology*; New York: Knopf; by permission of the publishers.)

which is motionless. At the same time the whole wheel seems to go uniformly forwards, although there is always part of it going forwards twice as fast as the hub, and one point of it is not moving at all.

We may well pause to ask in this connexion what are the functions of the eye and brain in perceiving. They are not to present the percipient with data as they would be represented by the mathematical physicist, but to keep him in touch with objects in the environment in such a way that they are directly meaningful for his thought and behaviour. When we say "eye" or "ear" in relation to perception, it is important to appreciate that we are speaking of the whole system of the sense organs and brain acting together. Thus it is clear that all attempts to represent the psycho-physiological system as a complex calculating machine which simply reflects the objective facts or elements of physical reality are bound to fail.

Stabilised Retinal Stimulation

As described in the earlier section on vision (cp. p. 98) there are three classes of normal eye movements, (1) large voluntary movements of changing fixation, (2) small drifting movements which are involuntary, and (3) minute involuntary "saccadic" movements. It is possible, by means

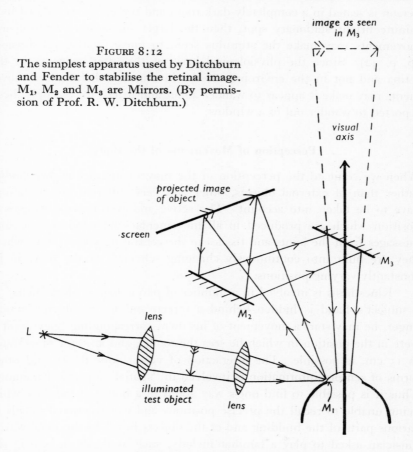

FIGURE 8:12
The simplest apparatus used by Ditchburn and Fender to stabilise the retinal image. M_1, M_2 and M_3 are Mirrors. (By permission of Prof. R. W. Ditchburn.)

of an optical arrangement including a minute mirror attached to a contact lens on the subject's eyeball, to compensate automatically for involuntary eye movements so that the image remains stationary on one part of the retina (Fig. 8:12). As already noted, under such conditions the image tends to vanish but is restored as a continuous perception if the stimulus pattern flickers at about the critical fusion frequency. In other words, not only is seen movement the result of stimuli separated in time and space, but also the normal perception of stationary objects is the result of interrupted stimuli, and the object is seen as stationary provided the successive stimuli are not separated in space beyond certain limits. More recent observations on the stabilised retinal image have suggested that vision is not completely eliminated. After a short interval large outlines and big areas of light may tend to return vaguely. In normal vision the saccadic movements promote continuous excitation but do not produce a conscious impression of movement of the objects seen. If, however, a person is seated in a completely dark room and the eye is stimulated by a minute bright stationary spot, then the larger involuntary drifting eye movements may make the stimulus seem to move (oculogyral illusion, cp. p. 42). Since the physiological basis of the after-image is in the retina and not in the environment, the involuntary drifting eye movements may make it appear to wander about and it has, for example, been reported to wander out of a window.

Perception of Movements of the Body

When we come to the perception of the movements of our own bodies rather than of external objects, other and very different considerations have to be taken into account. The active and even passive changes of position which are produced in all movements send combined sensory messages from the joints and tissues to the central nervous system where they are built into continuously changing schemata of the body in its constantly varying positions.

Kinesthesis is involved in a number of psychological phenomena. If a subject's hand is hidden behind a screen and he is shown a model finger, he may start a movement of his own, corresponding finger as if it were in the position in which he sees the model, and an error of as much as 15 cm. is possible. The interaction of vision, kinesthesis, and other forms of sensory information is involved in "spatial" aspects of memory. Thus it is possible to find one's way about in a house in the dark while being unable to recall the precise positions and constructional details of various parts of the building and of the objects in it. In the same way, a musician asked to play a familiar melody, such as the horn solo in the Nocturne of Mendelssohn's *Midsummer Night's Dream*, might be able to do it from memory quite correctly, but if he were asked to play a single note which occurs in it at a specified place, say its tenth note, without running through it from the beginning, he might not get it right. Old people with loss of memory can cope successfully with a familiar environment, but if they move into new surroundings the loss of capacity for accurate recall may lead to confusion and disorientation.

In general, movement is consciously referred either to our own bodies or to the environment according to which appears as the figure and which the ground under the special conditions of the moment. On this it is difficult to generalise, but often it we initiate a movement ourselves our body seems to be the figure which moves, whereas when the body is moved passively it may seem to be the ground, and objects around us seem to move suddenly towards or away from us. This is well illustrated when a person who has been knocked down says that the road "came up suddenly" and hit him.

When there is a confusion of figure and ground, disorientation and nausea may result. People vary very much in their tendency to suffer from sea, air, and in general from motion sickness, but experiments have shown that a swinging movement up and down of about 16 feet every 2 seconds will reduce almost anybody to nausea if continued long enough.

Perceptual Consciousness of Causality

In speaking of the perceptual consciousness of causality we refer to those situations where the percipient observes or seems to observe causality. As explained more fully in Chapter 14, the point of saying "he was perceptually conscious of" causality is to avoid implying either that causality was objectively present (as "he perceived it" would imply) or that it was not so present (as "he seemed to perceive it" would imply). Sometimes the phrase "impression of causality" is used in this way, but that would be confusing here since Hume used the word "impression" for what was immediately or directly perceived (a sense-datum) (cp. p. 269).

Michotte has shown that if an illuminated or dark patch, or a spot of light, or a dark spot, coloured or otherwise, is made to approach another and "touch it," and at the same time the second is made to move away in the same direction, then it appears to the majority of observers that the movement of the first has been imparted to or has caused that of the second. This is illustrated in Figs. 8:13 and 8:14.

There are many variations of this fundamental experiment. The first spot may follow the second in contact with it as far as its new position. Alternatively, when the first almost touches the second it may stop while there is still a slight gap and the second may move off in front of the first before it is touched. The first may reach the second and then return, while the second either moves away in the same direction or follows the first back again. All the many experiments can be carried out with rotating disks. The lines on these disks are drawn in such a way that the effect

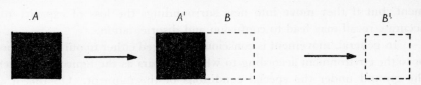

A   A'   B   B¹

FIG. 8:13. In Michotte's experiment the object *A* is made to
move towards *B* and apparently to touch it. Object *B* is then made
to move away and its movement appears to be caused by the movement of object *A*. (Similar to a figure in Krech, D. and Crutchfield,
R. S., *Elements of Psychology*; New York: Knopf; by permission
of the publishers and of Baron A. Michotte.)

desired for a particular experiment is obtained, and all of the disk except
the "spots" must be hidden. All the effects can also be obtained by
cinematograph methods.

The various psychological aspects may be summarised by saying that
the speed of movement of the first spot may be controlled, together with

FIGURE 8:14 (*a*)
This diagram shows the hidden disk in Michotte's
experiment, by means of which objects A and B are
made to move as shown in Figure 8.13. (By permission
of Baron A. Michotte. Similar to a figure in Krech, D.
and Crutchfield, R. S., *Elements of Psychology*; New
York: Knopf; by permission of the publishers.)

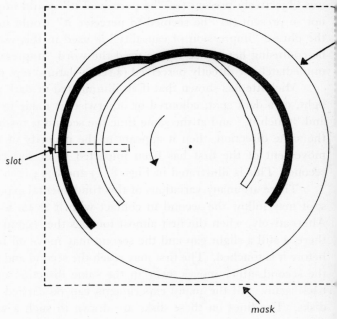

slot

mask

the distance it travels before reaching the second. The duration of its contact with the second may be controlled and so may be the direction and speed of movement of both the spots subsequently. Michotte showed that if the first spot remained motionless when it touched the second there was usually the consciousness that it had launched, pushed, or propelled the second. When the first followed the second and remained in contact with it, then there was the consciousness that it carried the second along with it. Perceptual consciousness of other relationships could be produced, such as unconnected movement, fixed continuous movement, "running away," "tunnelling under," "transportation," and "releasing" or "triggering off" a latent force of motion. A single spot which swells and then contracts several times in motion may give perceptual consciousness of spontaneous or animate causality. Sounds or touches may be made in such a way that the apparent contacts of the spots may also seem to cause them.

The essence of these experiments is that perceptual consciousness of causality is produced when there is possibly no "real" causality between

FIGURE 8:14 (b)

tte has found that the best effect of the "launch-
f B by A is obtained if B moves off at a somewhat
speed than that of A, as in Figure 8.14 (b), and
made to disappear behind a shutter at the end of
t. (Diagram presented by Baron Michotte.)

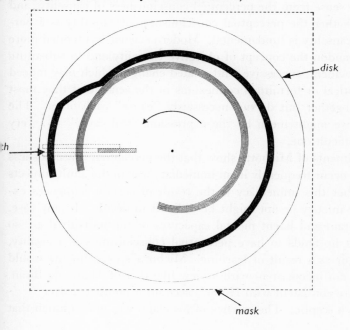

the two spots, or at least not of a kind of which the percipient is conscious, and that the variations of the objective conditions of the experiments lead to consciousness of different kinds of causality. The fundamental questions at issue are: (1) How is consciousness of causality affected by variations of the experimental conditions? (2) Can the perceptual consciousness of causality under these conditions be said to be perception of real causality?

As for the first question, there is no doubt that it is one of very great interest for psychology and that it can be answered by experiment. It is upon the second question, however, that attention may be focused.

In most or many of these experiments the consciousness of causality is immediate, and it is not an inference from data separately observed. According to Michotte, the results of his experiments are opposed to the theory of Hume, who claimed that causality cannot be directly perceived but is a relation which we "infer" (or, rather, are compelled by "instinct" and custom to suppose) to exist between events we have perceived to be constantly conjoined in time and space. Michotte also considered that the results were opposed to the theory of Maine de Biran, with which that of Berkeley should be coupled, that the perceptual consciousness of causality is the result of our projection upon external objects of our own subjective impressions of voluntary action, and the feeling that one object had caused the changes in another, just as we feel that we cause our limbs and other objects to move by means of our intention.

In this discussion it is necessary to be careful to distinguish causality in the objective sense from the perceptual consciousness of causality, and the question whether the perceptual consciousness of causality is a perception of real causality is fundamental. Modern science has tended more and more to abandon the concept of objective causality and to substitute a system of coincident, successive, and related changes which may indeed have only statistical or fortuitous connexions in the sense that they most frequently go together but do not necessarily "cause" each other. The question what we might mean by the expression "real cause" is a very complex and difficult one.

The experiments of Michotte show that the perceptual consciousness of causality can occur frequently in an immediate way in the adult subjects studied. Whether this immediacy is the result of certain sequences experienced since infancy or not might be difficult to decide. In any case, however, the brain and latent mental capacities of the individual are so constituted that he tends to have perceptual consciousness of causality, either innately or as a result of learning. Michotte's experiments would therefore seem not inconsistent with a view like that of Maine de Biran. Whether they are consistent with Hume's account is another matter.

Hume was a sceptic. The essence of his claim was not so much that perceptual consciousness of causality was in itself inferential, as that we can have neither proof nor even a clear idea of the existence of objective causality at all; that our idea of causality, a necessary connexion between cause and effect, is due to our customary expectation of the "effects" once the "cause" has been observed, and has no other basis. There is some doubt whether his aim was to prove the nonexistence of objective causality, or to show that it is meaningless to assert its existence, but he certainly claimed that what we think is an objective causal relation is in fact the product of our mental habits.

All the results of any experiments which depend on the perceptual consciousness arising from the manipulation of perceived objects would be open to Hume's strictures, and in the end there is no other kind of experiment, because all experiments depend on perception. While Michotte has successfully shown that the consciousness of causality is or can be immediate, and not what present-day psychologists would call an inference or deduction, this is not necessarily contradictory to Hume. He lived in a time when psychology was far less elaborated than it is today, and had he seen and understood the experiments he would have regarded Michotte's perceptual consciousness of causality as being our immediate reaction to the present succession of events, and so covered by his theory.

There are, of course, many situations in which the attribution of causality is inferential and due to reasoning. For instance, when a motor car is seen beside the road badly damaged and partly overturned, it is a legitimate deduction that the differences between it and a car of the same make in good condition and running on its wheels were caused by an accident. The deductions are, however, probably always based ultimately on generalisations from consciousness of causality on other occasions which may have been immediate in Michotte's sense. Nevertheless, it cannot be said that Michotte's experiments, however brilliant from a phenomenological point of view, have any bearing on Hume's claims that causality, as opposed to constant conjunctions or regular sequences of events, is not experienced directly and, indeed, that we have no direct evidence that it exists at all. Hume's theory undercuts Maine de Biran just as much as it undercuts Michotte, because both appeal to sensory observation and this, in whatever forms and under whatever names, is just what Hume said did not reveal objective causality.

Whether the perceptual consciousness of causality in Michotte's experiments is immediate or not, it is still an inference in Hume's sense, that it is not a direct observation of an objective relation. He would argue that it is the linking in the mind of two events as the result of our having observed events to succeed each other regularly in the past. This linkage is supplied by us, but it may be supplied so readily and habitually that causality seems immediately perceived even if it does not exist as an objective relation. Even if we claimed, as we might, that the perceptual consciousness of causality in the experiments and elsewhere was a spontaneous and immediate product of neuropsychological functioning, quite apart from experience in the past, Hume's strictures would not be met. Although he wrote in terms of habitual associations and previous experiences of events occurring together, if he were here today he would be able to say that even neuropsychologically produced linkages in perceptual consciousness, of an immediate kind not based on associated experiences, were no evidence of the existence of objective causality.

It may be claimed that in Michotte's experiments perceptual consciousness of causality occurs where causality does not exist. The so-called blocks or objects in his disk experiments are only the illuminated and visible parts of continuous bands. The first object does not actually "hit" the second, and even when we say that it touches the second we are doing so in what might well be called a metaphorical sense. There is no "hitting" at all. In the film the objects are only moving spots of light. The sense in which we can say that two spots of light are in contact, in these experiments, is quite different from that in which we could say that two billiard balls are in contact, because one spot of light could not cause another to move.

All this might seem to some people to accord with Hume's scepticism about the external world, and it might seem that we can test Hume's views by experiments in which there might be only associative relationships between certain impressions or sensory data. However, in the experiments the seen movements are due to a complex machine, so constructed that they are caused in a predetermined manner. These experiments are, therefore, further illustrations of the extraordinary powers of the perceptual system to abstract and generalise, and to put the percipient in touch with external relationships in the most direct and economical manner possible. The perceptual system is perfectly right in signalling "causality" in Michotte's experiments provided we can silence Hume, although it does not reveal all the intricacies of the machine at work unless further investigations are made. Thus it must be said that it is even impossible to set up any experiment on perceptual consciousness of causality in which what is usually called objective causality is excluded or does not exist in some way, although it may be very complex and indirect; and yet, in relation to every experiment, although one cannot exclude the possibility of causality, Hume would be able to say that there could never be proof of that objective causality itself, but only the idea of it.

BIBLIOGRAPHY

BEARDSLEE, D. C. and WERTHEIMER, M. 1958. *Readings in Perception.* Van
    Nostrand, London and New York.

CORNSWEET, T. N., CORNSWEET, J. C., RIGGS, L. A. and RATLIFF, F. 1953. The
    disappearance of steadily fixated visual test objects. *J. Opt. Soc. Amer.*,
    43, 495-501.

DITCHBURN, R. W. and FENDER, D. H. 1955. The stabilised retinal image. *Opt.
    Acta.*, **2,** 128-133.

GELDARD, F. A. 1953. *The Human Senses.* Wiley, New York; Chapman and Hall,
    London.

HUEY, E. B. 1924. *The Psychology and Pedagogy of Reading.* Macmillan, New
    York.

ISAACS, N. 1949. *The Foundations of Common Sense.* Routledge and Kegan Paul,
    London.

KRECH, D. and CRUTCHFIELD, R. S. 1958. *Elements of Psychology.* Knopf,
    New York.

MICHOTTE, A. 1946. *La Perception de la Causalité.* Publications Universitaires
    de Louvain, Louvain.

——1962. *The Perception of Causality* (3rd Edn.). Tr. Miles, T. R. and E.
    Methuen, London.

PIÉRON, H. 1952. *The Sensations : Their Functions, Processes, and Mechanisms.*
    Muller, London.

VERNON, M. D. 1931. *The Experimental Study of Reading.* Cambridge University
    Press, London.

——1952. *A Further Study of Visual Perception.* Cambridge University Press,
    London.

9

Learning and Special Conditions in Perception

Perceiving, Recognising, and Recall

In experiments on perception, recognition, and recall, Bartlett used cards on which were a variety of line drawings, simple diagrams, patterns, and partly representational material. The cards were exposed for the subject's perception in a tachistoscope, which is an apparatus with a shutter or other mechanism by which the object is revealed for a short and controlled period of time. In Bartlett's experiments the times of exposure ranged from about one fifteenth to one quarter of a second. The subjects reported on what was seen, and wherever possible reproduced it immediately by drawing it. They also reported introspectively on their mental processes in perception. Illustrations of some of the types of patterns and designs used are given in Fig. 9:1. One of the representational drawings was of a five-barred gate with a notice beside it: "Trespassers will be prosecuted." Fig. 9:1(d) was the first of a progressive series ending in a crown. Other

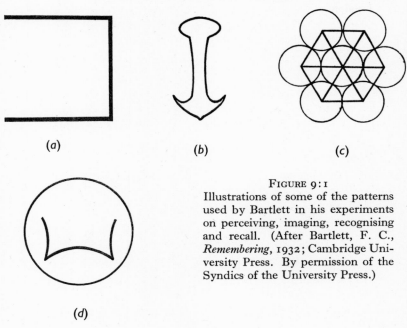

(a) (b) (c)

(d)

FIGURE 9:1
Illustrations of some of the patterns used by Bartlett in his experiments on perceiving, imaging, recognising and recall. (After Bartlett, F. C., *Remembering*, 1932; Cambridge University Press. By permission of the Syndics of the University Press.)

progressive series were also used, and these revealed the development of perceptions in successive steps.

While perception seems to be the most immediate of experiences, it can be very complex and is influenced by a great variety of conditions. These conditions include the effects of details in the object perceived, the mental setting which makes perception possible, attitude factors, and quasi-inferential processes. The experiments showed that there is no perceptual situation which is not dominated by some part of the material such as an odd or apparently incongruous aspect or feature, the disposition of figures and their relative emphasis, or the suggestion of familiar objects. Thus perceiving, although in a sense unitary and immediate, at the same time always tends to break the object or pattern into parts.

Under the heading of the influence of the mental setting was included the tendency to name material or to fit it, even unwittingly, into pre-existing patterns in the person's mental life. When perceived objects are more complex or less familiar, then there is a tendency to find analogical material or to name them, and a more conscious process of perceiving develops. Where the objects are very complex or unfamiliar there is hesitation, and sensory imagery of relevant material may enter conscious-ness. Where the material in a number of exposures forms a sequence of growing complexity, then a new attitude involving expectation of the direction of development and change will arise and will influence percep-tion, making it much easier.

In all perceptual processes the temperament, interests, and attitudes of the subject will influence his reactions to the material in a great variety of ways. Finally there is no difficulty in showing that perceiving often takes on the appearance of inferential construction (cp. p. 298).

It is easy to show that the recognition of objects once perceived is much easier than their precise recall. If a series of ten patterns or figures is first presented and then recalled by drawing and verbal description, probably less than half will be clearly remembered. If now these ten patterns are mixed in an irregular order with ten more, different but of the same general kind, at least nine of the first ten will be picked out by recognition, and possibly all ten.

Perceiving equips us to react with appropriate adjustments to specific objects in the environment, these objects being picked out and particu-larised in terms of their outstanding features, membership of certain groups or series, and in terms of our own past experience. Recognition equips us to react to them readily again and again, but recall enables us to identify particular objects from past experience and to anticipate their appearance again in the future. Recall, however, is very much less certain and efficient than recognition. Probably the psychologist must think of perceiving as

HSP O

a biological system of adjustment which has developed out of the organism's primitive reactions to regular and repetitive series of changes, such as those associated with the rise and fall of the tides for animals which live in tidal water. The limpet, for example, makes its regular round looking for food every day at high tide and returns to the same resting place at low tide. Since it makes almost the same reactions to the same objects every day, even perceiving hardly enters into its life and recognising very little, while memory probably does not enter at all. It only has to learn to react to an almost unchanging sequence of situations. With any marked changes in these sequences, which were certainly met with in the evolution of a land fauna, perceiving single objects, recognising them out of sequence, and later recalling them for anticipatory adaptations in behaviour, were necessary. Thus, perceiving, imaging, recognising, recall, and the higher mental processes must be thought of as specialised forms of adjustment to more complex, variable, and unfamiliar objects and events. Although the psychologist speaks of these mental functions as if they were "separate," in fact they must have evolved continuously out of each other, and the qualities of the most elaborate mental process are implicit and present to a small extent in an undifferentiated way in the most simple ones. Thus, perceiving often has some quality approximating to inferential construction.

Learning in Perception

It is clear that perceiving is a special form of the isolation by the organism of objects in the environment for response and mental manipulation, and Koffka brought this out very clearly when he distinguished between the "geographical" and the "behavioural" environments. The objects isolated in perception do not necessarily correspond exactly with objects which are real in the physicist's sense. No philosophical problems about the theory of knowledge are raised by this statement. Many examples of behavioural objects have been seen in Chapter 7. In its capacity as a functional system for providing the organism with behavioural objects, perceiving is subject to changes as a result of experience, or learning. Imaging, recognising, and verbal and other forms of remembering and also thinking are further processes which have adaptive functions on higher levels.

Drever has suggested four approaches as essential landmarks for the study of learning in perception. In the *"judgmental"* approach, perceiving is regarded as essentially analogous to thinking. In the *"stimulation"* approach there is an attempt to give an orderly account of how things look under various conditions of sensory excitation, and how the organism learns to exploit the wealth of stimulus variables offered by its environment. The *"association"* approach considers learning as association if we accept that concept as a basic general principle of explanation in psychology. The "*adaptation*" approach includes changes in perceiving which result from readjustments in functioning. This last notion will be mentioned later in the discussion of learning to see upright with inverting spectacles.

Here are some simple examples of the ways in which perceiving is subject to learning influences. Many people who have heard and even enjoyed birds' songs for years cannot tell the difference between the song of the blackbird, thrush, and missel thrush. If they had to learn, in addition, to distinguish the American robin which is another kind of thrush, the American wood thrush, and other thrushes, their difficulties would be greatly increased. These and similar perceptual differences cannot be learned without careful and repeated attention and depend upon some form of interest or motivation. In visual perception the position is essentially the same. The expert microscopist learns to discriminate between numerous kinds of tissues, the appearances of which are not different to the beginner. The musician learns to identify chords and their inversions in complex passages of music, even when passing dissonances are added and resolved. The different chords announce their identities to him as clearly as the blackbird or thrush announces itself to the bird watcher. Such skills acquired in perceiving are almost certainly based on native special abilities as well as upon learning by experience.

We may also note other examples in which highly skilled adaptive behaviour is involved as well as perception itself. "Road sense" is a necessary condition of driving a car efficiently without frequent accidents. The competent driver does not think elaborately of all the possible moves of the other vehicles on the road, estimate their speed in miles per hour, judge whether a slight hesitation or change of direction in a certain car's movements implies that the driver must have seen another car approaching from the side road, and so on. These points and many others may come into consciousness and call for special attention on occasions of difficulty, but for the most part they are dealt with by the flow of perceptual processes and their continuous linkage with adaptive behaviour in an almost unconscious manner.

To return to a musical example, the expert conductor, faced with a complex score in which there are several different clef signs and also numerous different transpositions for various instruments which transpose differently, can read the whole in his own mind, and sing or whistle the separate parts to show players what to do, and this is the result of an elaborate perceptual learning process, usually based on special aptitude.

Experimental psychology seeks to bring such examples within the bounds of laboratory control and to establish detailed facts about them. Frequently we have to deal with what might be called perceptual unlearning. James explained many years ago that the artist has to learn to see with an "innocent eye." In place of the objects seen by the ordinary person he must be able to see all the essential components of them in the visual pattern before him, to manipulate these components so that he can build up an aesthetically satisfactory picture, and to represent them by what might be called patches of paint on the canvas. Thus, the artistic imagination and behaviour in painting untie ordinary perceptual parcels and tie them up again for us, interposing aesthetic selection. Many pictures by modern artists, to whom the convention of perfectly smoothing over the patches out of which their structures have been made is less important than it was in the past, show us what the many appearances of ordinary objects may be under various conditions. For example, when examining a modern portrait such as one by Kokoschka, the viewer may find it difficult to believe that the patches of paint taken singly could possibly contribute what they do to a brilliant and penetrating representation of character. Examination of a classical portrait will then reveal that essentially the kinds of fragments are employed, but in a more smoothed and polished manner.

A familiar joke illustrates the close inter-relation between learning to perceive and not to perceive at the same time. A would-be purchaser of a picture of two female figures said to the artist: "It's an odd picture. I never saw women such an ugly shape before." The artist replied: "But think of the wonderful shape of the space between them. That's what I was really painting."

Some artists draw shapes "as they appear," rather than as they are to the physicist. The perspective shape of the chair and floor tiles in Van Gogh's famous painting of a yellow chair illustrates this. The conventional artist must represent objects by lines and areas adjusted for perspective so that when viewed they appear as if seen from a particular point in space. Modern artists, like Van Gogh and Matisse, often represent objects as affected by size constancy and phenomenal regression in general. Then to the viewer these pictures, although more psychologically correct in one way, present him with a new set of problems, namely to undo his own constancy functions and substitute those of the artist. In this way a new range of artistic vision is opened up, and the artist can show us what objects look like to him rather than as under conditions of strict geometrical perspective. Problems of artistic technique and convention may therefore involve problems of learning to perceive by both artist and spectator. Questions arise about how effectively the appearances of solid objects or their perspective shapes can be represented on flat surfaces at all. The history of art, however, provides many illustrations of the fact that drawing as we see, rather than as we ought to see according to the laws of perspective, has been found all over the world, in primitive as well as in modern art. The problems of perception in relation to art will be mentioned again in the next chapter.

Vision with Inverting Spectacles (cp. p. 79)

Apart from the direction of gravity on the Earth, presumably there is no such thing as the "upright," except on other planets where it might be in any direction at all in relation to the Earth. In fact, the upright at the Earth's equator is sideways for us, and at the opposite side of the Earth it is upside down. In any case, consciousness cannot be thought of as an "upright" person looking in on the brain, like an individual looking at a television set to see what is represented there.

Should it be said, therefore, that each of us learns to see the "upright" from infancy onwards? This may be partly true, but it is more than likely that the sensory-motor co-ordinations between vision, the organs sensitive to gravitational direction, and the muscles involved in balancing, standing, and moving in adjustment to gravity, are determined innately in part and also by maturation and development. Learning is superimposed on this basis. It would not matter how many times the optical image on the retina was inverted and re-inverted, or even if it were sideways, provided this basis and the subsequent learning were adequate for harmoniously co-ordinated movements. In a spaceship between planets, where there was no gravitational force, any position in which a person stood would seem as much "upright" as any other, and he would be able to stand sideways on a wall or upside down on the ceiling effortlessly without falling or feeling giddy, and always feeling "upright."

When inverting spectacles are worn the individual has to learn to reverse all normal and habitual adjustments to what seems upright. Stratton carried out experiments with inverting lenses, and more recently Erismann and Ivo Kohler used a flat mirror held in a suitable frame above the eyes as illustrated in Fig. 9:2. The effect can readily be tested by any reader who holds a plate glass mirror horizontally above the eyes. A simple lens system can be used to produce essentially the same effect, (Fig. 9:3). The subjects of these experiments had the task of learning to reverse all their normal and habitual adjustments. At first they seemed to themselves to be in an upside-down world. A man wearing inverted spectacles tried to pour tea upwards into a cup held upside down, with disastrous results. He lifted his leg to step over an archway seen upside down on the floor, instead of going under it. It is said that these subjects suffered from nausea, giddiness, and headaches at first and had to take strong sedatives. During about a month, two changes gradually took

place. The subjects slowly became able to make correct adaptive movements in relation to objects which, nevertheless, still seemed inverted, and
later they found that the objects no longer even seemed upside down. At
this stage the subject of Kohler's experiment could ride a bicycle safely
along a crowded street while wearing the inverting spectacles.

The new adaptations of vision and movement, however, were never
so well established as the old ones, and Pronko gives an illuminating
example of this. When his subject was standing on the parapet of a high

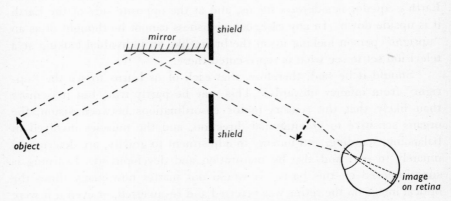

FIG. 9:2.   This diagram illustrates the method of inverting the
retinal image by means of a mirror above the eyes.

FIG. 9:3.   This diagram illustrates the inversion of the retinal
image by means of a simple lens system.

building looking at other buildings and saw nothing abnormal, he was
asked whether the scene before him looked upright. He immediately
exclaimed that as soon as this question was posed it suddenly seemed as if
inverted. After the inverting spectacles are removed the subject is confused, apparently sees things upside down, and makes false movements;
but in a few days he returns to his normal conditions of perception and
adjustment, just as if the experiment had never taken place.

Shigeoka has recently shown that there are no statistically significant
differences in size, shape, or brightness constancy between vision with
inverting spectacles and normal vision, and that the constancy of localisa-

tion of objects in space when there were head movements was not different with and without inverting spectacles.

We are quite accustomed in daily life to many side-to-side mirror reversals which do not disturb the relation to gravity. Most men can shave in a mirror, and the dentist has perfect sensory-motor adaptation to the reversals produced by the mirror he uses to view the patient's teeth. When looking into the driving mirror of a motor car there is no danger of seeing vehicles coming as if towards us on the wrong side of the road, and it is even possible to drive a car backwards while looking in the mirror. In other words, perceptual learning has enabled us to see the reflected objects as they are actually situated.

Our visual functions are so highly organised that we can react correctly at the same time to objects coming towards us from behind, as seen in the car mirror, and coming towards us in front, as seen without the mirror, within the same forward field of view in the windscreen. After some practice it is possible, keeping both eyes open, to look down a monocular microscope with, say, the left eye and to see the magnified object projected upon the surface of a sheet of paper alongside the microscope as if seen with the right eye. What exactly is happening here is difficult to explain. With any relaxation of attention the image vanishes from the paper, and it is obvious that this image was not dependent on stimulation of the right retina. Few marksmen close the left eye when aiming with a rifle or shot gun.

Blindness

Blindness is an extreme condition, and it is said to lead to perception dominated by kinesthesia and by the feel of objects, instead of vision. Revesz has suggested that art dominated by non-visual modes of perception has many of the characteristics of some kinds of modern sculpture and painting. Spatial relationships are much distorted from the visual point of view, and many curves and distinctive lumps on objects are exaggerated. This kind of art has been called "haptic" art and is supposed to reflect the perception of the blind, as distinct from visual perception.

We usually conceive of space as if modelled on visually perceived relationships, and experiences of objects and spaces founded on tactile, kinesthetic, and even auditory perception are subordinated to them. A tendency to refer freely to tactile qualities and to have strong emotional experiences about them may suggest the persistence of perceptual adjustments of origin earlier in infancy than those dominated by vision, but not necessarily abnormal.

If blindness occurs in the first two years of the person life tends to have no visual imagery later and does not dream in visual images, but if it occurs after the visual modes of perception have been well established, then visual imagery and visual modes of thinking tend to be retained, and the blind person may dream in visual images.

About 66 persons have been investigated who were born blind owing to cataracts in both eyes, and upon whom operations were performed to restore vision. It is generally agreed that such persons are at first confused when vision returns, but immediately see unitary figures differentiated from their backgrounds. They are able to fixate objects and follow them with their eyes. However, they find much difficulty in identifying familiar objects by vision and in correctly naming objects and their qualities when they have been known only by touch previously. Days or weeks may go by before the person can name objects correctly, and there may be great difficulty in generalising and abstracting qualities in the world of vision. If a square which is white on one side and yellow on the other is perceived as a square when one side is exposed, it may not be recognised as a square at all when turned over to expose the other side, because the one colour and squareness had become linked in the first visual perception and were not readily separated. There was, however, no case in which difficulty in learning the application of colour names by themselves was reported.

Colour Blindness (cp. p. 105)

Colour blindness obviously restricts perception in certain ways. To the few people who are totally colour blind—the monochromats—the world is a place of blacks, whites, and greys. Monochromats learn to use colour names and often use them correctly because they hear other people say the sky is blue, and so on; but in moments when they are not on their guard they will admit that the sky might as well be called green or red, since no colour names refer to any quality which they can perceive.

It is generally agreed that there are two kinds of total colour blindness. In one kind, the subject has vision which is almost the same as night vision, which is believed to be exclusively mediated by the rods. These subjects usually have to wear dark glasses, show a characteristic nystagmus or fluttering movement of the eyeball, and have a marked shortening of the red end of the spectrum. In the other kind of total colour blindness there is apparently normal tolerance for bright lights and the spectrum is very little shortened at the red end; nystagmus is not apparent. In these subjects the cones seem to be in action but not in such a way as to signal colour differences.

Red/green blindness is a condition found in about 7 per cent or

8 per cent of men and in 0·45 per cent of women among European whites. It exists in six clearly marked forms, and in varying degrees of severity in four of them. The forms are as follows: the "protan" group, including protanopia, extreme protanomaly, and simple protanomaly; and the "deutan" group, including deuteranopia, extreme deuteranomaly, and simple deuteranomaly. Protanopes and deuteranopes are dichromats and see only two colours, probably green and blue for protanopes, and definitely yellow and blue for deuteranopes. The work of Graham and his colleagues on a woman who was a deuteranope in one eye and normal in the other has established the latter point, because with the colour-blind eye she was able to match all spectral reds, yellows, and greens with yellow, as seen with the normal eye, and all blue-greens, blues, and violets with blue. Protanopes have marked shortening of the red end of the spectrum, while it is not shortened in deuteranopes.

The remaining groups are called anomalous trichromats. The extreme protanomalous and deuteranomalous have some ability to distinguish reds, yellows, and greens, but very much less than in normal people, and in the protanomalous the red end of the spectrum is shortened. In the simple protanomalous and deuteranomalous colour discrimination may be almost normal in precision, but it is widely different from the normal in quality, since yellow for the simple protanomalous is strongly deviated towards the normal green, and the normal yellow looks red while for the simple deuteranomalous it is strongly deviated towards red and the normal yellow looks green. All these subjects will fail absolutely on any competent test of colour blindness. The inheritance of red/green blindness follows the well-known sex-linked pattern in which the mother of a defective man will be a conductor, but will not show the defect fully herself unless her father and mother both gave her defective genes of appropriate kinds.

There are minor degrees of red/green defect less marked than colour blindness, and these can be detected with an instrument called an anomaloscope. In this, a mixture of red and green lights, which look yellow, is matched with a standard yellow light, and the deviations and small errors of colour matching made by various subjects can be used as measures of their defects. These minor defects are important in occupations in which fine colour matching is required, like colour printing and dyeing. The anomaloscope is also the best single testing instrument for all kinds of colour vision defect and variation, large or small, and its invention, in 1881, was due to Lord Rayleigh. A simple type of anomaloscope is illustrated in Fig. 9:4.

It is astonishing how many colour-blind people do not recognise their defects, and how often they think their difficulties are due to errors of naming or to unfamiliarity with "modern" shades, and so on. One deuteranope succeeded in convincing himself and some other people that he was sensitive to colours they could not see. Other red/green defectives,

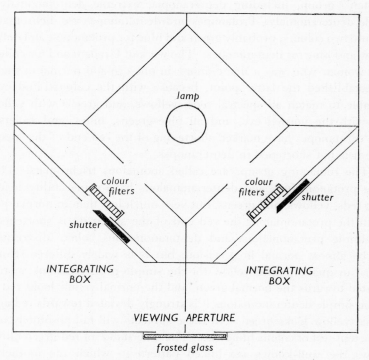

FIG. 9:4. Diagram of the Pickford-Nicolson anomaloscope for measuring and testing colour vision variations and defects. (After Lakowski and Pickford, by permission of the editor of the *British Journal of Physiological Optics*.)

since they have unusual difficulty and are therefore slow and cautious in making colour matches and comparisons, have earned the name in their family circles for being exceptionally good judges of colour.

Yellow/blue blindness is very rare, but mild degrees of variation in sensitivity to yellow and blue make themselves felt in daily life and are not uncommon. The well-known dispute about whether Cambridge blue is green or not, is maintained by mild blue defectives who are slightly less sensitive to the blue in this blue-green colour than most people, and who tend to identify it with greens in consequence. A man who had a mild yellow deficiency according to standard tests, was unable to distinguish a bale of yellow cloth which had been sent back from China, because it was a false match, when he compared it with others which had been accepted as correct. The best standard test for yellow/blue defects is an anomaloscope test in which a mixture of yellow and blue is matched against a neutral light, or in which a mixture of blue and green is matched against a blue-green light.

Marked differences in the frequencies of various kinds of colour vision defects are found among the populations of the world. It is a very difficult question how far the numbers and kinds of colour names provided in various languages reflect the colour vision peculiarities of the people in question. The presence or absence of colour names corresponding to those we use is a very unreliable guide to the colour vision of another people. Unless tests of naming are reinforced by reliable colour discrimination tests, no conclusions can be drawn. A people who used the same generic name for green and blue, as many do, might be just as good as ourselves at distinguishing these colours in a critical test. Myers has summarised the position admirably. There is no definite word for blue or brown in the *Iliad*, and this and other peculiarities of colour terminology found in Homer occur in other ancient writings such as the Zendavesta and the Norse Edda. The Uralis and Sholagas of Madras have a word for green which may also be used for brown and grey, but they have no special words for brown, violet, or light blue. The Todas of Madras and the Murray Islanders of the Torres Straits also have no word of their own for blue, but are beginning to use the English word. The Welsh may use "glas" (green) for blue. In Scottish Gaelic the word "gorm" (blue) may be used for the green of grass or for dark grey like the colour of a grey horse. "Glas" (grey) may be used for the green of trees and hills. "Gormghlas" is used for sea-green. Rivers found that more among dark-skinned peoples were slightly weak in the blue and yellow vision than of our own population. This has been confirmed by recent studies on small numbers with the anomaloscope. These differences, however, would not be sufficient to account for the complete absence of a name for blue and other important differences of language in colour naming. It is also established now that red/green blindness is less frequent among dark-skinned peoples, especially Australians, than among Caucasian whites, and apparently the human race has not maintained better colour vision consistently for all hues. Indeed, red/green blindness is much less frequent among the most primitive peoples and, since red, yellow, brown, and green are important indicators of ripeness, overripeness and rottenness in many edible fruits and meat, it is not unlikely that colour-blind children or infants have been killed by food poisoning in primitive peoples more often than among ourselves, and thus the frequency of colour blindness in our population has increased with growing civilisation.

The Modes of Appearance of Colours

Katz showed that there are three modes of appearance of colours. "Film" colours are produced in the spectrometer or a section of clear sky and seem to have a certain but indefinite distance, and are neither voluminous nor transparent. They are always frontal to the eye.

"Surface" colours are seen on any object which has texture, and they are located on its surface and may shift in distance and position, and in angle to the line of vision as the surface moves. They are not transparent or voluminous.

"Volume" colours are seen in a cloud of smoke or steam which is illuminated by a coloured light, or in a transparent medium like a bottle of coloured fluid. They are not localised except by the boundaries of the medium in which they inhere, cannot change in angle to the eye, and are both voluminous and transparent.

The conditions of perception, attitude, or physical state of the observer may change the appearance of colours very easily. For one patient, who had an injury to the parietal and occipital lobes, surface colours vanished and all colours were seen as film or volume colours.

Synesthesia and Physiognomic Properties

Synesthesia describes the identification or fusion of sensory experiences usually from two modalities. Thus, auditory/visual synesthesia means an auditory experience intimately linked with visual qualities so that hearing is "coloured," while visual/auditory synesthesia would refer to vision which was intimately linked with ideas of sound. Presumably in all cases the modality excited by the stimulus experiences is associated, revived, or imaged, although none of these words is wholly adequate. There are many types of synesthesia, including threefold combinations. A difference exists between the true synesthesias, where there is a fusion of the stimulus and the associated experience, and false synesthesias in which, for example, the percipient simply thinks of a colour as appropriate to a particular sound. It is easy to invent coloured pictorial fantasies to go with music, and many people always think of music in terms of associated visual and kinesthetic imagery. On the other hand, true synesthesia is rare. It is said that the Russian composer Scriabin had true auditory/visual synesthesia and that he actually composed music in terms of the colours he thought appropriate to the sounds. Many people think of the notes of the major and minor scales or of particular chords as being coloured, or have colour experiences connected with the sounds of certain instruments. Thus, the timbre or tone quality of the flute might be pale

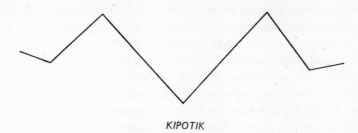

KIPOTIK

blue or white, that of the oboe scarlet, of the clarinet rose or crimson, of the violin sky blue, and of the viola green, and the 'cello and double bass purple, violet, or black. The tone of the trumpets might be golden yellow, of the horns orange, and of the trombone and tuba various orange-browns. Then an orchestral combination might suggest fascinating colour effects. Few people will agree about the so-called colour qualities of the tones of musical instruments, of chords or notes of the scale, or of particular keys, and it is not possible to arrive at a universal colour harmony.

Synesthesia brings us to a more general and very remarkable group of attributes of perceptual experience which have been called physiognomic qualities. A group of subjects is provided with a series of simple designs, some flowing and others angular, such as those shown in Figs. 9:5 and 9:6, and a list of as many nonsense words, some smooth-sounding and others jerky, like Kohler's words "maluma" and "takete." The subjects are then asked to pair the nonsense words with the designs. There is a surprising amount of agreement, and the flowing outlines tend to be paired with the smooth-sounding words and vice versa. It is possible that great artists who have exploited vast combinations of perceptual experiences, as in orchestral music with solo and choral singing, stage decorations and dancing, and used them to form settings for literary works, as in the music drama of Wagner, have drawn upon physiognomic properties very extensively to build up their principal aesthetic effects.

OLULO

FIGS. 9:5, and 9:6. Two or more figures, some angular, like 9.5, and others rounded, like 9.6, are shown to a group of subjects. They are asked to pair the figures with nonsense words either of the types shown, or like Kohler's "maluma" and "takete". There is a strong tendency to associate smooth-sounding words with rounded, and harsh-sounding words with the angular figures.

The question how far these physiognomic qualities are universal and innate, or individual and due to experience, training, and cultural patterns, is just as difficult as any other perceptual problems involving individual and social influences and the effects of learning. It is well known that many words are expressive in their auditory and kinesthetic qualities. Most swear words are explosive, while soothing words are smooth and flowing. It would, however, be naive to suggest that aesthetic values are themselves nothing more than the physiognomic properties of certain objects, designs, patterns, and perceptual organisations in general. Although in immediate experience we do not feel that the qualities of beauty or ugliness are added attributes, but are associated inherently with certain forms, designs, or colours, whatever sensory modality they may exploit, nevertheless, beauty and ugliness are values of which objects or perceptions may be said to partake, or which they may express, rather than properties of those objects or perceptions themselves.

Synesthesias might be aspects of artistic or musical technique employed by individuals such as Scriabin, but their works would have to be adequate aesthetically, apart from these synesthesias, which are very individual. On the other hand, an artist, composer, or architect would be able to rely on physiognomic properties of his works as aspects of his technique which would affect most interested people in the ways he intended. Le Douanier Rousseau, for example, has employed his jagged though highly integrated patterns to reinforce what might be called the latent savagery of the very static wild animals in his imaginary forests in a most fascinating way. This, however, is only a means to an end, and could not be regarded as an aesthetic value in itself.

Perceptual Facilitation and Defence

It is general knowledge that physiological needs, memories, and subjective attitudes have a considerable effect on perception and that, for example, the deaf are often surprisingly good at hearing statements of personal interest while, on the other hand, those who are not deaf often fail to hear, or misinterpret, statements which are not in accord with their views or wishes. It is very difficult to bring these phenomena within the bounds of laboratory experiment because we have to invent suitable experimental procedures and materials for groups of people sufficiently large for statistical analysis. Such groups will almost certainly include wide individual variations, thus reducing the chances of controlled experiment. A few examples will illustrate this.

In many subjects with red/green colour blindness a reinforcement of certain colour differences by other means than colour may make test figures temporarily visible. If a man who cannot see certain figures in the Ishihara test for colour blindness is shown one of its plates, and the figure is now outlined with the butt-end of a pencil or a dry paint brush, he may suddenly see it quite clearly, but it usually fades in a few moments. The sensory receptors must be working to a certain extent, but in a way which is below the threshold for conscious perception. When the reinforcement of the outline of the figure is applied without drawing it, the two modes of stimulation interact so that the figure is temporarily visible, but in what colours it may be difficult to say.

In an experiment on perceptual facilitation by Bruner, Postman, and Rodrigues, the subjects were asked to match the colours of certain familiar objects cut in paper, such as a tomato, a tangerine, a lemon, and a non-representative oval shape. The matching was done under experimentally controlled conditions with red and yellow sectors on a colour wheel in such a way that the subject had to turn his gaze through 80° from the patch to the wheel and back. The results were given in terms of the proportions of red and yellow required to match the colours of the paper patches. When the paper patches were neutral grey, but on a sheet of blue-green paper, a slight orange colour was produced in them by simultaneous contrast. In matching them, however, the subjects used much more red than the average for the non-representative patch when looking at the patches like red objects, and much more yellow than the average for the patches like yellow objects. Other very interesting variations of the experiment were carried out, but when the matching conditions were at their optimum and the colour wheel and the patch were side by side, the differences in matches due to the known colours of the objects disappeared.

Another experiment was reported by Postman and Crutchfield in which skeleton food-words were presented to hungry and non-hungry students. If one such word were used, the numbers who filled it in as a food-word were not significantly different for the two groups, but the more words such as L U N – H, which could be filled in only as food words, that were introduced in a series before the test words, the greater was the tendency of the hungry group to fill in the test word with a food name in comparison with the non-hungry group.

In an experiment with adequately controlled physical conditions, Dixon measured the proportions of red and green required to match a neutral background with one eye and the differential thresholds, *i.e.* the amount of red and green to be added to the mixture to make it appear different from the background for that eye. These amounts were affected more by emotionally toned words such as "cancer" than by neutral words such as "stance," which were presented at a subthreshold intensity to the other eye in a stereoscopic arrangement. The main effects were that during the subthreshold presentation of the anxiety word in red in one eye, a raised threshold for red was produced in the other eye, although during its subthreshold presentation in green for one eye the threshold for green in the other eye was lowered. Whether his results support a theory of perceptual defence or not may remain an open question, but they are consistent with the finding that adrenaline decreases sensitivity to red-orange light and increases it to green-blue light. Adrenaline secretion into the bloodstream is increased in anxiety-producing situations.

The Effect of Drugs on Perception

The influence of drugs on visual and probably other modes of perception may be considerable. The effects of alcohol on the perception of size, distance, and movement would be well worth investigation. In order to illustrate the experimental study of this kind of problem a research by Steinberg, Legge, and Summerfield may be mentioned. It was found that nitrous oxide caused subjects to judge the lengths of lines at a distance as being consistently longer than the judgments of the "air" or control group of subjects. Some schizophrenics made the same kinds of judgments, apparently judging lines as if they were very far away, and therefore longer. This might be related to the reduced contact with the environment, which is characteristic of schizophrenics. Chlorpromazine, however, failed to induce any changes in comparable judgments of size at a distance.

Subthreshold Stimulation

Some work on perception has centred about the possibility that stimuli presented below the threshold for conscious experience may influence feeling, perception, or behaviour. There are several ways of producing such stimuli. One method is to have lettering or other visual or auditory messages or patterns of such low energy value that they are consciously imperceptible. Another method is that of introducing occasional frames in a cinema or television performance and, since they are of very short duration each, they are not perceived. The conscious thresholds for different people vary widely and, in addition, the thresholds for one person are subject to considerable change owing to a variety of causes.

Dixon showed that verbal responses to words presented below the threshold of awareness tended to be symbolic associations to these stimulus words. Where a word could be changed to a more emotionally toned word by altering one letter, if both were presented below the threshold of awareness there were more correct guesses for the word which had the greater emotional tone, to a statistically significant extent.

Many people who have been interested in this subject from the point of view of influencing overt behaviour by advertising have carried out experiments, the general results of which appear often to be equivocal or unproved, although in some cases there may have been statistically convincing results.

In general, it may be concluded that there is little possibility of profoundly influencing behaviour or thought by such means, and we do not need to fear that cinema and television performances will be able to include unconsciously presented suggestions which will have more than a very slight or temporary effect on us.

From the philosophical point of view it is an interesting question whether these phenomena should be included under the heading of perception at all, because the person does not consciously apprehend the stimulus as a recognisable word or object. However, this is an insoluble problem because the threshold for conscious perception is a fluctuating range rather than a precise and constant limit, and much ordinary conscious perception is undoubtedly affected by many unconscious factors, both internal and on the stimulus side.

Extrasensory Perception

Much valuable research has been carried out, notably by Rhine, Pratt, Whately Carington, and Thouless, on extrasensory perception. Again it is philosophically doubtful whether the term "perception" is properly applied to these phenomena, because the person who "perceives" by clairvoyance the next card to be turned up in a pack by an experimenter not visible to him, does it perhaps by a guess, "hunch," or intuition, and not by any clear form of cognition for which the term perception could be used. Similarly, in thought transference or telepathy, the "percipient" does not use ordinary sensory means of perception. It is because ordinary perception is not used that the expression extrasensory perception has been adopted.

Statistically orientated experiments have been carried out on extrasensory perception, in particular making use of the "Zener" cards. Five different line diagrams were employed in a pack of 25 cards, five of each, and with these sets it is easy to calculate the probabilities in guessing, and to test the hypothesis that the result may favour clairvoyance or telepathy. The five diagrams are shown in Fig. 9:7. Those who object to the findings, which appear in general to support extrasensory perception, must face the fact that in many experiments there is strong statistical evidence of a positive kind. Thouless has stressed that in some experiments the statistical evidence favouring extrasensory perception is of the order of 10^{17} or 10^{35} to 1. Odds like this against chance are overwhelming. Doubt, however, might be based on the possibility of intentional deception, which might be true in some experiments, or, more likely, on that of unknown flaws in the techniques. It seems unlikely that even these possibilities would account for all the evidence supposedly favouring telepathy or clairvoyance. There remains, however, the apparent impossibility of formulating any physically satisfactory theory to account for extrasensory perception, and Whately Carington has tried to work out non-physical concepts. It would be unreasonable, however, to assume that all we know about physics today must be adequate to account for all the phenomena of the physical universe. Most scientific psychologists are devoted to a behaviouristic-materialistic standpoint and simply exclude extrasensory perception from their province on principle.

Whately Carington claims to have shown that extrasensory perception cannot be attributed to any ordinary form of radiation, because in experiments conducted with the experimenter in Cambridge and observers in London, Manchester, Edinburgh, or Glasgow, positive results were obtained which were not affected by the inverse square law. That is to say, the effects of the supposed influence of extrasensory perception did not diminish in proportion to the distance and definitely not to the square of the distance, which is always found with ordinary types of physical radiation such as light and sound unless a narrow and precisely directed beam of rays is used. In an experiment carried out on about 35 students by McElroy in Glasgow on card-guessing or clairvoyance, about 51 per cent or 52 per cent of positive guesses were obtained against about 49 per cent or 48 per cent negative. This is a very small difference, but in proportion to the thousands of guesses made it was significantly different from zero in the statistical sense.

FIG. 9 : 7. The Zener cards used extensively in experiments on extrasensory perception. (By permission of Prof. J. B. Rhine.)

BIBLIOGRAPHY

General

BARTLETT, F. C. 1932. *Remembering*. Cambridge University Press, London.

BEARDSLEE, D. C. and WERTHEIMER, M. 1958. *Readings in Perception*. Van Nostrand, London and New York.

BROADBENT, D. E. 1958. *Perception and Communication*. Pergamon Press, London.

DREVER, J. (2nd). 1960. Perceptual learning. *Ann. Rev. Psychol.*, **11**, 131-160.

KRECH, D. and CRUTCHFIELD, R. S. 1958. *Elements of Psychology*. Knopf. New York.

KOFFKA, K. 1935. *Principles of Gestalt Psychology*. Harcourt Brace, New York.

MYERS, C. S. 1925. *An Introduction to Experimental Psychology*. Cambridge University Press.

RÉVÉSZ, G. 1950. *Psychology and Art of the Blind*. Longmans, London.

SIMPSON, L. and MCKELLAR, P. 1955. Types of synaesthesia. *J. Ment. Sci.*, **101**, 141-147.

Visual Perception

BERGER, E., GRAHAM, C. H. and HSIA, Y. Some visual functions of a unilaterally colour-blind person. *J. Opt. Soc. Amer.*, **48**, 614-627.

BROWN, W. P. 1961. Conceptions of perceptual defence. *Brit. J. Psychol. Mongr.*, Supp. **35**. Cambridge University Press, London.

DIXON, N. F. 1958. Apparatus for continuous recording of the visual threshold by the method of "closed loop control". *Quart. J. Exptl. Psychol.*, **10**, 62-63.

——1958. The effect of subliminal stimulation upon autonomic and verbal behaviour. *J. Abn. and Soc. Psychol.*, **57**, 29-36.

——1958. Apparent changes in the visual threshold as a function of subliminal stimulation: A preliminary report. *Quart. J. Exptl. Psychol.*, **10**, 211-219.

——1960. Apparent changes in visual threshold—central or peripheral? *Brit. J. Psychol.*, **51**, 297-310.

——and HAIDER, M. 1961. Changes in the visual threshold as a function of subception. *Quart. J. Exptl. Psychol.*, **13**, 229-235.

GRAHAM, C. H. and HSIA, Y. 1959. Studies of color blindness: A unilaterally dichromatic subject. *Proc. Amer. Nat. Acad. Sci.*, **45**, 96-99.

KHERUMIAN, R. and PICKFORD, R. W. 1959. *Hérédité et Fréquence des Anomalies Congénitales du Sens Chromatique (Dyschromatopsies)*. Vigot Frères, Paris.

PICKFORD, R. W. 1951. *Individual Differences in Colour Vision*. Routledge and Kegan Paul, London.

——and LAKOWSKI, R. 1960. The Pickford Nicolson Anomaloscope. *Brit. J. Physiol. Optics*, **17**, 131-150.

SENDEN, M. VON. 1960. *Space and Sight* (tr. P. Heath). Methuen, London.

SHIGEOKA, K. 1961. Experimental Study of Perceptual Constancy under the Condition of Inverted Glasses and Bodily Movements. *Kyushu Psychological Studies*. Ed. by Y. Akishige, No. II, Experimental Researches in the Structure of the Perceptual Space, iv, xxviii.

SNYDER, F. W. and PRONKO, N. H. 1952. *Vision with Inverting Spectacles*. University of Wichita Press, Wichita, Kansas.

STEINBERG, H., LEGGE, D., and SUMMERFIELD, A. 1961. Drug-Induced Changes in Visual Perception. Ed. by E. Rothlin. *Neuro-Psychopharmacology*, **2**, 392-396.

VARLEY, A. N. C. (Chairman of the Committee on Subliminal Communication) and ABRAMS, M. (Chairman of the Technical Sub-Committee). 1958. *Subliminal Communication*. Institute for Practitioners in Advertising, London.

VERNON, M. D. 1957. Cognitive inference in perceptual activity. *Brit. J. Psychol.*, **48**, 35-47.

Extrasensory Perception

CARINGTON, W. 1945. *Telepathy: An Outline of the Facts, Theory, and Implications*. Methuen, London.

MONCRIEFF, M. M. 1951. *The Clairvoyant Theory of Perception*. Faber, London.

RHINE, J. B. 1948. *The Reach of the Mind*. Faber, London.

——and PRATT, J. G. 1958. *Parapsychology, Frontier Science of the Mind: A Survey of the Field, the Methods, and the Facts of ESP and PK Research*. Blackwell, Oxford.

RHINE, L. E. 1962. *Hidden Channels of the Mind*. Gollancz, London.

THOULESS, R. H. 1952. Psychical Research Past and Present. Eleventh F. W. H. Myers Memorial Lecture. *Soc. for Psychical Res.*, London.

——1954. Problems of design in parapsychological experiments. *Proc. Soc. Psych. Res.*, **37**, 299-307.

10

Individual and Social Factors in Perception

Individual Factors

There are considerable differences from one individual to another in what
is perceived when the stimuli are identical. These differences are due to
a number of factors. In the first place there are variations in the physiological basis of perception. Some people are blind or colour blind, others
are deaf or partly so. Dallenbach studied a girl born without any sensitivity to pain, and the difficulties she had in avoiding burns, cuts, and
bruises. Other differences are due to innate variations of temperament,
or inborn disposition to a high or low degree of emotionality. These,
however, cannot in practice be distinguished from acquired differences
between individuals in personality because we have no efficient means of
separating the two experimentally, and it is only a theoretical conjecture,
although a very likely one, that innate differences of temperament underly
personality differences resulting from the influence of experiences from
infancy onward. It is clear, however, that wide variations occur in certain
aspects of perception, such as the constancy phenomena. The more
analytic and introverted persons are less subject to them than those who
are more extroverted and objective. Probably the phi-phenomenon and
Michotte's experiments would also divide people roughly into similar
groups, readier perception of movement or causality being found among
those of the extroverted, non-analytic, and objective types.

Emotional Factors

In addition to the special ways in which learning processes sensitise us
to perceive objects in certain ways, so varying emotional states give us
special tendencies in perception. This is illustrated by the difficulty of
obtaining consistent evidence from persons witnessing or involved in
accidents.

In a court of law conflicting statements are frequently met with and,
while sometimes it may be that one or both parties were consciously mis-
representing the truth in their own favour, frequently they believe what
they say, and are simply describing their own impressions. Allowing for
the very great differences known to be introduced into recall by subjective

217

factors, even when there was every opportunity for clear perception, it seems that different people perceive the same event in widely different ways as a result of emotions such as fear and anger.

There is a simple laboratory experiment, called the "Aussage" experiment, on the accuracy of impression and fidelity of report. A fairly complex picture, large enough to be seen clearly by about 10-20 people, is exposed for 5 to 10 seconds and then the subjects are asked, (*a*) to write a report on what they saw in the picture; (*b*) to answer about 20 questions concerning it, half of which, in random order, will be leading questions conveying a suggestion such as, "Was the yellow dog barking?" and (*c*) to estimate their confidence on a 3- or 5-point scale. A study of the results, comparing the reports for a group of subjects and showing how they varied in accuracy of observation and fidelity of report, how far they were influenced by suggestion, and how confident they were of their own accuracy, is most illuminating. All persons concerned with the use of evidence from observations of events such as street accidents, should take part in and study the results of such experiments. They would almost certainly be astonished at the unrealiability of ordinary observation and testimony given confidently and in good faith. Those who are most confident are often enough the ones who are completely wrong. This experiment makes us wonder how much confidence to place in the statements of people who claim to have seen the Loch Ness Monster, or a flying saucer, or simply a very unusual bird.

Projection in Perception

No account of the psychology of perception is adequate without some consideration of projection. It is true that our perceptions of other people and objects are affected by our emotional sensitivity to minute modes of behaviour or qualities often imperceptible except to ourselves. Our emotional attitudes to other people and to environmental objects often lead to an exaggeration of some qualities and a diminution of others in or suggested by them. We perceive in other persons and in certain situations and events, various attitudes or intentions favourable or inimical to ourselves, and often simply characteristic of our own personalities in unrecognised ways. This is not by any means confined to visual perception, but may affect any sensory modality or all of them together.

Projection is most apparent when we are dealing with inchoate or relatively inchoate material. Vague sounds in a house at night may be perceived as an intruder unlocking the door, climbing in and walking stealthily across the hall and up the stairs. We may hesitate when we see two policemen approaching, because we see them as if they are about to stop us for questioning, although we have committed no offence.

It is not surprising that projection has been used widely in clinical psychology as the basis of tests of personality. Of these tests the best known are Rorschach's series of 10 ink blots and Murray's Thematic Apperception test. In the Rorschach test the person to be tested is asked what the blots look like to him, or what he sees in them. They are all quite non-representative, but are carefully chosen, and an analysis of the parts of the blots interpreted (location), the form, colour, or other quality of the blot (determinants) which gives rise to a thought, and of the human, animal, and other objects or ideas suggested by the blot (content), is used to assess the personality of the subject. Murray's T.A.T. consists of somewhat vague pictures open to a variety of interpretations, and the subject is asked to tell a story leading up to the event he sees depicted, to describe it, and to say what the outcome will be in completing his story. The personality assessment depends on an analysis of the underlying needs and forms of pressure which are brought to bear on the characters in the story. There are many other personality tests of the same general kind with various methods of assessment. One of Murray's pictures shows a man either climbing up a rope to a window or letting himself down. Whenever this test is used for class work it is found that the students are divided about the interpretation—some think the drawing is intended to show the man in the act of climbing up; others think it shows how his legs and arms would be placed if he were sliding down. In fact the picture is ambiguously drawn. The difference is due to projection and reveals a personality difference between the two groups. In a series of 120 childish drawings for use with children, one picture, illustrated in Fig. 10:1, shows a boy and a man and an object like a ball in the air. Some see the boy throwing the object at the man and others say that it is not aimed at him or would not hit him. In a meeting where this picture was shown to illustrate the method, there was a lively discussion about whether the artist intended the ball to look as if it would hit the man or not. Of course, the picture was carefully drawn so that it should be indefinite. What the subject perceives therefore reflects his personality in some way.

It might be said that projection is not truly perception, because the subject may have no clearly conscious representation or image of the content projected. He may, on careful questioning, for instance, say that what he was seeing was an ink blot but that it looked like an elephant squirting water from its trunk over an enraged tiger. However, there is no sharp division on one side of which we have perception and on the other projection, and there is every reason to suppose that some projective qualities enter into a great proportion of apparently ordinary perceptions.

For example, we may perceive a painter's ladder as dangerous and avoid it by walking in the road instead of going under it on the pathway, although the road may be much more dangerous. The difference is that the dangers

FIG. 10: 1   Projection in perception. Does it appear that the boy has thrown the stone in such a way that it will hit the man, or did he intend to miss him? The way in which a person perceives a drawing such as this depends on his own personality. (From *Pickford Projective Pictures*, London: Tavistock Press. New York: Springer. By permission of the publishers.)

inherent in the ladder are mainly subjective. There is, however, no objective way of defining the relative degrees of danger in a given instance for a particular individual.

Déjà vu

False recognition, or *déjà vu*, is an interesting experience allied to projection in perception. It may vary from sudden feelings of unexplained familiarity about an object or person, when it is known that the person or object has never been met with before, to extended emotional experiences, lasting perhaps for several hours, in which a whole situation or locality visited may be recognised although the individual knows quite well that he had never been there. *Déjà vu* although named as a visual experience, may affect any sense modality, and we may equally easily feel we have heard, smelled, or tasted something before, realising at the same time that it is unknown.

Since this experience involves recognition of a kind convincing but known to be "false" it is like a perplexity state. It might be said that *déjà vu*, since it is a form of recognition, is not a form of perception. All perception involves recognition, however, except those very peculiar experiences, the converse of *déjà vu*, in which we see something and feel it to be strange although we know it to be quite familiar.

A good example of *déjà vu* was reported by an adult student who, when he was in Persia and the Near East with the armed forces, experienced strong familiarity with every mosque he saw, although he knew he had never previously beheld them. Of course, he had seen photographs of such mosques, but this knowledge did not account for the remarkable subjective experience of *déjà vu*, because he could at the same time say to himself, "That's the mosque of so and so," of which he remembered the picture and for which he had a true recognition. It is important that *déjà vu* is not necessarily confined to objects we know to be unfamiliar, but may occur in relation to familiar objects. It is the peculiar intensity and unrelatedness of the emotional experience which distinguishes it from ordinary recognition.

MacCurdy put forward the view that *déjà vu* experiences are due to the excitation of latent emotional memories of early or infantile origin which are projected upon a present object or complete scene and give it the strange, intense, and unrelated feeling of familiarity, in spite of our knowing that it is new to us or even realising that it is not new. In the opposite experiences of false unfamiliarity it would be postulated that repression of memory traces, which would normally interact with incoming sensory data to give the feeling of familiarity, has taken place owing to some emotional complication. Banister and Zangwill have shown that *déjà vu* experiences can be produced by post-hypnotic suggestion. Here the latent memories and the situation in which they will act are established by suggestion when the subject is hypnotised, whereas in ordinary *déjà vu* this occurs spontaneously.

Personality through Perception

The influence of personality upon perception was revealed in a study by Witkin and others in which certain tests were applied to three groups of subjects. The tests were divided into two classes: firstly, tests of self-consistency in perception, and secondly tests of personality determinants of perception. The first group included the rod-and-frame test in which the subject attempts to give a correct determination of the position of a rod which he must dissociate from a tilted frame which surrounds it. In the tilted-room-tilted-chair test he must avoid being influenced by the tilted room in which he is placed if he is to succeed in making his body upright. In the embedded-figure test he is required to identify a figure hidden in a perceptual context. This is illustrated in Fig. 10:2. The

brightness constancy test showed the subject's ability to remain uninfluenced by the context in which an item is presented. The auditory-
visual conflict test required the subject to locate the source of a sound
when visual and auditory cues were in conflict.

The tests of personality determinants included a personality question-
naire of 78 items, a sentence-completion test of 75 items, such as, "There
are times when I . . . ," a clinical interview, a figure-drawing test, the
Rorschach test, fifteen cards of Murray's Thematic Apperception Test,

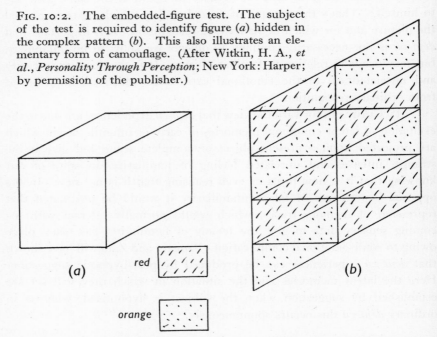

Fig. 10:2. The embedded-figure test. The subject
of the test is required to identify figure (a) hidden in
the complex pattern (b). This also illustrates an elementary form of camouflage. (After Witkin, H. A., et
al., Personality Through Perception; New York: Harper;
by permission of the publisher.)

and a word-association test. The subjects were normal men and women
volunteers and men and women patients from a mental hospital. The
development of perception was studied in five different age groups of
children.

The influence of the individual's personality may be considered
under three headings: (1) his relation to his environment and other people,
(2) the way he controls his strivings and impulses, and (3) his conception
of himself. Under the first heading passivity is associated with perception
dependent on the external world, while activity is associated with independent and analytic perception. Under the second heading a contrast is
found between people with a lack of self-awareness, fear of aggressive and
sexual impulses and poor control over them, and people with good self-
awareness and acceptance of and good control over sexual and aggressive

impulses. Under the third heading there are also opposing trends, namely low self-esteem and evaluation of the body together with self-acceptance and confidence. In general, dependence, lack of self-awareness, poor control and low self-esteem go together, while independence, good self-awareness and control and high self-evaluation are also correlated.

Women found it more difficult than men to resist the structuring influences of the external visual field. Men were more attentive to sensations of body positions, but women were more concerned with the relation between the body and the environment. Women tended to give more variable performances under different conditions than men, and were therefore less self-consistent. These differences in perception associated with sex may have been partly the products of the American culture in relation to which the results of the experiment must be considered, but they reflect the predominantly passive function of women in sexual relationships in contrast with the more active function of men.

Images and Percepts

Stout summarised the characteristic differences of sense impressions and images. He found that images are relatively more fragmentary and that they have less "force or liveliness" as mentioned by Hume, which may mean that the image is not necessarily less intense, but that the percept has an aggressiveness which does not belong to the image. The percept is more distinct whereas, in Fechner's language, images are "airy, unsubstantial and vaporous." Images are determined and carried on by inner mental activities and belong to this subjective sequence, whereas perceptions are produced by external events which compel attention. Lastly, perceptions vary with movements of the body, the direction in which the eyes are turned, and so on, whereas we can carry our mental images about with us and they are not dependent on sensory adaptation and adjustment.

In an experiment by Perky, arrangements of a very careful and ingenious kind were made for the subjects who took part to view certain correctly coloured representations of familiar objects at intensities increasing from subthreshold to suprathreshold brightness values, and slightly oscillating to imitate motions of a subjective image. The objects represented were: a tomato (red), a book (blue), a banana (deep yellow), an orange (orange), a leaf (green), and a lemon (light yellow). Each subject was asked to fixate a white fixation mark on a ground glass screen and to imagine a coloured object, for instance, a tomato, while at the same time the subthreshold representation of this object was made on the screen.

In the main experiment, on 27 subjects, all but three were sure that they had experienced mental images, generally of a particularly convincing kind, but the remaining three had to be eliminated owing to a fault of technique which they noticed. In an experiment on five subjects two of whom were practised in the observation of mental images, there was a tendency to think of the representations as rather more like perceptions or afterimages than true mental images, but all were convinced of their imaginary character.

This experiment confirms the conclusion that vague and nearthreshold perceptions would be difficult or impossible to distinguish from clear images. Some observers said they could continue to hold the images in attention after their eyes were closed, and one observer had the impression that he could move the images by moving his eyes. The distinction between an image and a perception, therefore, is not absolute or fundamental in experience, but is brought out only where the characteristic differences are emphasised, as they are in normal waking consciousness.

Illusions, Delusions, and Hallucinations

It might be argued that illusions and hallucinations are not aspects of perception, but illusions are always modes of perceptual "interpretation" of certain stimulus patterns, while even in hallucinations there may often be an absolute minimum of stimulation which is "interpreted." Delusions are distinguished from illusions and hallucinations in the sense that they affect thought rather than perception, but the distinction may not be absolute. It is an example of an illusion if on waking up in the semidarkness one perceives a dressing-gown as a man in monk's garments just behind the door. It differs from a projection essentially in the fact that one perceives a man dressed as a monk, instead of seeing a dressing-gown which looks like a monk's garment. Thus, some projection and *déjà vu* experiences may be illusions.

A good example of hallucination was given by a young woman who was frightened of being left to sleep alone when her husband was away on business. During the night a man in armour would enter her room and wander about. Then, with suitable clanking sounds he would get into bed with her and she, in a state of terror, found his armour was cold to the touch. After a while he would go away again. She was an example of what is very unusual, namely an hysterical patient who suffered from hallucinations. They were generally confined to the insane or to those under extreme influence of drugs or alcohol. Very likely the woman's hallucinations were stimulated by certain slight creaking sounds and had an almost imperceptive environmental origin. They were certainly due to psychopathological causes in her personality.

An example of delusory experience was given by a man who hardly dared to visit another town on business because he believed that the police were after him, even though it was more than ten years since a policeman saw him there. His delusions affected his relationship with women and the law in various ways. On the way home from work in a bus he read in a newspaper that a woman had been murdered and he immediately said to himself, "Well, I can use a good alibi if the police question me. I can prove I was out of the city at the time." Here we have delusory thought creeping into the patient's ideas and affecting them, although at times he had some insight and suspected that he was deceiving himself.

The question whether there is any special quality in delusions, illusions, and hallucinations which makes them distinctly different from true perception is important and interesting. As far as we can tell there is none. The person who can let himself think of such things as the examples given above, but does not have delusions or hallucinations, may be said to have insight, but insight is not a special faculty which enables us to see that our experiences are subjective. The difference implied by insight is that the person who has it is able to adjust himself to external realities and to follow his own thoughts and perceptions without confusing them with external realities. In conditions of emotional stress, or under the influence of alcohol and drugs, there may be a regression to a more infantile mode of functioning, normal at a stage at which the infant has not learned to make these distinctions. Then the subjective fantasies are imposed upon external reality, or interweave with externally originating stimuli and the person loses what is called insight. There are all degrees between projected ideas on the one hand, and illusions, hallucinations, and delusions on the other.

Social Influences in Perception

It is well known that most persons are suggestible and others are contra-suggestible, which is a form of suggestibility directed against rather than in favour of what is suggested. Many of the well-established phenomena of perception, such as various threshold differences, the influence of size, shape, and colour constancy, the phi-phenomenon, and perception of movement in general, as well as the impression of causality, are subject to suggestion. This can be illustrated by familiar experiments of which the following are examples. Several naive observers are brought into a dark room with others who have been instructed to make certain necessary suggestions. All are told to fixate a minute spot of light which, since the room is otherwise in total darkness, appears to hang in space. The observers who have been instructed now begin to report that the spot of light moves to one side, and many of the others then see the spot moving as suggested. In another experiment, about a dozen straight lines of slightly different lengths are drawn on separate pieces of paper and displayed before a group of naive and sophisticated subjects. Remarks are then made by the sophisticated subjects that certain pairs of lines look the same lengths, and the naive subjects are asked if this is not true. Again, many of them actually "perceive" the lines as if they are the same, although others will agree just to avoid being in a minority opposed to the general opinion.

A great variety of such experiments can be carried out and, at least in the two mentioned here, the effects depend on the influence of suggestibility upon a perceptual phenomenon. If a person is placed in a dark room alone and asked to fixate a spot of light, it is certain to appear to move after a time, and this is due to involuntary eye movements (cp. p. 98). The suggestion intensifies, negates, or otherwise controls an individual effect which might occur apart from the social influences. Essentially the same principle is true of the lines experiment. There are individual thresholds for the perception of differences between the lengths of lines and the sizes, shapes, or colours of objects, and a suggestion tends to increase or diminish these thresholds. In constancy experiments the effects are variable within fairly wide limits, and a suggestion will influence them quite considerably.

In psychological experiments it is important to give instructions in such a way as to avoid suggestions, and to adopt an attitude which will not convey to the subject the idea that the result to be observed has been attained. While results of observations and experiments may be greatly modified by intentional or unintentional suggestions, it is doubtful whether social suggestions can create new ideas or impressions which are not either possible to the individual or projections of his latent wishes. For instance, Malinowski reports being in a canoe with some Melanesians when all but he himself saw a spirit floating in the clouds. It is only fair to interpret this as an illusion or hallucination depending on their belief in such spirits, which he did not share. It was Janet who first pointed out that a suggestion must in some way exploit, activate, or utilise a latent impulse in the person to whom it is made. This is true of contra-suggestibility too, because here we inadvertently exploit a latent impulse to oppose, criticise, or resist, and sometimes, by making the opposite suggestion, we can make a person do what we want.

Perception in Art and Music

In visual arts the artist's interest in the object or scene may be predominantly representational, or he may make an abstract approach, and in either case his interest may be mainly in form or mainly emotional. Even the most rigidly representational artist, however, will have interests of a certain kind, either subjective or objective, and there are a few pictures or other objects of art which do not select and emphasise a special aspect of what is represented. If his approach is abstract, the artist may be said to provide the essential material out of his inner fantasies, or as products of his analytic thought processes, organised into a work of art. This kind of art represents the artist's subjective material rather than external objects. In fact, a very large number of works of art necessarily have more than one function. An artist may start with an object or scene and use it to express an inner mood or thought, or turn from his inner experiences to something objective which can convey them to others. Even if the artist has no interest in expressing something for other people his products will, if at all successful, be a kind of crystallisation of his mental states into an objectified form. Current social and aesthetic attitudes will play a large part in determining what the artist does and how he does it.

From the viewer's standpoint works of art must excite experiences of comparable interest to those felt by the artist, even if they are not the same, which they are very unlikely to be; and therefore good art must have a degree of generality in its appeal which, in most cases, will extend only within a certain cultural or historical circle. There is a famous story about the Shah of Persia who was taken to hear a European symphony concert. After it was over he asked for an encore, and when invited to say which item should be repeated he asked for the first. This was duly played again, but he was disappointed and said it was not the one he wanted. After some discussion it was discovered that the first item, which he wanted to hear again and liked most, was the tuning-up. No doubt this was nearest to what he had been accustomed to think of as good music. It is not unlikely that a good deal of modern music would appeal more to the Shah of Persia than it does to those who have been brought up on eighteenth- and nineteenth-century European music. The art which is most likely to have a wide general appeal will be conventional, and probably not very original, while, if the artist concentrates on being original, which he must if he is to be creative, then his public may be very small. Similarly, the art of earlier periods, such as early harpsichord music, requires that we should learn to perceive it in the right way if we are to understand it.

Sculpture may be viewed from all points of physical space, and could be artistically interesting from every angle, but in practice this is not likely, any more than it is likely that a piece of music could be equally interesting if played backwards, although this technical feat has been achieved sometimes. Most works of sculpture will be conceived, and the objects they represent will be perceived by the artist, from a certain position in space and in relation to certain settings, perhaps high up outside a cathedral, in a garden among trees, or in relation to other buildings or objects. Our museums and art galleries contain many objects of art which were never planned to be in such places.

Binocular Vision in Art

A group of psychological problems centres round the representation of solids in perspective in two-dimensional pictures. An actual scene changes in appearance, as explained in Chapter 7, for a single eye as it moves in space. However, the objects depicted in a two-dimensional drawing are in fact all in one plane on the paper, canvas, or other medium, and as the viewer walks past the picture he does not see a changing view of each object but only of its perspective outline, and the objects cannot overlap and occlude, or reveal each other more from one viewing position than another. There is only a single position in space, somewhere in front of each picture, from which its perspective outlines are geometrically correct. In all other positions its geometry is incorrect, but the viewer's perception adapts him to these objective falsities to a very large extent. It is very probable that in much modern art in which perspective outlines are not rendered faithfully for a single viewing point, the viewer actually gains a better general impression from the variety of positions which he is likely to adopt.

The normal viewer has two eyes, one of which must always be in a geometrically wrong position for perspective from a single point. In looking at flat pictures, binocular vision with the two eyes at different positions in space does not help to give a solid effect. The second eye must be a hindrance to seeing solid effects in perspective on flat surfaces. It is not surprising that one often gains a better impression of the perspective effects of a flat picture by looking at it with one eye closed. Those stereoscopic effects which the artist loses by his monocular representation he must make up by exploiting the other well-known factors in solid vision, namely the overlapping of objects, diminishing sizes with increasing distance, varying colour effects, varying clarity of outlines, and so on. Here again, the modern artist who does not attempt to give geometrically accurate renderings of perspective shapes and outlines may have a real advantage for the binocular viewer, and objects and scenes may even look more convincing when they are less "accurately" drawn for single-point perspective.

Binaural Hearing in Music

The existence of two ears separated in space presents similar problems for the musician and the listener. Many sounds reaching the ears when we listen to a large orchestra come from different places in space, and the perception of these differences is part of our normal experience in the concert hall. When orchestral music is recorded and reproduced through a loudspeaker, all the sounds are made to come from a single source. Binaural hearing of music and other sounds may be imitated to some extent by having two sound tracks on a recording made by microphones at suitable and separated positions in space at the concert, and coupled with two loudspeakers separately. In this case, both ears receive sound waves from both loudspeakers, but a better effect would be produced by earphones coupled separately with the pick-ups on the two sound tracks. Such devices make music sound more like real music in a concert hall than it does from a single loudspeaker (cp. p. 63).

The problems of the acoustics of concert halls are very complex. Many compositions were devised for a particular church or opera house or for a small room, and would probably have been composed or orchestrated somewhat differently by the composer for the room in which we have to hear them. In addition to the differences between halls, however, most concert rooms have defects in their acoustics which are often very difficult to overcome. Sounds are reflected from the walls just as light is reflected from mirrors, and there is an optimum persistence of echo which is suitable for the spoken voice or for music. If this length of echo is exceeded then the effect is blurred and overwhelming. If the echo is too short the effect is very dull and colourless. Music rehearsed in a big empty hall will not sound the same when the hall is full of listeners, whose clothes and bodies have a considerable damping effect on the echo.

Another kind of difficulty for the listener is the presence in many halls of areas within which at least some of the sounds made on the stage are nearly inaudible owing to the effects of differential reflexion. The planning of a hall or theatre in which sounds from every point of the stage will be equally audible in every part of the building, and in which the echo will be at its optimum, presents the architect with some difficult problems. The study of the acoustics of halls and theatres is a special science today. The old-fashioned kind of theatre which is full of sound-dispersing mouldings, including such things as plaster cherubs playing trumpets, virgins dancing, and so on, is probably better acoustically than the type with flat or curved reflecting walls and no sound-dispersing ornaments. The highly ornamental coffered ceiling is much better than a smooth barrel dome. Nevertheless, hearing, like vision, is astonishingly adaptable, and the processes of perception adjust us to many inadequacies of the stimulus patterns presented.

Divergent Perspective in Art

In the study of art all historical and cultural interpretations of perception are dependent on indirect evidence and speculative interpretation, and it is difficult to be confident about the conclusions. In addition, traditions and conventions of representation are very powerful factors in art. Although, as Thouless pointed out, it is well known that in Chinese and Eastern art there is often an avoidance of what we should regard as true perspective, it does not necessarily follow that people in the corresponding cultures perceived objects in these ways. For example, a coffer may be drawn as if apparently wider at the back than the front, as in Fig. 10:3, but it is not to be inferred of necessity that it was perceived as of that shape by the artist.

Zajac has shown, however, that the apparent reversals of perspective shown in Eastern and primitive art may have a genuine basis. If, as in

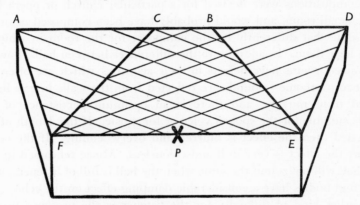

FIG. 10:3. Divergent perspective in art. If the point P is fixated in viewing a solid object like a small box, the right eye "sees" the view CDEF and the left eye "sees" ABEF. When they are combined the binocular view may be ADEF. (After Zajac, by permission of the Editor of the *British Journal of Psychology*.)

Fig. 10:3, the object was a small one like a matchbox, in which the width is less than the distance between the eyes, viewed at a distance of about one metre and fixated at the point P, the right eye "sees" the view $C D E F$, and the left eye "sees" the view $A B E F$. Then the right eye "sees" the right side of the box and the left eye the left side. This may be established readily by looking at a matchbox placed on a table about a metre from the eyes. Now, by combination of the two views, the binocular view as a whole tends to be *A D E F* and the object seems to have a divergent perspective. This may be proved by viewing it sometimes in monocular vision with either eye, and sometimes in binocular vision. If the reader then takes a flat sheet of paper about the size of a page of this book and views it in the same way, he may readily gain the same impression of divergence, even though the width of the sheet is greater than the distance between the eyes, simply because each eye gains a different view, as in the matchbox illusion. Divergent perspective may therefore in a sense be due to accurate rather than to inaccurate observation, even when it relates to objects wider than the distance between the eyes. It is only when we artificially reconstruct perspective, as it would be for a single or Cyclopean eye in the middle of the forehead, that divergent perspective is always wrong.

Cultural or Racial Influences in Perception

It may not be possible to delimit racial differences exactly because of the important effects of cultural and social pressures upon the individual. Nevertheless, it is a fair presumption that racial differences may underly many social and cultural factors, although they may be too greatly changed and obscured to be measured independently.

Thouless and Beveridge have shown that there are differences in size and shape constancy between European whites, Indians, and Africans. The Indians showed significantly greater constancy than the British group. Thouless suggests that the frequent absence of perspective or shadows in oriental art may be caused by racial differences in perception and not merely by traditions of representation.

Beveridge tested West African men for constancy of shape and he showed that in comparison with Europeans they had significantly greater constancy. He also showed that West African men had significantly less constancy for brightness but more for whiteness than British subjects. In the estimation of the horizontal from inside a closed box which could be tilted, West African men were more accurate than the Europeans. Beveridge considers that Africans are on the whole less affected by visual clues than Europeans.

A cross-cultural study of "closure" (cp. Chapter 7) was reported by Michael. In this experiment white Americans of New Mexico and Navaho Indians of the same district were tested with a series of circles of varying degrees of completeness by a lantern method of exposure for one-tenth of a second. They were asked to draw what they saw. The results confirmed the hypothesis that if closure is an innate tendency it should not

be affected by cultural influences, because no significant difference
between the whites and Navaho Indians was found. It appears that in the
Navaho culture there is a fear of "closed" patterns. All artistic patterns
are left "open" in order to let out evil spirits. Apparently, however, this
had no effect on the results, because no differences from European whites
were found.

LeShan has examined the hypothesis that there are different time
orientations at various levels of social class. The differences postulated
were that in the lower-lower class time orientation is one of quick sequences
of tension and relief; in the upper-lower, middle, and lower-upper classes
the time orientation is one of much longer tension-relief sequences; in
the upper-upper class the individual sees himself as part of a sequence of
several generations and time orientation is towards the past based on
traditional patterns of social regulation, as well as towards the future.

Evidence was obtained from data about child-rearing practices and
types of reward and punishment, and also from the stories of children
of 8 to 10 years of age given in response to the request "Tell me a story."
Of the children who told stories, 74 were of lower class and 43 of middle
class. In general the data supported the hypothesis. It might be added
that since the upper-upper class time orientation also involves the individual's conception of himself as belonging to a sequence which leads into
the future, he is often willing to forego immediate satisfaction of an
interest or impulse because he realises that a plan of action less satisfying
to him at the moment will lead to his successors gaining more of what
they will need after his death.

It might be expected that physiognomic qualities or, in particular,
the fitness of names to drawings such as mentioned in Chapter 7, might
vary from race to race or culture to culture. Experiments by Davis,
however, suggested that this is not the case. Native children in the
Mahali peninsula, Lake Tanganyika, were asked to match nonsense names
with abstract drawings after the fashion of Kohler's "maluma" and
"takete." They carried out this task in a highly consistent manner and
their choices were similar to those of a group of English schoolchildren.

Vision and the Pilot or Motorist

There are important problems about perception connected with the
control of a fast-moving vehicle, and some of these can be studied by
experimental psychology. Ludvigh and Miller tested 200 incoming U.S.
Naval Aviation cadets, 18-25 years of age, who were an unselected sample
of the cadet population, with tests of dynamic visual acuity (the ability

to see moving targets). The subject viewed a Landolt ring (cp. p. 91) monocularly in a moving mirror placed close to the eye. It was found that all the subjects had static visual acuity of 20/20 with the Snellen Chart, but their dynamic acuity was shown to deteriorate as the angular velocity of the test object was increased. The effect of training was found to be substantial at a high angular velocity of the test object, but the rate of improvement varied greatly among individuals. A significant difference was found at the first and at all the subsequent trials, between the thresholds for dynamic visual acuity of the twenty subjects having the highest and the twenty having the lowest initial thresholds.

Different mechanisms may underly static and dynamic visual acuity, and an individual's static acuity is no guide to his dynamic acuity. This brings out an important point about the perception of moving objects —or of stationary objects seen from a fast-moving vehicle—which is not generally recognised.

The problem of vision at night, when the illumination is very low and falls between mid-mesopic and low photopic levels of luminance, are important. At dusk seeing becomes difficult. The sky is still quite bright, while objects on the road seem to merge with their shadows and fade into the darkness. In twilight objects seem to be further away than their actual distances. With greater darkness, changes in the appearance of objects are more rapid and momentary, and a second look for rechecking becomes less and less possible. Transition zones at tunnels or the ends of brightly lighted streets are dangerous unless so lighted as to ease the adaptation of the eyes.

In night driving, brightness values change, colours fade, visual resolution decreases, and large objects must be distinguished from patches of light or shadow. Close objects are seen directly by the light they reflect, but when they are 25 feet or more away they can be seen only in silhouette against the slightly brighter surround.

An experiment showed that veiling glare, viz. the diffused light reflected back into the eyes from a mist or fog, reduced size constancy so that size judgments for disks of equal diameter at different distances approached what would be expected on the law of inverse squares. A second experiment showed the disturbing nature of veiling glare in binocular vision for simple judgments of equality of size and distance of circular disks. The binocular veiling glare was obtained by an apparatus illustrated in Fig. 10:4, in which light from one or other of two lamps illuminated a milk glass screen at right angles to the line of vision and was graduated in intensity from left to right, or from right to left, according to which lamp was used. The glare from the milk glass screen was reflected into the eyes from a piece of plate glass at 45° to the line of vision and

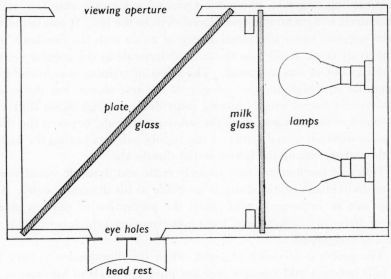

Fig. 10:4. Apparatus used to produce a veiling glare in binocular vision, graduated from left to right with one lamp, from right to left with the other lamp, or uniform if both lamps are used. (After Pickford, by permission of the editor of the *British Journal of Psychology*.)

the subject, looking through the eyeholes, saw the test objects at a distance through the veiling glare.

In normal perception, apparent size tends to follow the law of constancy, while distance tends to be perceived directly, and the two are thus integrated to accord with the requirements of adaptive behaviour because it is important to be able to estimate accurately the relative distances of objects one may be trying to grasp, but to perceive them as if in their real sizes. One of the most remarkable effects of the veiling glare was that the subjects found that they could use either "size" or "distance" methods of adjustment separately. Thus, veiling glare disturbs perceptual adaptation.

A third experiment tested the efforts of coloured veiling glare, produced in binocular vision with the apparatus described above, but with the addition of Ilford spectrum red, yellow, green, and blue filters according to a prearranged experimental plan. The colour of the veiling glare had almost no influence. The effects of veiling glare vary from individual to individual, and this is important from the point of view of perception in conditions of fog or haze because, as with dynamic visual acuity, individuals are affected in ways which would not be predicted from their performances under normal conditions. This may explain why some ordinary capable motorists become over-confident and erratic drivers in fog, while others lose their confidence completely and hardly dare to move.

The Development of Perception[1]

Thanks to thirty years of developmental research, mainly by Gesell on the one hand, using a natural history, normative, approach documented with photographs, and by Piaget on the other hand with his *méthode clinique* which combines phenomenological observation with experiment, certain facts have been established.

There is a distinction between instantaneous perceptions which are relatively passive, and a "perceptual activity" connecting them with each other. This is not inconsistent with the Gestalt view that there are certain basic "given" aspects of perception such as the figure-ground experience, but it also recognises the importance of early learning.

There is substantial agreement by a long line of investigators that movement and its experience are specially important for perceptual development. Piaget outlines six stages in the first two years of life by which a child comes to perceive objects, self and others, in spatial, temporal, and causal relationships, from an originally diffuse global state which consisted only of changing or repeated movements accompanied by visual, tactile, and kinesthetic "happenings." "Gradually these images are detached from the activity itself, are externalised and inter-related. . . . Above all the child discovers his own body and locates it in space with other objects." Evidence of this differentiation can be found in the child's recognition of himself in mirrors, his ability to imitate another person, and the increasing discrimination of his smiling response to different people.

Clinical studies by Bender of children with retardation of development show these developmental tasks "writ large." Drawings are a rich source of information on both normal and abnormal perceptual development after infancy. Meili has used the Rorschach ink blots to study development of perceiving and has found a diffuse global response, followed by a stage involving perception of details without integration and then of wholes perceived as integrations of parts.

For the primary school years, in addition to work on perceptual development with regard to judging length, weight, and volume, there is a body of experimental research concerned with constancy of size, shape, and colour. Individual differences appear to be greater than differences

[1] We are indebted to Miss L. R. Bowyer, Psychology Department, Glasgow University, for the material in this section.

due to age or intelligence trends and also constancy for the same individual may differ for different sense modalities.

Other research concerns perception of apparent movement, causal effects using the Michotte disk technique with children 4-8 years old, visual depth discrimination in infants, susceptibility to illusions, perception of quantity and of velocity, time perception, and the perception of expressive qualities of persons.

There are still only a few developmental studies of auditory, olfactory, and tactile-kinesthetic perception, and there is a need to continue the study of development, in its complete sense, through adolescent years beyond maturity to changes which may take place in old age.

BIBLIOGRAPHY

General

ALLPORT, F. H. 1955. *Theories of Perception and the Concept of Structure.* Chapman and Hall, London; Wiley, New York.

BEARDSLEE, D. C. and WERTHEIMER, M. 1958. *Readings in Perception.* Van Nostrand, London and New York.

STOUT, G. F. 1938. *Manual of Psychology* (5th Edn.). University Tutorial Press.

WOODWORTH, R. S. 1958. *Dynamics of Behavior.* Methuen, London.

Projection and Personality in Perception

BANISTER, H. and ZANGWILL, O. L. 1941. Experimentally induced visual paramnesias. *Brit. J. Psychol.*, **32**, 30-51.

BOWYER, L. R. and PICKFORD, R. W. 1949. The three haystacks—Notes on an experience analogous to Déjà Vu. *Brit. J. Med. Psychol.*, **22**, 117-21.

KLOPFER, B. and KELLEY, D. M. 1946. *The Rorschach Technique : A Manual for a Projective Method of Personality Diagnosis.* World Book Co., New York.

MacCURDY, J. T. 1925. *The Psychology of Emotion.* Ch. 43. Kegan Paul, London.

MURRAY, H. A. *et al.* 1938. *Explorations into Personality* (and Plates). Oxford University Press, London.

PHILLIPSON, H. 1956. *The Object Relations Technique* (with Plates). Tavistock Press, London.

PICKFORD, R. W. 1942. Rossetti's "Sudden Light" as an experience of Déjà Vu. *Brit. J. Med. Psychol.*, **19**, 192-200.

——1944. Déjà Vu in Proust and Tolstoy. *Int. J. Psycho-Analysis*, **25**, 155-65.

——1963. *Pickford Projective Pictures.* Tavistock Press, London.

RORSCHACH, H. 1942. *Psychodiagnostics* (Text and Plates, 2nd Edn.). Huber, Berne.

STEIN, M. L. 1955. *The Thematic Apperception Test : An Introductory Manual for its Clinical Use with Adults.* Addison Wesley, Cambridge, Mass.

TAGIURI, R. and PETRULLO, L. (Eds.). 1958. *Person Perception and Interpersonal Behavior.* Stanford University Press, Stanford, U.S.A.

WITKIN, H. A. *et al.* 1954. *Personality through Perception.* Harper, New York.

Visual Perception

EVANS, R. M. 1959. *Eye, Film, and Camera in Color Photography.* Wiley, New York; Chapman and Hall, London.

GOMBRICH, E. H. 1956. *Art and Illusion: A Study in the Psychology of Pictorial Representation.* Phaidon, London.

LUCKIESH, M. 1944. *Light, Vision, and Seeing.* Van Nostrand, New York.

LUDVIGH, E. and MILLER, J. W. 1953-59. *A Study of Dynamic Visual Acuity* (and other reports). U.S. Bureau of Medicine and Surgery, Project Nos. N.M. 001 075.01, 01-08, N.M. 001 110 501.09-10, and N.M. 17 01 99 Subtask 2, Reports 13 and 16. U.S. Naval School of Aviation Medicine, Naval Air Station, Pensacola, Florida.

MARTIN, T. M. and PICKFORD, R. W. 1938. Effect of veiling glare on apparent size relations. *Brit. J. Psychol.*, **29,** 91-103.

PICKFORD, R. W. 1943. Some effects of veiling glare in binocular vision. *Brit. J. Psychol.*, **33,** 150-161.

——1944. Some effects of coloured veiling glare in binocular vision. *Brit. J. Psychol.*, **34,** 89-103.

RICHARDS, O. W. 1952. *Vision at Levels of Night Road Illumination.* Highway Research Board, U.S.A., Bull. **56,** 36-55.

——1953. Yellow glasses fail to improve seeing at night driving luminances. *U.S.A. Highway Res. Absts.*, **23**: 7, 32-6.

——1957. *Vision at Levels of Night Road Illumination.* Highway Research Board, U.S.A., Bull. **146,** 58-66.

——1958. Night driving seeing problems. *Amer. J. Optom. and Arch. Amer. Acad. Optom.*, Monograph **241.**

——1960. Seeing for night driving. *J. Amer. Optom. Ass.*, **32,** 211-14.

ZAJAC, J. L. 1961. Studies in perspective. *Brit. J. Psychol.*, **52,** 233-340.

Cross-Cultural, Social, and Racial Differences

BARBU, Z. 1960. *Problems of Historical Psychology.* Routledge and Kegan Paul, London.

BEVERIDGE, W. M. 1935. Racial differences in phenomenal regression. *Brit. J. Psychol.*, **26,** 59-62.

——1939. Some racial differences in perception. *Brit. J. Psychol.*, **30,** 57-64.

DAVIS, R. 1961. The fitness of names to drawings. A cross-cultural study in Tanganyika. *Brit. J. Psychol.*, **52,** 259-68.

THOULESS, R. H. 1932. A racial difference in perception. *J. Soc. Psychol.*, **4,** 330-9.

Development of Perception

BENDER, L. 1958. Emerging patterns in child psychiatry. *Bull. New York Acad. Med.* (2nd Series), **34,** 794-810.

GESELL, A. 1948. *Studies in Child Development.* Harper, New York and London.

GIBSON, E. J. and OLUM, V. 1960. Experimental methods of studying perception in children, Ch. 8. In *Handbook of Research Methods in Child Development.* Ed. by P. H. Mussen. Wiley, London and New York.

INHELDER, B. and PIAGET, J. 1956. *The Child's Conception of Space.* Routledge and Kegan Paul, London.

PIAGET, J., INHELDER, B. and SZEMINSKA, A. 1960. *The Child's Conception of Geometry*. Routledge and Kegan Paul, London.

SOLLEY, C. M. and MURPHY, G. 1960. *Development of the Perceptual World*, Basic Books, New York.

VERNON, M. D. 1960. The development of perception in children. *Educational Res.*, **3**, 1-11.

WAPNER, S. and WERNER, H. 1957. *Perceptual Development*. Clark University Press, Worcester, Mass.

11

Conclusion

Psychological Theories of Perception

In a brief consideration of psychological theories of perception we might return to the landmarks for perceptual learning—the judgmental, stimulation, association, and adaptation approaches. Perception is concerned with the influence of judgments about experiences and the external world, and it is clear the psychologists have not been able to exclude something very like judgment from their studies of perception, although they might well have tried. Again, perception is the product of the stimulus pattern interacting with inner functions, processes, and stresses, and its study entails an account of how the stimulus pattern appears under various conditions. Thirdly, in perception it is still true that associative processes play a large part, even if the traditional theories of mental association, which had such a long reign in psychology, must be translated into other, and mainly neurological, terms. Lastly, perception is intimately connected with varying and complex conditions of conscious and unconscious adjustment and adaptation. It might be said that every change or new development in perception involves adaptation of the organism as a whole to new conditions, social or individual, while every mode of resistance to change in perception implies an absence or failure of adaptation.

A psychological theory of perception must be flexible and comprehensive enough to account for all the influences of sensory excitation and of appetite, interest, attention, recognition, memory, and conscious and unconscious factors, including repression, dissociation, and other ego-defence functions, and the many aspects of thinking and problem-solving. It is closely tied up with racial, social, and cultural influences. In order to give an adequate psychological account of perception, therefore, it is necessary to deal with the entire psychological functioning of the organism as a whole and within its social setting.

In the last twenty years there have been many new psychological theories of perception. Floyd Allport, for instance, discusses no less than thirteen of them and tries, with quite a considerable measure of success, to integrate them into a coherent scheme. All these theories have some basis in fact and something to be said in their favour on general grounds, and the attempted integration has been a valuable contribution to psychology.

239

In these chapters no attempt has been made to discuss all these theories, but Gestalt psychology, which has illuminated perception more than any approach in the last half century, has been dealt with briefly. Psychologists now await much more complete knowledge of the brain functions at work in perception and in other fields, and the understanding of the ways in which these functions underlie conscious experiences will be fundamental.

PART III

12

Scepticism and the Representative Theory

Traditionally philosophers have approached the study of perception in two ways. First they have enquired whether and to what extent perceiving is a form of knowledge, how far, if at all, the senses can be trusted to reveal the nature of external reality; secondly, they have sought a satisfactory explanation of the action of the senses as intermediaries between human beings and the external world, and have examined the role the relevant physical and mental processes play in perception. These two types of enquiry are closely linked, since the first provides data and problems for the second, and the second throws light, and doubt, on the first.

Scepticism with respect to the Senses

Grounds for Scepticism

Very often the answer to the first enquiry was a sceptical one, for doubts about the senses are easily induced by illusions, hallucinations, and distortions. We must therefore consider these phenomena to see whether they justify scepticism, and for this purpose it is most convenient to distinguish them as follows, even though this involves some departure from the use of the term "illusion" normal among psychologists (cp. p. 143).

Illusions: In these the percipient is mistaken about the nature or properties of the objects perceived, or even if sophisticated enough to know the actual situation is often still unable to <u>perceive it correctly</u>.* Thus he may misidentify an object or person, especially if looking casually or in a poor light; he may mistake an object's colour or size, may be taken in by an imitation, wax fruit perhaps, or by the misdirection of conjurors. Every visit to the cinema is a prolonged illusion: we seem to be seeing a three-dimensional scene with people or horses moving across it, but there is actually projected on the flat screen a rapid succession of slightly different "stills." Cases of reflexion can be very deceptive, while in mirages refraction of the light rays misleads one as to the distance of the oasis seen (though some mirages are hallucinations); even if we know it is a mirage <u>the eye is still deceived</u>, as it is when the straight stick half

242

* meaning precisely what?

immersed in water still looks bent. Psychologists have provided us with compelling illusions, *e.g.* the Müller-Lyer illusion in which we misjudge the length of lines or the Distorted Room in which a man may look smaller than a boy. Again, we may see double as a result of disease or alcohol, or if mescaline is taken startling effects may occur—the carpet may seem to undulate or pyjamas seem edged with flame.

Hallucinations: Here the distinguishing feature is that the ostensible object of perception is not actually present or within view, nor does it resemble any object present. "Resemble" is inevitably vague, for between pure hallucinations and pure illusions there is a gradation of "triggered hallucinations," *e.g.* where a shadow or patch of light is taken to be a person—it apparently sets off a train of imagery which is confused with genuine perceptions. (Similarly, many dreams are "triggered," *e.g.* if the eiderdown falls off we may dream that we are crossing Antarctica.) Classic cases among pure hallucinations are Macbeth's dagger, the pink rats or snakes the drunkard may see, or the apparitions of delirium. Also notorious are "phantom limbs," where the patient feels pain in the toes of an amputated leg or may feel the missing limb still there but lying in an odd position. But there is a range of instances—one may hear voices, smell burning for long periods, or by taking mescaline enjoy a remarkable phantasmagoria. It is important to note that hallucinations, whether pure or triggered, may be perfectly well integrated with a genuine background —the pink rat may be seen to run along a real bedstead.

The relativity of perception: Examples of this are unspectacular and normally cause no deception, but they are very common and present theoretical problems. Sometimes they are included under illusions, but since deception is absent or irrelevant we have classified them separately. The essential point is that in a large range of cases, the properties perceived in an object are relative to factors extraneous to it, *i.e.* to the position of the percipient, to the distance and media between object and percipient, to the lighting, to the state of the percipient's health or sense organs, or to his psychological state. A common example is that of perspective distortion: a square table may from certain angles look diamond-shaped or trapezoid. Similarly the distant green hills may look blue or grey, the same water may feel cool to one person and warm to another, and food may taste quite different when we have a cold or a hangover. Other examples are the effects of colour blindness, fog, or short sight, of lenses and microscopes, or of inattention or past experiences, on what is seen.

The Simple Sceptical Argument

Most of these phenomena have been adduced by certain philosophers as grounds for scepticism with regard to the senses. In its simplest form their claim is that, since illusions and hallucinations occur, the senses cannot be trusted and perceiving is not a form of knowing. An illusory perception or hallucination or vivid dream seems perfectly genuine and indistinguishable from the real thing; so whenever we try to discover the nature of objects by the senses, our perception may be quite deceptive, however convincing it seems—indeed we may not even be perceiving and there may be no object there.

It may be objected that this is unrealistic—the possibility of illusions and hallucinations causes no serious difficulty in practice since they are comparatively rare and can be ruled out by various precautions and tests. We can avoid taking mescaline or too much alcohol; we can use the evidence of one sense to check another—if we think we hear someone at the door we can go and see, if hallucination or refraction is suspected we can try to touch the object concerned; movement will reveal distortions, reflexions, and mirages, while measurement of the lines can dispose of artificial optical illusions; we can always compare notes with other persons to rule out dreams and hallucinations or establish the characteristics of a thing. All this is obvious enough, but will not worry the sceptic. He will still say that a possibility of doubt remains; the various tests are satisfactory for practical purposes, but mere practical success is not enough; what we seek here is absolute certainty beyond any possibility of doubt, and this the senses cannot provide even when supplemented by tests. If one sense supports another, it too may be deceived; measurement and movement are not final criteria to justify observation because they only offer support by affording further observations, which may also be illusory; if you compare notes with another person he also may have been tricked by his senses. Indeed, there is still the *possibility* that he does not exist, that you are having an hallucination of his presence or dreaming that he appeared with confirmation. In short, however much we reduce the likelihood of error by various tests, we can never *finally* prove that we have attained absolute certainty and that some further observation or occurrence will not throw doubt on the supposed facts.

This simple sceptical argument was not usually advanced on its own. Rationalist[1] philosophers like Plato and Descartes supported it by the claim that there is by contrast an absolutely certain method of obtaining knowledge of reality, viz. by the intuition[2] and reasoning used in mathematics—we can intuit without any doubt that two straight lines cannot

---

[1] In philosophy a Rationalist is not an agnostic but a person who holds that knowledge must be attained by intuition and deductive reasoning, not by sensory observation.

[2] Intuition is not a feminine guesswork, but means here the immediate intellectual grasp of a self-evident truth with full conviction of its certainty. The problem is to distinguish it from a pseudo-intuition where the belief is immediately convincing but false.

enclose a space and prove without any possibility of error that $7 + 5 = 12$ or that the sum of the angles of a triangle is 180°. Furthermore, this knowledge is universal in character—it applies to all objects and all triangles, while perception is always particular, can tell us only of this object or that. The only way, the Rationalists thought, that science and philosophy could advance in true knowledge was to avoid the blandishments of the unreliable senses and to apply mathematical intuition and reasoning to a wider field. Gradually, however, it became apparent that this would not work: mathematical methods are only successful in so far as one is dealing with an abstract and close-knit system, *e.g.* a geometry, whose basic elements and structural principles are stated and precisely defined in one's premises; the certain and demonstrative knowledge that one obtains is then of the detailed ramifications of the system granted these elements and principles. But that anything exists in the world with the same kind of elements and structure as the abstract mathematical system, or that one mathematical system rather than another fits a given part of reality—this has to be discovered by sensory observation. In the complex world of concrete reality one will also be faced with many fields, *e.g.* human relationships, to which the abstract systems are inappropriate. The Rationalists did not realise these limitations because they thought that they knew by intuition that the basic mathematical principles held true of all reality—everything physical must obey Euclid and the rules of arithmetic. To them the only problem seemed to be to find more intuitions of this kind. But the development of non-Euclidean geometries and of modern physics undermined these supposed intuitions, while confidence in the discovery of any others has dwindled.

In its heyday this Rationalist claim made the simple sceptical argument seem serious, but with its collapse one no longer seems justified in abandoning the senses for some chimerical "absolute certainty." The only way of learning about the real world is by sensory observation and reasoning based on it, and if this does not give a final irrefragable certainty it comes close to it, since by various checks and tests we can normally reduce this possibility of error to an infinitesimal amount. If we seek absolute certainty we can only find it in tautologies or within some abstract system, one divorced from the real world or whose application to it has to be established by observation. It is worth while raising these doubts, however, not only on historical grounds—so much of philosophy has been devoted to trying to find more reliable sources of knowledge than sense perception—but also on practical ones. Even if seeing is believing it isn't knowing—at least not without great care and confirmation. Untested and unconfirmed perception may also deceive in unexpected ways: this is notorious in the law courts with the contradictions of eye-witnesses and the dangers of misidentification; and many advances, *e.g.* the work of Pasteur, were only made possible by more careful and accurate observation. Further, even in science observed "facts" are always subject to reassessment in the light of newer theories and discoveries.

Further Implications of the Relativity of Perception

The principle of the relativity of perception is that the qualities perceived in an object, while no doubt dependent on its nature, are greatly affected by extraneous factors such as distance and light or the state of the percipient. A further sceptical conclusion was drawn from this that perception, even in genuine cases where there is no illusion or hallucination, does not reveal to us the real intrinsic properties of external objects; all it reveals are perceived qualities which may be very different indeed owing to the action of these extraneous factors. This kind of argument dates back to the Greeks, was popularised in the seventeenth century, and is still influential. Let us take a few traditional examples: (*a*) Have three bowls of water, one hot, one cold, and one of intermediate heat; place one hand in the hot and one in the cold water; after a few minutes transfer your hand from the hot water to the intermediate one which will then feel cold; then transfer your other hand to the intermediate water which will feel warm to it. But this water cannot *be* both warm and cold, which would be a self-contradiction. Therefore, warmth and cold are not intrinsic properties of the water which we directly perceive: they are subjective feelings induced in the percipient by some quite different property[1] in external objects. (*b*) A wine or a fruit may taste sour to one person and sweet to another; it cannot be both sweet and sour; so sweet and sour, and presumably other tastes, for they seem to be of the same generic nature, are not intrinsic properties of external things but are our reactions to some evidently different property. (*c*) The colours that we see are dependent on the light and so cannot be intrinsic to external things. It is well known that a coat or a tie may look one colour in the shop and another in daylight. Which then is the real colour—the daylight one? or is that an arbitrary standard chosen for convenience? And even daylight varies with season, weather, and location. Again, the object may look one colour to you and another to Jones who is colour blind; and however brightly coloured it may be, it will lose its colour and look grey in the dim twilight.

These arguments were supported by various scientific considerations tending to show that the counterpart in external objects to perceived

---

[1] To be more exact the "different property" is the relation between the heat or temperature of the water and that of the skin, but the argument does not depend for its validity on the scientific details.

* what is the criterion for something's being an 'intrinsic property'?

qualities must often be quite different. Heat is regarded as a form of energy and explained in terms of atomic or molecular movement, something unlike sensations of warmth; colours <u>are associated with</u> waves of a certain frequency, the object property being the power to reflect waves of certain frequencies, a matter of texture perhaps; the objective counterpart of sound is something unlike it, vibration at a certain frequency. Even if the scientific account changes, as it changed between 1700 and today, its support for the relativity argument remains provided a difference between perceived qualities and intrinsic object-properties survives.

but not identical with?

Primary and Secondary Qualities

From the seventeenth century onwards a common conclusion from these arguments has been the distinction of Primary and Secondary Qualities. Colours, sounds, tastes, smells, hardness, softness, warmth, and cold were called secondary qualities; this means that these qualities as perceived, as we experience them, are not intrinsic properties of external objects but are subjective reactions to properties of the object quite different in character. But spatial properties in particular (shape and size or extension), also motion, number, and solidity, were called primary qualities, because although we must still distinguish between the perceived quality and its counterpart in the object, the perceived shape, size, motion, etc., do in favourable circumstances accurately resemble, and so reveal, the intrinsic shape, size, and motion of the object; and even when this is not so and the perceived qualities are only "apparent," there is still a rough or global resemblance, <u>the perceived shape for example being a projection of the intrinsic one.</u>

could the secondary qualities also be projections?

The belief that there are qualities which are primary in this sense was challenged by Berkeley who argued as follows: perceived shape varies with position as colour does with distance or light; sensible size and details of structure vary with the distance of the object, and change if you use a microscope; perceived motion varies with your own motion or with distance (parallax); so there is no logical ground for treating them differently from the others and supposing that they resemble supposed intrinsic object-properties. But this relativity is merely the ground for distinguishing perceived quality and object-property: the claim to resemblance between the two rests on other evidence, chiefly measurement. Even if a coin looks elliptical from some angles we can establish that it is really or intrinsically round (and that the roundness that we see from directly above it <u>accurately</u> <u>resembles</u> its <u>intrinsic shape</u>) by measuring its various diameters and finding that they are all equal. And this may be confirmed by other operations: rolling the coin, fitting it into a drawn circle, trying to fit several into a square box, etc. Size is more complicated: we can show that one object is larger than another by measuring them, but length, breadth, and size generally may seem to be only relations between objects or between object and standard; however, they are not just this, for although a standard is necessary for numerical expression of measurement there are also length, breadth, and size as a physical extension, a space-occupying, which is measured and which is presupposed by the relative size of objects. One can also measure different speeds or agree as to what is moving and what is stationary on the earth; mass also can be measured and the number of objects present settled by touching and counting. On the other hand, one cannot obtain direct measurements of tastes and smells; nor indeed can one do this for colours and sounds, since any measurement there is is of physical properties (light quanta or wave amplitude) not of perceived colour or sound. Relativity physics may introduce difficulties about motion, for example, but provided one can assume the earth as a frame of reference and insist that one is concerned with macroscopic or large-scale properties, not with sub-atomic structure, it does not seem to invalidate the general argument. Indeed, physical theory as a whole supports the distinction. In so far as science can explain the world in terms of measurable properties amenable to mathematical treatment, it suggests that they are basic and intrinsic, the only properties even. But reliance on physics should be cautious: for example, seventeenth-century theory was responsible for the dubious inclusion of "solidity" (impenetrability) in the list of primary qualities.

The Representative Theory

Statement of the Theory

For a proper assessment of the reliability of the senses as a source of knowledge of the world, we must also consider how perception works and how convincing illusions and hallucinations can occur. We must therefore turn to the second line of philosophical enquiry, which is an important study in its own right. The dominant seventeenth-century attempt at a general explanation of perception and attendant phenomena was the Representative Theory; and this, with slight modernisation, is worth close examination not only for its plausibility and dangers, but because it is in essence the same theory as is advanced by many modern neurologists under different names: "Physiological Idealism," "Two-world Theory," or, confusingly, "The Sense-datum Theory."[1]

The starting-point of the theory is the fact of causal transmission from object to percipient's brain, e.g. in sight, light waves→retina→ex-

---

[1] The philosophical Sense-datum Theory is quite different, see Ch. 13, and the term "sense-datum" is perhaps best reserved for it.

citation of optic pathways→cerebral cortex. Even where there is "direct contact" with the object, as in touch, there is still a causal transmission from nerve endings in the skin to the appropriate areas of the brain. The theory claims that the transmission is continued to the mind,[1] that for all the senses the brain activity aroused by stimulation of the sense organ causes the mind to be directly aware of mental representations of the properties of the external objects which initiated the whole process. A wide range of names has been given to these representations: originally called Ideas or Representative Ideas, they were later referred to as Impressions, Sensations, Percepts, or Sense-data. But whatever their name, it is agreed that these representations are objects of direct awareness, that they are quite distinct from external physical objects, that they are private to the percipient concerned, that they are generated or created by his brain (normally on stimulation of the sense organ), and that they are mental or "in the mind"; they are exemplified, usually, by patches of colour of varying shape, by sounds, tastes, smells, feelings of pressure, warmth or cold. Normally there is the further refinement that they are synthesised by the mind, so that one is aware not of shapes, colour patches, sounds, etc., but of wholes or units possessing these shapes, colours or sounds as qualities, just as the external objects they represent are conceived of as possessing corresponding properties. In older versions the two types of representations (colour patches, etc., or whole objects) were distinguished as simple and complex ideas; a more modern way would be to distinguish them as sensations and percepts respectively. But some versions cut out this stage of mental synthesis or construction of percepts out of sensations; they assume that the pattern of brain activity normally gives rise directly to percepts or representations of an object-like character.

The essential point of the theory is thus that the physical and physiological causal process from object to brain causes, as a further step, mental representations of the external objects and properties initiating the process. "Perception of external objects" as ordinarily understood is thus claimed to be mediate or indirect; it is really the direct perception of the effects of these objects, viz. of the mental representations they ultimately cause. This direct perception of representations, not external objects, is stressed in all the versions by analogies: the percipient is said to be like a king in his audience chamber seeing a representative of a

[1] By "mind" the older exponents of the theory usually meant the true self or person, which they conceived as a spiritual or non-physical being associated with the body (cp. p. 250). Some of the difficulties associated with this notion are discussed in pp. 261-3, and an alternative concept of mind is outlined in Ch. 15. Modern neurological versions are vaguer and more cautious, but if fully worked out would probably approximate to the older ones: at least they seem to suggest that there is an order of being, a "mental world" or events in a "mental space," different from but affected by the brain and physical world.

foreign country, like a man seeing a mental map of the external world or a mental cinema or T.V. picture of it, like a radar operator looking at the representation of the outside world on his screen.

bad analogies

Advantages of the Theory

This theory has survived for four centuries because it can account for a wide range of phenomena.

As a causal explanation it gives due weight to the causal transmission in perception and can explain how certain physiological events are conditions of perceiving. If the eye is damaged, the optic nerve cut, or the visual cortex of the brain destroyed, then sight is lost; and similar necessary conditions hold for the other senses. Clearly this is because such damage interrupts the causal transmission and prevents the brain activity by which the mental representations are produced. On the other hand, it suggests that the earlier stages of the causal transmission are not necessary to perceiving if the appropriate brain activity can be caused in some other way, and this can be shown experimentally to a large extent. Direct electrical stimulation of the cortex can cause sensations, and knowledge of the points stimulated and sensations caused has been used to draw "cortical maps" (cp. p. 30). (The sensations concerned are not exactly like normal ones, being vaguer and of a different quality, but this can be explained by the difference in the stimulus; direct electrical stimulation excites a large group of cells at fixed frequencies, while the normal nerve impulses of perception are trains of impulses rising and falling in frequency.) Ability to account for the causal conditions of perception is a virtue of the theory, for some theories of perception largely ignore them; but this may not be the only way of accounting for them.

Interactionism: In continuing the causal transmission to the mind, the Representative Theory is attempting an answer to the questions of how mind and body are related—a problem which cannot be evaded if one is to understand man and his nature. If, as is commonly done under the influence of Plato and of Christian theology, you regard the true self or person as a spiritual being, a soul or mind imprisoned in a material body for the duration of his earthly life, then it is orthodox to suppose that interaction occurs between the soul or mind on the one hand and the body on the other; in conduct generally, the mind, having decided on a course of action, excites the motor areas of the brain and sets up there activity which in turn causes movement of the muscles and the body; conversely, in perception, stimulation of the sense organs sets up brain activity which causes mental sensations. Thus the Representative Theory takes its place as part of the widely held Interaction Theory of the relation of mind and body, and it is supported by the latter's theological and philosophical popularity. How can the interaction take place if the Representative Theory is false? And if there is no interaction, what substitute account of mind and body can be offered?

Time-lag: As a causal theory of perception, the Representative Theory is able to explain the time-lag which is noticeable in certain perceptions. It is well known that the flash of the firing of a distant gun can be seen appreciably before the sound is heard, even though they both occur simultaneously at the point of origin. The explanation seems simple: sound waves travel much more slowly than light waves from the source; hence they are later in stimulating the sense organ and causing their characteristic mental representation. A notorious problem about time-lag is that as light travels at finite speed the light from the stars takes years to reach us—4·27 years from the nearest star, *Proxima Centauri*, and up to millions of years from distant galaxies. Hence when we look at a star we do not see it as it is: indeed, it is theoretically possible that it disintegrated and disappeared years ago. Even the sun is seen as it was eight minutes before, and there is always some time-lag in perception, though it is normally of the order of milliseconds: it takes a finite time for waves from objects to reach us and for impulses to travel from sense organ to brain. All this fits the Representative Theory's claim that we do not directly perceive external objects: strictly we perceive a mental representation caused by the external object, and this representation need not be simultaneous with the state of the object it represents. When we seem to see a star which no longer exists, strictly we see a mental representation of the star caused by light which left it several years ago. No problem at all for this theory—but a serious difficulty for any naive or common-sense view which supposes that we perceive external objects directly. *

Illusions, hallucinations, and relativity explained: A well-known difficulty concerns the nature of what is perceived during an illusory or hallucinatory experience. When the drunkard sees a snake and it is not a real snake, what is it? A man with double vision sees two bottles when there is actually only one. What then is the second bottle? Of what does he see two? Again, what are the visions of mescaline? Indeed this kind of question can be asked about cases of relativity. When the round table looks elliptical or the distant green mountains look blue, we seem to be seeing something elliptical or blue respectively, it may be argued, and these are not the table, which is round, or the mountains, which are green, so what are they? Or what is the black or grey thing the colour-blind man "sees" and identifies as a "red" pillarbox?

question-begging.

The Representative Theory has a ready answer to all this. What the percipient perceives or is directly aware of in all these cases is a mental

where "directly" means .... without any causal mediation? Has this view been seriously maintained by philosophers, or even "educated" plain men?

representation; this representation may be of some object not present, *e.g.* of a snake or second bottle, or it may differ in quality from the object present and causing it, as in the cases of relativity. The table causes a representation of round shape if the percipient looks from above, or an elliptical one from certain other viewpoints; the water causes a representation of warmth via one hand and of cold via the other, in the bowls of water example; the pillarbox causes a red representation in normal people and a black or grey one in the colour blind, and so on. This is not a complete explanation in itself. In the cases of relativity it needs to be supplemented by an account of how perspective, distance or media alter the stimulus to the sense organ, or defects affect the response of the organ, so that the brain activity and hence the representation is changed. And for hallucinations one may suppose that the deceptive representation is caused by brain activity which would have been due to the object represented had that been perceived, but which in this case arises from some quite different internal or external cause. But though leaving various details unsettled, the theory does deal with the main philosophical difficulty of the nature of what is perceived in all these cases and offers a reasonable prospect of an ultimately complete explanation. It may similarly accommodate dreams and the mental imagery that occurs in memory and day-dreaming: these too are private mental representations, presumably due to the revival or recombination of patterns of brain activity which have occurred in past perceptions.

Primary and secondary qualities: The theory can easily accept this distinction of qualities and was normally advocated along with it. As perceived qualities are always mental representations, according to the theory, a large step has been taken towards the distinction; and the question of which of them actually resemble the corresponding properties of external objects can be settled by measurement or other operations and by scientific considerations. It may also be pointed out that there is nothing in the conduction of nerve impulses from sense organ to brain that could resemble or transmit qualities such as perceived colour, warmth, or sound. The nerves from the different sense organs are all similar, and the only variables are the spatio-temporal pattern of the impulses, the pathways used, and the cortical destinations; the main determinant of the quality of the sensation or mental representation seems to be the location of the activity excited in the brain. This confirms the earlier point (p. 247) that, so far as we can tell, what corresponds in the external objects to these secondary qualities differs greatly from them. The transmission of certain primary qualities seems easier to understand: shape of object→spatial pattern of light rays and retinal excitation→spatial pattern of excitation in the brain. But even here the case is not simple since the brain pattern seems not to be "isomorphic" but to differ in shape from the object and the representation. Hence the main evidence for the resemblance of the last two must still remain that of measurement.

A Fundamental Weakness and Resultant Scepticism

The chief difficulty in the theory lies in its main conclusion, that we are never directly aware of external physical objects; strictly all our direct perception is of mental representations which, though they are supposed to be caused by and in part resemble external objects, are nevertheless quite distinct from them and form a private world for each percipient. The question then is: how does the percipient ever get out of this private mental world to which all his sensory awareness is confined? If his direct perception is only of representations how does he ever come to know that the external objects they represent do actually exist, still more how does he know what these external objects are like, or which representations they resemble? Normally one would say that A was like or unlike B, or that A was a picture or representation of B, by observing the two and comparing them; similarly the statement that B caused A would be based on observation of both. But here one is in the strange position of being able to observe only A, never B: we can only perceive the representations, and whenever we may think we are observing external objects to compare them with the representations or discover their intrinsic nature, we are only observing more and more representations; we may suppose that there are external objects causing the representations, but we can never *know* this because we can never directly perceive such objects. The theory is in fact having to assume a set of strictly unobservable, and so unknown, causes for the private mental world towards which all our perception is really directed.

This may be underlined by consideration of the proffered analogies. We can make and understand maps only because we can perceive the country which is represented on the map as well as the map itself; if we could see only maps and had never seen the real countryside or anything like it, the map would not be a *map* for us and we should not realise that it was a representation. Similarly, the person watching the film or T.V. or radar screen can readily go outside and compare similar scenes or objects; the film or representation would probably not mean much to us (particularly the radar picture) unless we had had experience of direct observation of the kind of scene portrayed; and we also have the evidence of those who designed the representational device. But on the Representative Theory we see only the map, are never out of the cinema, or spend all our lives glued to the T.V. or radar screen.

An even more serious aspect of this fundamental difficulty is that many versions of the theory are self-refuting. In the early part of the exposition, when the causal transmission is being established, it seems assumed that we can directly observe objects, sense organs, nerves, and brains, and so can observe causal processes outside the mind; but by the time the conclusion is reached all we can perceive are mental representations, so that the "brains," "nerves," etc., directly observed and described in the early stages must, it seems, have been mental representations only, and the causal relations observed must have been between such representations. The theory has "cut off the branch on which it was sitting" by disallowing the direct perception of objects in the external world on which its premises rested. It has the logical structure "if p is true then p is false"—if it is true that we observe brains, sense organs, etc., then further investigation shows that we observe only mental representations of brains and sense organs, not the things themselves.

Measurement and physical theory are used by the Representative Theory to justify its account of the external world that we never directly perceive, but this too is open to attack. Measurement is itself a perceptual process, merely revealing more representations. Take, for example, measurement of a coin. If the theory is correct we never directly see or feel the coin; we are directly aware only of mental representations of it caused by contact of hand and coin. When we bring up the ruler to the coin all that our perceptions amount to are more visual and tactile representations "in the mind" together with some sensations of movement; we may claim to see coincidence of the edges of the coin with marks on the ruler, but what strictly we are seeing is a complex group of mental representations in which the brown colour-patch we attribute to the coin is adjacent to the yellowish shape we attribute to the ruler, and the edges of the former coincide with marks at the edge of the latter. Never have we passed over the barrier of mental representations—we have only got more and different representations. Similarly, what is the supporting physical theory but a system of hypotheses co-ordinating and explaining various observations? And observations of what? If the Representative Theory is correct and is strictly applied, they are not observations of external objects: they are observations only of mental representations. So physical theory is really the systematic correlation of a whole host of mental representations, but it never enables us to make direct perceptions outside the representations and so never gives us first-hand evidence of the external world.

The Representative Theory, if correct, thus seemed to imprison us within a world of mental representations and made it difficult to see how the claim to knowledge of the external world could be sustained; granted the theory, this claim is to knowledge of something of an entirely different type or category from the representations which alone we perceive. They are supposed to be private, mental, transitory, and rich in qualities primary and secondary, while the objects of the external world are supposed to be public (accessible to many people at once), material, enduring, but possessing nothing resembling secondary qualities. So it was suggested that perhaps the unseen causes of representations were more like their effects and were not material or physical but mental or spiritual. Berkeley even claimed that our various mental representations or sense impressions are ordered and caused by God, and that there is no need to suppose "matter" as an anomalous and mysterious intermediary—a position difficult for those to refute who had made matter an *unobservable* cause and all our supposed perception of it perception merely of more representations. An even more radical step was taken by Hume who claimed that, as we can never observe anything behind "representations," there is no reasonable ground for supposing that anything does exist behind them. Hume did accept, however, from the evidence of illusions, that our immediate perception is of private mental "impressions" or sense-data, and so was equally opposed to the common-sense view that there are external physical objects capable of persisting unobserved. He maintained that the way our sense impressions are grouped and follow one another leads us to attribute external and continued existence to them as "objects" and thus to adopt what is merely a convenient myth.

These positions were worked out with much ingenuity but carried little conviction. The more common result of these theoretical difficulties was greatly to increase scepticism as to the reliability of the senses: even when apparently genuine and non-illusory, perception seemed unable to reveal reality or to carry us beyond private representations; hence the temptation to develop a more speculative metaphysics and seek knowledge of reality by intuition and abstract reasoning.

Defences

By Lord Brain. This fundamental difficulty has been stated at length because it is not fully appreciated by many scientific expositors of the theory. Some, like J. C. Eccles, do not mention it at all, while others briefly dismiss it. Lord Brain claims that there is a complete answer to it, namely: "that awareness of objective elements is given in perception. Assuming that in general the number, discreteness, and movement of objects we perceive are objective, science infers a structure of the physical world such that some perceptual elements are shown to be subjective. The self-contradictory view that begins with objects and ends by making them entirely subjective is a misrepresentation of the . . . theory." Again: "We do not need to ask how we become aware of things outside ourselves because it is with that awareness that we begin."[1]

But all this begs the question. If the conclusion of the Representative Theory is correct, what right have we to assume that number, discreteness, etc., are objective? If we conclude that perception is strictly only of mental data, of a perceptual world constructed by our minds or brains, how can we claim knowledge of the external world? Maybe the theory begins with awareness of things outside ourselves, but its conclusion means that this was not a true beginning; we began with *what we thought* was awareness of external things, but which turns out to have been really awareness of mental representations. Also the term "objective" as used by Brain is misleading. It might seem to suggest "truly real and external to us" but on the theory that is impossible; the number, discreteness, etc., *i.e.* the primary qualities a person perceives, are still subjective in that they are mental representations private to him and created by his brain; all that is really claimed as objective about them is that they are accurate representations of external properties. But how do we know that they are accurate since we can never compare them with the original?

Two necessary amendments: For a more plausible attempt to rehabilitate the theory one must make two amendments: (1) distinguish explicitly two types of perceiving, viz. a direct perception of representations and an indirect perception of external objects, and (2) claim that the resultant theory is the best hypothesis to explain the order of our sense experience (*i.e.* of our direct perceptions).[2]

1. *Two types of perceiving*: This avoids the danger of formal self-refutation: the premises of the theory still assume that we perceive external objects, but the conclusion does not deny this by saying that strictly we perceive only mental representations; it still insists that we perceive the external world, but maintains that we do this indirectly by means of a more direct perception of representations of it. One should note this claim that direct perception is the *means* to indirect perception and that the latter is not just the inference of external objects from directly observed data, for those versions of the theory that say we infer the existence of external objects from representations contradict their premises by thus denying that we perceive external objects such as brains and sense organs. (Even if this denial is not explicit it is implied, for if you claim that we discover the existence of E by inferring it from D you imply that E is not

---

[1] *The Nature of Experience* (1959), pp. 42, 31. Brain speaks of the "sense-datum theory" but it is in essentials the Representative Theory. He adopts the radar screen analogy, p. 41.

[2] A convenient version which does this is J. R. Smythies' *Analysis of Perception*, but more defence and development is needed than he gives.

being perceived, otherwise the claim is pointless.) It may sound little better to say that the way in which we perceive external objects is by perceiving representations of them, that the latter is the means to the former, but any oddity is due to the common-sense assumption that to perceive is to be directly confronted with, to look at face to face. "Perceive" in "indirectly perceive" must be understood without that suggestion of direct confrontation and must mean "ascertain by means of the senses the existence and essential properties of an object." The theory then claims that the way we do this is by direct awareness of a mental percept which is a true representation, so far as primary qualities are concerned, of the external object causing it and which we in fact take to be that object.

2. *The claim that the theory is the best hypothesis*: This is necessary to deal with the doubt that still remains about the existence of external objects. For even on this new version the observation which led to the theory are still only direct observations of percepts which we take to be external objects or to be essentially exact representations of them; there is no guarantee that *all* or *any* direct observations of percepts which we take to be or to represent objects is in fact perception, *i.e.* the ascertaining of the properties of real objects. It may only be direct awareness of percepts which have been caused by God or by other percepts in such a way that we *think* they are due to external physical objects; *ex hypothesi* we can never get behind the percepts to check this. What the Representative Theory must then reply is that if you consider the order and sequence of the various directly observed "representations" then by far the best, *i.e.* the simplest and most satisfying, explanation is that, except for illusions and hallucinations which can easily be identified and excluded, they are in fact caused by the external physical objects that they seem to represent. (Simplest of all would be the common-sense notion that they *are* external objects, but that is ruled out by the scientific observations which establish a causal transmission and show that representations are distinct from physical objects.)

Furthermore, once it is admitted to be the best hypothesis that the sense experiences ordinarily accepted as veridical, *i.e.* as not illusory, are in fact caused by the objects of which they seem to be perceptions, the objection concerning measurement raised p. 254 is also met. We may now assume that when we claim to measure a table we are in fact doing this: we are observing the coincidence of the table edge with a mark on a ruler and not just the coincidence of certain sense-data; and from a series of such observations we can work out the dimensions of the table and its distance from other objects, and can explain by laws of perspective how the representations or directly perceived shapes vary with one's position. Similarly the evidence for the causal processes in perception is validated, once one accepts as the best hypothesis that supposed investigation of brains and sense organs is in fact this and not simply the correlation of mental representations; and the physicist's account of the atomic characteristics of matter may also be accepted as complementary to the evidence of perception and measurement. Also as the measured shape and macroscopic dimensions of objects are invariant despite variations in the directly perceived shape, we can maintain that such shapes and dimensions are "real," *i.e.* are intrinsic properties of the objects concerned; thus shape and size are "primary qualities" in that there are objective counterparts resembling the shape and size directly seen in favourable circumstances. By contrast colours and sounds are "secondary," for neither measurement nor physical theory reveals any resembling objective counterparts for them.

Comparison with Alternatives

This claim of the Representative Theory to be the best hypothesis should really be supported by a full comparison with the various alternatives, but it will be sufficient here to refer to its general advantages already given and to indicate the main points of its superiority to the alternatives, (*a*) that nothing exists behind the representations as their cause, and (*b*) that they are caused by other minds, especially God.

Solipsism is the strong form of (*a*) and is the view that only one's own stream of representations exists. This is difficult to state without self-contradiction, for expressions like "one's own" and the existence of language generally as a mode of communication imply other persons; one would have to imagine that one talks only to oneself and that apparent communication between people is as in a dream. The main weakness of this view is that the only reason for rejecting the almost irresistible assumption that we are aware of other persons and objects would be the belief that the evidence of physiology and hallucinations shows such awareness to be really only of representations or that all experience is a dream. But the former belief rests almost entirely on the evidence of other persons, *e.g.* of scientific observers, while the latter is nonsensical. If all experience were a dream we should not be able to conceive of it as such: the concept of "dream" and its contrast with "waking reality" are meaningful only if we have experienced some waking reality, and the solipsist's waking reality presumably involved the perception of other things or even persons. Furthermore, we can usually tell when we have been dreaming or awake by a continuity criterion: there is a simple continuity of causal laws between two waking states but not between two dream states or between a dream and waking state—if you really backed the car hard into a wall last night the damage will have continued and be only too plain today, but if you only dreamt it then the rear bumper will be unsullied. The solipsist would have to explain this away by saying that evidence seeming to support continuity was only dreamt also, but that is not very convincing. Finally, it is very difficult for him to explain away the sequence of experiences involved in education or in what would ordinarily be described as being given information by another person and verifying it for oneself.

Phenomenalism is a name given to a weaker form of (*a*): it admits the existence of other persons but claims that there are no physical objects as entities different from persons and representations (or sense impressions): the concepts of "chair," "table," etc., or of "physical object," have been developed to distinguish or refer to patterns and sequences of actual and possible sense impressions. The main difficulty for this view lies in explaining how several people can perceive or act on or be affected by the same object at one time, or how an object may persist even when it is unobserved, *e.g.* the floor is supported by unseen joists, fire warms the room when no one is in it. Since no actual impressions occur when no observation takes place the notion of possible sense impressions was introduced for the latter cases—the unseen joists are thus collections of possible not actual sense impressions—but this is most odd: how can groups of possible sense impressions have actual effects? Indeed, any attempt to explain everyday situations in terms of impressions or representations alone becomes very complex and unconvincing compared with the alternative that such public objects do exist and may act causally when unobserved. Consider for example a simple case of the publicity of objects. You give a bus conductor 6*d.* and receive a ticket in exchange: the Representative Theory claims simply that physical objects (coin and ticket) pass from hand to hand and in doing so affect our sense organs and give representations of the objects concerned; but if there are no such objects, the facts that the conductor should get representations of receiving the money and giving the ticket, and that you and other passengers should simultaneously get corresponding impressions, seem an unexplained coincidence; why do he and they not get the impressions if you merely imagine that you are paying him? If everyday life is not to be a series of incredible coincidences of different people's sense impressions, there must be some external and public physical objects to act as a focus and cause of the coinciding impressions.

Berkeley's view, (*b*), is also weak. He may criticise the Representative Theory for postulating directly unobservable causes, but he had to postulate equally unobservable ones—spiritual or divine causes. And as the causes are directly unobservable the representations give no ground for deciding what kind of spiritual causes they are—minds, ghosts, demons, gods or God—and such causes may have little in common with the observable representations, so that we are still in the dark about the nature of reality. But perhaps the main objection to this alternative is that it is unscientific. Just as the Greek dramatists sometimes introduced one of the Olympian Gods into their plays to unravel a hopelessly tangled plot by supernatural means, so Berkeley seems to try to solve his problem of a continuing cause of our impressions by bringing in his God. This seems perilously near cheating and is certainly to abandon science and philosophy; if one can "solve" theoretical problems by postulating God's intervention and attribute to him just the powers and intentions necessary to fill the bill, then scientific investigation and reasoning are nullified, for any theory you like can be patched up in this way.

Further Difficulties

Duplication or circularity: By such arguments the Representative Theory can make a fair reply to the main charge levelled against it. Claiming to be the best hypothesis to explain the nature and order of our sense experiences, it does not or should not deny our perception of external objects, but explains how we achieve this perception by means of a direct awareness of mental representations caused by these objects. This reply does lay the theory open to a different criticism, however, viz. that it merely duplicates perceiving in its attempt to explain our perception of external objects in terms of a second perception of representations caused by them. The addition of "direct" or "indirect" does little to disguise a duplication which makes the explanation offered neither simple nor satisfying. To put the point in another way: if this perception of representations is similar to perception of external objects, then it must in turn require an inner perception of inner representations caused by inner sense organs, and this inner perception requires a further perception, and so in an infinite regress. The only escape is to maintain that the perception of representations is substantially different from the perception of external objects. This difference is hardly borne out by the analogies —we use our eyes to see maps, cinema, or T.V. pictures, just as we do to see the outside world. But if it is maintained, what kind of process is this inner perception supposed to be? Why, for example, does it not need sense organs? By leaving this in obscurity the amended Representative Theory loses plausibility.

It may be objected that the theory does say something about it, namely that it is direct and mental. But these are not much help. Leaving the "mental" side for the next section, we may point out that the directness is suspicious in that the ordinary common-sense notion of perceiving is that it is mostly direct—a direct contact in touch or taste or a sort of face-to-face confrontation with the object in sight; but that is direct perception of external objects, and it looks as if the theory, unable to allow common-sense direct perception of such objects because of the causal process, introduces it without justification at the end of the process where it is accepted unquestioningly because ostensible direct perception of objects is familiar and rarely questioned. Indeed, the alleged direct inner perception so resembles ordinary notions of perception of external objects that it cannot be used to elucidate them; the theory has a circularity similar to the "definition" of a horse as an equine quadruped, for perception is "explained" in terms of itself.

Furthermore, the theory claims to be the best and simplest explanation, and if these terms are taken in their technical sense it is claiming to account for phenomena with the least postulation of types and orders of entity. It is therefore a serious weakness that it has to suppose not only a second inner perception but also a second, private, world of objects (the representations) in addition to the external physical world. And where can this private world be located, for it can hardly be in the brain or anywhere in physical space?

Its concept of mind (cp. pp. 249-50): It may be replied that some of these points are easily met: the percepts or representations are mental objects in mental not physical space; similarly the inner perception of them is mental, thus requiring no sense organs and physical intermediaries. But this general reliance on mind and a mental world is one of the less satisfactory features of the Representative Theory and impairs its value as an explanation, quite apart from the weakness of introducing a second perception and second world.

First, it nullifies the claims of the theory to be in accordance with science and observed fact. Scientific investigation and the public observation it presupposes cannot be undertaken of the mind, or of its perceiving, or of a mental world of representations. We can observe the percipient as a person behaving in various ways, but not as a mind; we can investigate the causal chain from object to brain, but so far as scientific observation is concerned the causal chain ends with brain activity. (One might claim that a further stage is often observed—behavioural reactions in the percipient, or motor activity in his nervous system—but there is nothing mental about these and they may not occur.) Furthermore, since mental perceiving and its objects are quite different in character from all the other physical and publicly observable processes in perception we cannot legitimately extrapolate them from those processes. What then is the evidence for them? The percipient perhaps—we rely on our introspection as percipients or we stimulate the patient's brain and ask for his sensations. But such methods can afford evidence only of the quality of the experience, not of its status as mental or physical, object or event. There is nothing in auditory or visual <u>sensations</u>, for example, to tell us that they are purely private and mental; indeed normally when we perceive and are introspectively aware of our perceiving, we seem clearly to be perceiving external objects, so if introspection did give evidence of the status of what is perceived it would run quite contrary to the supposition of private mental objects or sensations throughout perceiving. Sometimes we say we are day-dreaming or imagining a scene, "seeing it in our mind's eye"; this may be because we know that it cannot be true or because we are conscious of picturing, *i.e.* of inducing the experience, or it may be because of its elusive quality; but these verdicts are no evidence for mental awareness in normal perception—quite the contrary, for reference to the "mind's eye" is pointing to a difference from normal. So the percipient's evidence is of no help to the theory. Also it would be evidence different in character from that of the causal chain, for it would be from the inside as it were, from the percipient's "immanent" viewpoint, and not be publicly and scientifically observable like an eye movement.

Furthermore, introspection does not reveal that the self that is seeing or thinking is a mind, *i.e.* is an immaterial mental substance temporarily lodged in a body. It may reveal that "I" am seeing X or thinking Y, but not what kind of a being "I" am. Indeed, our natural assumption seems to be that the "I" or "self" that sees or thinks is not a mind but a person —the same person who walks and performs other bodily activities and who can be perceived or jostled by other persons. So it may quite well be claimed that the percipient, and person, is a conscious physical organism, not a separate mental substance lodged in the organism, and that the duplicates, the mental perceiving, mental percipient, and world of representations, are merely inventions of an extravagant hypothesis.

Secondly, it is not an illuminating hypothesis: the notion of mind and mental perceiving are so vague, empty indeed, that we are being offered an explanation *per obscurius*. What is mind? There is an initial confusion between substance (in the philosophical sense of an entity like a person or thing) and faculty: for whereas most versions talk of the mind observing percepts (as if it were a little person in the head like the person in the cinema or watching T.V.) they slip into talking of perceiving *in the mind*, which despite its suggestion of place—in the cinema or in the T.V. room—probably means *with* the mind or mentally, a suggestion of faculty or mode. Philosophers have of course spoken more strictly and specifically of mind as a mental substance, but the more explicit they get the more difficult the theory becomes.

The two classical differentiae of mind are that it is unextended, *i.e.*

does not occupy or extend over physical space, and that it is essentially a thinking being—thought, or more plausibly consciousness, is its characteristic and defining activity. The first of these raises difficulties when it is remembered that percepts or mental representations are said to resemble physical objects in primary qualities. These qualities are mainly spatial, so percepts must be physically extended, as indeed introspectively they seem to be; but then how can they be mental, be part of the unextended, non-spatial world of the mind? Some modern theories try to avoid this by saying that percepts are extended in their own mental space different from physical space. This destroys one of the differentiae of mind, is puzzling in itself, and introduces enormous complexities, especially when one tries to work out the causal relations between brain events in ordinary physical space and their alleged effects in mental space. If, for example, mental space is treated as one unified space similar to physical space, how would this mental space be linked with the different minds or the different brains of the various percipients? While even if one neglects relations with others and simply supposes that each person has a different private mental space at a point within him, events in this space can hardly be related causally to the brain activity which is spread out physically over an area of the cortex. And once private spaces are admitted, why stop at one per person? Co-ordination of sight and touch has to be learned, so might not each sense have its own private space?

As to the other differentia, one can claim that it is the person, either as a physical organism or as a union of mind and body, that thinks and is conscious. All the evidence suggests that a properly functioning brain is essential for thought: concussion, disease, drugs, or interruption of the supply of blood to the brain, may produce unconsciousness and prevent thought or perception. So it is more plausible to conceive of the thinker or percipient as a whole person, predominantly physical, and not as a non-physical mind. Also, the more the difference between mind and body is stressed (and on the classical distinction they are complete opposites, unextended thinking substance as opposed to extended and unthinking substance) the more difficult it is not only to observe but even to conceive their interrelation and mode of interaction. It would thus seem that the introduction of mind, as a mental substance, raises more problems than it solves.

Mental activity in perception: There is considerable vagueness in the various versions of the theory as to the mental activities which are held to be involved in perceiving. Two main types of activity have been suggested: first a synthesising one in which we construct percepts or ostensible objects out of the sensations which the brain processes cause, and secondly a passage from private to public—we are said to infer from experiment and communication with others that the private percepts are externally caused, or simply to treat them as public external objects. Both have been challenged. Thus, especially as the result of the work of the Gestalt psychologists, it seems very unlikely that we build up from atomic sensations, each one containing "nothing but one uniform appearance and not distinguishable into different sensations" (to adapt Locke's formula); the more probable view would be that our first experience was of an undifferentiated whole in which objects were gradually distinguished, and that from the beginning of these powers of discrimination binocular vision would make ostensible objects stand out as wholes. There would still be scope for the correlation of impressions of one object by different senses, but no need for synthesising within sight, an activity for which there is no introspective evidence. Nor is it very plausible to suppose that we start with sensations or percepts perceived as private representations and then we go on to infer that they are externally caused or otherwise to refer them to the external world. There seems no evidence that we ever were aware of a private world of representations either as private or as consisting of representations only. It is so difficult to regard colours, shapes, or sounds as private and mental that probably they have always seemed external; even pains, which are more clearly sensations, normally seem located outside the mind somewhere in the body. And later (pp. 301-4) we shall consider reasons for rejecting the supposition of inference by the percipient from private data to public external objects. Some versions of the theory are closer to introspective evidence and maintain that our experiences "reach consciousness already stamped with externality" (Lord Brain's phrase), and for them the inner perception of what are in fact private representations seems to the percipient to be direct confrontation with external objects; but it is left obscure how this happens, and the unexplained gap between brain activity and conscious experience seems wider than ever.

Even when postulating inference and synthesis these various versions of the Representative Theory take little notice of important psychological factors in perception such as recognition or misinterpretation, stereoscopic vision and object constancy, or the effect of attention, learning, and past experience on what we perceive. These omissions are particularly unfortunate in view of the stress the theory lays on illusions and the relativity of perception. Whereas it is plausible to say that an object looks round to one man and elliptical to another in a different position because of different patterns of light striking the retina, or to explain some differences in perceived colour by physiological defects like colour blindness, it is not enough. Object constancy, for example, greatly modifies the effects of relativity, while many variations from person to person in how an object looks are not obviously due to physiological factors or sensation differences: they may be due to differences in attention or in past experience, or in what we want to see. These factors are discussed more fully in Chapter 14: here we may simply note that the Representative Theory is thus probed at one of its weak points, the inner perception of sensations or percepts. On its assumption that this inner perceiving is simple, direct, and immediate, how are these psychological factors to be accommodated? *Prima facie*, attention, recognition, and the influence of interests and past experience belong to the mental world and should affect the inner mental perceiving; but the theory offers no account of how this occurs. Some might claim that these factors affect the sensations or percepts "given" to the mind, but one would still wonder how this comes about—perhaps it might be attributed to a modifying activity in the brain or even the sense organ, a suggestion which might accommodate object constancy but which if applied to the other, *prima facie* mental, factors, would make nonsense of the clearcut distinction between mental and physical which the theory presupposes.

Conclusions

We may conclude, therefore, that the Representative Theory cannot be accepted. It has important merits in the prominence it gives to the causal transmission in perception and in the explanations it is able to offer of time-lag, hallucinations, imagery, illusions, and the relativity of perception; it also succeeds in accommodating both the traditional view of the mind/body relationship and the general scientific picture of physical objects and of the physics and physiology of perception. Defence is possible against the traditional charge of self-refutation, and one may avoid its more sceptical rivals by arguing that it offers the best hypothesis to account for the order and repetitions of our sense-experiences. But even in its most plausible form the theory has grave weaknesses. It can avoid self-refutation only by explaining perception of objects in terms of an inner perception which seems just to be a replica of the original perceiving as ordinarily conceived. To this fundamental circularity must be added a lack of simplicity in the postulation of a percipient mind and a mental world of private objects of awareness which seem but duplicates of the real world of persons and things. Thus the accommodation of traditional notions of mind, which seemed a virtue, is actually a serious defect in the theory, if it is assessed as a scientific attempt to explain the observational evidence. It introduces new obscurities and perplexities, and it is vague on key points such as the relation of mental and physical factors in perception or the scope and mode of operation of the psychological, and so *prima facie* mental, ones. Perhaps some of these defects are inevitable in the present state of our knowledge, but, for all its popularity among neurologists, we must at least seek to improve on this theory by examining some philosophical alternatives and by reconsidering the evidence on which it is based.

BIBLIOGRAPHY

General Introductions to Philosophy

HOSPERS, J. 1956. *Introduction to Philosophical Analysis*, Ch. 6. Routledge and Kegan Paul, London.*

RUSSELL, B. 1912. *Problems of Philosophy*. Oxford University Press, London.

WHITELEY, C. H. 1955. *Introduction to Metaphysics*. Methuen, London.*

Classical Statements of the Topics of this Chapter

BERKELEY, G. 1713. *Three Dialogues between Hylas and Philonous*.

HUME, D. 1739. *Treatise of Human Nature*, Bk. I, Pts. 2 and 4.

LOCKE, J. 1690. *Essay Concerning Human Understanding*. Books II and IV.

For a brief account of these writers' views on perception see:

HAMLYN, D. W. 1961. *Sensation and Perception*. Chs. 5-6 and 10.* Routledge and Kegan Paul, London.

Modern Works

AYER, A. J. 1956. *The Problem of Knowledge*, Ch. 3. Macmillan, London, and Penguin, London.*

BELOFF, J. 1962. *The Existence of Mind*, Ch. 3. MacGibbon and Kee, London.

BRAIN, Lord (then Sir Russell). 1951. *Mind Perception and Science*. Blackwell, Oxford.

——1959. *The Nature of Experience*. Oxford University Press, London.

HIRST, R. J. 1959. *The Problems of Perception*, Chs. 1, 2* and 6. Allen and Unwin, London.

RUSSELL, B. 1927. *Analysis of Matter*, mainly Pt. II. Allen and Unwin, London.

——1948. *Human Knowledge*, Pts. I, III and VI. Allen and Unwin, London.

SMYTHIES, J. R. 1956. *Analysis of Perception*. Routledge and Kegan Paul, London.

* Also relevant to Ch. 13.

13

Sense-Data and Common Sense

Impressed by the weaknesses of the Representative Theory, especially of those earlier versions which seemed to lead to self-refutation or gross scepticism, philosophers sought some other approach to the problems of sense perception and of our knowledge of the external world. We shall now consider the two most influential approaches of the last forty years, viz. the Sense-datum Theory and the Revival of Common Sense. The second of these has now become associated with what is often called "Linguistic" or "Analytical" Philosophy, but one should bear in mind that these labels do not indicate any rigid or closely organised school of thought.

The Sense-datum Theory

Outline of the Theory

Its aims: Two aims may perhaps be singled out as most prominent in the minds of the chief advocates of the sense-datum approach to perception. One was the search for a new starting-point free from the logical difficulties of the Representative Theory. It was felt that the basic error of that theory had been to begin with a fairly naive acceptance of the validity of perception and then to use the facts allegedly discovered by it to build up a theory which undermined it. This they regarded as a "gross fallacy"; empirical science can never be more trustworthy than the perception on which it is based and which the scientist uses in his observations of eyes and nerves, meters and microscope slides; it cannot therefore be employed to throw doubt on our perceptually-based beliefs concerning tables and chairs, cats and cabbages. Furthermore, the scientist has not really explained what perceiving is or justified its validity. (When you examine his proffered explanation it is all in terms of light rays, sense organs, or the cerebral cortex, *i.e.* it concerns processes which are the *causes* of perceiving and does not tell us what perceiving itself is. And as his descriptions of causal processes are themselves perceptual beliefs, they afford no grounds for accepting (or rejecting) such beliefs.

If then science is no help in the quest for the nature of perception some other method must be adopted. To find out what perception really

267

is we must, they claimed, "examine it for themselves"; all of us have considerable first-hand knowledge of perceiving and we must make use of this, adopting an "immanent" viewpoint akin to that of introspection. We must examine and reflect on our own experience as percipients, starting with the first-hand inside story, not with what we can observe (from the outside) of processes in other persons. This distinction of viewpoints is of first importance in the study of perception and leads to another diagnosis of the ills of the Representative Theory, viz. that it started from the outside viewpoint by amassing evidence of an externally observed causal chain leading up to the brain, and then added as a final link the percipient's own experiences of sensations or percepts; in doing this it changed viewpoints without realising it and so produced theoretical confusion. The Sense-datum Philosophers hoped to avoid this by starting with a reflective examination of their own experience as percipients. Their approach had some similarity to that of the introspective psychology which reached its zenith some years earlier, but their examination was not just a careful report of experience; it included questioning and analysis, comparisons and arguments.

The second aim was to find an absolutely certain basis on which to build up perceptual knowledge and by which to assess our more complex and questionable perceptual beliefs. The search for certainty is a constant motivating force in philosophy, but the novel point here is the insistence that knowledge and certainty can be found in perception, not as a characteristic of the perceptual act as a whole but within it as an element. It was claimed that within any perceptual situation there is a "given" element, something which we are directly acquainted with and so can be absolutely certain of, however illusory the full perception or the beliefs arising out of it may eventually prove to be.

Its initial analysis: The Sense-datum Theory thus begins with a reflective examination of a familiar perceptual situation and seeks to isolate within it the given element of which we have a direct awareness amounting to knowledge. As an example of this analysis we may take Price's discussion, of seeing a tomato:

"When I see a tomato there is much that I can doubt. I can doubt whether it is a tomato that I am seeing, and not a cleverly painted piece of wax. I can doubt whether there is any material thing there at all. Perhaps what I took for a tomato was really a reflection; perhaps I am even the victim of some hallucination. One thing however I cannot doubt: that there exists a red patch of round and somewhat bulgy shape, standing out from a background of other colour-patches, and having a certain visual depth, and that this whole field of colour is directly present to my consciousness. What the red patch is, whether a substance . . . or an event, whether it is physical or psychical or neither . . . we may doubt about. But that something is red and round then and there I cannot doubt."[1]

The "directly present" or "given" elements, in this case the red round patch and the other patches in the background, are called sense-data, and the awareness we have of them when they are directly present to us is called sensing. ("Direct" means here "without any intellectual process such as inference or synthesis".) Other examples of sense-data would be the tactile data, of something cool, smooth, and fairly firm, obtained by touching the tomato, the characteristic taste obtained on biting into it, the soft "plop" heard on dropping it, etc. It is sometimes difficult to describe these data but we are all familiar with them.

Sense-data are defined as the given or directly present elements revealed by this kind of analysis; they should thus be distinguished from the representations discussed in the Representative Theory which, though they may be similar in how they seem to the percipient, are defined causally as the effects of brain activity. Also, sense-data should not simply be identified with sensations: the strict meaning of "sensation" is too narrow, covering only borderline examples of sense-data such as itches, pains, or feelings of warmth, while wider usages, being confined generally to a causal context, suggest the representations again. Other differences are: "sensation" especially in contrast to "percept" suggests something "atomic," the smallest uniform appearance, whereas the visual sense-datum is all that is seen of one object from one viewpoint, the ostensible front surface however variegated; in some writers also "sensation" is used to refer to the whole experience, the sensing of the sense-datum or the awareness of the representation.

The Immediacy Assumption: This initial analysis is partly phenomenological, *i.e.* an attempt to give a careful description of the quality of the sense experience without being committed to judgments as to what objects are actually present. Hence statements like "there exists a red patch of round and . . . bulgy shape." Yet the object might be deceptive in this light and might in fact be orange and ovoid, so strictly all one can say with certainty is that something *looks* red and round, or something red and round *appears* to exist. But as it would be tedious to keep repeating "looks" or "appears" one may in such a description say there exists a red patch or something is red, it being understood that the description is of appearances only. Price however is not simply using a conveniently elliptical expression: he emphasises the "exists" and the "is." Sensing is not just direct awareness, but possesses certainty and is an apprehension or acquaintance amounting to knowledge; and the existence claimed for sense-data is one distinct from and independent of the act of sensing. He

[1] *Perception* (1932), p. 3.

is thus going beyond phenomenological observation in supposing that "given" or "directly present" amounts to "certainly exists with the qualities it appears to have," and that the sense-datum in question exists as something actually red and round, not just something looking red and round. Price holds that this is directly revealed by a reflective examination ' of one's own perceiving. The belief involved, that givenness or direct presentation in perception implies certain existence as presented, may be called the Immediacy Assumption and is very pervasive in philosophies of perception. It underlies the Representative Theory, which assumes that inner perceiving is likewise immediate and certain: there is no suggestion that the representations may in fact possess qualities different from those they appear to have. The directness of inner perception is assumed to guarantee its accuracy.

In fact, this is usually specifically denied, often with argument.

 Evidence for sense-data: Once the Immediacy Assumption is made, implicitly or explicitly, one has to distinguish sense-data (or representations) from physical objects. An argument for this is sketched in the initial analysis: I may not be seeing a real tomato or even a material thing at all—it may be a fake or an hallucination—but some sensible existent, the red round datum, is indubitably present; consequently such existents, *i.e.* sense-data, are not, or not always at least, material objects. The stronger conclusion, that they are never material objects, comes from the following argument similar to those given in the last chapter. In an hallucination we are aware of something, a pink rat for example, which is not a present physical object; but it is certainly a sensed existent, a pink rat-like sense-datum. Again, in perceptual relativity or illusions the observer is aware of something other than the material object. For example, the argument continues, if the table looks elliptical to you and round to me it cannot *be* both round and elliptical (one need not assume that the "real" shape of the object is known); if it is round you are having something elliptical directly presented to your consciousness, *i.e.* are sensing an elliptical sense-datum which cannot be the table, for that is round; while if the table is elliptical then my round sense-datum cannot be the table. Similarly, the grey or black shape the totally colour-blind man sees on looking at a red pillarbox, or the second candle of double vision, is a sense-datum which cannot be a physical object. Then the final steps: the hallucinatory data or those of relativity are perfectly convincing at the time, *i.e.* seem just like genuine perceptions; furthermore, the hallucination may be integrated with a real background, or you may pass from the situation where the table looks round to one where it looks elliptical without any abrupt change such as would be expected on passing from seeing a sense-datum to seeing a public physical object. Hence, in both kinds of case we have an experience of the same type—they are *as criterion at least as old as Descartes.*

introspectively indistinguishable and similar in given character. In the one kind, hallucination or misleading perception, we must be aware of sense-data which are not physical objects, so probably in all cases our awareness is of such data, of existents which are neither physical objects nor the surfaces of such objects.

Elaboration of the Theory

Once the existence of sense-data as objects of awareness different from physical objects has been accepted, further steps are necessary to establish their full nature, their relation to physical objects, and the part played by sensing in perceiving.

Further properties of sense-data: All that has been claimed so far is that they are existents distinct from the act of sensing, that they exist as presented; examples such as coloured shapes, tastes, or sounds, have been given. From hallucinations and relativity it is clear that some sense-data are private to the percipient, and from considerations of continuity and similarity presumably all are, even though two people may sense similar sense-data belonging to the same physical object. They also seem transitory: a sound or taste or sensed colour only lasts a short while and there is no evidence that even coloured shapes last longer than the sensing of them. Also they have no causal characteristics—colour patches or tastes cannot act on other things, and although the sensing of them may influence a person's actions, that is a different matter. By contrast physical objects are public, *i.e.* can be perceived by or may affect a large number of people at once; they may persist and act causally when unobserved, *i.e.* when presenting no sense-data. Sense-data also often seem spatially extended or located, but this raises difficulties to which we shall return later.

Perceptual consciousness: Perception must be more than sensing sense-data: it is an actual awareness of physical objects—or at least it involves the assumption or tacit belief that one is aware of such objects. There is a difficulty here in that "perceive" and similar words, *e.g.* "see," especially when used in the third person, have the implication that what was perceived was "really there." Thus when a person mistook a wax imitation for a tomato one would not say that he saw a tomato but only that he thought he saw a tomato; yet his state of mind would have been just the same as if he saw a real tomato. So if one is investigating perceiving as a state of mind or consciousness and is paying special attention to how it seems to the percipient, it is convenient to introduce the term "perceptual consciousness" to cover both perceiving and seeming to perceive. Thus even though the object was a piece of wax the person in the example was perceptually conscious of a tomato: had the object been a tomato he would both have perceived and been perceptually conscious of a tomato. This usage avoids the confusion that might arise because some writers would say in the first case that he perceived wax and others that he perceived a tomato: if it is adopted, the percipient in that case perceived neither wax nor tomato—he was not perceptually conscious of wax and there was no tomato.

Perceptual consciousness of objects is thus a necessary but not a sufficient condition of perceiving them. Price defines it as sensing a sense-datum (or data) and taking for granted that it (they) belong to a physical object; sensing is as it were the central core of activity overlaid by a further mental process of taking for granted. This is in opposition to many theorists (psychologists as well as philosophers) who have regarded perceiving, or rather perceptual consciousness, as the interpretation of sensations or judgment concerning sensations. Any theory will have to decide whether judgment is involved in perceptual consciousness, so Price's view is worth consideration even if one rejects sense-data. He claims that nothing so explicit or discursive as judgment or inference is involved; there is rather a taking-for-granted, an immediate unquestioning acceptance that sense-data belong to a physical object; the two states of mind, sensing the sense-datum and consciousness of the tomato, for example, arise together. There is no distinction at the time by the percipient between sensing and perceiving, between red datum and tomato; that distinction is only the work of subsequent analysis. This account may be applied to the other theories with small changes, *e.g.* the substitution of sensations or percepts for sense-data. It certainly seems more plausible, so far as the evidence of introspection goes, than those views which claim inference or interpretation in perceiving.

Sense-data and physical objects: A physical object (or "material thing") is claimed on the theory to be primarily a "family" or ordered group of sense-data, actual and obtainable. The structure of such a family has been worked out with great ingenuity; it consists of nuclear or standard data at the centre, *i.e.* those which fit together and show what we take to be the real shape of the object, and of series of gradually more distorted ones radiating from these.

Some holders of the theory claimed also that, since sense-data have no causal properties, there must be in physical objects some hidden element as well as the family of sense-data; this element being responsible for the object's causal properties and persistence unobserved. This view was attacked by others who argued that it postulated unobservable causes as did the Representative Theory; on the contrary, the physical object was simply a family of sense-data, and what were regarded as causal relationships were merely regular sequences of actual and possible sense-data. This theory, Phenomenalism, was discussed on p. 259 (though with the substitution of sense-impressions for sense-data) as one of the alternatives to the Representative Theory. Among its many difficulties perhaps the most serious is that it cannot avoid gross implausibilities in the analysis of unseen causes.

Objections to the Sense-datum Analysis

It seems unnecessary here to attempt a detailed exposition of the full development of the Sense-datum Theory; it is sufficient to show that the postulation of sense-data is mistaken.

As phenomenology: Price claimed that reflective analysis of a perceptual situation, *e.g.* seeing a tomato, shows that one is certainly aware of sense-data, *i.e.* of existents such as colour patches or shapes, sounds, tactile feelings, all of which have existence distinct from the act of sensing them and which are different from physical objects. This view has been attacked in two ways as a phenomenological account. First it has been claimed that the sensed or given data are not distinct existents, but depend for their existence on the sensing; hence they are indistinguishable from it intro-spectively in the way that a feeling cannot exist or be told apart from the feeling of it. This view has been called the Adverbial Analysis of sensing (as opposed to Price's which is an Act/object Analysis); according to it, "I sense a blue expanse" or "I hear a shrill sound" are really statements about *how* I sense or experience. Indeed, "I sense bluely" or "I hear shrilly" would be truer descriptions of the situation, though these, and especially cases like "I sense circularly," sound awkward because our language was developed to describe the perception of independent external objects. The influence of language has led Price and others mistakenly to treat sense-data as objects, as colour patches like bits of a patchwork quilt, when really sensing a blue sense-datum is just sensing in a certain way. If one wants a less awkward expression of the adverbial view one can say that the shrill sound or blue expanse are internal accusatives like "jig" in "he danced a jig" and have no more independent existence than a dance has from the dancing of it; and to avoid confusion it is usual for supporters of this view to speak of sense-contents rather than sense-data, though there is no hard and fast rule about this. Adoption of this adverbial analysis results in the variation rather than the rejection of the Sense-datum Theory; it avoids the difficulties outlined in the next section, but intensifies the problem of the relation between sense-contents and physical objects—one can hardly say that physical objects consist of ways of sensing or experiencing. A form of the Representative Theory might be adopted in which the sense-contents were effects of unobservable physical objects, but usually the more radical, but no more satisfactory, Phenomenalist view was preferred, which claimed that there were no physical objects as independent public entities—all that existed were persons having sequences of actual and possible sense-experiences.

In any case the existence of this disagreement about phenomenological analysis is a weakness in the sense-datum approach. It is particularly intractable because the act/object analysis seems justified for visual sense-data, most of which do seem distinct, external, and "set over against us," while the adverbial one seems more plausible for tastes and many tactile data, e.g. feelings of pressure or warmth.

A second and more fruitful criticism is that the discerning of colour patches or shapes, of the quality of sounds or tactile data, is an act of abstraction requiring special effort, and so does not do justice to the character of the normal perceptual situation. What one would normally be conscious of in the tomato situation would be not a round red patch of colour but a tomato or at least something looking like a tomato. Awareness of a colour-patch as such is a different act from perceiving a tomato and cannot be claimed as a central core within it. Perceptual consciousness is indivisible in that it cannot be split up, even retrospectively, into conscious elements of sensory awareness and interpretation or taking-for-granted.

As revealing existents: We have already seen that the Sense-datum Theory goes beyond phenomenology by maintaining that its analysis reveals existents different from physical objects; it can do this because of its Immediacy Assumption, that what is directly "given" to us in perception exists as presented or, since direct immediate awareness is the converse of givenness, that what we are directly aware of in perception exists with the qualities it appears to have. We can realise what is involved here by considering the resultant explanation of the relativity of perception. The common-sense assumption would be that we do not always see things as they are—the round table may look elliptical, the green mountain look blue, the red box appear grey. In these cases we are still seeing the table, mountain, or box, but perceiving is a process which varies greatly in efficiency and we often do not perceive properly or correctly. The supporter of a sense-datum analysis does not deny this but claims that it is inadequate; it does not do justice to the immediacy of perception—in the situations mentioned we do seem clearly and directly aware of an elliptical shape, a blue or grey colour—and it requires explanation both as to what the elliptical shape or blue colour are and as to how the perception varies in efficiency. His theory explains these as already suggested—the shape and colour are sense-data, and perception varies in efficiency according as the physical and physiological conditions cause us to sense veridical or distorted sense-data from the large "family" belonging to the object. It is still left unclear how the conditions do this, so the strength of the theory lies in its Immediacy Assumption; granted this, then the elliptical shape or blue colour do exist as existents different from the physical objects, and on considerations of continuity all our awareness is in the first instance of such data not of physical objects. But can one accept this assumption? Certainly many philosophers (and those neurologists who hold the Representative Theory) have been drawn to it. The more one tends to rely on introspection the more it seems convincing that the elliptical shape or blue colour do exist, are something; we seem to have a direct awareness of them which cannot be mistaken, and it seems difficult to believe that we are aware merely, and inefficiently, of a round table or green hill, *i.e.* that the elliptical shape is a round table misperceived or the blue colour is green looking blue.

As against its introspective plausibility, the Immediacy Assumption has distinct weaknesses. First it forces us to postulate a fantastic number of existents in order to account for the relativity of perception. We have already made this point against the Representative Theory's postulation, partly based on the same assumption, of a host of private objects as representations. The Sense-datum Theory, relying explicitly on the assumption and not on causal considerations, is similarly embarrassed. On every different view of an object one is said to be sensing a different sense-datum belonging to it, and every object is thus a family or an infinite number of differently shaped and coloured sense-data, together with differently feeling and sounding and tasting and smelling ones (to cover relativity to other senses). This is scarcely conceivable—remember that the sense-data are all existents—and seems to put the theory out of court on the test of simplicity and economy. This objection will be greatly strengthened when in the next section we consider the queerness of the existents thus lavishly multiplied.

[margin note: Not unless a simpler one meets the requirements better.]

Secondly, the Immediacy Assumption means that the direct awareness is mistake-proof and always excellent. This was true of the inner perception of the Representative Theory and applies also to sensing. But it does not seem plausible when one considers psychological processes or sensory defects. For example, when we attend to some object or scene, and look more closely at it, its ostensible character may change: we notice things in it we did not see before. This may equally apply to the awareness of an alleged sense-datum, *e.g.* on looking attentively at a coloured expanse we may see that it is not a uniform shade, as we had thought, or that its shape is irregular. Now this clearly seems to the percipient to be a change in his mode of awareness—it is his observation not its object that has changed. But if sensing (or direct perception) is always perfect, then the change must have been in the data: by looking more carefully we do not change its efficiency, but we just equally efficiently sense different sense-data belonging to (or perceive different representa-

[margin note: question-begging]

tions due to) the one object. Similarly, learning and past experience must be claimed to affect not the sensing but the sense-data sensed. As to sensory defect, it is difficult to believe that a person suffering from colour blindness, short sight, or deafness, still senses with unimpaired excellence, and that his condition merely makes him select different sense-data belonging to the external object, *e.g.* if shortsighted he senses perfectly clearly a fuzzy-outlined sense-datum belonging to it. One must remember here that the Sense-datum Theory is trying to discover what seeing and hearing themselves are without introducing causal considerations. Hence this point is more embarrassing for it than for the Representative Theory.

We can now dispose briefly of the other arguments for the existence of sense-data. The one sketched in the passage quoted from Price's initial analysis does not amount to much. If the putative tomato is a real one or if it is a piece of wax or similar fake, it is still a physical object; even if it is a reflexion in a mirror it is still a reflexion of a tomato, and it may be argued that we are still seeing the tomato, although reflected in a mirror. Even if the putative tomato is just an image thrown on a screen we are still seeing something material—the screen with a round area of its surface coloured red—and we need not invoke sense-data. The only exception is an hallucination, so an alternative analysis would be that we are seeing something which looks like a tomato and which is either an hallucination or, more probably, a physical object of some sort. Price's claim that in each case it is a red sense-datum depends on the assumption that one is aware of the *same* kind of existent in both hallucination and perception. This runs contrary to the common view, which we shall discuss on pp. 284-5, that hallucinations are realistic mental images taken to be real things.

The queerness of sense-data: The first problem here is: what kind of entities or existents are sense-data? The terms used for visual sense-data, viz. shapes or colour-patches, suggest that they are entities or things of some kind, as though the visual scene were a patchwork quilt or jigsaw puzzle made up of sense-data; but although some tactile data are of something solid and resistant, others, together with sounds, smells, and tastes, seem more like events (if that term may be used to cover feelings as well as other occurrences). In general it was maintained that sense-data were events, since even colour-patches were transitory so far as sensory experiences went. The problem then arose: what were they events of? For at least so far as the Aristotelian category system goes, and this is the system presupposed by common sense, events cannot exist on their own: they must be phases of, or happen to, some substance, *e.g.* person, animal, or physical object—one cannot have a game without players, or an accident without persons or without some object such as a tool or machine or tree.

[margin handwritten note:] why more embarrassing? if causal considerations are set aside, this point is a strength of the theory — though from a causal point of view it seems odd.

The theory did not want to say that sense-data were purely mental events, happening in or to a mind, like the sensations of the Representative Theory, for then they could no longer "belong" to material objects, and the latter would be reduced to unknown external causes with all the traditional epistemological difficulties. Nor could it say that sense-data were events occurring in or to external physical objects; for some are hallucinatory, and many, as perceptual relativity shows, are dependent on the position or sense organs or physical and mental state of the percipient; indeed, the main line of the theory was that sense-data are all dependent for their ultimate nature on the nervous system and brain, being "generated" or brought into being by them. The ultimate compromise solution was: sense-data are events which happen to nothing but are nevertheless closely connected with persons and external objects. This is most unsatisfactory on the normal conception of events. A few examples were claimed of events happening to nothing, e.g. lightning flashes or sounds, but in so far as these are distinct events (and not just experiences of the percipients) they are occurrences in the atmosphere. A possible solution would be to adopt a non-Aristotelian category system, a metaphysics in which events and not substances (or things) are basic; some systems of this nature have been developed, notably by Whitehead, and it might even be argued that they fit atomic physics better. But they are obscure and controversial and do not easily accommodate sense-data. At any rate the Sense-datum Philosophers have not dealt convincingly with this question or argued in any detail for a change in our category system.

The second main problem is that even if sense-data are admitted as events of this kind they still seem to be almost self-contradictory, or at least to be in two places at once. They are all said to belong to physical objects, to be part of the family which is the main constituent of such objects; and the nuclear data in particular are supposed to fit together to make the "real" physical shape of the external object and so must be outside the body in physical space. And yet all of them, and particularly those in distorted perception, are supposed to be generated by the brain and so must inhere in the percipient as reactions in him. So the Sense-datum Theory has not surmounted the central difficulty of the Representative Theory, namely how can we know anything of the external world if all experience is of private data dependent on and caused by brain activity. To say that sense-data, while equally so dependent, nevertheless belong to and in some way form part of the structure of external objects, seems to be a paradox not a solution.

Ingenious attempts have been made to mitigate this by claiming that sense-data are in a space of their own, sensible space. But then, just as on some versions of the Representative Theory mental and physical space could not successfully be related (cp. p. 263), so the problem remains of the relation between sensible and physical space. If the latter is primary, as we ordinarily assume, and physical objects are in it at some distance from the body, then at what point does sensible space impinge on physical, or from where is it a projection? If the point is in the external object, then how can sense-data, in sensible space, be generated by the brain? If it is in the person or brain, then there is a different private sensible space for each person (perhaps, indeed, one for each of his senses), and it is difficult to see how data in these spaces can belong to external objects in physical space except as representations of them; the traditional difficulties about knowledge then recur. On the other hand, if physical space is secondary, just a construct out of our different sensible spaces and not an objective medium or set of objective relations, then physical objects, as supposed entities different from sense-data and in physical space, are also just constructs without objective existence. We are then back in Phenomenalism with all its difficulties; we cannot explain how the experiences of different persons coincide so that we can correlate them and construct physical space; the evidence of causal processes in perception is reduced to other strangely coincidental sequences of sense-data; and in what space do percipients move and act on each other? Perhaps they or their activities are illusions too—but how could sets of experiences exist as self-subsistent events and not be experiences *of* persons?

Sense-datum Language and Ordinary Language

It is now generally accepted that the Sense-datum Theory has failed. With it must go a tempting method in the philosophy of perception of which it was the most sophisticated example: namely, the isolation of some given or directly apprehended element in our experience, and the attempt on the basis of this to construct an account of perception and of the physical world. Apart from exposing the inadequacies of this method, the theory had some valuable lessons which we must attempt to apply later— the importance of distinguishing one's viewpoint, of distinguishing perceiving from its causes, of examining the non-sensory processes in perceptual consciousness, and of the possibility of adverbial and act/object analyses of sense-experience.

Sense-data still survive in certain quarters, not as supposed existents different from physical objects, but as concepts or elements in a terminology. Partly this is due to the encouragement the original theory gave to phenomenological description. It is thus maintained that by using a sense-datum language, *i.e.* by speaking of visual and tactile sense-data, or of red round bulgy sense-data, etc., one can make phenomenological descriptions, particularly of hallucinations, more conveniently than by using ordinary expressions. This may be so, although it may also mislead by suggesting that the sense-data are some kind of private existent.

Others have spoken of a sense-datum language from a different motive. They have maintained that the so-called Sense-datum Theory and indeed all "theories" of perception, were not theories at all but merely alternative languages or terminologies for describing the agreed facts of perception. This view is based on an unduly narrow conception of "theory" as something which leads to experiments by which it can be verified or rejected, a theory of natural science in fact. But the advocates of the Representative or Sense-datum Theories were doing philosophy not science, and so they each produced a *philosophical* theory, *i.e.* a comprehensive account of a set of phenomena which interprets or explains them; the explanation is partly a systematic ordering of all the facts, partly an indication of the significant relations between them (*e.g.* causes and necessary conditions), and partly a putting in perspective, a stressing of what is important and basic.

This strange suggestion that philosophers were producing languages not theories was one of the first signs of a movement which has become quite fashionable among philosophers in this country, the view that the main concern of philosophy is with language and the analysis of language, not with discovering facts or propounding explanatory theories. Nowadays however, the language meant is "ordinary language" (especially English), and the claim is not that philosophers should invent new descriptive terminologies but that they should analyse ordinary language and investigate how we use words. The chief motive for this inquiry is the belief that the main problems of philosophy originated in a failure to understand the logic of our language. Philosophers have spread confusion or built up unsound metaphysical structures because they have used words incorrectly, have been misled by ordinary expressions, or have failed to appreciate the various functions of language. Once these mistakes have been exposed and understood the seemingly intractable problems of philosophy will be seen to be pseudo-problems and will no longer trouble us.

Sometimes this claim has been expressed in a dogmatic and paradoxical manner, as if philosophers should be amateur grammarians or lexicographers, but its main exponents do stress that they are concerned with use not usage and are in fact analysing and displaying the logical geography or interrelations of concepts. Thus when they appear obsessed with ordinary language their concern is not with the words or expressions so much as with the meanings or ideas which they are used to convey. Now in so far as these modern philosophers are trying to clarify the meaning of "mind," "perception," "knowledge," etc., and to analyse and relate the concepts concerned, they might seem to be performing a traditional philosophical task of explaining what mind, perception, or knowledge are, of putting forward theories of them in fact. But they differ from past philosophers in two main ways. First they regard the meaning of a word as its function or use, not as the quality, situation or thing to which it refers; hence analysis of concepts or meanings is in their eyes largely a linguistic matter—the analysis of how the word is used, or what "jobs" it does. Secondly they stress that the language and the word-use are *ordinary*. Other philosophers, outside ethics, have despised both ordinary language and the ordinary notions or concepts it is meant to convey; they have sought not to analyse existing notions so much as to propose new concepts, *e.g.* "sensing," or extensions and refinements of old ones such as "mind," in order better to account for the facts. This made their use of the words concerned incorrect by ordinary standards, but it did not worry them because they thought the ordinary use was developed for practical convenience only or was based on ignorance; similarly the scientific use of "energy," "mass," or "cell" is different from the ordinary one. Hence in claiming that the ordinary use of words is correct, and in seeking to analyse rather than replace or refine our every-day concepts, this new movement in philosophy appears really to be defending a common-sense view of the world or at least of the topics discussed by philosophers. (There is no wish to supplant science, but there is a tendency to assume that it is creating a complementary view of the world for its own purposes, one which does not affect philosophers.) It seems supposed that when we have grasped the common-sense concepts enshrined in our ordinary language we shall find them fully satisfactory; presumably it is then that the traditional philosophical problems will be seen to amount to nothing.

Hence the new movement has been associated with an attempt to revive and defend a common-sense view of perception against the Sense-datum and Representative Theories. Earlier philosophers had dismissed the common-sense view as "naive realism," but in this century of the common man his notions of perception have been advocated with a good deal of sophistication. We must now consider whether these can be developed into a superior theory of perception.

Common Sense

Common-sense Tenets

First we must outline the main points of such a view. For this a Gallup Poll is of little help; we need to render explicit what seems to be taken for granted, if not clearly appreciated, by intelligent persons before they study the scientific and philosophical arguments on the question.

"Perceiving (seeing, hearing, touching, etc.) is the normal way in which we find out about the world and its contents." This vague statement can be made more specific as follows:

1. "We"—the percipients are persons like you and me (animals also, but that is unimportant), not just minds.

2. "The world and its contents"—*i.e.* other persons, animals, plants, physical things and substances of various kinds, all conceived of as interacting and enduring entities in a common spatio-temporal system; we also perceive events which occur to these entities and their various qualities and relations. The factor common to all these objects of perception (in the widest sense of "object") is that in general they can be perceived by several persons at once and can be photographed, recorded, or measured. This may be called their "publicity"—they are public in being available to various percipients even at the same time. In this they differ from dream objects, the images of memory and imagination, or "sense-data" or "representations," which are private to the person concerned. A subsidiary point is that the objects of perception tend to be neutral between different senses—a clock, for example, may be seen and touched and heard. A corollary of (1) and (2) would be that perceiving is a relation between a person and various public objects; also, as perceivable, a person is to that extent one of those public objects, one of the entities in the world.

3. "Find out"—the assumption here is that, although we may make mistakes, we are generally right and do ascertain the real existence and characteristics of objects of perception; we can always achieve certainty by simple checks and tests.

4. "Normal way"—by using elaborate instruments, calculations, and inferences scientists can discover many other characteristics of objects, but this does not invalidate the characteristics we discover by perception. The qualities—colour, taste, smell, and sound as well as shape—that we perceive under normal conditions are possessed by the object as we perceive them.

We may add two points less obvious but probably involved:

5. Perceiving normally seems a simple straightforward relation with the object perceived, a direct awareness or confrontation or contact not mediated by other types of entity.

6. For all this simplicity and directness perception is a variable relation in that we may see clearly or dimly, hear distinctly or indistinctly, etc.

Defence of Common Sense

Concerning certainty: A position such as this has to be defended against the arguments from illusion, hallucination, and relativity that we have already outlined, and must be able to account for the causal and other processes in perception. Various methods of meeting these requirements have been suggested by modern writers, and we may take first the attempts to deal with the general sceptical argument that, owing to the possibility of deception by illusions and hallucinations, perception cannot give certain knowledge. We earlier suggested (p. 245) that this claim, while true, does not amount to much: absolute certainty on matters of fact is not obtainable by any means, being found only in tautologies or within an abstract system, yet there is no reason to suppose that the possibility of error over well-tested observations is other than extremely small.

This does not satisfy some philosophical defenders of "common sense." They declare quite bluntly that we ordinarily say that many perceptual statements are certain and that we know them to be true (e.g. "the dog is in his basket" or "this rose has got greenfly" when we are observing them); this ordinary use is correct use; therefore to say that they are not certain or known, or worse still that no such statements are ever certain, is just to misuse the words "certain" and "known." The sceptic can reply quite simply that the words are used in such contexts because the plain man is not aware of the possibilities of illusion and hallucination or because he disregards them for practical purposes; but as soon as the facts are realised we have to admit that strictly no perceptual statements are absolutely certain.

The more sophisticated defender will then say that the sceptic is redefining "certainty" and is really talking of logical certainty; a statement is logically certain if it would be self-contradictory to deny it, examples being "a triangle has three sides" or "2 + 2 = 4." A perceptual statement, e.g. "this page is white," is always logically uncertain as it can be denied without self-contradiction, but it may be certain in the normal sense of the word. "Certainty," or rather "possibility" if we define "certain" as "without possibility of error," are too fundamental to define easily; but we all know what they mean and how to apply them correctly in everyday language. Further, if we go on pretending that perceptual statements are uncertain, we shall destroy the useful and well-known distinction between "certain" and "uncertain": it would be nonsensical to say that "this page is white" and "the surface of the other side of the moon is white" are both uncertain; if we are not allowed to differentiate them by saying that the former is certain, we shall merely have to invent new words to state the distinction.

To this the sceptic will say that he is not meaning just logical certainty. He is using "certain" strictly in its normal meaning of "without any possibility whatever of error," and owing to illusions and hallucinations there is always some possibility that a given perceptual statement is erroneous. Nor is the distinction between "certain" and "uncertain" being destroyed in this way—it can still be maintained for practical purposes: we can say loosely that "this paper is white" is certain, or say strictly that it is "virtually certain," while "a triangle has three sides" is certain *simpliciter* or absolutely, because it affords no possibility of error. He also has a reply to other defences. Thus it may be argued that it is nonsensical to assert that all our perceptions may be false; our only reason for suspecting that some are false or hallucinatory is that they differ from those which are true or are contradicted by later experience which we accept as true. But the reply could always be that even if some perceptions are in fact true we still cannot be certain *which* these are; and if subsequent experience condemns what was previously accepted, then it in turn may be condemned by later experience.

So it would appear that there is nothing in these modern arguments to alter our conclusion that the sceptic's claim is true but trivial. But they suggest that a different criterion of certainty would be more appropriate here. If we can say that the possibility of error in a well-tested perceptual statement is purely logical, *i.e.* that to say it is uncertain is *only* to say that it can be denied without self-contradiction, then we could propose a theoretical criterion of the certainty of such statements, viz. that the possibility of error was only logical. The sceptic might still claim that his doubts amount to more than this, but one should then ask whether he is proposing any new kind of test or merely a repetition of an old one. If we doubt whether we are seeing a tomato or a wax imitation, we can feel it or cut it or bite it, or can get other people to do these things; but soon no further tests can be conceived. All the sceptic can then do is to say if you look or cut again you might get a result contrary to the hypothesis that it is a tomato; and whatever the result if you complied, he could always say "Well, if you did that again. . . ." This might be as good a ground as any for saying that he was merely asserting the logical possibility of error. And so it might be a better criterion of certainty in such statements, and show up the triviality of further doubt, if we were to say that they were certain if they had passed all conceivable kinds of tests and if the possibility of doubt was consequently only logical.

The sceptic may now shift his ground and argue that even when there are no illusions perception is inadequate because it does not (or may not) reveal the world as it really is. He can point to the discrepancy between the world as we perceive it and the scientific account of its nature, a discrepancy traditionally formulated in the distinction of primary and secondary qualities (cp. p. 247). The properties in terms of which physical science describes and explains the world can all be objectively measured and mathematically stated: colours, sounds, tastes, and smells form no part of them and so should on principles of economy be regarded as purely subjective and not as intrinsic to the physical world. Even if this positive conclusion is not accepted there is certainly ground for sceptical doubts as to whether secondary qualities are objective.

A reply commonly made to this, *e.g.* by Ryle, is that if these secondary qualities do not enter into the scientific account of the world the reason simply is that this account is partial and abstract, of an aspect only of reality. The physicist's description of matter is thus merely complementary to normal perception and does not supplant it. The trouble with this answer is that the physicist's account is normally regarded as *superior*, because it depends on instruments of greater range and accuracy than the naked eye, because by reliance on measurement it avoids the relativity of perception, and because it is not merely description but is explanatory also—it provides interlocking laws and hypotheses to cover many diverse phenomena. Furthermore, defence of perception as valid and complementary will have to deal with the argument, based on the causal processes in perception, that the qualities we directly perceive must be sharply distinguished from the intrinsic properties of objects. To clear the way for this last question we will first deal with possible replies to other sceptical doubts about hallucinations and relativity.

Concerning hallucinations: What are the drunkard's pink rat or the visions of mescaline? Can common sense's sophisticated defenders explain what we are aware of in these cases, in such a way that we need not follow the arguments of the Sense-datum or Representative Theories into a denial of common-sense tenet (2)?

Perhaps the dominant psychological view of hallucinations is that they are mental images which the victim confuses with perceived objects; this confusion is made easier because of the special circumstances that are found in almost all cases. Generally the victim is suffering from fever, madness, *delirium tremens*, starvation, thirst, or at least fear or acute anxiety; these may clearly affect his judgment and may also enhance the imagery. (In the hallucinations induced by mescaline the subject is said to preserve his intellectual powers unimpaired; but as a result he is not deceived into thinking he is perceiving normally, even if the unusually vivid imagery is not specifically identified as such.) Probably in many hallucinations the imagery is not merely vivid, it is eidetic. Eidetic images are particularly detailed and realistic ones which may be projected on to the visual field and may be seen with the eyes open; under normal conditions they are obtainable only by children and are reproductions of that which has recently been before the eyes; it may be assumed that these limitations do not hold in the special circumstances of hallucination, *e.g.*

when one is drugged. If hallucinations are eidetic or otherwise very vivid mental images, they are not sense-data, not the same sort of thing as is given in normal perception; nor do they seem to require any special theory of perception—it would certainly not do to say that normal perception was imagery, however much they resemble each other, for the notion of imagery implies the earlier perception of something which was not imagery but, relative to it, an original.

It is dubious, however, whether this defence is ultimately satisfactory. In the first place it offers no account of what mental images really are or of how they occur; and as soon as one attempts this, one is led to suggest reactivation of the kind of brain or nervous activity that occurs in perception (or in action if it is motor imagery), and the existence of such activity can be detected in imagery as action potentials. One is thus involved in the causal processes which, as will be seen, are a grave embarrassment to common-sense theories. Secondly, the defence does not really dispose of the continuity argument, that perceptions are in the first instance private, because hallucinations must be private objects of awareness (mental images are private) and perceptions so closely resemble them. The Representative Theory can still claim an inner perception of objects which though not mental images are like them in being private and mental; the images must have an original relative to it, but this original may still be a representation of the external object. And where this continuity argument is so strong as to endanger common-sense views is in the case of integrated hallucinations. It seems difficult to suppose that a mental image can be integrated with a real background, that a private and mental imaginary snake can be seen to crawl along a real bedstead. Projection of imagery on to a seen background as in eidetic imagery may go a good way to explain this, but can hardly account for the degree of integration which may occur. Similar problems arise in "transformed perception" where a poor or ambiguous perception is merged with or overlain by imagery, although not to the extent of a full hallucination; examples would be when you mistakenly identify a person as the one whom you expected to see or similarly, owing to priming, mistake the number on a bus or misread a word. The union of imagery and perception seems too intimate for one to be private and mental and the other public and physical.

Phantom limbs present a different problem for common sense. The pain and feelings seem genuine, not images of genuine ones, and the explanation of the error seems to take us straight into causal theory.

Relativity and variability: The common-sense defence here has already been mentioned (p. 274) and is a development of tenet (6). Perceiving, though awareness of public objects, varies in efficiency so that we do not always perceive a thing clearly or distinctly or properly. In the examples of relativity given, the percipient still sees a round table, green mountain, or red pillarbox, but does not see them properly, so that they look respectively elliptical, blue, or grey. To maintain this it is necessary to reject the Immediacy Assumption in the way suggested; it is particularly necessary for any defender of common sense to be clear on this and not to admit the existence there of anything elliptical, blue, or grey (according to the example). He must say that in claiming such existents the Sense-datum Theory was misled by the apparent immediacy and directness of the perception into reifying, *i.e.* treating as independent existents, the looks of the physical objects concerned; but in fact there was only the round table looking elliptical and so on. (In some cases this may seem forced owing to unfamiliarity; it may appear easier to say in double vision that one sees two bottles rather than one bottle looking double. But one is not seeing two existents, *e.g.* two bottles on a single background, with the same reliability and accuracy with which normal observers see only one bottle. The bottle and the background have a doubled, slightly de-focused appearance, which makes it reasonable to say that they look double.)

This account is made more plausible by the fact that in cases of relativity various concomitant factors can be pointed to as responsible for the variations in the efficiency of the perception. Position, distance, and angle of sight affect the accuracy with which we perceive real shape or size; distance and intervening media affect our perception of the colour of mountains; defects in the sense organs spoil the perception in double vision, short sight, colour blindness, and so on; and if we are inattentive or wrongly "primed" we may not perceive correctly. So common sense can claim not only to avoid postulating unnecessary existents but also to avoid the Sense-datum Theory's dubious notion of a constantly excellent awareness in perception.

But whereas this kind of explanation seems plausible, even obvious, it is not a final deliverance for common sense. It is scarcely consistent with tenet (5) that perceiving is a simple direct awareness, a face-to-face confrontation or contact. The more one stresses and develops detailed accounts of the effects of distance, angle of sight, intervening media, defective organs, inattention, etc., the less plausible it becomes to suppose that perceiving is either simple or direct; on the contrary, it is variable and complex, mediated by organs and nerves and by whatever lies between percipient and object. Thus though introspectively it may seem a simple direct confrontation with an object, that must be dismissed as illusory.[1] Some people have great difficulty in doing this, and we have seen the result of their inability in the Immediacy Assumption, which not only

---

[1] Not even a pain is a simple unitary experience: see p. 34.

maintains the immediacy of perceiving but extends it as a guarantee of certainty. Common sense does not go so far in its unreflective assumption that perceiving is a simple direct confrontation with an external object, but even this lesser assumption has to go. It could anyhow hardly be maintained along with the variability, even before the latter was developed into a necessary defence against the relativity argument; and we shall find other objections to it. Nevertheless, this abandonment of simple directness still leaves the main common-sense position intact.

The other difficulty here is that, though an admirable first step, the explanation of relativity in terms of variability is not finally adequate. We need to know how distance, position, media, and the other factors affect the quality of our perception, and we can only learn this by studying the behaviour of light rays and the operation of the causal processes in perceiving. So a fully satisfactory explanation even of relativity raises what is anyhow the most serious difficulty for common-sense views, namely how to account for these processes.

Common Sense and the Problem of the Causal Processes

Generative and selective theories: The existence of a causal transmission as a necessary condition of perceiving, and the time-lag it involves (cp. p. 251) are a minor difficulty for common sense in that they are further and compelling ground for rejecting the notion of the simple directness of perceiving; but they create a more formidable problem as well, namely that it seems *prima facie* impossible to give any explanation of the role of the causal processes without saying that the pattern of activity caused in the brain by stimulation of the sense organ gives rise in turn to private representations (or sense-data, or sensations, or percepts) which are the immediate objects of the mind's awareness. This account of the effects of brain activity is often called the Generative Theory, viz. that private objects of direct mental awareness are generated, brought into being, by the nervous system and brain. This name is useful in that it does not commit one to any specific account of these objects or of their relation to the external world. Both the Representative Theory and, in most versions, the Sense-datum Theory, adopt this Generative theory or explanation of the physiological processes. It does, however, mean the end of any common-sense view. One might still maintain that perception (or at least indirect perception) is the awareness of public objects, but the Generative explanation of how this is done completely transforms tenets (1), (2), and (4) as well as (5), for they amounted to denials of private objects, of perceived qualities distinct from the intrinsic qualities of external objects, and of perception by minds. For common sense, perceiving is primarily and only a relation (of awareness) with public objects which possess the qualities we perceive in them exactly as we perceive them in favourable circumstances.

Attempts have been made to save the common-sense assumptions and to provide an alternative explanation of the causal processes in perceiving. One is the Selective Theory which maintains that the role of these processes is not to generate private objects, sense-data or representations, but to disclose, and so give us direct access to, the intrinsic properties of public objects. The processes are selective in that they determine (i) which if any of the available public objects are disclosed to the observer, and (ii) which of the properties of the revealed objects are disclosed. The relativity of perception is then explained by saying that the public external object possesses all the various properties we perceive in it, *e.g.* the table possesses not only a round shape but an elliptical one, the mountains have a blue colour as well as a green one, etc., and the percipient selects one of these; which one he selects depends on his position, the distance and media, the state of his sense organs, and so on.

This may sound an odd or outrageous theory to those who have studied the details of the causal processes and the Generative Theory which is normally interwoven with the accounts of these processes; but if one can approach the question without prejudices thus acquired, or if one is overwhelmingly impressed by the objections to the Representative Theory and to other developments of the Generative account, then it may seem plausible; at least it has been seriously advocated by some philosophers, *e.g.* Professor Mundle. But it has fatal defects.

1. Even the Generative Theory admits that the sense organs and nervous system have some selective functions. Which object you perceive, and to some extent which part and which properties of it, depend on where you look or feel, and how attentive or clear-sighted you are. But the Generative Theory offers an account of how this selection occurs: you see a chair rather than a table because, as the result of the direction in which the eyes are turned, light rays from the chair not the table strike the retinae; this causes one pattern of excitation rather than another in the brain and so in turn generates the representation of a chair not a table. If you are short-sighted the image of the chair on the retina will be blurred and so the mental representation will not be as clear as that of a normal person; if the retina is deficient it will not produce representations of red colour, etc. In so far as these can be called selections, they are due to the kind of stimulus or brain activity and so to the kind of representations thereby caused. To be a true and satisfactory alternative the Selective Theory must offer a different account of how selection occurs, and this it fails to do.

2. The Selective Theory explains relativity as due to the percipient's

selecting different qualities from those actually possessed by external objects. But this makes the latter very queer indeed. Not only must each possess a wide variety of colours, shapes, and sizes; it must also possess qualities revealed by the more bizarre cases. If under mescaline the carpet is seen to undulate, if you are giddy and the room seems to go round, if you have double vision, you are not attributing to external objects representations caused by your disordered brain; you are selecting actual properties of things—the carpet is undulatory as well as flat, the room is rotating as well as still, everything is double even if we normally select a single appearance. Indeed there is self-contradiction as well as queerness in this, even in simple cases. For there to be selection of qualities a table must be both round and elliptical, which is a self-contradiction; if it is round its diameters are equal, if it is elliptical they are not, so how can it be both?

3. To avoid this self-contradiction it is said that the properties concerned are really relational. The table is round from here, elliptical from there; the mountains are green from close to, blue from far away; the pillarbox is red to us but grey or black to a colour-blind man. They are not round or green or red *per se* and without relation to percipients or points of view. Thus, though they are still intrinsic properties, there is no self-contradiction because they are relational not absolute.

But this is still unsatisfactory. First, self-contradiction remains over the claim that the properties are intrinsic and relational, for the meaning of "intrinsic" in these contexts rules out relational. If a thing's shape is its intrinsic property, then it possesses that shape objectively and quite independently of any observer. Secondly, the nature of the relation claimed for these properties is obscure. The natural way to understand "the table is elliptical from there," "the mountains are green from close to," and so on, is to regard the "is" as an unusual way of saying "looks" —"the table looks elliptical from there," etc. But if so, nothing is explained: all agree on this "looking," which is one of the data of the problem. Another difficulty is that the theory originally conceived of percipients as selecting different non-relational properties—X selecting round and Y selecting elliptical from the table's properties. But if the property of the table is that of being round from here and elliptical from there X and Y would seem to be perceiving this one property, not selecting from two. Perhaps the only way to make sense of these alleged relations would be to interpret them as causal; "round from here" meaning "causing a round representation or sense-datum in an observer here," "elliptical from there" meaning "causing an elliptical datum in an observer there," and so on. But that would be to relinquish the Selective Theory for the Generative one.

Perception as instantaneous success: We must consider one more attempt to deal with the causal processes in perception without adopting the Generative Theory. In his *Dilemmas* Professor Ryle criticises the common scientific and philosophical conclusion that seeing and hearing are the mental end-stages of an otherwise physical and physiological process: he points out that this is unsatisfactory, (*a*) to common sense, because it suggests that what we perceive must be some happening inside us and not outside us as we ordinarily suppose, and (*b*) to the scientists themselves, because they cannot observe in the laboratory this mental end-stage or the changeover to it. His diagnosis is that this perplexity is due to a misconception of the nature of perception. Seeing and hearing are not inexplicably unobservable phenomena because they are not phenomena or activities at all, not the sort of thing that could be observed; in particular they are not states or processes and so cannot be the mental or physiological end-stages of processes. We must distinguish between those verbs which describe activities or processes and those whose function is to declare a terminus or signify that something has been accomplished. Examples of the latter are winning a race, scoring a goal, finding something, detecting, or solving. The criteria proposed for this distinction are mainly linguistic: the second class of "achievement words" is such that I can say "I have won it (found it, solved it)" as soon as I win, find, or solve it, and the verbs are not normally used in the continuous present—we do not say "I am finding the book (or solving the anagram)." But the underlying point is that these achievements are instantaneous: it does not make sense to ask how long they last, and one cannot be occupied in doing them or carrying them out. Ryle claims that "perceive," "see" and "hear" (as opposed to "look" or "watch") belong to this class. Perceiving is the scoring of an investigational success, and is not an activity or process but the successful completion of one. It is not an experience, *i.e.* not something I go through or am engaged in, and it is not a "sub-stretch of my life-story."

If this account of perceiving is correct one would have to amend the suggested common-sense tenets. Assuming ordinary language to be the clue to ordinary assumptions, one would have to say that perceiving is not so much a relation between percipient and object as the successful completion or forming of one. But the important points are whether Ryle is right about perceiving, and whether this releases one from the theoretical perplexities produced by the study of the causal processes.

On the whole he is right about the normal use of the words "see" and "hear"—at least we do not often use them in the continuous present, though "I have seen it" is not a natural utterance to mark seeing as "I've found it" is when one finds something, and we can say "I am touching" or "tasting" or "smelling" (perhaps because these words also correspond to "looking" or "listening"). But whether this means we regard perceiving as instantaneous, a successful completion without duration, is more doubtful. We can say we gradually become aware of our surroundings, and in some situations seeing or hearing last a long time, *e.g.* seeing a film, seeing someone cross the road or "I heard the noise slowly die away."

But the essential point is that even if he is right about all this it does not remove the basic perplexity. It would only show that the plain man speaks as if perception is a successful terminus not a process, and that he would presumably accept this if it were put to him. But this does not mean that perceiving is not a process: the common-sense opinion may be based on ignorance of the causation of perception or of the time-lag involved in it. And even if we reserve the term "perceive" for the achievement, this does not conjure away the experience or the perplexing causal process. That there are experiences in the various perceptual situations seems clear from introspection or retrospection; whatever we call them there is a succession of sensory or perceptual experiences making up stretches of our life story. Also, even Ryle admits some processes, *e.g.* looking and listening, but more important, he cannot dispose of the causal processes which have been scientifically established as conditions of our perceiving at all, and so of success in use of the senses. If perceiving is not a process it cannot be the end-stage of a process, assuming "end-stage" implies duration and means the last sub-stretch of the whole process, although the experiences may. But perceiving may still be the end or the effect of the process. A process may terminate in an instantaneous or near instantaneous occurrence which is its effect, *e.g.* the detonation ends the burning up of the fuse, scoring a goal ends and is the effect of a series of moves, as may be solving a problem or finding something. So to show that perceiving is not the effect of the causal process or transmission, it is not enough to claim or show its instantaneity—one would need to subvert all the scientific evidence, which Ryle does not attempt and could not achieve.

Conclusion concerning Common Sense

We may conclude then that even with its modern variations and defences a common-sense view cannot give an ultimately satisfactory account of hallucinations or of the relativity of perception; above all, the causal transmission involved in perception as a necessary condition presents such a view with insuperable difficulties and seems to require some kind of Generative Theory. There is also a further group of phenomena which leads to the abandonment of common-sense tenets: the psychological processes involved in recognition, priming, and attention, the use of cues and of interpretation and imaginative enrichment in perceiving, the influence on it of learning and past experience, and the operation of object constancy—all these exclude simple direct confrontation with external objects and show an immense complexity in perception unrealised by common sense. Some account of these has already been given but their philosophical significance needs further consideration; this will be attempted in the next chapter, where there will also be discussion of some other issues where physiology and psychology interact with philosophy. Then in the last chapter we shall attempt a comprehensive philosophical theory of perception; in the main it will be an improved version of the Representative Theory, one that will take account of points raised by the other philosophical approaches we have discussed.

BIBLIOGRAPHY

The works starred in the references to Ch. 12, also:

Sense-datum Theories (several variants)

AYER, A. J. 1940. *The Foundations of Empirical Knowledge.* Macmillan, London.

——1954. *Philosophical Essays.* Macmillan, London.

BROAD, C. D. 1923. *Scientific Thought.* Pt. II. Kegan Paul, London.

——1925. *The Mind and its Place in Nature*, Ch. 4. Kegan Paul, London.

MOORE, G. E. 1953. *Some Main Problems of Philosophy.* Allen and Unwin, London.

PRICE, H. H. 1932. *Perception.* Methuen, London.

RUSSELL, B. 1914. *Our Knowledge of the External World*, Lectures III and IV. Allen and Unwin, London.

——1918. *Mysticism and Logic*, Chs. 7-8. Allen and Unwin, London; Penguin, Harmondsworth (1953).

Critics of Sense-datum Theories or Defenders of Common-sense Theories

ARMSTRONG, D. M. 1961. *Perception and the Physical World.* Routledge and Kegan Paul, London.[1]

AUSTIN, J. L. 1962. *Sense and Sensibilia.* Oxford University Press, London.[1]

HIRST, R. J. 1959. *The Problems of Perception*, Chs. 2-5. Allen and Unwin, London.

MUNDLE, C. W. K. 1959-60. "Common Sense versus Mr Hirst's Theory of Perception." In *Proceedings of the Aristotelian Society*, Harrison, London.

RYLE, G. 1949. *The Concept of Mind*, Ch. 7. Hutchinson, London.

——1954. *Dilemmas*, Chs. 5-7. Cambridge University Press, Cambridge.

[1] These two were published too late to be discussed in this book.

14

Perceptual Consciousness

Terminological Points

Before we can profitably discuss the mental processes which occur in perceiving two terminological points must be made.

Perceiving and perceptual consciousness: First, we may take over from Price's Sense-datum Theory the distinction between perceiving and perceptual consciousness (p. 271) without thereby being committed to his other views. To say someone perceives a tree, for example, is normally to imply both that he is conscious of a tree and that there is a tree (or light, etc., from one) affecting his sense organs. But as the same consciousness of a tree might occur when some other object, or none at all, was causing it, one should distinguish it from the causal relations obtaining. Perceptual consciousness of an X, then, is the mode of consciousness which occurs normally in veridical perception of X but also in a range of possible illusions; it is distinguished from consciousness of Y or Z only by, or on the evidence of, the person concerned. Our main concern in this chapter will be with the mental activities which underly or comprise such a mode of consciousness.

Stimulus properties and percipienda: Secondly, in discussing the kind of evidence from which such activities may be inferred, psychologists often distinguish between the phenomenal, the physical, and the stimulus properties of an object. If we were to observe two trees which differ in physical size, *i.e.* in measured height and girth, and physical (measured) distance, then they may appear of similar size to the percipient if the larger is farther away (*i.e.* they will possess the same phenomenal size); but from our knowledge of the laws of perspective and of the distances and dimensions involved we may conclude that the stimulus size of the farther and larger tree is smaller than that of the other. This concept of stimulus property is complex and ambiguous. It normally refers to the pattern of light rays striking the eye or of sound waves striking the ear (or equivalents for other senses), patterns which would also act on a camera or microphone substituted for the percipient. Thus if the stimulus size and shape of two objects A and B were the same, the pattern of excitation set up on the retina by light rays from A would be the same in size and shape as that set up by light rays from B; similarly equal would be the size and shape of *A* and *B* on a photograph taken from the same point as the percipient's eye. It is further often assumed that the percipient's awareness sometimes corresponds exactly to this pattern of excitation, so that there is a temptation to speak of his observing the stimulus shape and size, or of his observing the stimulus as opposed to the object.

A dangerous ambiguity arises here. The word "stimulus" may be used for the object arousing the perception, whether something touching the body or a more distinct object; in this case "stimulus properties" would more naturally suggest the physical properties of the stimulus. Furthermore, when the whole causal process in perception is taken into account, it seems that the stimulus in the sense of the light ray (or retinal) pattern is strictly never seen by the percipient; he sees the external object or, on the Representative Theory, sensations or percepts caused by the brain activity set up by the excitation. So if he is said to perceive stimulus properties, he is perceiving not the stimulus with its properties but either the object as possessing properties corresponding to those supposedly possessed by the stimulus or, perhaps, some sense-impression corresponding to those supposed properties. It is less confusing, therefore, to reserve "stimulus" and "stimulus property" for the external observer's account of perceiving, *i.e.* for what the psychologist observes or supposes is happening to the percipient; he may describe the percipient as being affected by a stimulus of such and such kind. But when we pass over to the "immanent viewpoint" to describe what the percipient is or may be conscious of, then we need a different term for these properties which, from the nature of the stimulus, should theoretically be apparent to him —"percipienda" perhaps. Thus we may contrast (i) the physical object actually present and its physical properties, (ii) the phenomenal properties or *percepta*, *i.e.* what the percipient is perceptually conscious of, and (iii) the *percipienda* or theoretically apparent objects and properties, *i.e.* what a normal percipient would be expected to be conscious of, this expectation being based on knowledge of the objects present, their properties, distance, and position, the media and lighting, the evidence of cameras and recorders, etc., all the knowledge in fact that has led to talk of stimulus properties.

The Evidence

Introspective Characteristics of Perceptual Consciousness

If we seek a general account of the nature and contents of perceptual consciousness, the first step is to question a percipient or, as we are all percipients, to reflect on our own experience. From this we might suggest the following for the normal case:

(1) It is, or seems to be, awareness of external object(s) and properties,

not of imagery, sensations, or adverbial experiences. This is not as trivial as it may sound, for in view of the Phenomenalist or Representative Theories it is important to stress that perceptual consciousness is usually of objects distinct from and external to us. (This does not mean that there are in fact such objects present: we are only discussing the percepta or contents of perceptual consciousness). Occasionally these percepta or contents may be simple smells or sounds or flashes of light and not objects smelt, heard, or seen; but even then they seem distinct and externally localisable—we smell a funny smell in the cupboard, hear a loud noise coming from over there, see a flash of red behind the trees, etc.

(2) It is intuitive, *i.e.* immediate and undoubting at the time, involving no discursive thought such as inference or interpretation; we are simply conscious of the object without any intervening stages. Even in abnormal cases when we are puzzled or only succeed in identifying the object after some tests or reasoning, there is usually some simple immediate perceptual consciousness as a basis—we see something red (some red object) but don't know what it is; we hear a loud thump in the hall and then find that Tommy fell downstairs.

(3) Nevertheless, perceptual consciousness may in fact be erroneous or inadequate; we may be quite wrong about what object was present or may miss most of its characteristics (often the omissions do not matter as it is the identification or main features only that interest us).

(4) It often issues in judgment, *i.e.* in a remark out loud or a proposition merely thought or spoken to oneself: "That's the Jones's dog," or "Here's the postman now." Some have claimed that such a judgment is an essential part of perceptual consciousness, but it seems better to say just that it commonly supervenes on it (see p. 304).

These characteristics do not take us very far, and this introspective evidence is only part of the picture; worse still, it seems contradicted by other evidence. The first three characteristics correspond roughly to the common-sense view of perception which we have rejected; although perceptual consciousness seems to the percipient to be direct immediate awareness of external objects, it cannot be this in view of the multi-stage causal processes involved in it and of the possibility of error and hallucination. Further, and this is our particular interest here, the introspective evidence that perceptual consciousness is immediate intuitive awareness implies that it is simple and unanalysable, that "perception is one state of mind or nothing" as William James claimed. Yet there is a wealth of evidence, which we must now review, to show that perceptual consciousness, at least if regarded as the mental activity or state of mind in perception and hallucination, cannot be simple but involves a range of complex processes, processes moreover which are not purely sensory.

We shall then seek to resolve this clash of evidence, not by analysing perceptual consciousness into more elementary conscious processes of which it is supposed to be composed (for *qua* mode of consciousness it is simple and unitary, as the introspective evidence shows), but by putting forward a genetic hypothesis that perceptual consciousness is the product of various unconscious processes, sensory and non-sensory. We shall argue that although it is convenient to talk of these postulated unconscious processes *as if* they were conscious, they are in fact cerebral ones which combine and interact to produce the complex of brain activity which "becomes conscious," *i.e.* which corresponds to or produces the mode of consciousness which occurs in and characterises perceiving.

The Complexity of Perceptual Consciousness

All this evidence turns on a series of discrepancies between the percipienda and the percepta in different kinds of perceptual situation, predominantly cases of seeing (for it is on our eyes that we mainly rely for information about the world). Usually the contents of perceptual consciousness of different people or of the one person at different times (the percepta) differ while the external objects, their properties, and the percipienda they produce, do not; although in the constancy phenomena the reverse is the case.

Attention and selection: Once we have allowed for the changes in percipienda brought about by the eye movements and focusing involved in voluntary attention, there still remains a great difference between the percepta and percipienda in a given situation. In almost all seeing there is much that goes unnoticed—minor features of the object, its texture perhaps or blemishes on it, which are revealed on careful inspection and which we have no doubt were "there all the time," *i.e.* were represented in the pattern of light rays reaching the eye. Similarly, in a complex sound, *e.g.* of an orchestra, we can, if experienced, pick out special elements such as the woodwind which others never notice. But we may also miss quite prominent features of an object or scene if our interests lie elsewhere or we are preoccupied. "Priming" or "set" in a particular case or resultant habits of attention generally, will lead to great variations from time to time and from person to person in what is observed of a given scene—percepta vary while percipienda do not. Now if perceptual consciousness were a simple immediate awareness, whether of external things or of sense impressions corresponding to the nature of the stimulus and closely reproducing it, this variation would not occur. In such intuitive awareness there would be no place for variations in quality and degree, as the Sense-datum Theorists saw: you would either grasp the nature of the object completely or not at all.

Error: Constant reference has been made to mistakes and illusions in perception, but again if it were intuitive they should not occur. The simple direct confrontation with objects which common sense assumes allows no place for them: the Sense-datum Theory did in fact claim intuitive and mistaken proof awareness of sense-data, but maintained also that in perceptual consciousness this was overlaid by a "taking-for-granted" in which error could occur, though it had to admit that the sensing and taking-for-granted were not distinguished by the percipient at the time. Similarly, any Representative Theory has to allow that there is more to perceptual consciousness than direct awareness of sensations which reproduce the object or stimulus. Some errors can be attributed to faults in that reproduction due to defective sense organs, bad light, or distance, but others cannot. Among the latter are those due to careless or inattentive observations, or to the supplementation of some ambiguous percipiendum by imagery or thought:[1] thus we may misidentify a person, "recognising" or "seeing" him as our acquaintance X when he is not; the anxious mother may "hear" her baby cry when it is sleeping quietly, and so on. Even when not erroneous, perceiving is often "enriched" by imagery or thought (cp. pp. 313-5), and this means that perceptual consciousness is a complex activity; if it were simple and intuitive it would always be literal.

Another point about the possibility of error in perception is that it suggests some conceptual or intellectual process of an interpretative kind is involved. Thus some philosophers have claimed that as perception may be true or false it must be a mode of judgment, for only judgments (*i.e.* assertions) can be true or false. This goes too far in that not all error is false assertion, *e.g.* the mistakes which occur in playing a game or an instrument or in constructing something, and it would be better to say that perceiving was correct or incorrect rather than true or false; but it is difficult to deny some conceptual element, something akin to but less developed than judgment, particularly in perceiving *that* so and so, *e.g.* seeing that the glass is cracked, the bus is coming, the coat is too large, etc.

Learning and experience (cp. pp. 199-201): These factors affect all perceiving to some extent, but are especially required for recognition and discrimination; perceptual consciousness is therefore complex in that it involves the application of what one has learnt—it is not just a matter of simply opening one's eyes and looking, even if the skill is, from much practice, automatic and unnoticed. Thus a scene looks different to an expert, or a piece of music sounds different, in that he can discern ordered structure, patterns, or rhythms which the layman cannot; and this ability

---

[1] Cp. also the operation of projection and suggestion, pp. 218 and 225-6.

is normally acquired by training and experience. Experiments with inversion lenses or distorted rooms, and the evidence of blind men who recover their sight, show that one has to learn to harmonise sight and touch, though this learning was for most of us done easily in childhood by handling and playing with objects. Again the study of stereoscopic vision and of the perception of distance shows that there are a large number of "cues" which we come to learn to use, *e.g.* shadows, aerial and linear perspective, interposition of objects, texture gradients and relative movement (parallax) (see pp. 147-50). Even if secondary to the effects of binocular vision, these still play a significant part.

Figure-ground and constancy, time, and motion: The cues we have just mentioned might easily have come under a separate heading, for their importance in the argument is as much that they are used (*i.e.* that some quasi-interpretative process occurs in perception) as that their use is learnt. The factors we shall now consider introduce another and pervasive complexity into perceiving. In the figure-ground drawings, when reversals readily occur, it would seem that the percepta (phenomenal properties) are changing while the object properties and probably the percipienda do not; the drawing, together with the light rays from it, stays constant while the percipient sees it first as two faces and then as a goblet (Fig. 7:1). Similar discrepancies between percipienda and percepta occur when sets of dots are grouped differently by different people or incomplete figures are completed by the subject. On the other hand, in the size, shape, and brightness constancies (see pp. 156-62) the percipienda differ widely, while the percepta stay roughly constant (granted the background of the object is visible) or become a compromise between percipienda and physical properties. Again, the discussion of the perception of time and motion (Ch. 8) has shown the wide divergence between the stimuli and the contents of perceptual consciousness. In all these examples perception is seen to be not a simple intuitive awareness, whether of object, property, or of percipienda.

The Traditional Explanation

Statement

Although only some of the above phenomena have been appreciated by philosophers, there has been offered a traditional explanation which should easily be extended to them all: it is that perceptual consciousness involves the synthesis and interpretation of a "sensory given" (*i.e.* of sensations or sense-data), activities which have become swift and unnoticed through practice. There have been many variations on this basic theme: thus synthesis was prominent in Locke (as "compounding") and, with the additional notion of structural organisation, in Kant also; while more recently, as atomic sensations have fallen out of favour, more emphasis has been placed on the interpretation of or inference from sense-data. But it will be sufficient here to consider only the general principles of this traditional kind of explanation.

First let us apply it briefly to the phenomena mentioned.

It is strongest in explaining errors, recognition, and identification in perception, though it can claim fair success in dealing generally with the effects of learning and experience. Thus even without the claim that perceiving is true or false, it is easy to maintain that erroneous perception consists in wrongly organising the sensory data or in misinterpreting them and making faulty inferences from them; and one could claim also that similar though correct processes would be involved in correct perception. Given the sense impression of certain coloured shapes moving together, we may synthesise and interpret them as a blonde girl in a red dress; we may get this right but may also "recognise" her as Mary Jane, making a further very fast inference which may be wrong. Any perception of any object may be said to go beyond the given pattern of sense-data or sensations in this way—by synthesis and interpretation we see that it is a bush not a bear, a tomato and not an apple or a piece of wax. Similarly the use of cues, a concept on which many psychologists rely, is regarded on this explanation as the making of inferences from them. Furthermore, since our powers of perceptual discrimination, of noticing and recognition, develop with our interests and experience and may be improved by learning, it may be argued that they involve (quasi-)intellectual powers of interpretation; if perceptual consciousness were automatic and unintelligent, quite free from thought and reasoning, these factors should not influence it. Indeed, some philosophers have even claimed that perception of an object is controlled, not merely influenced, by our ideas, by the "mass of meaning with which we greet it."

The other phenomena are more difficult to explain in this way. It has been said that the constancy phenomena show that our visual perception of shape, size, and brightness, involves a judgment: thus because we know the real physical shape we interpret the percipiendum (or stimulus shape) so as to see the object correctly. But although familiarity and pre-knowledge have a little effect, the constancies are mainly due to the visible presence of the background, including background illumination. It might then be claimed that we are still reasoning from what we see of the background—we mentally allow for distorting factors, having learnt their effect. Against this it may be pointed out that if so the reasoning involved must be very rudimentary, for the experimental evidence suggests that chickens, fish, and other unintelligent creatures can see things with constancy; furthermore, if the background is cut off by a reduction screen or if the distortion is too great, reasoning or knowledge of the real properties will not enable us to see the object with constancy.

It is also said that the grouping of dots and the continuation of incomplete figures are matters of interpretation and inference, but this seems so to widen the meaning of those terms as to destroy their explanatory value. The traditional view could still rely here on its second but now rarely emphasised principle of synthesis, maintaining that the mental process involved is an integrative one in which the various elements presented are so combined as to give an intelligible structure to the whole. (The usual objection to the theory of perceptual synthesis, namely that there is no evidence that the mind is presented with incompletely organised material or atomic sensations to work on, does not apply in these cases where the percipienda do consist of sets of dots or incomplete figures.) Even the outlines used in figure/ground experiments might be regarded as needing some sort of integration, although there it is simpler to say that they are interpreted, as for example, faces or goblets, and that we keep unconsciously trying different interpretations until satisfied.

Lastly, with respect to attention and selection the traditional view can claim that noticing is controlled by intellectual factors such as our interests or thoughts at the time, but this sort of control would hardly amount to inference or interpretation; and the theory would need to suggest a further intelligent mental process in perceiving, namely selection or discrimination from an overwhelmingly detailed "given."

To sum up then, the traditional explanation would be that perceptual consciousness involves, and is often governed by, intelligent and quasi-intellectual mental activities; of these the most important by far is an interpretative process, normally a form of inference, but this may be aided or replaced by synthesis or selection. These activities are learnt effortlessly in childhood, and so in adults are extremely swift and virtually automatic; they are thus unnoticed, although in certain circumstances, e.g. when faced with an unfamiliar object, an indistinct scene or a photograph from an unfamiliar angle, we can obtain a slow-motion experience of these interpretative processes at work. Such a view has two corollaries: first, where there is inference the conclusion of it must be a judgment, so that in these cases at least perceiving is a form of judging. Secondly, an inference must have its grounds or data, and synthesis, interpretation, or selection must have raw material on which to work; we are thus forced to recognise or postulate a "sensory given," namely sensations or sense-data; this "given" will be immediately due to the brain activity caused by the excitation of the sense organ, and may be supposed to reveal the percipienda, i.e. to correspond to the stimulus properties.

Criticism of this Traditional Explanation

There is no "sensory given": (a) Introspective grounds. A common criticism of the traditional explanation is that the "given" or grounds of inference on which it relies do not exist. For there to be inference or interpretation the percipient must not only be aware of a sensory datum; he must be fully conscious of it, or else no intelligent, quasi-intellectual process occurs, and he must be aware of it as distinct from the object or properties whose existence is the alleged conclusion of his reasoning. But introspection shows that we are never normally aware in perception of any such distinct sensory given; our consciousness is simply of objects possessing various properties, not of sensations or sense-data. Admittedly there are occasions when we do interpret or infer in order to discover the identity of what we perceive, but then we usually start not with sensations but with a perceived object or person of some indeterminate kind: in "I wonder who (or what) that is?" we are already seeing "that" as a person or thing. Sometimes we do talk as if we are aware merely of sense-impressions, of colours, shapes, noises, tastes or smells. But this does not mean that they are pure data free from all interpretation; they are usually recognised and named, often being labelled as from some kind of object. And even when we cannot identify the object or event to which they belong, or are indulging in close phenomenological investigation, we still perceive them as external and distinct from us.

(b) Difficulties about sensations. Often the supposed sensory data are simply referred to as sensations, but there have recently been strong philosophical attacks on the view that sensations are omni-present elements in perceiving. Thus Ryle argues: (1) The claim that perceiving or observing entails awareness of sensations involves an infinite regress; for the awareness of sensations is treated as though it were seeing or hearing, a form of observation in fact, and so in turn should involve the observation of more sensations, and so on (compare the duplication objection, p. 260). (2) Sensations are not the sorts of things we can see, hear, or observe; we may "have" sensations but this "having" differs from perceiving or observing—it is not, for example, characterised by the kind of process discussed in this chapter—and those who regard it as a form of awareness of grounds of inference must justify their claim. (3) The sensations which we do recognise and "have" are very limited in scope: they are pains, tickles, itches, feelings of suffocation or thirst, etc. The theoretical "visual and auditory sensations" are quite different in character; even when we perceive the texture or temperature of things by feeling them, this active feeling differs from feeling pain or discomfort as it is a skill that can be learnt and it may be done carefully or carelessly. (4) If we abandon the

word "sensation" in these theoretical contexts and speak of sense-impressions or sense-data as the "given," there is still the regress objection and the objection that we are conscious of no such given. Distrusting appeals to introspection, Ryle supports this last point by arguing that there is no ordinary language for reporting sense-impressions or sense-data and distinguishing them from objects; if there is no ordinary language for them we are not conscious of them. He points out that words like "glimpse" or "whiff," which might seem to name sense-impressions, merely indicate the fleeting nature of our perception of objects. Unfortunately, he does not account for our having words for sounds, smells, and tastes, and our distinguishing them from objects, but the arguments of our preceding section might be brought in here.

Ryle's conclusion is that, except for the feelings mentioned in point (3), sensations are simply postulated on theoretical grounds and have no support in ordinary language and experience. This may well be so, but we cannot accept his further point that these theoretical grounds are mistaken; the problem which the postulation of sensations sought to solve still remains, namely the occurrence of causal and interpretative processes in perception. We have already rejected Ryle's main argument for dismissing the problems presented by the causation of perception (pp. 290-1). Another of his arguments is that the postulation of sensations in order to explain these causal processes rests on a confusion. Theorists realised that the causal processes up to and including brain activity were not enough to answer all the questions about perceiving, but did not see that the remaining questions were simply questions about the technique of perceiving, its art or craft. The answer to this is that the remaining questions are not simply these; they are, and this the theorists saw clearly, problems about how it is that the *experiences* which we have in perceiving, and which are essential to it, are related to or depend on activity in the brain, nerves, and sense organs.

As to the interpretative processes, Ryle simply claims that perceiving is an acquired skill and that though it involves the exploitation of past experience and knowledge this exploitation is not thinking, still less inferring. The weaknesses in this are: (i) He offers no suggestion about how the exploitation occurs if it is not by thought. He has little comprehension of the range of interpretative processes involved, and also seems to assume that thinking must take an appreciable time—he glosses it by "pondering." (ii) Other skills are exercised on a perceived subject-matter, *e.g.* tennis balls, musical instruments, raw materials like wood or cloth; might not then the raw material of perceptual skill be the sensations that are synthesised or interpreted? If it is replied that perceiving is not a manipulative skill requiring a material but a performative one like swimming or dancing, the answer would be that perceiving has an end-product, the conscious experience of external objects; it is not just performing or using one's muscles in a certain way. (iii) Whereas we can speak of a skilled observer we do not speak of a skilled perceiver, so if linguistic considerations are as important as Ryle thinks, perceiving is not a skill. That observing is one may be because it involves organising a series of perceptions, avoiding illusions, disregarding irrelevancies, etc.

(c) *Difficulties in modern versions.* Although we have now disposed of the simpler traditional notions of a sensory given, there are more sophisticated views. Idealists like Blanshard claim that the data from which inference takes place in perception are implicit grounds not normally distinguished at the time. Thus when we see a plane in the sky only a speck is sensorily given and we infer that it belongs to a plane. Normally it is only afterwards that we realise that we strictly saw only a speck; at the time our consciousness was only of the conclusion of the inference, namely that we were seeing a plane in the sky.

The main difficulty in this is that although it is only afterwards that one is supposed to distinguish the datum or ground, *e.g.* the speck, the inference from it is supposed to take place at the time, in fact to be the perceiving. But is this possible? Can one infer that *A* belongs to *B* without at the same time distinguishing *A* and *B* in some way, or at least being aware of *A* as *A*? And even granted that we are somehow subconsciously aware of the datum, this is really a subconscious *perception* and so there is a regress: we "strictly see" only a speck, but we see it as something public and external to us up in the sky. Sometimes we do consciously "see a speck in the sky" and infer a plane, but our conclusion is then that the speck *is* a plane, not belongs to one; we are aware of a speck-like external object, not of a sensory datum.

Price's Sense-datum Theory is similar in claiming that the sensory given or datum is not distinguished by the percipient at the time, but is only revealed on subsequent analysis. He differs in maintaining that perceiving is not judging but merely gives a subject for judgments, and that no inference from datum to object is involved; we merely take for granted that datum belongs to the object, *e.g.* that the red round bulgy sense-datum belongs to a tomato. This view seems an uncomfortable halfway house, for "taking for granted" is not easy to distinguish from implicit judgment of the kind maintained by Blanshard. Admittedly it is sometimes plausible to speak of the percipient as taking something for granted; but then one would say that he took for granted or assumed that, for example, a piece of wax was a tomato, not that a red datum belonged to one. Such references to percipient's taking for granted are not concerned with the data before his mind but are descriptions of the situation

by someone wise after the event or more knowledgeable than the percipient. Price seems to be conflating this with his analysis in terms of
certainty (cp. p. 268), and so his account really amounts to: the percipient
took for granted that [what if he had made an epistemological analysis he
would have realised could only be characterised with certainty as] a red
bulgy datum belonged to a tomato. But this is to read back into the
percipient's mental processes an analysis and distinction which, even if
correct, can only be made afterwards.

Perceiving (or perceptual consciousness) is not judging: The main
reasons for this objection to the traditional explanation are: (1) Perceiving
may occur without any introspectible judgment or assertion, even to
oneself, *e.g.* when listening to music, or watching some event, or where the
perception leads to immediate action. (2) The term "judgment" suggests
an intellectual process, one which is explicit, considered, and deliberate,
accompanied by consciousness of the evidence for one's assertion; in all
this there is a marked difference from normal perception. (3) Our judgments are, if we are honest, governed by our knowledge of the facts and
are amended when an error is made clear to us. But in many perceptual
illusions this is not so: we may know that the lines in the Müller-Lyer
illusion are equal but we cannot see them as equal, we know that the railway lines are parallel but see them as converging in the distance. (4) Even
when judgments are made while perceiving (or rather supervene on
certain perceptions) they often differ from what is perceived. We may
judge that it is going to rain when all we see are clouds massing. And
what supervenes on the perception may be a question; "I wonder who
that is?" (On this last point it may be alleged that the question presupposes the judgment "That is a man I do not know," but this seems
far-fetched.)

Perceptual consciousness does not involve inference: This objection
follows from the last one, at least to the extent that the conclusion of an
inference must be judgment or assertion. Furthermore, some of the same
detailed points apply. We are not normally conscious of any inference,
and it is difficult to see how even swift unnoticed inferences can be postulated in aesthetic contemplation or in everyday unconsidered casual
perceiving. Also, one would expect the inferences, like the alleged judgments, to be governed by our knowledge of the facts and so to correct our
perceptions in illusions that we know are illusions. Nor apparently is
there any correlation between a person's ability to reason, or make inferences, and his ability to perceive things. But the main point is that if
perceiving is inferential there must be some grounds or datum, from
consciousness of which we pass to the conclusion. And this has already
been rejected.

A Genetic Explanation in terms of Unconscious Activities

General

So far we have established concerning perceptual consciousness that: (1) It is consciousness of external objects and their properties, in the sense that they are its contents. This does not mean that they are necessarily present, or that perceptual consciousness is the same as perception. (2) It is apparently, *i.e.* so far as introspection goes, intuitive (simple, immediate, and undoubting), though in fact it may be erroneous and must be complex. There is a large and varied range of phenomena pointing to its complexity. (3) It involves no awareness of sensations or sensory given as such, nor can it be explained as the interpretation of or inference from such a given.

The essential problem facing any theory of perceptual consciousness is therefore twofold; to reconcile its apparently intuitive character with its complexity, and to give a plausible account of processes or activities involved in this complexity. The reconciliation must be achieved by providing a genetic rather than analytic hypothesis. The theories we have criticised tended towards the latter, and spoke as though one could break down perceptual consciousness into separate activities—awareness of sensations, interpretations, etc. But this has proved impossible, and the only alternative is to regard perceptual consciousness as unanalysable at the conscious level, as a unitary awareness of objects or scenes, but at the same time to suppose, first that it is the product of various interacting unconscious activities which cannot be brought forward into consciousness as elements coexisting within it, and secondly that if these activities could become conscious they would be of two main types, sensory and interpretative.

A hypothesis of unconscious activities of this nature should not seem paradoxical or outrageous, as it is a commonplace to talk of unconscious wishes or fears, but it does require some explanation. It must be emphasised that it does not require one to propose a new realm of mental existents, an unconscious mind or ego as a counterpart to a conscious mind or ego, both somehow distinct from the physical world of the body or brain. More will be said later on the nature of mind, but all that is being postulated here is the occurrence of certain unconscious *brain* activities; however, one is forced to distinguish and describe these postulated activities *as if* they are conscious, because at present the various brain activities cannot be adequately identified and differentiated in neurological terms.

To elaborate this a little. It is plausible to assume that perceptual consciousness, like any other form of consciousness, is always accompanied by a corresponding and concomitantly varying complex of brain activity. So far as the latter is concerned the traditional formula, perceptual consciousness = sensation + interpretative activities, can be applied as perceptual brain activity = activity in receiving areas + activity in association areas; although it does not make sense to regard the activity in the association areas as interpreting that in the receiving areas, it may modify it or at least will integrate it within a complex which can produce or correspond to a mode of consciousness. But on the conscious side, whereas it would make sense to speak of interpreting sensations we cannot discover such a process; perceptual consciousness is not normally capable of resolution into separate parts, and the interpretations we can find are of shapes, sounds, or indeterminate objects apprehended as public and external, *i.e.* of the contents of perceptual consciousness, even if of a less developed kind. The only answer seems to be to leave perceptual consciousness intact as a mode of consciousness and to regard its corresponding brain activity as the complex which can be analysed into two modes of activity, sensory and non-sensory, in order to meet the requirements of the psychological evidence. Though the main division, sensory and non-sensory, accords with the neurological evidence, we must, pending further advance in this field, differentiate and describe the postulated component activities, particularly the various modificatory or non-sensory activities, as if they were conscious activities of selection, integration, or interpretation, while recognising that they are in fact below the level of consciousness and so are only activities in the percipient's brain.

It does not seem possible to confirm this hypothesis by reproducing the modificatory and the purely sensory activities together in consciousness—indeed if what has been said is correct that is a theoretical as well as a practical impossibility; but it should be possible to inhibit many of the modificatory activities and so reduce perceptual consciousness to a form approaching the form which it is supposed the pure sensory activity would take if it could be made conscious. One will in fact be extrapolating from the experience of the modification of simple perceptual consciousness to the modification of pure sensation.

Modificatory Activities

(*a*) *Conceptual*: We have already rejected the view that perceiving is or involves judging, but we still have to account for the characteristics of perceptual consciousness which led to that view, namely its liability to certain kinds of error and the way it seems often to amount to a recognition or identification of the object concerned. We have in fact to agree that perceptual consciousness has a conceptual aspect and to some extent shares the characteristics of thought; but not that it amounts to a fully-fledged judgment, or even taking-for-granted, in which A, the datum and subject of the judgment, and B, the predicate assigned, would be distinguishable; still less that there is any passage of the mind from A to B. Thought of the object, or of the property or characterised object (*e.g.* bent stick), must be held to enter into perceptual consciousness of it; but only thought of it, not thought or judgment that a datum is it or belongs to it. In perceiving the tomato or the plane, thought of a tomato or a plane occurs along with the sensory element due to them; in misperceiving the wax as a tomato or a bird as a plane, the thought of the tomato arises with sentience, as we shall call it, due to the wax, and thought of a plane along with the sentience due to a bird.

What this conceptual element or aspect, the "thought of the object," amounts to in a given situation will vary: sometimes it is a naming or verbal identification; sometimes less than this, a feeling that one could name or make judgments or act appropriately; sometimes more like imagery, whether representative of a definite object or of motor responses to it. The sensory element or aspect we conceive of as something akin to the experiences obtainable in phenomenological observation and discuss more fully below; we call it sentience in order to avoid confusion with traditional sensations or sense-data, which were supposed to be conscious or potentially distinguishable elements within perceptual consciousness. It must be emphasised that attempts to describe the thought and sentience are speculative, and are simply suggestions of the minimum hypothesis necessary to explain the recognitional and other characteristics of perception, including its liability to error. They are speculative because the thought and the sentience are not introspectively distinguishable elements within consciousness: they have been fused or merged below the level of consciousness so that all the percipient experiences is a unitary product that, as it were, possesses the flavour of both; and this unconscious fusion is in fact the combination of brain activity in the sensory receiving areas with the kind of brain activity which is normally associated with thought of a thing. Whether the perception is veridical or not will depend on whether it is activity associated with thought of an object similar to that which is actually producing the brain activity in the receiving areas.

The terms "fusing" and "merging" are unfortunately vague and metaphorical, but this is inevitable; they do at least seem suitable both for combination of brain activity in different areas and for the production of the unitary perceptual consciousness that we know. Eventually more precise neurological description may be possible, but the hypothesis must not be dismissed as pointless without that. It is an attempt at suggesting how perceptual consciousness, though introspectively intuitive and a unity, can be mistaken and involve misidentification and wrongful "recog-

nition"; the possibility of error requires a combination of two types of
activity, and the intuitive unity requires this to be unconscious, at the level
only of brain activity. Fusing or merging does not suggest anything
considered or intellectual, which fits the facts of normal perceptual
recognition. Also, it may be easily understood to be assisted or governed
by learning and past experience in that a certain fusion or combination of
brain activity is easier and more likely to happen if it is a repetition of
combinations and neural connexions already made in the past. This
facilitation by repetition will apply to the other modificatory processes
suggested as well as to conceptual supplementation, and so no separate
section will be needed for the effects of learning, habit, and past experience.

(b) *Selection*: We have mentioned the large part played by priming
and inattention in perception, the many cases where the percepta (phenomenal object or properties, *i.e.* the contents of consciousness) fail to
reproduce many features of the percipienda (the stimulus object or
properties). Apparently selection from the percipienda occurs, so that
much is rejected and only part appears in consciousness, such selection
being normally unconscious and involuntary, though governed by emotion,
interest, expectancy or habit. The difficulty is that "selection" suggests
some person who selects and a mass of material presented to him from
which to select. But one can hardly say that the percipient selects in that
he is *ex hypothesi* unaware of the rejected material and fails to notice it;
nor does one wish to conjure up the extravagant notion of selection by
the "unconscious", as though there were a hidden censor in the head who
is aware of all the percipienda but passes on only some of them. This
difficulty arises from taking "select" in the sense of "make a choice" with
its implication of deliberate choice by a person. Instead we need here
more the notion of a filter or of a tuned circuit in a radio—some device
which lets only some data or patterns through, which can be operated
deliberately by a person, although he would then only be aware of the
results of the selection, and which more often will be preset and act
automatically in a given situation. The presetting will be the priming by
interests, expectation, etc., and will vary as they vary. One cannot press
such analogies too far, but filters and tuned circuits do carry the essential
feature of allowing only some signals through and of doing this without
conscious personal selection. What this would mean neurologically is not
certain: perhaps there is activity in the receiving areas corresponding to
all the percipienda, but only some of it is able to influence or join in the
complex of activity over wide areas of the brain which one supposes is
the correlate of conscious experience; but perhaps the centrifugal fibres
(see p. 33) play a part, affording some selection at an earlier stage.

(c) *Organisational activity*: Activity of this type must be postulated to explain the figure/ground reversals, the grouping of dots, and similar features of perceiving emphasised by the Gestalt psychologists (who unfortunately neglect the selective and conceptual ones). In the perceptual consciousness of an object or scene the parts do not have equal force: some stand out, and within the whole there is an organisation or pattern in which some elements are subordinate to others. This organisation may change when it is not clear-cut or does not accord with other information or past experience—hence the reversals. Like these the organisation is to a large extent involuntary and unconsciously made. It can be assisted by learning or effort but is not usually governed by it; thus in Boring's wife/mother-in-law picture (Fig. 7:10) some persons see both, now one now the other, others see only one, and others again can be assisted to see one or the other by being told what to look for or by having the outline traced in a certain way. But in all such figures the picture as it were "clicks" into one position or the other automatically. These figures are artificial in that they are drawn ambiguously so that reversals readily occur, but the various examples do seem to provide evidence of organisational activity. In practice that activity is associated with selective ones. It is assisted by binocular vision (for real things not drawings) and by the conceptual element: in some circumstances it may aid recognition, in others the object stands out more clearly once it is recognised. Again, the neurological side is not clear. There seems, however, little need for the elaborate forces postulated in Gestalt psychology; perhaps no more is needed than that the activity associated with certain parts of the picture should be stronger and more widely linked in the brain than that of others, since the result will also be affected or effected by selective filtering and the activity associated with the conceptual element.

Much the same may be said of the other phenomena mentioned, *i.e.* the integration of activity due to separate stimuli which gives rise to perception of motion and succession; the adjustments for seen background responsible for the constancy phenomena; and the use of cues like perspective or parallax in perception of depth and distance. In all these the modifications which result in the marked discrepancy between percepta and percipienda are brought about unconsciously and automatically. Presumably the brain activity in the receiving areas, and so the sentience, were it to become conscious, correspond to the percipienda and to the pattern of excitation of the sense organ, if one could be directly conscious of that; but in its linkage with the rest of the cerebral activity of the conscious experience, this sensory activity is modified or distorted so that the percepta are different; it would not be necessary that the sensory activity itself should be altered, only that its connexions with the rest should filter, integrate, unevenly amplify or otherwise modify its influence.

HSP X

But however one may speculate on the modificatory mechanism, and whatever may eventually be discovered, it does at least seem to be a cerebral one, and not to be a process in the percipient's mind; as it is not conscious and deliberate, and perhaps even if it were, to attribute it to the mind would be to say nothing.

Sentience

Three main types of unconscious activity have been suggested as so underlying perceptual consciousness that only their results appear in it; their function is to supplement, as in the conceptual activity, or to modify, by selection or organisation, a basic sentience (though the term "organisation" may in fact cover a range of activities of integration, differential emphasis, etc.). Unlike the traditional sensations or sense-data this postulated sentience is neither conscious nor distinguishable, even after the event, within perceptual consciousness. When it is supposed to occur, all that is really occurring is activity in the receiving areas of the brain due to the external object; but it is convenient to refer to this activity in experiential terms as if it were conscious, *i.e.* to refer to it as sentience.

One can also try to give cash value to the notion, by indicating what it would be like if it were to become conscious and how this experience can almost be obtained. The route to it is by "perceptual reduction," which results in a kind of phenomenological observation: observe attentively the object or scene, putting aside all conceptual supplementations, *i.e.* all thought of what objects are being perceived; try to notice all features equally, *i.e.* to inhibit the selective activities; also allow for and discount the various cues of perspective, background, lighting, etc., and inhibit the constancy adjustments. This is not a task which can be fully performed, such is the difficulty of discounting or inhibiting habitual and automatic processes; but one can go a fair way, at least so far as the first two groups of activities are concerned. A measure of success in phenomenological observation is necessary for painting (cp. p. 200). (It is not quite the same in that there one usually seeks a single-eye view.) If one is to reproduce a scene realistically one has to observe shadows, patches of light on rounded surfaces, textures and graining, blemishes, percipiendum- or stimulus-shapes, etc. (Many of these features are seen more easily on a photograph, if one observes that in the same attentive way.) Further, there are devices like reduction screens (cp. p. 158) which enable one to overcome constancy effects, though they limit the field of view on the object concerned. Although one may thus approach the postulated visual sentience, it is not completely attainable, even in a static scene—at least one could not be sure of noticing all features and of discounting all cues or organisation; also, the coloured shapes, etc., are seen as external. But as the reduction consists in inhibiting various selective and modificatory activities, one may imaginatively extrapolate beyond what can be attained in practice and may thus conceive what pure sentience would be like; at any rate one can get close enough to give meaning to the concept of sentience.

It must be emphasised, however, that such perceptual reduction does not give one the traditional sensations or sense-data. It does not reveal the sensory core, as it were, of the normal perceptual act, for it is a special process which substitutes for normal perception a subsequent and different form of consciousness, one which is moreover still perceptual and not purely sensory so far as it is attainable in practice. But even if it did reveal a purely sensory awareness, this would not be anything that survives as a distinguishable element in normal perceptual consciousness which is unitary and unanalysable *qua* mode of consciousness. The sentience revealed by reduction would simply be the conscious correlate of activity in the receiving areas of the brain; its only connexion with perceptual consciousness is indirect, via the brain, in that the complex of brain activity which is correlated with perceptual consciousness can theoretically be distinguished into sensory (corresponding to sentience) and modificatory activities. This is in contrast to the traditional account where perceptual consciousness was held to be due to interpretation by the percipient's mind of sensations present to it, even if this mental awareness and interpretation of sensations had rather mysteriously to be dubbed "unconscious" or "implicit."

As if your explanation were not mysterious.

Qualifications

(a) *Stereoscopic vision*: Two important qualifications must be made to the above account. The first is that stereoscopic vision has not been considered. We normally see a scene with depth and with objects that seem three-dimensional: this is to some extent facilitated by the use of cues, *e.g.* shadows or aerial perspective, and is thus far covered by the organisational processes postulated above; but the main factor involved in it is retinal disparity. The operation of this factor is often unfortunately described by saying that the two eyes get slightly different views of the same object or scene, and that the brain responds to these views by seeing the object as solid and three-dimensional. But the eyes and brain in themselves cannot see or get views of anything, only the person can do this. The patterns of stimulation of the two retinae differ, but neither the eyes nor the percipient see them; nor is it possible to find two patterns of excitation in the brain, each corresponding to that on one retina. So there is no reason to suppose that the postulated sentience consists of two single-eye views which are combined by integrative forces; the com-

really?

bination that gives stereoscopic vision is already complete in the receiving areas of the brain and so the sentience would be of one scene with depth and solidity in which object-shapes to some extent stand out.[1] This means that the organisational forces postulated will need to be less potent, and sentience more complex, than might have been expected. At any rate visual sentience would not seem positively private and adverbial as some doctrines of the projection of sensations seem to suggest; on the other hand it need not be assumed to be awareness of objects, or shapes even, as positively public and external. The notions of public, private, external, etc., introduce a conceptual element and so indicate perceptual consciousness, even if a rudimentary one.

The difficulty is, of course, that one cannot do more than speculate about a pure sentience, about what activity solely in the receiving areas of the brain would be like if conscious. There are a few further phenomena which might seem to throw light on it: the experience produced by electrical stimulation of those sensory areas, the coloured field obtained by pressing the closed eyes, and perhaps after-images and "spots before the eyes." But these would be treacherous guides, for the first two are due to a crude and undifferentiated stimulus very different from the normal one, and the last two show the marked difference that they "follow one around," i.e. do not change or disappear as the head is turned. But it might be that the contents of visual sentience have the sort of distinctness without full externality or objectification that the first two show.

(b) Non-visual sentience: Secondly, our discussion has been primarily about visual perception, partly because that is for the great majority the most copious and important source of information about the world, and partly because it involves the widest range of non-sensory activities. But similar activities occur also with the other senses, particularly hearing. Attention, noticing and failing to notice, are found with all of them, while selective and organisational activities (temporal rather than spatial grouping) occur when a theme is picked out from an orchestral background (see also pp. 141 and 173). Recognition, which can be greatly developed by learning and experience, is also widespread, e.g. identifying sounds, tea-tasting, or connoisseurship of wine or perfume, telling a cloth by its feel), while the experience of a sound or smell, and thought of its object, frequently arise in one complex. The main differences from sight are that the conceptual or imaginative supplementation is relatively weaker and that sentience is to this extent more easily approached: a sound or a taste or smell is readily isolated from its source and may be "savoured" and

[1] Cp. the evidence of the congenitally blind who later regain their sight, p. 204; they immediately see unitary figures differentiated from their background, though perhaps even that is not pure visual sentience.

experienced on its own without thought of what its source is. But even then it is not certain one has quite got pure sentience, and at any rate there is a difference from the traditional sensations. Sounds are normally experienced as at or from a point outside us, and though this would be like visual sentience with depth in that it is primarily a matter of aural disparity, it is difficult to be sure that external placing of a conceptual kind or use of cues is not involved. Smells are also normally experienced as public and external, and tastes as in the mouth, while in touch one often seems to be feeling, *e.g.* a cold rough object rather than a cold rough sensation. And while it is easy to savour all these experiences without knowing or thinking what their exact source is, it is difficult to isolate them from the thought that they possess some sort of public external source.

Scale of Perceptual Consciousness

The non-sensory activities we have discussed may merge with or modify sentience in various degrees, and so it is possible to construct a theoretical scale of perceptual consciousness, a continuous gradation from the one extreme or ideal limit of pure sentience to the other of independent and self-maintaining imagery, as in hallucination. Largely according to the strength and differentiation of the percipienda and to the attentiveness of observation, any particular perception will have a position on this scale, though the next may occupy a different one. This has been recognised to some extent by psychologists who have distinguished "literal" and "enriched" or "literal" and "schematic" perception, but there are not just two grades as those distinctions might suggest.

We may start with literal perception, which is in the middle of the scale and not at the bottom. Here the percipienda (stimulus properties) are relatively strong and clear, and we recognise the object and observe it carefully and attentively, taking care not to overlook or misperceive any of its characteristics. Although involuntary selection is thus controlled as far as possible, object constancy will operate and cues will be used, so that the percepta will accord with the physical properties of the object. *which are ...?* To judge from the successful behaviour to which it leads and the part it plays in the foundation of science, this kind of observation is successful in revealing what objects are present and in indicating their properties.

To move down from literal perception we must strip off, so far as we can, the conceptual additions involved in recognition and identification, not only maintaining a general attentiveness but looking very closely in an effort to become aware of the various percipiendum features which are normally used as cues, or for constancy, without conscious grasp of them.

Thus we arrive at reduced perception of phenomenological observation, and may approach pure sentience.

Returning to literal perception, we can move in the other direction to levels at which the foundation of sentience becomes less and less important. Sometimes this is because the perception becomes casual and sketchy, the selective processes cutting out all but the grossest features of the perceived object. But quite often it is because the perception is being enriched by the modificatory activities: perhaps the percipienda are partial and ambiguous and so have to be completed and "organised"; perhaps the conceptual supplementation required for the recognition of what is seen is more extensive. Relatively weak or undifferentiated percipienda will also encourage imaginative as well as conceptual supplementation, whether to remedy gaps and defects in the picture or just because the imagery is attractive or obsessive, and once set off this may be little controlled by the percipienda.

As these kinds of enrichment become more prominent at the expense of sentience the resultant contents of consciousness may differ widely from the object or scene present to the senses; we may then pass to the level of what may be called transformed perceptual consciousness, which may often be illusory. Its nature will vary with the person and the general context of events, and may be largely conceptual or largely imaginative. In the first case one has a perceptual consciousness which is largely thought of an object, and as any perception may lead to supervenient judgments this passes readily into thought or judgment about the object seemingly present; indeed, one's consciousness may be filled with a series of judgments. An extreme case of this would be when one is reading, or listening to a speech, and is scarcely conscious of seeing or hearing the words at all; but in more straightforward cases where symbols are not involved one may simply "jump to conclusions" about what one is perceiving. On the other hand, the supplementation may be imaginative, more of the nature of sights and sounds. The sensuous (pictorial, auditory, etc.) character of this supplementation no doubt means that it corresponds to or involves activity in the sensory receiving areas of the brain, and so while it differs from sentience in not being directly caused by an external stimulus its similarity in other respects means that it will readily merge with sentience and may quite overwhelm it.

The supplementation may be sufficiently close for this transformed perceptual consciousness to be correct as to the object present, if not as to its properties, but when the supplementation is very different as well as marked, the result will be an hallucination. Indeed it is not easy to draw any hard and fast line between transformed perceptual consciousness and hallucination, and many hallucinations are in fact extreme cases of the former. The bush dimly discernible in the shrubbery may appear to be a man in hiding, the sigh of the wind will sound to be the baby crying, the beam of light will be seen as the expected ghost—in all these cases the experience will be set off by something in sentience and so we may call it either transformed perceptual consciousness or triggered hallucination. Similarly, hallucinations may be perfectly integrated with a veridically perceived background, *i.e.* one may have a complex mode of consciousness in which a normally modified sentience is merged with mental or eidetic imagery. And then at the end of the scale as its upper limit will come pure hallucination, vivid imagery which is not triggered off by anything that is acting on the sense organs and which may oust rather than be integrated with any perceptual consciousness.

BIBLIOGRAPHY

BLANSHARD, B. 1939. *The Nature of Thought.* Vol. I, Chs. 2-3. Allen and Unwin, London.

HIRST, R. J. 1959. *The Problems of Perception,* Chs. 8-9. Allen and Unwin, London.

PRICE, H. H. 1932. *Perception.* Methuen, London.

RYLE, G. 1949. *The Concept of Mind,* Ch. 7. Hutchinson, London.

    1956. "Sensation." In *Contemporary British Philosophy* III. Ed. by H. D. Lewis. Allen and Unwin, London.

15

Philosophical Conclusions

Orthodox Theories Unsatisfactory

Common-sense and Sense-datum Theories: It will be apparent from the discussion in Chapters 12 and 13 that none of the usual philosophical theories of perception is satisfactory. The Common-sense view, even as recently revived and restated, cannot ultimately account for hallucinations, particularly those which are closely integrated with a perceived background; and though acceptance of the variability of perceiving goes a good way to meet the traditional arguments from illusion, this is not easily reconciled with the widespread common-sense assumption that perception is direct confrontation with the physical object, nor can one explain without recourse to science how this variability occurs. But the dependence of perceiving on causal processes, especially when these involve significant time-lag, is perhaps the most serious difficulty a common-sense approach has to face, since a generative explanation and its attendant epistemological difficulties seems unavoidable; and the complex psychological processes just discussed are a final blow to the notion that perceiving is a simple direct awareness of external physical objects.

The Sense-datum Theory must likewise be rejected; whichever of its versions is taken, its phenomenological analysis does not do justice to how perception seems to the percipient; but its main faults lie in its immediacy assumption (which forces it to postulate a host of private existents, awareness of which is always incorrigible) and in the general status and spatial relations attributed to sense-data—allegedly belonging to physical objects but nevertheless generated by processes in the human brain, these "events which happen to nothing" are too paradoxical for the theory which fathered them to be convincing.

The Representative Theory: Passing over the implausible and complicated "analyses" of Phenomenalism, whether that is considered as a development of the Sense-datum Theory or of earlier views, we are left with the Representative Theory as the strongest and best able to survive. In its traditional seventeenth-century form this appeared self-refuting and so became in the tuition of young philosophers an Awful Warning of the dangers of dabbling in science. But scientific discoveries and the problems they raise have rightly been a challenge not a bogy to the greatest philosophers of the past, and the sterile ingenuities of recent philosophical analyses should in turn be a More Awful Warning against neglect of the physiological and psychological evidence. Moreover, the more modern versions of the Representative Theory have avoided the classical accusations of self-refutation and of imprisonment within the barrier of representations by two amendments: (1) two types of perceiving are distinguished, namely the direct perception of representations and the indirect perception of external objects which is mediated by it, and (2) it is claimed that the resultant theory is the best hypothesis to explain the nature and order of our sense experiences.

Nevertheless, the following difficulties still remain (cp. pp. 260-5):

(a) The inner direct perception it proposes seems to be just a duplicate of what common sense thinks the perception of external objects to be—a direct confrontation with an object. It thus gains a spurious plausibility as an explanation by referring us to something familiar; but this means that it is really circular in that it explains perceiving in terms of perceiving; nor is it clear why this inner perceiving requires no sense organs. The defence is offered that this inner seeing, which should more properly be called "having sensations or percepts" is different from the outer seeing of physical objects, and so there is no duplication; the former is simply a part of the latter, not a copy of it. This hardly meets the more damaging part of the circularity charge, that the alleged inner seeing is a duplicate of (outer) seeing as ordinarily and mistakenly conceived, not of the complex indirect outer seeing proposed by the theory. But even as regards duplication within the theory itself, one should note that in all the analogies offered by its proponents the person who sees the inner representation, e.g. the T.V. screen, the radar screen, the map, sees it in exactly the same way as he would see the external world represented by it. To the counter that this is pushing the analogies too far, one can reply that this is an obvious, not a recondite, feature of all the analogies, and that if it is removed it is difficult to see what is left of them.

(b) Apart from this, the inner perception is supposed to be a direct awareness (or having) of sensations or percepts, and whether or not it is just a copy of the confrontation supposed by common sense, it allows no scope for the complex of organisational and interpretative processes considered in the last chapter. Even if otherwise satisfactory, the Representative Theory would have to be amended to include these.

(c) Its concept of mind is obscure. Apart from splitting up the person into two radically different entities, a body and a "pure ego" or mind, it involves postulating a mental realm in which the representations, i.e. the objects of inner perceiving, can exist. Not only is this unecon-

omical and unenlightening, but it raises the notorious difficulty of how
the mind and mental world are related to the body and physical world.
This is alleged to be a two-way causal interaction, but it must then be a
unique type of causal relation, the cause being unconscious, physical, and
extended, and the effect being conscious, non-physical, and not in physical
space—or vice versa. Furthermore, this relation cannot be observed. So
far as external observation goes, the causal process from the object via
the sense organs terminates in brain activity. And if the percipient's
introspection is admitted as a form of observation, all it reveals are the
conscious experiences, which seem to him to be awareness of external
objects not of mental sensations or brain processes, and which are themselves the result of an intermediate state of unconscious mental modificatory activities. The link between the conscious experiences and the
brain activity is thus forever mysterious: might it indeed not exist *as a
causal one*? Normally cause and effect are both publicly observable by the
scientist; to put mental awareness of mental data as a further stage at the
end of an otherwise publicly observable and physical causal process is to
abandon the scientific standpoint and to make an unnoticed and unjustified
switch from publicly observed processes to introspected ones private to
the percipient.

These difficulties seem sufficiently serious to warrant the exploration
of a new kind of theoretical approach. This will now be attempted, and
on page 331 a return will be made to what is common ground between
the new suggestion and the Representative Theory.

An Alternative Theory of Mind

"Mind" as a Group of Faculties, not an Entity

The first step is to adopt a different concept of mind from the orthodox
Interactionist one assumed by the Representative Theory. One may turn
to another and almost equally ancient theory of mind, which was on the
whole the one preferred by Aristotle and which has recently been revived
and restated in various ways. Its basic claim is that the person or self is
not a mysterious mental entity lodged in the body or a compound of two
disparate substances, mind and body, but is the human living organism
itself; furthermore, the human organism is a conscious one, and it is to
this consciousness, the power of the organism with a sufficiently complex
and developed brain to be aware of itself, its history, and its environment,
that we refer when we speak of "mind." Mind is not an entity or substance, but is a set of dispositions, faculties, activities, and tastes possessed
by the human being. If we take the person, *i.e.* the essentially conscious

organism, we can by observation distinguish a whole range of activities and capacities: some of these, *e.g.* locomotion and digestion, we ordinarily label "physical" and others, *e.g.* perceiving, thinking, desiring, we label "mental." The ordinary principle of division between the two is not very clear, but on the whole the former are completely observable by public scientific procedures, while the latter are in an important sense only accessible to the person concerned, for they are primarily conscious, involving experience as well as activity. All that need or should be meant by the term "mind" is the complex of dispositions, faculties, and activities which are mental in this sense; it is a shorthand way of referring to a part of the activities and faculties of the person, the part distinguished on an empirical basis as above. (The distinction is not entirely consistent in that we distinguish mental and physical pain, while even the latter is mental in the sense of being a private conscious experience; it is the supposed origin of the pain that makes that distinction. Another difficulty is in unconscious mental activities; though they may be no more than brain activities they are labelled "mental" because they are most easily described as if they were conscious, though history and theory influence terminology here.) By contrast, Interactionism claims more than a purely empirical distinction of mental and physical activities: the former are mental because they are performed by a mental, *i.e.* conscious and not physically extended, entity, while the latter belong only to an unconscious physical entity, the body. But this presupposes the theory in that it affords no independent criterion for deciding if a given activity is mental or physical, especially as "mental" activities involve physical (brain) activity and cannot, it seems, occur without it. And Interactionism is in worse difficulty over unconscious mental activities—if the essence of mind is consciousness as Descartes claimed, then they are self-contradictory and impossible, and if the essence of mind is not consciousness "mind" becomes an empty term with no positive meaning.

An extreme form of this faculty and activity notion of mind is Behaviourism, which limits mental activities and abilities to certain publicly observable behaviour and behaviour patterns, including sub-vocal speech. This seems implausible in its denial and neglect of conscious experiences. On the view suggested here, that to speak of a person's mind is to refer to his mental activities, abilities, and dispositions, the characteristic feature of mental activities is that they are not wholly open to external observation and are conscious (or best described as if they were conscious). The problem then remains, and it is a transmutation of the old "mind/body" problem, what is the relation of these mental activities, or at least of their conscious or experiential character, to brain activity?

[margin note: but locomotion is perceptible by proprioceptive senses — so it could be partially "mental" — (despite the "volitional" aspects of it)]

The Two Aspects of Mental Activities

If we say that the relation between mental and cerebral activities is a causal one, we are liable to the very objections we have made against the Representative Theory. The causal relation postulated would have to be unique and unobservable, involving a switch from external to internal viewpoints in the description of the one causal chain. And what could mental activity then be if it is to be different (either as effect or cause) from brain activity and if the person is to be regarded as a living organism with a developed brain? There could be no place for these extra activities in the physical world of organisms and objects, and so like Interactionism we should be reduced to inventing a non-physical world in which they could take place and a non-physical entity which could perform them, thus destroying the unity of the person. The only possible conclusion would seem to be that the cerebral activities *are* the mental activities, or rather that they are the outwardly observable aspect of them.

This needs some explanation. We have distinguished certain activities of a person which are ordinarily labelled "mental" and have supposed them to be activities of the human organism which differ in various characteristics from the "physical" activities of the organism. Perhaps we might adopt the term "whole activities" for thinking, perceiving, imagining and the like, to remind us that they involve experiences and cerebral processes, in this way being activities of the person or organism. The next step is to ask how do we get to know of the occurrence of these activities? We do this in two main ways, (*a*) by observing a person's behaviour (including what he says) and (*b*) by being the person concerned and so performing the activity and introspecting one's experience. You can tell that I am perceiving or thinking from my behaviour; I know that I am perceiving or thinking from carrying out and experiencing the activities. We might therefore say that my behaviour and my experiences are two aspects of these whole activities, the one an externally observed aspect, the other an internally observed one. But more exactitude is needed for "behaviour" is very vague, and much of the behavioural evidence consists in consequences or inessential accompaniments of the activity. If I am thinking of a problem you may see my furrowed brow, my doodling on paper, may hear what I say I am doing and then hear me announce or act on the solution. But all this behaviour is caused by brain activity, especially in the motor areas and speech centre; if I am a good actor it may be suppressed when I am actually thinking or simulated when I am not. So it would be very loose to call it an aspect of the thinking—it consists merely of common consequences or indications. But there will be something externally observable, in principle at least, whenever the thinking occurs, namely the brain activity that would occur even when the overt signs do not; there is no doubt that one cannot think or perform "mental" activities without a properly functioning and developed brain, *i.e.* without brain activity; what extent of brain activity and in what areas is a question that does not concern us here, for we are attempting only a general theoretical elucidation. Let us say that there is activity in the association areas and, so far as the thought is verbal, in the speech centre; the claim would then be that such activity is the external aspect of the person's thinking, is what can (in principle) be observed of it from outside. Similarly perceiving, or rather perceptual consciousness, will present an external aspect, namely brain activity in the receiving and other areas, as discussed in the last chapter.

We can now provisionally state a double-aspect theory of "mental" activities. It is that such activities are "whole" activities of the person *qua* living organism, and that they present two aspects: an outer one which consists of a complex of brain activity and is on principle, at least, externally observable; and an inner one, the various experiences which the person has, and can introspect, in the actual performance of these activities. This latter aspect is available only to the person concerned; it is the actor's view as it were, not the spectator's, of the whole activity. "Mind" therefore is not a non-physical being or entity: it is a convenient term for referring to activities of this type and particularly to the ability or disposition to perform them which a person possesses; and the characteristic feature of these activities is that they present these two aspects. This is not quite enough to justify the ordinary mental/physical distinction, for one might say that there is a conscious or inner aspect of walking or other physical movements; but this can be met by the riders, (*a*) that in the "mental" activities it is the inner aspect which differentiates them and give us most information about them, the outer aspect being difficult as yet to determine in any detail, and (*b*) that the outer aspect is strictly or primarily cerebral, though this will have to be qualified later.

Identity and Modes of Access

Further theoretical development is required, even though it is an advance to regard conscious (or introspective) experiences and brain activity as co-ordinate aspects of whole activities of the person rather than as cause and effect. For it might still be supposed that they were aspects of some third thing, of some process of a different character forever unknown to us except for its misleading appearance in these aspects. And then one would have a theory as uneconomical as Interactionism in postulating a special order of being. But that would be unnecessary as well as undesirable; the logic of the term "aspect" is such that when we are said to see an aspect (or view) of anything we are seeing the thing in question; the point of the term is not that we see some screen behind which the real thing hides, but that we do not see the whole of the thing or of its characteristics. When we see the southern aspect of a building, or get a bird's eye view of it, we are still seeing the building. So when the person concerned is having or introspecting the experiences which constitute the inner aspect of thought, he is aware of himself thinking, of his "whole activity" of thinking; and in so far as one can observe or record the corresponding outer aspect, *i.e.* the brain activity, one is observing the person's thinking. The experiences *are* the "mental" activity as observed from within, the brain activity *is* the "mental" activity as observed from without. If then thinking of Z or perceiving X is one whole event in a person's life, his conscious experience at the time and the concomitant brain activity are both that one event as revealed to different observers—or rather as revealed on different modes of access or observation, for the person might be able to adopt the external viewpoint and observe his own brain activity. Instead then of a mysterious causal relation one has a partial identity; conscious experiences and brain activity are not two distinct whole events between which one must postulate or discover a causal relation; they are co-ordinate aspects of one whole event or activity in a person's life, *e.g.* his thinking, perceiving, etc.; they are that one event or activity differently revealed. The difficulties of Interactionism arose because it took two aspects of the one event to be two quite different events and identified the person's thinking or per-ceiving with only one of them, so that the other, the brain activity, became an embarrassment.

Difficulty may be felt in accepting this because of the apparently very different nature of conscious experiences and brain activity; surely occurrences so radically different must be separate, even if simultaneous, events? The answer to this is that the difference lies in and is due to the radical difference in modes of access. To this extent the ordinary analogies of aspect and view are inadequate, for they presuppose the same sort of mode of access, namely sight, and only a difference in viewpoint. But there is an immense difference between inner private awareness of one's "mental" activities by performing, experiencing, and introspecting them, and the outer public awareness which some other person or even oneself may obtain by use of sense organs and scientific instruments. And it is because of this difference that the one event or activity presents different appearances. If the same or similar mode of access revealed appearances so disparate one would have to say that they were two distinct events; but that does not hold. Interactionism assumed that they were distinct events because it did not realise or allow for the difference in modes of access.

Appreciation of this point may be assisted by two analogies. First, the perception of one object by different senses gives us modes of access which differ markedly. We may see the wine as a red transparent liquid, and taste it as cool, smooth, and tangy; we hear the ringing of a bell as a constant note, feel it as vibration, see the blurred contact of striker and rounded metal; we may hear the collision as a series of sharp sounds, see it as the impact of two cars. Disparate as are transparent red and cool tang, as are a note or sound and the seen contact of metal, we have no compunction in saying that we see and taste the same wine, hear and see the same bell ringing or the same accident, and we can accept the difference in perceived characteristics as due to the radical differences in the senses by which we perceive it. Even here some Interactionists made an analogous error to that concerning brain and mental events by supposing that the different perceived characteristics were different objects of perception, so that the wine or the bell was an unknown substratum or thing-in-itself concealed from us by them; but there was not the temptation to identify the true wine or bell with the qualities perceived by one sense and to dismiss the others as cause or effect—though the primary/ secondary quality distinction got near to this—for both kinds of observation were public and via sense organs. Thus the analogy cannot go all the way—the different sense modalities are not different enough to afford a true parallel; the modes of access to the inner and outer aspects of mental activities differ further in that one is private and not via sense organs.

Secondly, there is the notorious wave/particle duality in modern physics: in certain experimental situations electrons behave as particles, in others they behave as waves. Now it would be out of place to attempt to go into the controversies surrounding the interpretation of this; but one can say, without necessarily claiming that they are right, that some physicists have given an essentially double-aspect account of this. They have asserted a Complementarity Principle, that the wave aspect and the particle aspect are two complementary and equally valid aspects of an electron. In some experimental situations the wave aspect is revealed, in others the particle one, but there is no sense in asking: "Are electrons really particles?" They are at once both waves and particles, possessing these disparate but complementary characteristics. This claim is analogous in that waves and particles are *prima facie* as different as conscious experiences and brain activity; but it is even more paradoxical in that the experimental situations in physics do not differ as markedly as do introspection and external neurological observation. Some physicists reject complementarity on the ground that the wave and particle characteristics appear in the same experimental situation. We cannot pronounce on this, but the objection does not hold in the mind/body situation. The subject's conscious experience is of the inner aspect only, available only to him. His brain activity is available only to observations from without, and if he can be aware of it, that is only because he uses sense organs and apparatus and so adopts the external mode of access.

Criteria of Correlation

On a double-aspect theory the question naturally arises of how we can be sure that we do in fact have two co-ordinate aspects, that the two modes of access do reveal one and the same whole activity. The criteria of the correlation of experience and brain activity thus sought are similar to those we readily adopt for deciding that one and the same object is being perceived by different senses, viz. identity of spatio-temporal co-ordinates and concomitant variation. We might, for example, determine which of several birds it is that is singing by locating the origin of the sound as a certain branch where there are several birds and then observing that the song starts or stops as one of them opens or shuts its beak. Similarly, if we are to correlate as aspects of the one whole activity both certain experiences of the person and certain brain activity, we must establish first that the two are occurring at the same time and in or to the same person, and secondly, if possible, that the brain activity starts, stops, and varies as the experience does.

Both these present problems. Location can only be rough, because a large amount of brain activity will be occurring before, after, and during the experience in question, and one can say little more than that within a certain complex is the activity required. Also, causal relations within the body are involved. One may have a pain in the big toe and the toe may be visibly inflamed, but this does not mean that the painful experience and the inflammation are the two co-ordinate aspects of the situation of having the pain. The lesion in the toe causes excitation in the appropriate part of the brain, and it is the latter which should strictly be co-ordinated with the experience, for if the nerve is blocked (anaesthetised) the experience ceases even though the inflammation continues. Similarly, we may detect impulses passing along the optic nerve when a flash of light is seen in a dark room, but the visual experience must be co-ordinated rather with the end in the brain of the causal chain of which the observed impulses are only a link.

Establishment of concomitant variation also involves causal inferences of this kind. There are two main types of variation: (1) Starting and stopping. The sensory experience begins as the stimulus is applied to the sense organ and ends as it is removed, and we can infer from observable nerve impulses, etc., and from experiments of direct stimulation of the brain itself, that certain brain activity starts and stops with the stimulus and is the appropriate correlate of the experience. Also, there is the evidence of electroencephalograms: as perceiving or certain other mental activities begin the alpha rhythm ceases and more complex rhythms take over, and then as the subject subsides to a relaxed inattentive state the alpha rhythm returns (cp. p. 109); the inference is that the complex rhythms indicate the brain activity which is the correlate of the attentive perception. (2) The experience may vary in intensity and quality as the stimulus, and hence the inferred brain activity, varies. This is only true within limits owing to the operation of the various factors discussed in the previous chapter, but it is enough to support correlation, e.g. as the sound frequency changes and hence the area of brain excited, so does the heard tone.

The various difficulties are practical ones and scarcely affect the theoretical claim that the brain activity which corresponds to a certain conscious experience is a co-ordinate aspect with it of the whole activity of the person, not a cause or effect of it. In fact the detailed evidence is equally required on either theory. An Interactionist must equally wish to establish the precise brain activity which he claims causes a given perception; the double-aspect theory simply claims that this activity is not a cause but a co-ordinate aspect. Similarly the Interactionist may investigate psychosomatic diseases and claim that a certain mental state causes certain bodily effects. On the double-aspect theory this is equally correct but is reinterpreted. The mental state presents two aspects, feelings of anxiety perhaps and corresponding brain activity, but the feeling of anxiety is not the cause of, say, the contraction of the bronchioles; the cause is the mental state of which that feeling is one aspect and brain activity another. Hence observable causal relations should be sought between the brain and the contraction. Again, mental disease must be regarded as a disease of the whole person, presenting conscious and cerebral aspects, and may be treatable by drugs or by psychological methods (though it may happen that one is more effective than the other in practice). Interactionism, however, apart from its theoretical extravagance, has more difficulty in certain cases: it is not clear why a purely mental activity, e.g. working out a sum, should cause brain activity which is detectable on an electroencephalogram. There seems no point in this —surely the mind should think on its own without causing brain effects? Again, in the psychosomatic case unconscious worry might cause the contraction; in this as in many other situations, there is the danger of inventing an unconscious mind as well as a conscious one. But if mental activities are activities of the whole person, then some may be such that they are brain activity only and do not present any conscious aspect.

HSP Y

Application of this Theory to Perception

So far we have suggested that the various "mental" activities, *e.g.* perceiving, thinking, feeling emotion or pain, are activities of the whole person, and that there are two radically different ways of observing or having access to these activities. On the one, observation from without by instruments and sense organs, they are essentially brain activity, though activity elsewhere in the nervous system may be involved; on the other, the subject's private mode of access by performing, experiencing, and introspecting them, they are the various conscious experiences we are familiar with in these situations. Thus the brain activity and the experiences are not cause and effect: they are co-ordinate aspects of the one whole activity of the organism or person, and so, as suggested on p. 322, they *are* that activity as revealed on the mode of access in question.

If this is applied directly to perceiving one should say that the conscious experiences are the inner aspect of perceiving an object, are what it is like to perceive one, while the corresponding brain activity is the perceiving as observed by the neurologists or external observer. But there are some qualifications which have to be made to this.

First Qualification : Content and Object

There is a general characteristic of mental activities which we have been able to leave in the background so far, but which is particularly important in perceiving. This is the distinction between the theoretical description of a mental activity, *i.e.* what a theoretician correlating the two aspects would want to say of it, and the inner aspect or subject's description, how performing the activity seems to the person concerned. Whereas perceiving (not perceptual consciousness) or observing involves a causal process in which the agent and his act of perceiving are quite distinct from the perceived external object, most other mental activities are not transitive in this way; they are not linked by any observable causal relation to any external object, and so may be said to be "adverbial," to be modes of activity or ways of experiencing on the part of the person concerned. This is particularly clear in imagining, thinking, dreaming, wishing, or emotional states generally; it must also be true of hallucinations and of perceptual consciousness, as opposed to perceiving, for they may occur without an external object; strictly also it applies to feeling a pain, for that similarly may occur without any causal relation to a lesion in the part of the body where the pain seems to be.

On the other hand these various mental activities or states do not seem adverbial to the subject at all. In dreaming or imagining there seems to be a scene dreamt or imagined, something distinct from oneself;

desiring ?

this is still so even if we say it is only an image or a dream picture and not real; in thought also, even if from the real thing thought about we distinguish the image, words, or other symbols by which we think of it, these symbols too seem to stand out as distinct from us; and much the same seems true of desiring or fearing in that they presuppose perception or thought of their object. Even pain seems normally to be located in the body and somehow dissociated from oneself.

We may express this fairly generally and neutrally by saying that these various activities have an experienced *content*; this enables us to keep the word "object" for external physical objects, and in discussing thought or hallucination it is particularly important to be able to distinguish the content (pictorial or verbal imagery, etc.) from external objects. Also one needs to be able to distinguish the awareness of the content from observing or perceiving of objects; the latter is transitive, involving sense organs and causal relations, whereas the former clearly does not involve these. Interactionism claims that this awareness of contents is in fact a transitive awareness of distinct mental objects (images, representations, ideas, or sense-data), but if so it would be an unusual kind of transitive awareness with no organic or causal process between subject and object. It seems better for this reason and on grounds of economy (the avoidance of the supposition of a distinct world of mental objects) to say that these contents are not in fact distinct from the experiencing subject and are not like objects separated by a transitive relation; they and the experiencing of them are really merged in one activity. It just seems to be a pervasive characteristic of "mental" activities that, though they seem to the subject to possess a distinct experienced content, yet they must be judged to be adverbial activities by anyone taking into account outer and inner aspects and trying to form a general theory of the whole activity. (In saying that the contents are mental objects one would also be forming a hypothesis as to their status, not describing observed fact. The datum is not that these contents are distinct objects, only that they *seem* to the subjects to be this, and saying that they are mental, if this means any more than what both sides would agree, viz. that they are not external objects, is just as much theorising as saying that they are not really distinct objects.)

It is not clear just why mental activities, though really adverbial, involve an experienced content. Perhaps it is connected with the reflexivity of consciousness; if conscious experience is an inner aspect of the whole mental activity, is how that activity seems to the actor, it must involve some distinction of the self (as actor) and not-self. More likely it is because perception of distinct objects is biologically necessary, and it may arise out of the fact that the neural (and even cerebral) processes

involved extend over a distance: they have a point of origin and end some
way away from it, and this may tend to give a distinction in consciousness
between "self" at the end and "content" set over against it at the beginning
of the process. Thus pain, as a content, seems to be at the origin of the
neural processes which cause the brain excitation properly identifiable with
the feeling of it, and likewise the content of visual, auditory, and other supposed sentience would seem to be at their neural origin, the sense organ.
Also perceptual consciousness is not just simple sentience; hence if the
latter can give some distinctness of content, it is reasonable to suppose
that the various modificatory activities intensify this, so that the complex
activity seems to be an act/object awareness of an external object—particularly since these other activities are in part conceptual, i.e. involve
thought of an object, a characterisation and identification of what is
perceived. Once the idea that one is faced with distinct objects is acquired, however dimly, from the sensory distinctness of content, and is
continually confirmed by behaviour and by manipulating or otherwise
dealing with those objects, this idea must react on and intensify the sensory
discrimination so that full perceptual consciousness seems in itself to be
a relation with those objects. Moreover, dreams or imagery seem primarily
to be duplicates of the range of activity that occurs in perception, even to
the extent of involving some processes in the nerves and sense organs
as well as the brain, hence they too will reproduce the distinction, though
less markedly.

this is just speculative science

Second Qualification : Perception and Perceptual Consciousness

This distinction has been introduced already (see p. 271) and the
difference between the two is one of whole and part, perceiving consisting
of perceptual consciousness plus a causal relation; in normal perceiving
the subject's perceptual consciousness is caused by the corresponding
external object, in illusions it may be caused by a different object, in
hallucinations there may be no external cause at all. (By "corresponding
object" is meant the object which corresponds in its characteristics to the
content experienced in the perceptual consciousness.) It will thus be
seen that perceiving differs significantly from the other mental activities
in that it does involve an observable transitive relation, a causal process
between subject and object. Perceptual consciousness, however, resembles
them closely in that it is theoretically adverbial, a mode of activity, but
possesses an experienced content which seems to the subject to be distinct
and external (though more clearly external than the content of the other
activities). In fact the discussion of the previous section applies properly
to perceptual consciousness, not to perceiving.

Thus perceptual consciousness is a whole activity of the person and

*   what sort of "characteristics"? And "corresponds" how?
** is this a phenomenological comment?

presents two aspects: an inner one which is the conscious experience possessing a distinct-seeming content, and an outer one which is a complex of brain activity. To perceive is to have perceptual consciousness caused ✳ by the corresponding object, and one might say that it too presented two aspects, an inner one the same as the perceptual consciousness which is part of the perceiving, and an outer one which consists of the whole causal chain from object to brain activity. But this would be a loose way of speaking; the double-aspect theory, with its implication of the identity of the co-ordinate aspects with the whole activity presenting them, cannot strictly allow a causal chain within one aspect—both aspects need to be theoretically adverbial. One must emphasise also that to say that the perceptual consciousness (a whole activity) is caused by an external object, does not mean that the conscious experience is caused by brain activity; the experience is a co-ordinate aspect, along with the brain activity, of the whole activity of the person caused by the effect of the object on the sense organs.

In speaking of the inner aspect of perceptual consciousness as a conscious experience with a distinct-seeming content, we are adopting the position of a theoretician correlating the aspects and activities. If one asks simply for a description of that experience and content in any particular case, i.e. asks how the perceptual consciousness seems to the person concerned, the answer, e.g. "I see a red tomato on a plate," would refer to an object or scene. To the person concerned perceptual consciousness seems to be awareness of a distinct external object, but owing to the possibility of hallucinations it cannot be this strictly; such consciousness is adverbial like the other mental activities and its link with the corresponding external object is per accidens, not essential to its occurrence. However, since it normally occurs as part of perceiving, i.e. when there is a causal relation with the corresponding external object, this misconception does not often matter in practice. It is an important mistake, however, if this common-sense assumption, that the content of the experience is an external object and that the experience of a content is a transitive relation with an external object, is made into a theory of perception, i.e. into the claim that perceiving or perceptual consciousness is a direct confrontation with an external physical object. ✳ ✳

Holders of the Representative Theory should be sympathetic to this point, for they also claim that the percipient is mistaken as to the nature of perceiving, and that his mistake is of little practical importance being significant only if made into a theoretical claim. On their view, though the percipient is right in thinking that he has a transitive awareness in all perceptual consciousness, he fails to realise that this awareness is always primarily of mental objects; direct awareness is only of them, and any

[margin note:] wouldn't this be biologically maladaptive?

[footnote:] ✳ surely: "caused in the proper way"

✳ But why couldn't perceiving (but not perceptual consciousness) be a direct confrontation with a m.o.? It depends upon what one means by "direct confrontation".

awareness of external objects is only of a mediate and indirect kind and is not essential to perceptual consciousness. We must, however, indicate in much greater detail the similarities and dissimilarities between the suggested Double-aspect Theory and the Representative Theory.

The Aspect Theory and the Representative Theory

Differences

Although the account of perceiving suggested here has its own complexities and difficulties, it avoids the major weaknesses of the Representative Theory. It is more economical in that it does not involve a second order of entities, viz. a mind, as a mental substance or entity different from the observable living organism, and a host of mental objects, distinct from physical objects, for the mind to perceive or be aware of. It avoids postulating a strange causal relation between physical brain and totally different mental entities, namely mind affected by, and representations produced by, brain activity—a relation not only strange but unobservable by any scientific means. It avoids the unnoticed shift of viewpoints from that of scientific observer of the physical and publicly observable causal process up to the brain to that of the percipient introspecting or having private experiences. Instead of ignoring the enormous difference in mode of access of percipient and external observer, the suggested theory makes integral use of it in claiming that the experiences and the brain activity are co-ordinate aspects of the "whole activity" of the living organism. Finally, it avoids the duplication or circularity of the Representative Theory, for perceptual consciousness as conceived by it is strictly adverbial, a mode of activity, and so is not a duplicate either of the supposed transitive relation between person and external object or of perceiving as understood by common sense.

These advantages have their price, namely the difficulty of the notion of perceptual consciousness as adverbial yet possessing a content, though one can hardly expect a thorny problem like that of perception to yield without difficulty, and difficulty of explanatory concept seems preferable to the lavish multiplication of entities. The notion may seem hard to accept because of a prior assumption that any kind of awareness must, like perceiving itself, be transitive or "act/object" in character, i.e. must be a relation with objects that actually are distinct and confronting one. Thus the Representative Theory assumes that the perception of representations must be like this and so has to make them distinct mental entities. And if perceptual consciousness were of this kind, i.e. the "objects" of it qua mode of awareness were distinct entities, then it could not simply be adverbial. But a different conception or type of awareness is being proposed here, namely a mode of experience with a content, one in which there is *in fact* no separate object or entity, for experienced and experiencing merge into one, even though there seems to the percipient to be a distinct content and so he might in a sense be said to be aware of, but not to perceive, a content. Perhaps the term "adverbial" is too narrow here—it would ordinarily suggest a mode of feeling like an emotion or sense of well-being. But between adverbial experiences of that kind and the act/object perception of external objects there must on any view be a range of experiences, *e.g.* located pains, mental images, and dreams. The traditional theories suggest that the gap be filled by supposing these experiences to be act/object awareness in fact, like perception seems to be, but with mental objects supplied; the present suggestion is that the gap is filled by an intermediate type of state which, although it is only a mode of experiencing or reacting of the person as a whole and does not involve distinct objects, nevertheless seems to that person to be act/object awareness because of the nature of its normal basis of sentience and because of the occurrence of conceptual and organisational activities underlying consciousness. Both sides are agreed as to absence (or possible absence) of external objects in these experiences: the question is whether we then supply "mental" replicas of such objects, though strangely perceived without sense organs, or try to enlarge our conception of experience and awareness.

Similarities

The suggested Aspect Theory resembles the modern type of Representative Theory in many ways and faces the same epistemological problem of how far on the theory we can be said to have knowledge of external objects and their nature. Thus, (1) if perceptual consciousness is an activity of the person concerned, which may occur without causation by a corresponding external object, how do we know that there are such objects since our "verification" of their existence consists of further perceptual consciousness which may likewise be hallucinatory? (2) Even granted that it is veridical to the extent of being caused by an external object, what knowledge does it give us of that object? True it involves an experience which has a content, *i.e.* may seem to the percipient to be awareness of an object or scene with certain characteristics, *e.g.* of a red tomato on a white plate; but these characteristics may be purely of the nature of the conscious experience and may be quite different from those of the corresponding external cause.

The first of these problems may be dealt with on the same lines as those suggested on pp. 257-60 for the modern Representative Theory. First one must rule out those perceptual experiences which would ordin-

arily be regarded as hallucinations or illusions because they do not pass
the tests for genuine perceptions and do not square with subsequent or
more careful public observations. Then one must say that our supposition
that the remaining or "veridical" experiences are genuine perceptions is
the best hypothesis to explain their patterns or sequences; to suppose that
they are in fact caused by the physical objects corresponding to their
content is more plausible than any of the alternative hypotheses such as
Solipsism, Phenomenalism, or Common-sense Theory. Reasons for
rejecting all these have been given. We may repeat that the present
suggestion avoids the danger of duplication or circularity: there is no
distinction of two kinds of perceiving with the claim that the one is the
means to the other; the theory simply is that perception of external
objects *consists in* having an activity, namely perceptual consciousness,
caused by the action of the object on the sense organs. Being thus perceptually conscious or active is not a duplicate of perceiving as a whole
because it is in fact adverbial.

The second problem may also be dealt with as it would be by a modern
type of Representative Theory, viz. by means of a refined form of the
distinction of primary and secondary qualities. So far as the characteristics of physical objects are concerned, the Representative and Aspect
Theories may agree on the following:

(*a*) That such objects are external and public, and possess causal properties which persist even when not observed (this is accepted by all theories
except Phenomenalism, Solipsism, and some forms of Idealism).

(*b*) That most of them are perceptible, *i.e.* possess among their causal
characteristics the property of causing human beings to have perceptual
consciousness corresponding to them. The analysis of this human
reaction or experience will then vary according to theory, *e.g.* that it
is a mental perception of mental representations of the external cause
or that it is an activity whose inner aspect is an experienced content
corresponding to them. In either case the representations or content will
show a range of qualities (colours, shapes, sounds, etc.) according to the
properties of the object causing the experience.

(*c*) Thus it can be said that an apple, for example, is red, round, firm,
and sweet in that it causes in normal human beings under normal conditions the sense experiences indicated by those epithets. But the main
problem is whether we can describe the properties of the external object
in some way other than by their effects; merely to say that this apple is
red in that it causes consciousness of red colour does not get us very far,
for it may be that the causal properties of the apple are quite unlike its
effects, so that its true intrinsic nature is not revealed to us by perception.
(These sceptical doubts may be supported by the arguments advanced in

Chapter 12: (1) The relativity of perception shows that the qualities of which we are perceptually conscious often cannot be the intrinsic object properties. This can be met by the common-sense defence that these variations, being due to various factors which impair the efficiency of perception, do nothing to show that perception when working at its best does not reveal objects as they are. But such a defence merely emphasises the role of the causal processes in perceiving on which the variations depend, and so leads to the sceptic's next point. (2) From the causal processes it is clear that the qualities of which the subject is perceptually conscious, *i.e.* the contents of this consciousness or its mental objects, must be distinguished in all perception from the intrinsic properties of physical objects, *i.e.* they are not numerically identical; further, that it is unlikely that the two are always qualitatively identical, or at least evidence of this would be required, because the latter are characteristics of material, and usually inorganic objects, while the former are, according to theory, mental non-physical qualties or experience-contents co-ordinate with human cerebral activity. Also, examination of the neural processes involved in their causation shows that, as the variables involved are frequency, pathways and destinations only, they can hardly transmit or respond to secondary qualities. (3) There is the support of general physical theory which claims that the objective counterparts of experienced colours, sounds, heat or cold, etc., are quite different, being light quanta, sound waves, atomic or molecular motion.)

(*d*) Such scepticism only applies to the secondary qualities. So far as the primary ones are concerned we can supplement direct perception by measurement and thus establish macroscopic shape, structure and size (or degree of extension). Not only are these measured properties independent of human beings, but they can fairly be regarded as intrinsic properties of the objects concerned. (Admittedly the dimensions have to be stated in terms of some standard such as a yard or a metre, but it is only the description or labelling that is thus relative; the shape or extension labelled is intrinsic.) We can also compare the measured shape or size[1] of an object with the corresponding part of the content of perceptual consciousness (or, if preferred, with the shape or size of the mental representations) and see when they resemble each other. Similarly measurement can establish other primary qualities such as motion or mass. There is some difficulty about temperature, however: it seems objectively measurable, but what is measured is the causal property of causing expansion of fluid or metal, and this in no way resembles felt

[handwritten margin note: But how can such a comparison be made? Surely we can only compare contents with one another.]

---

[1] Relative size that is; the resemblance is between the relative sizes of different parts of the content (or representations) and the relative sizes of different objects in the external scene.

[handwritten note: * But what now is direct perception?]

warmth; moreover, physical theory shows that the intrinsic characteristics responsible for this causal property are something different again. So it would be better not to include it on the primary list. There may also be difficulties about mass, but the physical considerations involved are too complex to discuss here. So far as the other primaries are concerned, scientific theory gives a quite different account at the atomic level, but this is a complementary account and does not subvert the establishment of macroscopic shape and extension, or of motion relative to the earth.[1]

On the other hand this independent establishment does not seem possible for the secondary qualities. Colours and sounds can loosely be said to be measured, but that is not the point. For in sound what you normally measure is the frequency and amplitude of the associated sound wave, i.e. physical motion of a certain frequency—a primary quality and the cause of the heard sound—and in colour also the light wave may really be what is measured. There is another kind of "measurement," e.g. colour may be matched with a standard shade on an agreed shade card, or an instrument may be tuned so that it emits a note of middle C exactly; but in each case what is being done is equating or matching similar sense-experiences, one colour with a colour, one note with a note. But measurement of spatial properties is different in that it goes beyond pure perception and certainly beyond one type of sense experience. Measurement is an *operation* in which visual, tactile, and kinesthetic experiences concur; we feel as well as see that X is round, that the edges of the object and the ruler coincide, that A is larger than B. Also, measurement leads to con-clusions as to the dimensions and positions of objects in physical space which can be verified by further activities or operations, e.g. fitting the objects together, moving one's hand between them or over them, walking about between them or from one to the other, if they are large, and so on. In other words, there is a whole series of operations involved, and the only way of reducing them to order, i.e. the best hypothesis to explain them, is to suppose that the measurements have revealed intrinsic proper-ties of the objects concerned. And lastly, the measurements form the basis of general physical theories which do not undermine them but which, with other observations of physiology, neurology, and so on, do give rise to scepticism about the secondary qualities. (If this is felt to have an air of circularity, it must be remembered that any circle would not be vicious, for we are merely seeking the best hypothesis to explain the nature and order of many experiences, not to demonstrate some conclusion from premises that state or presuppose it.)

One final note of warning, however: one should not simply conclude

[1] Science also reveals other properties, e.g. electric charge, which may also be regarded as complementary.

from this discussion that objects are not really coloured, warm, or smelly. This word "really," or the similar "real/apparent" distinction by which it is said that colours, for example, are mere appearance and not real, is fertile in ambiguity and confusion, and contains many emotional and metaphysical overtones. It is thus best avoided, or if used must be made precise; as a chameleon adapts its colour to its surroundings, so the word "real" takes its meaning from its context. "Real" may mean genuine, *i.e.* not faked or counterfeit, not an imitation or substitute; it may mean actually existing, as opposed to fictitious, mythological, merely apparent, or ideal; and so on. Here one might interpret "real" as measured (in which case the apparent shape or size would be the shape or size which from simple perception we should wrongly suppose the object will be found to have when measured) or as intrinsic, *i.e.* at least as possessed by the object independently of human observation. Neither of these senses properly characterises the sensible shape which, as an experienced content or mental object, is never numerically identical with the measured intrinsic shape, though it may resemble it exactly or as a projection does. Nor does an object have a real colour or other real secondary qualities in these senses. On the other hand this does not mean that the colour, sound, or sensible shape is unreal in the sense of being some dream or illusion—they are all actually occurring contents of human perceptual consciousness of the object and characterise the object as perceived by us. Moreover, objects are coloured, noisy, smelly, etc., in the sense of causing the appropriate experiences or contents of consciousness. And it is legitimate to speak of real as opposed to apparent colour, taste, or sound, meaning the quality of which normal people are perceptually conscious under standard conditions such as daylight or absence of catarrh.

[marginal note:] ? .

[marginal note:] this seems like a category mistake *

[handwritten footnote:] * we presumably don't have perceptual consciousness of objects — on this view — only perceptual consciousness (caused by objects) containing contents. But the contents don't characterize anything — except perhaps classes of contents. But not objects.

BIBLIOGRAPHY

BELOFF, J. 1962. *The Existence of Mind*, MacGibbon and Kee, London.

BROAD, C. D. 1925. *The Mind and its Place in Nature*, Chs. 1, 2, and 14. Kegan Paul, London.

HIRST, R. J. 1959. *The Problems of Perception*, Chs. 6, 7, and 10. Allen and Unwin, London.

REEVES, J. W. 1958. *Body and Mind in Western Thought*, Introduction and Pt. II. Penguin, London.

RYLE, G. 1949. *The Concept of Mind*. Hutchinson, London.

16

Envoi

We have seen that, for the reasons summarised at the beginning of Chapter 15, the orthodox philosophical theories of perception must be rejected. The common-sense theories do not do justice to the scientific facts; the Sense-datum Theory postulates a range of unnecessary and unplausible entities; while, for all its latter-day popularity among neurologists and psychologists, the Representative Theory duplicates rather than explains perceiving, propounds an unclear and uneconomical theory of mind as an immaterial entity, and is quite unable to characterise the relationship it alleges between mind, so conceived, and brain. Consequently, if a solution is to be reached to the problems of perception that have exercised and defeated thinkers for centuries, one must make a fresh start and seek concepts of a radically different order. This is the aim and justification of the Aspect Theory here outlined. The essential steps are: (1) To regard the mind as a group of abilities and dispositions of the organism, thereby avoiding the postulation of any obscure immaterial entity; the mind/body problem is thus seen to be concerned with the relation between different kinds of activity of the one person. (2) To regard the cerebral processes as one aspect of "whole" mental activities of a person, and his conscious experiences as another aspect of those same activities; by the logic of "aspect," experiences and brain activities *are* those mental activities, and the apparent difference is due to the enormous differences in modes of access to them—external observations as a spectator on the one hand, and introspecting or carrying out the activities as agent on the other. The mysterious causal relationship between brain and mind alleged by Interactionism is thus dispensed with, the unity of the person is preserved, and the differences between immanent and external points of view allowed to play their full part. (3) In the application of this to perception one must realise a further difference according to points of view, namely that perceptual consciousness (the activity which when caused by a corresponding external object amounts to perception) is really, *i.e.* on the best evidence available to the theorist, adverbial activity, but to the person concerned has a content, *i.e.* appears to be transitive awareness of an object. That mental processes possess this dual character is perhaps the most difficult conceptual leap here required, but unless it is taken one

336

is forced to regard such consciousness as in fact transitive and its contents as in fact distinct objects—which means inventing a mental world in which to put them.

By these steps one may advance to a satisfactory solution to the traditional problems of perception. But even if the suggested solution is unacceptable, one thing at least is clear: the bankruptcy of the orthodox theories shows only that by some such radical revision of fundamental concepts can success finally be obtained.

Index